AF605824

Andrew H. Plaks and Michael Nylan, Series Editors

Exemplary Figures / Fayan
Yang Xiong, translated by Michael Nylan

Zuo Traditions / Zuozhuan
(*Commentary on Spring and Autumn Annals*)
Translated by Stephen Durrant, Wai-yee Li, and David Schaberg

Exemplary Figures

Fayan

Yang Xiong
(53 BCE – 18 CE)

TRANSLATED BY
Michael Nylan

UNIVERSITY OF WASHINGTON PRESS
Seattle and London

Publication of this book was made possible in part by a generous private gift.

Printed and bound in the United States of America
Design by Thomas Eykemans
Composed in Minion, typeface designed by Robert Slimbach
16 15 14 13 5 4 3 2 1

UNIVERSITY OF WASHINGTON PRESS
PO Box 50096, Seattle, WA 98145, USA
www.washington.edu/uwpress

LIBRARY OF CONGRESS CATALOGING-IN-PUBLICATION DATA
Yang, Xiong, 53 B.C.–18 A.D.
[Fa yan. English]
Exemplary figures = Fayan / Yang Xiong ;
Translated by Michael Nylan. — 1st edition.
p. cm. — (Classics of Chinese thought)
Includes bibliographical references and index.
ISBN 978-0-295-99289-1 (cloth : alk. paper)
1. Philosophy, Chinese.
2. Ethics—China.
I. Nylan, Michael.
II. Title.
III. Title: Fayan.
B128.Y313F313 2013 181'.11—dc23 2012046038

The paper used in this publication is acid-free and meets the minimum requirements of American National Standard for Information Sciences—Permanence of Paper for Printed Library Materials, ANSI Z39.48–1984.∞

This book is dedicated to Andrew Plaks, not for the extraordinary talents that he was given but for the large heart that he has cultivated all these many years, aided in this, no doubt, by the brilliantly human Lilly Plaks.

Contents

Acknowledgments

My first thanks must go to David Knechtges, whose knowledge of the *Fayan* is unparalleled, and to Anne Cheng, who not only encouraged me in this project but also alerted me to the need to take Yang Xiong seriously as a historian. Nathan Sivin, Marc Kalinowski, and Béatrice L'Haridon have all provided insights into aspects of Yang Xiong's life and works. I owe an enormous debt to Li Wai-yee as well, for she read the entire manuscript (then in penultimate draft) from beginning to end and corrected many of my most egregious errors and infelicities. Frederic Tibbetts was an invaluable friend and aide when it came to spotting ugly translations of phrases in classical Chinese and suggesting possible revisions; I owe to Rick the felicitous rendering of Yang's title. Christoph Harbsmeier also did me the very great favor of reading four chapters of the *Fayan* manuscript when it was in its final phases.

The anonymous readers for the University of Washington Press made fine suggestions, as did William G. Boltz, whom I consulted twice on questions about archaic rhymes. Thanks are due to Miranda Brown and Christian de Pee for conversations that (inadvertently or consciously) made major contributions to my thinking about the shape of this translation, along with J. Michael Farmer, whose work on Sichuan has proven useful at so many stages. Henry Rosemont is continually in my thoughts as I strive to do justice to a splendid philosophical text, and Michael Loewe, as I try to render the historical. Lorri Hagman, at the University of Washington Press, has been a model editor throughout the long process from birth to maturation of this particular project; it is no exaggeration to say that the translation would never have seen the light of day without her steady guidance and reliable good cheer.

Chronology of Dynasties

Five Lords	Legendary; traditionally third millennium BCE
Xia	Traditionally 2205–1766 BCE
Shang	Traditionally 1600–ca. 1050 BCE
Western Zhou Ca.	1050–771 BCE
Chunqiu	770–481 BCE
Zhanguo	475–222 BCE
Qin	221–210 BCE
Han	206 BCE–220 CE
Western	206 BCE–9 CE
Xin dynasty	9–23 CE (Wang Mang Interregnum)
Eastern	25–220
Sanguo	220–65
Jin	265–420
Western	265–316
Eastern	317–420
Nanbeichao	317–589
Sui	589–617
Tang	618–907
Song	960–1279
Northern	960–1126
Southern	1126–1279
Yuan	1279–1368
Ming	1368–1644
Qing	1644–1911

Introduction

In an era before strict genre distinctions, Yang Xiong 揚雄 (53 BCE–18 CE) wrote a work to which he gave the title *Fayan* 法言. From the beginning, scholars have variously treated Yang's text as a philosophical masterwork, a commentary on the *Analects* (Lunyu 論語) and Sima Qian's 司馬遷 (145?–86? BCE) *Shiji* 史記 (usually rendered as *Records of the Historian*), a sophisticated work of self-promotion, and a historical source.[1] Ban Biao 班彪 (3–54), one of Yang's more illustrious younger contemporaries, observed that the title clearly refers to the model of the sages.[2] The usual English translation of *Fayan* is *Model Sayings*. Like the Chinese, this rendering leaves open two possibilities: that the sayings issue from a model and that the sayings themselves are models of fine rhetoric. Still, *Model Sayings* is ugly in English (and hence a title that Yang would have abhorred). Besides, the word "model" carries unpleasantly prissy connotations for many. More importantly, the process of cultivation that the *Fayan* explicitly seeks to promote is more complicated than simply modeling oneself upon a person deemed superior. Among my working titles was *Exemplary Sayings*, which at least had the virtue of alluding to the similarities in grammar and style of the *Analects* and Yang's *Fayan*. Ultimately, however, I settled on *Exemplary Figures*.[3] "Figures," of course, can refer to "figures of speech," but the term encompasses "written symbols," "prominent people," "the impressions made by people," "images," "devices or patterns," "emblems," "embellishments," "portraying by speech or action," and "cutting a figure"—which are all important subjects in Yang's text.

In the best of all possible worlds, introductions to literary classics would always supply both a "degressive bibliography," explaining the original state of the text,[4] and a "progressive bibliography" (i.e., a reception history). While this may be possible with, say, the works of Shakespeare, no scholar of classical Chinese would dare claim that she is able to recover a Western Han (206 BCE–9 CE) text or ascertain the true significance of early textual variants among manuscripts compiled several millennia ago, in the time before printing. As a noted Han expert, Michael

Loewe, has remarked, "The curtain is firmly drawn."[5] One early editor of an *Exemplary Figures* manuscript boasted of having "corrected" some 500 separate items in the text. But a later manuscript, supposedly derived from Li Gui's 李軌 edition (compiled 335), to which Wu Mi's 吳祕 commentary (before 1081) was appended, still had many variant characters in it.[6]

The number of textual variants that can be culled from extant *Exemplary Figures* editions is huge. The earliest extant complete commentary to *Exemplary Figures* (excluding scattered remarks preserved in the received literature), that by Li Gui, dates to a time nearly three hundred and fifty years after the compilation of *Exemplary Figures*, by which time Yang's masterwork had already been adapted by many editors and commentators to new cultural contexts. Almost certainly, then, still more variants appeared in the early manuscript copies circulating among editors and commentators. Frankly, two millennia after the composition of *Exemplary Figures*, when multiple commentaries offer multiple readings, no translator can easily determine which variant more likely represents Yang's original argument, especially given Yang's love for double entendres and ambiguous phrases. Those versed in textual criticism typically argue the wisdom of an approach called *lectio difficilior*, in which "the harder reading" is thought more likely to be the earliest, since editors tend to revise manuscripts to make them more readable. In the case of *Exemplary Figures*, however, this approach often does not suffice, since there are several "hard readings," each backed by one or more authoritative commentaries. In the main, there is a tendency for editions and commentators in late imperial China to inject a sort of moral purism more reminiscent of the True Way Learning (Daoxue 道學) than of Han modes of thinking,[7] and so my translation reflects a general preference for earlier over later readings, unless cogent reasons militate against it. Major variants (defined as variants that give different meanings rather than simply different transcriptions) are usually cited in the footnotes to the Chinese text. Readers of classical Chinese may consult Wang Rongbao's 汪榮寶 1899 *Fayan yishu* 法言義疏 for a more complete list of variants.

Because so much of *Exemplary Figures* consists of dialogues between Yang and an unnamed interlocutor, the work is often described as "an imitation" of the *Analects*. However, substantial parts of *Exemplary Figures* are not in dialogues but are, rather, epigrams, rhymed encomia, and pithy historical judgments about key figures in Qin (221–210 BCE) and Han history.[8] Yang employed silences, ambiguities, incongruities, and non sequiturs to focus the reader's attention. He also loved games of witty wordplay in which he could best his opponents and interlocutors.[9] And indeed, Yang's desire to show off his enviable command of rhetorical skills may have dictated the final form of *Exemplary Figures* and Yang's "philosophical" poems as much as his intention to emulate the Kongzi 孔子 (Confucius 孔夫子) of the *Analects*. (Those rhetorical skills supplied

Yang with a broad array of defensive strategies; for example, accused of criticizing his betters, Yang pleaded his innocence by simply "invoking the argument of the simple formal exercise.")[10] Appreciating the subtle differences between these several registers of writing in *Exemplary Figures*, then, is a first step toward understanding the sheer virtuosity of the text. But the tone adopted in *Exemplary Figures* can be a barrier to understanding. Moderns do not generally expect our moralists or serious writers to be humorous, but Yang is invariably witty, by turns funny, ironic, or even caustic.[11]

Exemplary Figures, together with several *fu* composed by Yang late in life and Yang's two other masterworks, the *Supreme Mystery* (Taixuan 太玄) and the *Fangyan* 方言 (usually rendered as *Dialect Words*), show Yang to be the first highly self-conscious author in Chinese history.[12] In these mature works, Yang managed to displace the ruler as protagonist with a portrait of himself as a rhetorical master steeped in classical learning who has successfully emulated the legendary figures from antiquity. Before Yang, the only recognized profession (as opposed to occupation) had been that of the *shi* 士, the officer, the actual or potential "man of service."[13] Yang's self-portrait of the fiercely independent, if highly conservative, master offered something new, in the sense that Yang posited a superior authority for himself that was not tied to heredity or to public office, but was instead based on his superior knowledge of texts, his compilation of reliably superior manuscripts, and his superior understanding of what to do with texts.[14]

YANG XIONG'S LIFE

Yang Xiong composed a lengthy autobiography, which became (probably with emendations and additions) the basis for a lengthy two-chapter "biography" of Yang in Ban Gu's 班固 *History of the Han* (Hanshu 漢書; comp. ca. 92 CE).[15] Students of Yang's work regard this autobiography/biography as a blessing and a curse. A blessing, because this two-chapter work supplies a great many details of Yang's life and cites several of his *fu* in their entirety,[16] a curse because it is next to impossible to read Yang's writings except through the lens that Yang and Ban provided later readers. Since David Knechtges has done such a superb job of translating and annotating the entire *Hanshu* account, I will offer only a bare outline of Yang's life here, followed by a consideration of some questions raised by the autobiography/biography, by Ban Gu's concluding Appraisal to the biographical chapters (clearly framed as an apologia for Yang), and by tropes found in pre-Tang anecdotes about Yang as an inspired writer and classical master.[17]

Little is known of Yang's early life, other than that he studied with three of the most famous teachers in Sichuan: Yan Junping 嚴君平, Linlü

Wengru 林閭翁孺, and Li Hong 李弘. All three were experts in divination materials, in "strange characters" (probably transcriptions in seal script), and in important traditions that late imperial authorities tended to reclassify as "Confucian" or "Daoist."[18] Yang was supposedly over forty when he traveled from Shu (the Chengdu Plain) to the Western Han capital of Chang'an (near present-day Xi'an) sometime around 13 BCE, where he found an early patron in Wang Yin 王音, then marshal of state and cousin of Dowager Empress Wang. Yang was later appointed "courtier and servitor at the Yellow Gate," in which post Yang served alongside Wang Mang 王莽, nephew of the dowager empress, and Liu Xin 劉歆, a member of the imperial clan and son of Yang's chief mentor, Liu Xiang 劉向 (d. 7 CE).

The style of poetry most favored at the Han court at the time of Yang's arrival was the grand display *fu*. Given Yang's remarkable facility in composing such *fu* on demand, he soon secured imperial favor and went on to become court poet.[19] Once he became a fixture at court, Yang wrote dazzling occasional pieces depicting his emperor as a paragon of virtue, "equal in merit to that of the legendary Five Lords" of antiquity. But even the early *fu* pieces written during Yang's first years at court illustrate Yang's profound ambivalence as an onlooker and participant in court spectacles. He was both awestruck by the court's magnificence and appalled by its extravagance and waste,[20] especially when he considered the plight of ordinary farmers and artisans. As Yang matured as a poet, he struggled to break free of the old *fu* conventions, which typically glorified the august presence of the reigning Son of Heaven. The result was his *fu* pitting "Plume Grove" against "Ink Guest" in dialogues that nudged the figure of the ruler firmly offstage.[21] Wars and hunts should not become the "regular endeavor of state," he warned.[22] Only a fierce determination to conserve men and material would ensure that

> Farmers do not cease their harrowing,
> Nor weavers leave their looms, and [both empire and emperor]
> . . . .
> Truly earn their reward from the spirits.[23]

Yang had come to the court of Chengdi 成帝 (r. 33–7 BCE) when the emperor, who was himself well versed in the Classics, and other members of his court were beginning to seriously rethink older traditions premised on particular views of human nature and of good rule. At the level of both the body and the body politic, there was a partial turn away from the late Zhanguo period (475–222 BCE) models posited by Xunzi 荀子 (d. after 238 BCE) and the other pre-Qin masters, especially their presumption that the more centralized the power, the better. As it happened, Chengdi and his court were unusually receptive to new foreign and domestic policies, as well as new modes of scholarship and of interactions with the divine, if only because the cash-strapped court could no longer afford to continue the old ways inherited from previous reigns.[24] So freewheeling was the atmosphere in Chengdi's court that Yang at one point implicitly compared Chengdi with the archetypically evil last kings of the Xia (tradit. 2205–1766 BCE) and Shang (tradit. 1600–ca. 1050 BCE) dynasties; he also hazarded a satirical piece against wine that mocked Chengdi's bibulous habits.[25] Later, in *Exemplary Figures*, Yang would more constructively outline a series of methods by which classical learning at the Han court might be redirected to its proper ends (see below), while cleverly avoiding discussion of the tricky question of how true scholars such as Yang were to advise the court, since the very wisest men in antiquity, including Kongzi, had been hard put to save their skins, let alone promote their reformist programs, in similarly troubled times.[26] Much of *Exemplary Figures* reflects Yang's search for alternate classical models by which to "restore" harmony, dignity, and restraint to the late Western Han court.

By Aidi's reign (7–1 BCE), however, Yang was fed up with navigating the daily round of court activities and repulsed by a court that was pullulating with intrigues among consort clans (*waiqi* 外戚) and male favorites with few, if any, claims to special dignity.[27] Yang had attained such a degree of personal authority that he secured the equivalent of a sabbatical for three years, during which time he drafted *Supreme Mystery*, his neoclassic modeled upon the *Changes* (Yijing 易經) and its "Ten Wings." His mock defense of his decision to retire temporarily from court life declared that he preferred to abandon the rough-and-tumble of court life lest further engagement fail to "vermilion his wheel hubs" (i.e., elevate his official rank) and instead "turn his entire clan blood-red" (i.e., leave him liable to criminal prosecution as a traitor).[28] At the same time, he announced his sympathies with the increasingly powerful *haogu* 好古 (loving antiquity) faction, whose members boldly questioned the validity of many of the traditions transmitted by the Academicians charged with the supervision of classical learning at court.[29]

Twice—once in his autobiography and once in *Exemplary Figures*—Yang insisted that he had abandoned the writing of *fu* altogether around the time of Pingdi's accession in 1 BCE ("I stopped and never again engaged in writing them").[30] As Yang told it, "The *fu* is for the purpose of persuasion. It must speak by adducing examples, [but] by the time it gets around to the moral message, the reader has lost the point."[31] Despite such protestations, it is hard to see how Yang could have resisted entreaties and commissions, given his dependence on the court for a salary. If the received traditions are correct (always a big if!), Yang continued to compose new occasional pieces for the court, including three *fu* on luxury items, a eulogy for Dowager Empress Wang,[32] several formal "warnings" cataloging the duties and lapses of the major officers in the Han bureaucracy, and the poem "Excoriating Qin while Praising Xin," a single line of which seems to offer abject support for Wang Mang, who would later usurp the Han throne.[33] Not surprisingly, this last piece of writing, like the last line of *Exemplary Figures*, which also praises Wang, had disastrous consequences for Yang's posthumous reputation, but Yang himself offered an interpretive key to his work whereby his most hyperbolic praise was meant to indicate ruthless satire. In consequence, these works hardly present the ringing endorsements of Wang Mang that Yang's detractors claim.

Yang's last years, from Chengdi's reign through the first half of Wang Mang's Xin dynasty (9–23 CE), must have been incredibly busy. Sometime during the period 26–6 BCE, when the first imperial library collection was being put together, Yang worked under the direction of his mentor Liu Xiang, organizing and cataloging the library collection.[34] Reportedly, in those capacities he proved himself to be a good, if activist, editor, like Liu Xiang.[35] In a memorial to the throne, Yang characterized himself as a youth sadly deficient in learning; by his own account, he owed his erudition largely to the research he carried out in the Stone Chamber (Shiqu 石渠), one of the palace libraries.[36] He and his mentor were intent upon devising reliable methods by which to determine the best among several variant editions or characters in ancient texts.[37] (Yang and Liu Xiang have been dubbed the "twin fathers" of textual criticism in China.) During this time, one or possibly two beloved sons—one allegedly a child prodigy—died and had to be taken or sent back to Sichuan for burial. Yang's position at court as resident "wisdom bag" stuffed with encyclopedic knowledge also meant that learned men of every persuasion regularly consulted him on omens, historical figures, and "strange script."[38] (By his own account, the historical and literary allusions favored by Yang during these question-and-answer sessions became the core around which Yang built his *Exemplary Figures*.)[39] At the same time, Yang was tutoring several young men who were interested in pre-Qin script forms and fine literary expressions, and he functioned as official advisor to members of the court on a variety of matters relating to historical precedents, omen interpretation, and classical learning. As if that were not enough to occupy his time, upon two occasions, at least, Yang was pressed to defend himself against the threat of criminal charges (once for recommending to the palace a compatriot from Sichuan who turned out to be a thief, and once for being too intimate with members of a clique accused of treason). And all the while Yang was compiling and polishing his three masterworks.

Of these three masterworks, Yang's posthumous reputation rests primarily on *Exemplary Figures* and *Supreme Mystery*, in that order. Aside from linguists, few scholars today even bother to consult his third masterwork, now called the *Fangyan* (no longer in its original form), not to mention the fragments that survive from his radical expansion of the *Cang Jie pian* 倉頡篇 lexicon. These word lists represented the first steps in the search for ancient etymologies that eventually produced the much better known *Shuowen jiezi* 說文解字 (compiled 100 CE).[40] Although the lion's share of readers' attention in the twentieth century has gone to *Exemplary Figures*, it may well be that Yang considered *Supreme Mystery* or the *Fangyan* to be his finest writing. After all, Yang defended his *Supreme Mystery* at considerable length in two mature *fu*, "Dispelling Ridicule" and "Resolving Objections" (Jiechao 解嘲 and Jienan 解難),[41] as well as in *Exemplary Figures*, where Yang remarks on the pleasure he had in composing the *Supreme Mystery* with his beloved son Wu (Crow) and terms the work the equal of Kongzi's writings.[42] Notably, admirers of Yang in the pre-Tang and Tang (618–907) eras produced many more commentaries on *Supreme Mystery* than on *Exemplary Figures*.[43]

On the other hand, it was the *Fangyan* (or its precursor transcribed at least partly in seal script) whose painstaking compilation occupied Yang for a full twenty-seven years, roughly three times longer than either *Supreme Mystery* or *Exemplary Figures*. Determined to retrieve what he thought to be the core insights of the distant past, despite his belief that the pre-Han classics suffered from multiple interpolations, omissions, and errors introduced during transmission, Yang endeavored to devise trustworthy methods by which the Classics might be restored to something closer to their pristine states. Yang came up with a solution we might term his "ethnographic impulse."[44] Apparently, Yang (perhaps in concert with Liu Xiang) believed that if archaic phrases could be culled from the outlying areas far from the capital, at least some of those expressions would contain the aural and semantic clues needed to unlock the true meaning of passages in the older manuscripts and inscriptions that resisted ready decipherment and interpretation. Accordingly, for nearly three decades Yang, with notepad in hand, inquired of every envoy and official from the far-flung regions if they could tell him anything about word usage in their locality. The unusual expressions he duly recorded in the *Fangyan* could then supplement materials preserved in the *Erya* 爾雅 word list and together form a large database of genuinely early vocabulary items that would prove invaluable to scholars intent upon correcting the faulty traditions handed down from the pre-Qin period.

Completion of these three masterworks depended upon the superior access that Yang enjoyed to palace archives and libraries, not to mention the high officials bearing privileged information from distant parts. In any case, as one of a large group of advisers who longed to witness the implementation of the sort of sweeping reforms being touted right then by Wang Mang and Liu Xin, Yang would probably have been disinclined to quit the court during Wang's regency. By 9 CE, the year of Wang's accession to the throne, it was too late to retire, for retirement from office might well be read by Wang as a sign of dangerous disaffection. (As Hans Bielenstein has noted, very few officials *did* resign in protest over Wang's usurpation, if they could avoid it.)[45] Through it all, Yang perfected a style of writing that lent him an air of "plausible deniability,"[46] regardless of the political turmoil he witnessed daily at court.

Ban Gu supplied a fairly elaborate defense of Yang's decision to stay and continue serving the new Xin dynasty (9–23) founded by Wang. By Ban's account, Yang held too insignificant a post and was too dependent upon his meager salary to justify his quitting.[47] Besides, Yang suffered badly under Wang Mang, at one point attempting suicide because of the slanders aimed at him by Wang's toadies. But is Ban's defense true to the facts? While it is difficult to be certain about events so remote in time, it seems that Yang enjoyed considerable prestige at the Han and Xin courts as poet, thinker, and historian.[48] In addition to his regular salary, he was rewarded with ten units of gold by the Han court for submitting a memorial about Xiongnu policy that carried the day.[49] (Note that the *Huayang guozhi* 華陽國志, summarizing local Shu traditions about Yang, specifically says he was poor "*when young*.")[50] Yang moreover received a full three years' sabbatical from his activities as librarian and court poet so that he might compose his philosophical classics. Since people praised him even in his own lifetime as a Confucian master equal in erudition and character to the Supreme Sage Kongzi, it was hardly surprising that after his death he quickly gained a reputation as the most elegant, impressive, and versatile persuader among the early ethical masters.[51]

As I have argued elsewhere,[52] Yang's ties to Wang Mang have garnered far too much attention, especially after Zhu Xi 朱熹 (1130–1200) maligned his character, questioned the validity of his cosmological theories and views on human nature, and accused him of disloyally "serving two masters," Han and Xin.[53] Yang could hardly be expected to avoid all contact with Wang Mang, since (*a*) he had held the same post (Courtier) as Wang Mang and Liu Xin, who ultimately became one of Wang's strongest allies; and (*b*) Wang and Liu spearheaded a group of reform-minded classicists intent upon reshaping the institutions and operations of the Western Han bureaucracy. Notably, however, *Exemplary Figures* is not dedicated or addressed to any particular ruler or regent. Instead, it explicitly lodges an appeal to "later generations" of the governing elites, who are to reevaluate their priorities in life after recalculating the combined utility and pleasure to be gained from dedicating oneself to the higher ethical commitments of Yang's chosen Way. This explicit appeal to later generations of readers suggests a degree of uncertainty on Yang's part about whether the current power-holders (nominal or real) would heed his complex message and restrain their craven impulses. Subtle wording in the last chapter of *Exemplary Figures* supports the conclusion that Yang saw himself as a loyal servant of the Western Han imperial clan, perhaps because of his strong personal attachment to Liu Xiang, who was no friend of Wang Mang, or because he had doubts about Wang Mang's fitness for the highest office in the land. Equally germane are Yang's repeated warnings about the human propensity to confuse look-alikes and sycophants with true sages.[54]

MAJOR CONTRIBUTIONS AND THEMES IN THE TEXT

Along with all other major Han thinkers, Yang Xiong is today routinely, if unjustly, derided as an uninspired and unoriginal scholastic.[55] Famous thinkers of later ages incorporated in their own writings so much of what Yang Xiong wrote, thereby acknowledging his creation of admirable models combining superb rhetorical skills with sound Confucian ethics, that some of the most innovative features of *Exemplary Figures* strike readers now as less than original. Then, too, Yang wrote so disarmingly that a mere glancing acquaintance with his work does not permit readers to gauge the full depth and extent of the polemical content in his work.[56]

Arguably, Yang's foremost contribution in *Exemplary Figures* is his adaptation of the pleasure discourse inherited from the Zhanguo and early Western Han thinkers to the allied subjects of reading and classical learning; in Yang's view, the pleasures of the mind unquestionably could surpass those of the body. Other historians have stressed Yang's role, in conjunction with his contemporaries Liu Xiang and Liu Xin, in establishing the fashion for citation of the Five Classics (not just the *Odes*) in political pieces, particularly edicts and memorials.[57] Certainly, Yang insisted on the revelatory character of the Classics rather than using them merely as illustrations or ornaments in persuasions.[58] Fukui Shigemasa goes so far as to single out Yang as the first either to coin or to popularize the term "Five Classics,"[59] and while the loss of so many antique writings precludes absolute certainty on this point, it is obvious that Yang, Liu Xiang, and Liu Xin promoted the Five Classics corpus with such enthusiasm that they helped usher in new styles of writing and new ways of thinking about the distant past. Specifically, in *Exemplary Figures* Yang urged those in the governing elite to reexamine their presumptions about classical learning in general and Five Classics learning in particular. Among the most important claims he advanced were the following:

1. To the common objection that "learning is of no possible use," Yang replies that learning has the greatest possible utility, since without it humans can never learn to cultivate their defining qualities as human beings to engage in long-term constructive social relations.[60]
2. To an interlocutor who refines this blanket rejection of learning, arguing that the value of classical learning—in modern lingo, its cultural capital—fluctuates wildly, depending on the current ruler's interest in it, Yang replies that classical learning may be of greatest utility to the person when the "whole world is cold" (i.e., unfair and without comfort).[61]
3. To counter the prevailing notion that classical learning is simply one technique among many with the potential to bring fame and wealth to a professional, Yang crafts a five-part answer: (*a*) it cannot be true that all arts or skills are equally valuable, in that each mandates a stan-

dard "way" or skill, and the relative importance of the goal or product of each profession determines its value to mankind; (*b*) the arts wielded by men like Kongzi are manifestly superior to those of other professionals because they can improve the dispositions of the persons wielding them, while archers, cooks, charioteers, and carpenters exert mastery over the externals; (*c*) the goals of classical learning—and, most especially, Five Classics learning—are both broader and more ambitious in scope than other techniques governing other fields of endeavor; (*d*) classical learning properly wielded is more likely to attain its goal than other techniques; and thus (*e*) the value of classical learning does not lie primarily in its potential to win men tangible gains (high office, salary and rank, greater longevity, and so on), since it offers intangible benefits like security and cultivation.[62] (Readers may note similarities with Aristotle here.)

4. To the idea that the chief, if not the sole, use of classical learning is to prepare men for the qualifying examinations for entry into the bureaucracy, Yang replies that, as the examinations not only fail to locate men with true devotion to learning but even select the wrong people,[63] the dynasty would fare better if it would not employ the Classics when selecting men for careers in public service.[64]
5. To answer those who assert that the Classics are flawed, Yang retorts that they are still the most reliable guides for judging human conduct and the most discerning and elegant examples of rhetoric. Furthermore, errors, interpolations, and omissions introduced during the course of transmission can generally be corrected by reference to other genuinely early works, including the *Erya*.
6. To answer the objection that the classicists (Ru) in general and the proponents of the Five Classics in particular have never managed to usher in an era of "Great Peace," despite their long-term employment in high office in certain areas (e.g., the pre-imperial state of Lu and the Han dynasty itself), Yang replies that the right kind of classicists—those who teach power-holders that they must amend their ways—have never been employed in any polity. In other words, the court has all too often employed the wrong kind of classicists—those who wear the right clothes and talk the right talk but fail to act for the common good.
7. To complaints about the difficulty of mastering the Five Classics, Yang responds with certitude: "Were it [the Way] to be made smaller, then it would defeat the sages. How would that be?" In other words, the sages arranged their lives and their writings so that they might serve as perfectly adequate models for all times. Despite the sages' desire to make them as easy to understand as humanly possible, the Classics would inevitably be less versatile and less applicable to all situations if they were not in their present form and language. Obviously, this sort of experiential learning will be harder to master than the mere memorization, recitation, or drafting of texts.

8. After rebutting his peers' negative views of classical learning, Yang proceeded to frame a positive view of classical learning in general and Five Classics learning in particular, asserting that learning the moral Way embedded in the Classics is the only kind of learning in which single-minded effort is invariably repaid with the realization of the intended goal.[65] No natural impediment exists to any human becoming a sage through cumulative efforts, since people do not differ substantially in their capacities, but rather in the ways they evaluate, prioritize, and employ what they have learned—and these attitudes are amenable to good training. Even more importantly, a person's persistence in pursuing ethical solutions to life's dilemmas fosters an admirable state of independence that, being impervious to external threat and internal decay, elevates the person above his peers. Having broken free of ordinary travails, the person reaches a refined state of grace and power that Yang likens to divinity (*shen* 神) and to "clarity" or "light" (*ming* 明).[66]

While several of the foregoing claims that come together in *Exemplary Figures* had been advanced long before Yang, promoting these eight ideas as a coherent package was Yang's own contribution. The goal of learning, as Yang saw it, was to have the reading of superb texts strengthen the person's nascent desires for ethical behavior, as the memorization of each text inscribed body and soul with new edifying models.[67] In the early manuscript culture of Yang's day, reading typically entailed learning something by heart; as a result, reading became a contemplative or meditative act, less a purely intellectual activity than a transformative experience.

Turning from the sublime to the practical, *Exemplary Figures* stands out among extant Western Han works for its relative lack of interest in propagating the virtues of empire or the Han imperial ideology.[68] Instead, the text offers readers Yang's compelling, if somewhat idiosyncratic, notion of exemplarity (yet another reason to opt for the title *Exemplary Figures*), which reflects his determination to instruct members of the governing elite, who were the only people likely to command the requisite high cultural literacy to read and appreciate Yang's neoclassic.[69] In *Exemplary Figures* Yang pronounces judgments on a wide range of influential people and writings, even as he constructs himself, in passage after passage, as a figure well worth emulating—indeed, as a figure no less worthy of emulation than Kongzi himself.[70] (That self-promotional aspect of *Exemplary Figures* has provoked both strong praise and strong criticism down through the ages.)

Major themes of *Exemplary Figures* include timing and timely opportunity, providing conceptual overlap with Yang's *Supreme Mystery*, as well as with his *fu*.[71] Issues of timing were the primary focus of Han intellectual life, as is evident from the "Great Commentary to the *Changes*"

(Xici zhuan 繫辭傳), particularly among those scholars like Yang with a solid grasp of current astronomical theories.[72] Somewhat surprising, then, is the apparently curt dismissal of divination and star-consultation in *Exemplary Figures*. Given Yang's fame as an expert on omens, it seems doubtful that Yang questions the utility of all forms of divination.[73] But certainly Yang was wary of the tendency of unscrupulous officials and would-be rulers to manipulate divination results to give favorable predictions that seemed to confer the sanction of the gods (*fuming* 符命). More importantly, Yang prefers, whenever possible, to redirect attention to human responsibilities and those areas of conduct under people's control, especially the cultivation of their activities in society. In company with other Han thinkers, Yang evinces less concern with the complex interior processes that lead to efficacious social interactions, perhaps because he believed that little can be said about them.[74]

Another theme that Yang returns to repeatedly is that of the gap between the seeming and the real, a gap that ultimately leads him back to the real versus the false followers of Kongzi,[75] as seen in the following passage:

> Someone asked me about men.
>
> "They are hard to know."
>
> "Why so hard?"
>
> "It is hardly difficult to tell the difference between Mount Tai and an anthill or between the Yangzi and Yellow Rivers, on the one hand, and a rivulet, on the other. But the great sage and the hugely clever knave—those are very hard to tell apart. How sad! Those who can distinguish among similar things and people will surely experience no trouble."[76]

Literary scholars prefer to parse Yang's pronouncements on aesthetic values, which are still influential, rather than his views on timing, human agency, or fate. *Exemplary Figures* is famous for denouncing those who would reduce literary tradition to either the handmaiden of government or the merely ornamental. Yang criticized the grand display *fu*—the very genre in which he had made his name as a youth—for captivating listeners with their elaborate devices, gratifying the emperor's sense of self-importance, and encouraging him in immoral conduct. "Grown men do not engage in such activities!" he thundered.[77] In Yang's view, decor and decorum—the twin goals of all literary production, as of all communicative acts in society—should be the defining marks of every cultivated person and every composition. For it is "rituals and refinements" that ensure productive social exchanges between people of different status and temperaments.[78] Hence, Yang defined a sage as one "who adds ornamentation to the basic substance" through the institutions of rites and music.[79] As he argues in one exchange, "If jade was never really meant to be carved, then the precious *yufan* 璵璠 ornament would never have been fashioned into a ritual object. And if words were never really meant to be embellished, then neither the Canons nor the Counsel [chapters in the *Documents* Classic] would ever have become part of the Classic."[80] In numerous passages, Yang built the case that the Five Classics, in particular his beloved *Odes*, provided the very best models of elegant yet analytical rhetoric for all types of writing. Of the *Odes*, he wrote: "The rhymed compositions by the authors of the *Odes* are both beautifully balanced and properly regulated"; elsewhere he suggested that both ornamental phrasing and substantial content were necessary components of powerful rhetoric.[81] His own corpus of writings was likened, in later ages, to "strung pearls" whose individual parts shone gently on each other.[82]

No less significantly, Yang was the first writer to theorize the different uses of speech and writing:

> They say, "Speech cannot fully express what is in the heart, nor can writing fully express speech." What a difficulty! Only sages apprehend the true meaning of words and achieve the substantial embodiment [of standards] in writing. [Of Kongzi it was therefore said:] "The white sun shone down on him; the Yangzi and Yellow River cleansed him. So powerfully does [his example] flow onward that none have been a match for him."
>
> Nothing is as good as speech for exchanging remarks during face-to-face meetings, expressing the heart's desire, or communicating people's pent-up emotions. And nothing compares with writing for fully delineating the affairs of the whole realm, for recording events of the distant past or making one see what is geographically remote, for clarifying what has been obscured by the mists of time or transmitting whatever has been obscured by the distance of thousands of miles. Therefore, speech is the heart's sounds, and writing, its images. When sounds and images assume form, then the noble and petty appear in high relief, for sounds and images are surely the means, with the noble and petty alike, to see what motivates them.[83]

Later literary criticism often drew inspiration from this neat formulation about speech versus writing. (This seems the ultimate origin of Su Shi's 蘇軾 [1036–1101] dictum that "the writings *are* the person" [*wen ru qi ren* 文如其人].)[84] Nonetheless, Yang's stress on the special strengths of writing seems to be without precedent in his own era, when oral exchanges dominated many forms of social interaction. (Earlier Yang had advised the would-be student of classical learning to find a good teacher and, if the good teachers were dead, to consult their writings.) Notably, in *Exemplary Figures*, as well as in Yang's *fu*, some of the most pleasing effects depend as much on the graphic forms of the characters chosen by Yang as on their sounds and meanings, though translation inevitably fails to capture Yang's sublime virtuosity in such matters. It is no wonder that Yang shows unusual deference to book learning while refusing to be reduced to a mere scribbler or pedant.[85]

One final theme in *Exemplary Figures* that merits attention is Yang's unprecedented focus on Yan Hui 顏回 (Yuan Yuan 淵), a disciple of Kongzi. It seems nearly unthinkable now, given the honor that later Confucian tradition accorded him, that Yan did not always enjoy an extraordinarily elevated position as Kongzi's favorite and most worthy disciple. But Yan Hui is mentioned only three times in the *Mencius*, the *Xunzi*, and those lengthy compendia *Annals of Mr. Lü* (Lüshi chunqiu 吕氏春秋, compiled ca. 238 BCE) and *The Master of Huainan* (Huainanzi 淮南子, compiled before 139 BCE). If the Japanese scholar Matsukawa Kenji 松川健二 is correct, Yang Xiong, again perhaps in company with Liu Xiang, was one of the first to build a case for Yan Hui as a superior model for aspiring sages intent upon learning how to shape their physical persons and their inclinations.[86] Yan is praised as a superior model in no fewer than sixteen separate blocks of text in *Exemplary Figures* (sometimes with multiple mentions), and one entire chapter of *Exemplary Figures* is named after him. By way of comparison, the exemplary figure of the Supreme Sage Kongzi is praised in thirty-six passages altogether, while most other disciples of Kongzi are quickly dismissed as unpromising and unnamed students of the Way.[87] The virtues of Yan Hui are mentioned far more than those of any of the sage-kings.

In the pre-imperial and early imperial periods, high status was almost always a function of heredity. With considerable courage Yang built the case in *Exemplary Figures* that the true measure of a man's worth should be his aspirations and commitments (especially his dedication to classical learning) rather than his birth. Quite fittingly, then, later writers have tended to describe Yang Xiong as a latter-day Yan Hui, one whose poverty did not prevent his ardent dedication to the moral Way.[88] In any case, some suggest that it was largely due to Yang's influence that the *Analects*—as opposed to the *Annals* (Chunqiu 春秋) or the "Great Commentary" to the *Changes*, two other works ascribed to Kongzi—became over time the principal text to consult for a capsule record of Kongzi's teachings.[89]

YANG XIONG'S ROLE IN CATAPULTING THE *SHIJI* TO PROMINENCE AND HIS HISTORICAL WORK

Some passages in *Exemplary Figures* criticize Sima Qian for ignoring the teachings of the sages on history. Such criticisms appear to reflect Yang's deep and abiding suspicion of "thinkers who slander the sages with their strange and far-fetched arguments, hairsplitting debates, and paradoxical language, thereby introducing confusion into worldly affairs."[90] Such statements notwithstanding, Yang Xiong was an ardent admirer of Sima Qian and the *Shiji*, from whose content, he insisted, "even the sages could learn."[91] That admiration prompted Yang (probably acting under imperial orders) to "extend" the history recounted in the *Shiji* into the reigns of Yang's own lifetime, from Xuandi through Pingdi (74 BCE–6 CE).[92] It is therefore tempting to credit Yang with authorship of parts of the Basic Annals, Tables, and Biographies now included in Ban Gu's monumental *Han shu*, since echoes of Yang's judgments about Han figures appear frequently in that standard history, especially in the concluding Appraisals to the biographical chapters.[93] Even though any belated attempts to assign authorship of parts of the *Hanshu* to Yang, barring a relevant manuscript find from an excavated site, must remain firmly in the realm of speculation, it is notable that some of the earliest encomia dedicated to Yang cast him as a historian working in the "praise and blame" mode of the *Annals* ascribed to Kongzi himself.[94] There being no specific genre of history in Yang's era, Yang uses the term we translate as "history" (*shi* 史) much more broadly to denote "genuine transmissions from the past." But in the attempt to further clarify the recent historical record, the lengthy chapters 10–12 and parts of chapter 13 in *Exemplary Figures* provide historical judgments in the strictest modern sense, albeit in the highly compressed style reminiscent of the *Annals* appraisals.

It is well to remember that Sima Qian's monumental work might have been consigned to the dustbin of history, had it not been for the concerted efforts of Yang Xiong, Liu Xiang, and a second Yang, Yang Yun 楊惲 (d. 54? BCE), a grandson of Sima Qian.[95] A. F. P. Hulsewé and Michael Loewe share the opinion that the *Shiji* was not in wide circulation in the mid- to late Western Han.[96] They cite in evidence the Han court's refusal to grant permission to one Liu clan prince to see the text, which was then housed within the imperial library.[97] Possibly during the course of reorganizing the library, and probably under the anti-centralizing and anti-Wudi impulses that colored the reformist movement in late Western Han, Sima Qian's magnum opus came to be elevated to the status of classic around the time of Yang Xiong.[98] As one Jin dynasty (265–420) text puts it: "From the time of Liu Xiang and Yang Xiong, those who are broadly read in many texts have all said that Sima Qian had the talent of a true historian; they have admired the way he put in order the pattern of events, offering an acute analysis of them that does not suffer from overelaboration."[99]

Unfortunately, all too few modern scholars have taken the trouble to follow the advice of the historian Hsu Fu-kuan 徐復觀 (Xu Fuguan) to trace the critiques that Yang levels at the *Shiji* via a careful consideration of the pre-Han and Han political figures treated in both the *Shiji* and *Exemplary Figures*.[100] A close examination shows that Yang disputes many individual portraits found in the *Shiji*; apparently, he believes Sima

Qian to have been remiss in identifying the underlying moral issues, even as he deems the *Shiji* a "true record."[101] History is all too often conceived as a narrative, a story, when it is not employed simply as a heuristic device on which to hang names, events, and dates.[102] But Yang, following the lead of Sima Qian, conceived of history as a set of indisputable proofs attesting the ways in which character affects the course of a life, whether that "life" belonged to a state, a person, or a group. For Yang, character trumps plot and narrative in charting the course of history, since Yang holds that "in his every speech, the noble man brings to perfection his visible refinements of character, and in his every action, he perfects his charismatic presence."[103] The noble man makes speeches and writings that are "fit to be heard and . . . perused" and "inexhaustible" in their moral excellence and practical applicability.[104] That Yang, in the spirit of Sima Qian, did not hesitate to render judgments on the most controversial matters of his day and the leading figures of the Qin and Han dynasties tells us the lengths he would go to establish his own "true record," as does Yang's praise for many officials who had been demoted, dismissed, or even executed by successive Qin and Han courts.[105]

If Yang's *Supreme Mystery* made "reading the things of the world the basis for reading the Classics,"[106] *Exemplary Figures* chiefly examines human motivation as a main thread in the larger patterns of history. And while Yang's provision of "praise and blame" for historical figures can be read as commentary on the *Shiji,* it is equally possible to see Yang's remarks as extending Kongzi's traditional role as compiler of the *Annals* or affirming the *Documents*' injunctions about the necessity for power-holders to "know men."[107] In Yang's view the writing of history constitutes the most important contribution of the sages, insofar as the sages concentrated on the single topic of how to know men. Thinking all members of the governing elite needed to better understand human motivations, fears, and longings, Yang considered his own ability to "know men"[108] to be his principal claim to fame. Certainly, his own discussions of human strategies and capacities in relation to human agency impress historians even today with their cogency and nuance.

Yang would have accepted a distinction current among the early Greeks between two kinds of truth: *alêthês*, or accurate tales (corresponding to Yang's "substance" 實 or what is "right" 是 or "true" 正), and *etumos*, referring to beliefs that prove themselves "true" over time through the results they produce (typically rendered in Yang's work as *chuan* 傳, "[hallowed] tradition," or as "the Way" or Dao 道). Like most thinkers of his era, Yang was preoccupied with the way that traditions shape thought, speech, and action, and throughout *Exemplary Figures* Yang casts the second type of truth as a surer guide when arguing the superior value of the Classics or his own exemplary authority. The evaluation of any concept immediately entailed consideration of how that concept might be implemented in practice, and Yang insisted upon the potential of ethical persons to find a way of acting that would embody both moral purity and practical efficacy.[109] At the same time, Yang's *Exemplary Figures*—contrary to the "popular wisdom" that insists that premodern Chinese thinkers had little interest in or could not fathom the concept of "truth"—expends not a little time establishing the proper means by which to distinguish true from false, for such distinctions, in Yang's view, form the foundation and "moral core" not only for good government but also for social cultivation.[110]

YANG XIONG ON THE CLASSICISTS AND CENTRAL STATES CIVILIZATIONS

Many modern readers may find Yang's treatment of the classicists (Ru) and Central States (Zhongguo 中國; in modern times, "China") civilizations interesting. Given his admiration for Kongzi and a group of sages now deemed "Confucian," one might expect Yang to extol the classicists as a group. Instead, following the lead of Xunzi and other Confucian masters, Yang speaks with no little asperity about the role some, perhaps the majority, of the classicists have played at various courts. Early on in *Exemplary Figures*, commenting on the Ru, Yang remarks,

> The Way of Heaven—was it not invested in Kongzi? But the reins of Kongzi's carriage were set down [at his death]. Is the Way then not invested in these classicists? If one were to try to take up again the reins that were laid down, then the best way of doing this would be to cause all the classicists to make their voices ring out loud and clear, like wooden tongues giving voice to bells of bronze.[111]

Careful readers will note the character of Yang's advice to the classicists here: Yang never states that the classicists after Kongzi propagated his Way using the proper techniques. Other comments by Yang note that while many professional classicists bear a superficial resemblance to Kongzi or other sages of yore—they walk the walk and talk the talk—they still lack a moral core or a strong appreciation of ritual propriety, with the result that their superficial cultural attainments do not transform them into compelling persons on the model of Kongzi. Most of his fellow classicists, according to Yang's account, studied the masterworks of the past simply to improve their chances of attaining high office[112] or to lend themselves a refined air—not because they wished to emulate greatness. Another passage underscores this very point:

> Someone asked me, "Suppose a man were to take the surname of Kong and the sobriquet of Zhongni 仲尼 [like Kongzi]. If he then

> entered Kongzi's gate, ascended his hall, leaned on his armrest, and wore his robes, could he be rightly called Kongzi?"
>
> "The surface pattern would be right, but the substance would be wrong."[113]

To this reader's astonishment, Yang even praised figures like Ji An 汲黯 (d. ca. 105 BCE), who is known to history for "slandering the classicists" (*hui Ru* 毀儒). In Yang's judgment, Ji was one of the two best examples of the "straightforward" talker whose word can be trusted.[114]

While Yang ascribes a kind of godlike perspicacity to the sages, he also insists that, as human beings, they labored under numerous constraints, experiencing the normal travails and trials felt by other human beings. In other words, Yang is never idolatrous toward the sages of legend. For example, even charismatic figures like Kongzi cannot hope to avert death; nor can they hope to change the course of history unless they are lucky enough to meet with the "right time," when those in power are both politically and morally astute.[115] They can develop their powers of perception and foresight, chiefly through resort to history as a mirror, but no sage has uncanny prescience. Nor can the sages call upon any higher powers or magical devices to save themselves from the consequences of their actions and the actions of others.

On Central States civilizations, Yang offers an equally balanced picture. He speaks of the valuable legacy of the sage-kings,[116] who instituted rites and music, implemented sedentary agriculture,[117] and devised ways to school people in the techniques they need to realize their full potentials as social beings. Yet he also notes that those conversant with Central States civilizations often misconstrue the content and importance of this legacy and the ease with which it may be imposed on lands far outside the core regions in the Han realm. At the same time, for Yang the sage's construction of the Five Social Relations and the Five Virtues (the "Five Teachings," in Yang's terms) define what it means to become fully human and humane,[118] with the result that the gap between the less developed denizens of the Han realm and the finest examples of humanity living beyond the frontiers is very small and easily broached by those willing to make concerted efforts to this end.[119] Thus Yang Xiong, the ardent proponent of Central States civilizations, is no unthinking booster for empire's impulse toward expansionism, nor is he a patriot supporting his country, right or wrong. Like all the pre-Han and Han masters, he is instead intent upon delineating which matters are fated (i.e., subject to happenstance and coincidence) and which liable to amelioration through human agency.[120] That Yang always offers these views in constructed dialogues (monologic though these exchanges are) serves to remind us that Yang's views on the merits of Central States civilizations and the sages were probably developed in arguments with interlocutors raising precisely these sorts of questions.

RECEPTION HISTORY OF *EXEMPLARY FIGURES*

As noted above, Yang may not have believed *Exemplary Figures* to be the finest of his several masterworks. But like the *Analects*, one of the texts of Han "elementary education," *Exemplary Figures* set out for readers the "elementary" forms of classical learning that Yang hoped his readers would emulate. That probably accounts for its immense popularity, especially in the period from Eastern Han (25–220) through Northern Song (960–1126). Even during Yang Xiong's lifetime, his disciples and friends hailed him as "not only a Kongzi of the West" (since he hailed from Chengdu, in present-day Sichuan, southwest of the Western Han capital) but also "a Kongzi of Qi and Lu" (meaning, a sage for all times and places). When he died, disciples such as Hou Ba 侯芭 mourned him for six years, just as Kongzi's disciples had done before. And historians are hard put to find a critical word about Master Yang 揚子, as he was called, throughout the Eastern Han period or the post-Han Six Dynasties (220–589). Admittedly, Wang Chong 王充 (27–97) at one point registers a mild criticism, but most of Wang's *Discourses Weighed in the Balance* (Lunheng 論衡) is extremely deferential toward Yang Xiong, whom Wang ranks far above Kongzi and Mencius as an authority.[121] In the final years of the Eastern Han, an entire private academy was organized around the study of Yang Xiong's masterworks in Jingzhou 荊州 (Hubei), and it is through the Jingzhou curriculum and connections that Yang's ideas, particularly those in *Exemplary Figures* and *Supreme Mystery*, came to influence several generations of the Wang family, including Wang Can 王粲 (177–217), Wang Su 王肅 (195–256), and Wang Bi 王弼 (226–49)—hence the ultimate derivation of the term "Mystery Learning" (Xuanxue 玄學) in the Six Dynasties.[122]

While the clear majority of the extant sources from the Six Dynasties and Sui-Tang (589–907) periods cite Yang's *Supreme Mystery*, there are abundant allusions to Yang's *Exemplary Figures* during the same time. For instance, several of the most famous historians of the Six Dynasties allegedly modeled their writings on Yang's style of history writing, including not only Qiao Zhou 譙周 (fl. 221–263 CE) of Shu (who might be expected to favor a local hero) but also Pei Ziye 裴子野 (469–530), author of the *Song Digest* (Songlue 宋略) and a harsh critic of the now more famous historian Shen Yue 沈约 (441–505)[123] —not to mention Liu Zhiji 劉知幾 (661–721) in his masterwork of historical criticism. Liu Zhiji acknowledged at great length the profound debt he owed to Yang Xiong in his intellectual formation.[124] Yang's *Exemplary Figures* was also routinely consulted by those with access to power who were anxious to improve local customs and court policies. For example, the poet Xie Tiao 謝朓 (464–94) never mentions Yang Xiong by name in his Poem 151, "Allotting Fields to the Poor" (Fu pin min tian 賦貧民田), written ca. 495, but he hardly needs to, for the very air the poem breathes is borrowed from

Yang. The final line of the poem gives the game away because it mentions Zheng Pu 鄭樸 (known by his courtesy style name Zizhen 子真), who won renown largely thanks to Yang's unstinting praise for his steadfast refusal to join the ranks of the Western Han bureaucracy. Intriguing references tell of whole works devoted to Yang's writings by such luminaries as Yu Fan 虞翻 (164–233), Huangfu Mi 皇甫謐 (215–82), and Fan Ning 范寧 (339–401), but these writings now survive merely as titles or as short fragments preserved in early encyclopedias.[125]

Aside from frequent testimonials from men such as Han Yu 韓愈 (768–824), who traced the transmission of the Dao 道通 through Yang Xiong,[126] the best testimony to the continuing authority invested in Yang Xiong's neoclassical texts comes from Yan Lingfeng's 嚴靈峯 multivolume catalog, where one can see the great numbers of commentaries compiled for *Exemplary Figures* (not to mention *Supreme Mystery* and *Fangyan*) up through the Northern Song period. In confirmation of Yang's secure standing, Yang, along with Xunzi and Han Yu, was enshrined in the Confucian temple from 1083, at one rank below Mencius, where he received sacrifices on the grounds that he "elaborated and illuminated the former sages' Dao, thereby aiding all students."[127] In 1068 the Northern Song emperor Shenzong 神宗 (r. 1067–85) singled out Yang Xiong and Dong Zhongshu 董仲舒 (179?-104? BCE) as the two noble epitomes (*junzi* 君子) of old who combined classical learning with a talent for writing.[128]

Yang was probably too famous to have escaped censure entirely in the centuries before the Southern Song (1126–1279), when Yang's reputation took a severe beating from the adherents of the True Way Learning. Early denunciations tended to make Yang's *fu* in praise of Wang's short-lived Xin dynasty their starting point.[129] But there were other gripes as well. Liu Zongyuan 劉宗元 (773–819) did not feel any qualms about lumping Yang together with a number of Han writers (Sima Xiangru, Liu Xiang, Ban Biao, and Ban Gu among them) whom Liu blamed for following ludicrous old traditions.[130] (That censure notwithstanding, Liu thought highly enough of *Exemplary Figures* to compose one of the early commentaries to it.)[131] Su Shi, a second well-known critic, decried Yang's complicated arguments and ambiguous expressions in a famous letter to a friend.[132] But before Zhu Xi's era in the late twelfth century, sustained criticism of Yang or Yang's *Exemplary Figures* was rare.[133] Zhu—anxious to displace Yang as the premier master of classical learning after Kongzi and Mencius—excoriated Yang and his teachings on three main grounds: (1) Yang had shown disloyalty to the Han ruling house by supporting the usurper Wang Mang and then compounded that error through the arrogance that led him to claim the status of master for himself and of a Classic for his *Supreme Mystery*, which made all his writings suspect; (2) Yang's cosmology was "incorrect" and in need of revision by Zhu because it failed to distinguish the material aspects (*qi* 氣) from the immaterial principles (*li* 理) of the cosmos; and (3) Yang's theory of human nature did not follow that of Mencius, despite Yang's spirited defense of Mencius against his many detractors.[134] Given such criticisms, Zhu Xi was quick to suggest major changes to the wording of Yang's *Exemplary Figures* that would have dramatically altered its meaning.[135] Those who sought to condemn Yang typically elevated Dong Zhongshu, a relatively marginal figure in Western Han, to the rank of premier Han Confucian master.[136]

In 1371, as a result of such aspersions cast on Yang's character, the director of the Directorate of Education submitted a memorial suggesting that Yang Xiong, among others, be removed from the Confucian temple. Yang was eventually removed from the temple in 1393,[137] although he was apparently restored to the temple (perhaps in some form of secondary status?) sometime before 1488. In any case, in that year one memorial, swiftly followed by a second, spoke of Yang Xiong "committing crimes against the moral teachings" (*ming jiao* 名教)[138] as part of a broader attack against "the confused and unorthodox writings of the Han and Wei periods."[139] Although the dominance of True Way Learning associated with Zhu, along with its "exclusionary logic,"[140] faced strong challenges during the Qing and Republican eras (1644–1949), the damage had been done. Yang's reputation as a philosophical master was never fully restored, for two main reasons: first, the new nationalistic narratives forged in late Qing and the early Republican era continued to demand (even retroactively) that absolute loyalty be rendered to the nation-state; and second, the very influential narratives by such leading May Fourth figures as Lu Xun 魯迅 (1881–1936) and Hu Shi 胡適 (1891–1962) invariably assigned a single specialty to each period, with "philosophy" allotted to the Zhanguo period and the Han left with only the *fu*.[141] Until the post-Mao era, the Communist Party of the People's Republic of China also condemned avowedly "Confucian" thinkers as the "running dogs" of slave society.[142] Now that a series of Confucian Revivals has been encouraged by the governments of Taiwan, Singapore, South Korea, and the People's Republic, many scholars have begun to show greater interest in restoring the reputations of such long-lost Confucian masters as Yang Xiong.[143]

CONCLUSION

A modern American writer has written,

> Clarity is the enemy of self-deception and of the larger deception known as ideology. Style is not the ornament of thought but its very substance, and thinking is an ethical act. Humanism, which seeks a complex integration of disparate experience, requires the most difficult kind of style: a simple one . . . because to become great it must respond to, and thus force an awareness of, the whole of reality.[144]

These things Yang knew two millennia before our time.

Some may think Yang's *Exemplary Figures* incoherent, and so it is, if one looks in it for the same kind of systematic logical exposition of a given topic that the *Xunzi* supplies in its philosophical essays. However, Yang supplies his own definition of a Classic: a work that says neither too much nor too little, but has very wide application in human affairs. By these criteria, it matters not a whit how hard the reader of the *Exemplary Figures* must work to piece Yang's meaning together from different passages while weighing their import; after all, similar exercises must be undertaken with the *Analects* and other classics from other traditions. Passages may only seem convoluted and hairsplitting to the sloppy reader who prefers a quick sound bite or slogan—a preference that existed even in Han times.[145] It is these very acts of careful deliberation—likened to the slow process of grinding and polishing jade—that are meant to school the reader in the ways of "becoming a human being" who is compelling in his thinking, in his speech, and in his conduct.

By the Han era, custom dictated that rulers seek out the writings of all peoples (not just their maps), including those of alien and conquered lands, and, by translating them, render them acquisitions of the dominant culture. Thus could space be conquered intellectually as well as physically. Yang's idea of conquering the distant past, making it accessible not only to contemporary readers but also to later generations, was no less an act of supreme intellectual ambition. Of a comparable figure in the classical Mediterranean world, the famous poet-librarian Callimachus, one scholar has written,

> His poetry was a mix of different dialects that required the reader to be able to use commentaries, dictionaries, and scholia; it was inextricably linked to the philological work going on in the library. The language made this poetry both obscure and elitist, also loaded with connotations, stuffed with learned references and curios, religious and mythographic memories, as to become a veritable cultural game.[146]

Yang, who was so intent upon forging links between pleasure-taking and giving, reading and writing, and classical learning for "later generations," would doubtless have been gratified to see that this sort of comparison springs to mind in readers today.

Michael Nylan

NOTES

1 For Yang as a historian, see, for example, *Shitong* 12.306. There was, of course, no office of Historian at court until the Tang period (618–907), so, more accurately, Sima Qian is "Archivist." For the relation between the *Fayan* and the *Shiji*, see L'Haridon, forthcoming; Yang 2003, esp. 21–32.

2 See *Hou Hanshu* 40A.1325 (Ban Biao biography) for the phrase 依五經之法言, 同聖人之是非. Ban Biao, the father of Ban Gu 班固, knew Yang Xiong and Huan Tan 桓譚 well.

3 Yang's choice of title indicates his desire to borrow from Kongzi 孔子, Zhuangzi 莊子, and Xunzi 荀子, for all these texts discuss "model sayings" or "exemplary figures" (*fayan* 法言), as do the *Han Feizi* 韓非子 and the *Classic of Filial Piety* (Xiaojing 孝經), section 4. See *Analects* 9.24; *Zhuangzi* 10.4/46, 51; and *Xunzi* 16/6/26 ("To speak less but have the speech modeled defines the noble man" 少言而法, 君子也). Both the *Han Feizi* and the *Classic of Filial Piety* say, "If it is not the model sayings of the former kings, one should not dare to say it" 非先王之法言, 不敢道. When criticizing superstitions, the *History of the Han* mentions the "model sayings of the Five Classics" (*Hanshu* 25B.1260, the "Treatise on Suburban Sacrifices"). Waley's 1938 translation of the relevant *Analects* passage treats "model sayings" as a book title ("The words of the *Fayu* [a book of moral sayings?] cannot fail to stir us, but what matters is that they should cause us to change our ways"). The extant sources include no such title, however.

4 McKenzie 1986 defines "degressive" as "considering what the original was."

5 Loewe, personal communication, said of how little we really know of antiquity.

6 For the first example, see the preface by Song Xian 宋咸 to a manuscript dated 1037; for the second, see Sima Guang's 司馬光 comments in the preface to his *Zizhi tongjian* 資治通鑒 (usually rendered as *General Mirror for the Aid of Government*) dated 1081. See also Yan 1993, 5.328. It is very interesting how often Sima Guang relies on Yang Xiong's *Fayan* when rendering judgments on early figures; he also mentions Yang Xiong in his postface to *Zizhi tongjian*.

7 In comparison with True Way Learning (often dubbed "neo-Confucianism"), Han thought tends to be less interior, less abstract, less intent upon moral purity, and more intent upon efficacious action; it is also somewhat more egalitarian in spirit.

8 These pithy judgments, which seem to anticipate those in the *Shishuo xinyu* 世說新語 (A New Account of Tales of the World), recall those in *Analects* 11.2.

9 Some of these battles of wit most likely mimicked the court conferences, such as the famous Shiqu 石渠 conference on policy matters in 51 BCE (see below), where scholars sought to best their opponents.

10 David Knechtges, personal communication. Yang's elaborate account of his decision to imitate the Classics may have been, in part, a ploy to counter such potential criticism. See Genette 1997, 246.

11 *Wenxin diaolong*, *juan* 14, specifically points to the humor in Yang's "Dispelling Ridicule" *fu*, where Yang tries to account for his lack of worldly success, which is inexplicable, given his merits. See also Knechtges, in Loewe 1993, 100: "Most of the responses [in *Exemplary Figures*] . . . rely on wit and puns rather than on logical [i.e., systematic] exposition to make their point."

12 Yang's two other masterworks are the *Fangyan* and *Supreme Mystery*. See Nylan 1993 for a complete study of *Supreme Mystery*. The best study on the *Fangyan* remains Serruys 1959. On Yang as the first self-conscious author in Chinese history, see Taniguchi 2010. Taniguchi notes that the tragic figure of Qu Yuan is merely a creation by Sima Qian in the *Shiji*, and Sima Qian's "self-consciousness" as an author rests upon two pieces of writing, Sima Qian's autobiography (*Shiji* 130), part of which derives

from later authors, and *Hanshu* 62, "The Letter to Ren An," almost certainly a work of literary impersonation (prosopopoeia).

13 Loewe 2006, 71.

14 Nylan, forthcoming-a.

15 Most historians think that Ban Gu appended little to Yang's autobiography except the final exculpatory tale of Yang's arrest and attempted suicide under Wang Mang and an admiring appraisal by one of Yang's most famous disciples, Huan Tan 桓譚 (43 BCE–28 CE). Yang Xiong was close to Ban Zhi 稚 (father of Ban Biao). The Bans continued to sing the praises of Yang Xiong. See Ban Si's 嗣 "Sheng xian gao shi zhuan" 聖賢高士傳.

16 Yang has one of only three multi-chapter (*juan*) biographies for a single person in the *History of the Han*. The other two figures so honored are the poet Sima Xiangru 司馬相如 (ca. 179–117 BCE), who, like Yang, was from Chengdu (in present-day Sichuan) and the usurper Wang Mang.

17 Notably, opinions vary about Ban Gu's attitude toward Yang. I find it far more positive than Pitner (2010) does.

18 Shrines were erected to Yan Junping (aka Zhuang Zun 莊遵) and Li Hong, under the encouragement of Qin Mi 秦祕 (Three Kingdoms period). See *Sanguo zhi* 38.976.

19 For the importance of the *fu* at the Han court, see Kern 2003, esp. 383. But Kern notes the "virtual absence of the genre in Sima Qian's *Shiji*" and in the "elaborate *Hanshu* account of literary activities at the [court of] Emperor Wu" (397).

20 For example, Yang describes "the excursion lodges so unique and rare." Ma Jigao (1987, 138–41) submits that the tension between eulogy and admonition was not resolved in the Han *fu*.

21 E.g., *Fayan* 6.22.

22 See *Hanshu* 87B.2564, 87B.3563; Knechtges 1982a, 45, 44.

23 *Hanshu* 87B.3563; Knechtges 1982a, 44–45.

24 This portrait of Chengdi contradicts many of the prevailing stereotypes. As the last adult ruler of the late Western Han, Chengdi had to be blamed for the downfall of the dynasty. Chengdi was an ardent classicist and an innovative ruler. In Chengdi himself and in many prominent figures at Chengdi's court, Yang found people who were as sympathetic and open to Yang's neoclassical arguments as he could hope to meet, and yet the old ways proved far too tenacious for his liking. For Ban Gu's praise of Chengdi, which verges on the extravagant, see *Hanshu* 100B.4239. That Chengdi had less money than Han Wudi is not the only reason for his promotion of classicism. On this, see the forthcoming conference volume on Chengdi's reign to be edited by Michael Nylan and Griet Vankeerberghen.

25 In his "Sweet Springs" *fu*, Yang compares the building projects at Sweet Springs to the building projects of those bad rulers. See *Hanshu* 87A.3528. Yang's "Exhortation against Wine" was said to mock Chengdi (see *Quan Han wen*, 52.728). Similarly, once Liu Xiang compared Emperor Cheng to the "tyrants of the Qin." That Chengdi did not punish Liu Xiang is amazing. See *Hanshu* 10.330, 36.1956–57.

26 *Hanshu* 87B.3570; Knechtges 1982a, 49.

27 I speak here of the Ding and Fu consort clans, as well as of Dong Xian, reputedly the male lover of Aidi, who at least had the signal virtue, from the Eastern Han historians' point of view, of slowing the seemingly inexorable rise of Wang Mang at court.

28 *Hanshu* 87B.3565; Knechtges 1982a, 46.

29 *Hanshu* 87B.3569; Knechtges 1982a, 49. For the *haogu* movement, see Nylan 2011.

30 *Hanshu* 87B.3575; Knechtges 1982a, 53. See also *Fayan* 2.1: "Grown men do not engage in such activities."

31 *Hanshu* 87B.3575; Knechtges 1982a, 53.

32 Wang Mang decreed that Yang write this eulogy, according to *Hanshu* 98.4035.

33 See Knechtges 1977.

34 Earlier in Western Han, as in the Zhanguo and Qin periods, the throne had access to several archives. But a library is different. For this difference, see Nylan 2011, esp. chap. 4.

35 See *Yanshi jiaxun* 顏氏家訓 8, 1.36a ("Mianxue zhang"); Teng 1968, 64–84, esp. 83–84. This saying is often quoted by textual critics. This image of Yang persisted into the Six Dynasties; see Wu Chaoqing, *Collected Writings*, *juan* 1 (入蘭臺贈王治書僧孺), *juan* 2 (周承未還重贈). Yang is said there to have worked in both the Shiqu and the Linge 麟閣 libraries.

36 This remark is now preserved in a letter to Liu Xin 劉歆, in *Guwen yuan*; it is cited also in *Wenxin diaolong*, *juan* 38 (trans., p. 289); for a full translation, see Knechtges 1977–78.

37 See Nylan 2011, pt. 4.

38 *Hanshu* 87B.3585 (Knechtges 1982a, 60) presents some of these questioners as curiosity-seekers since Yang had survived being accused of treason.

39 Knechtges 1982a, 57. Readers may wish to contrast my translation with that of Wu Fusheng 2007.

40 A laudable exception is Greatrex 1994.

41 According to Liu Zhiji's preface to the *Shitong* 史通 (Anatomy of Histories), "When Yang wrote his *Exemplary Figures*, people of the time competed to fault its reckless foolishness, and so he composed the 'Jiechao' to set them straight. Clearly, this is because Yang criticized people of his own era."

42 Or possibly Tongwu (Child Crow).

43 According to Yan Lingfeng (1993, 5.323–36, 57–64), five commentaries were produced for *Exemplary Figures* in the pre-Tang and Tang periods (compared with eleven in the Song period). Eighteen commentaries were produced for *Supreme Mystery* during the pre-Tang and Tang periods. Moreover, the commentaries included many by the most famous writers and thinkers of the Wei-Jin period, such as Song Zhong 宋衷, Lu Ji 陸績 (d. 229 CE), Yu Fan 虞翻 (d. 233), Wang Su 王肅 (d. 256 CE), and Fan Ning 范甯 (d. 403 CE). The only person in this period to comment on both *Exemplary Figures* and *Supreme Mystery* was Song Zhong of the Jingzhou Academy (ca. 192 CE) (see below). *Huayang guozhi* (Ren Naiqiang ed.) 10A.533, adds the names of Zhang Heng 张衡 (78–139), Cui Yuan 崔瑗 (78?–143?), and several others to the list of commentators. We should not forget that many of Yang's *fu* also had commentaries written for them.

44 Liu Xin's primary reason for recommending that the *Zuozhuan* (Zuo Traditions 左傳) be officially studied in the Han Imperial Academy was that the text contained so many ancient characters and ancient phrases. Liu Xin wanted to use the text of the *Zuozhuan* to explain the Classics, in much the same way that Yang and Liu Xiang proposed to use the *Erya*.

45 This point was made repeatedly by Bielenstein (1953–59, 1980).

46 Wang Qicai (2009, 131) points to the practical utility of a new literary trope. Instead of speaking of inaction or new policies endangering the ruler, as the early Western Han writers did, Yang and others began to claim that they would happily endanger themselves for the sake of the dynasty. According to Wang Qicai, this accounts in part for the rhetorical turn away from making a show of one's bravery to making a show of one's classical elegance, with Yang Xiong a pivotal figure in shaping the new trend (ibid., 159).

47 See the concluding Appraisal to *Hanshu* 87B. A far more spirited defense, articulated by Zhang Heng, argued that since the length of a dynasty is tied to cosmic cycles, Yang's elucidation of those cycles in *Supreme Mystery* in some sense began the process which "restored" the Han after Wang Mang. See *Hou Hanshu* 59.1897.

48 The anecdotes circulating about Yang in early (i.e., pre-Tang) texts can be sorted into several categories: (1) those portraying Yang as a "wisdom bag"; (2) those portraying

him as a proponent of using the *Erya* to correct the Classics; (3) those commenting on Yang's love for technical matters, including astronomy and music theory; (4) those emphasizing his extreme poverty, including Huan's criticism of Yang as one who cared too much for wealth and status; (5) those attesting the brilliant writer's desperate search for inspiration and fear of writer's block; (6) those portraying his fondness for drink (another plausible excuse for disengagement?); and (7) those declaring Yang to be the best editor, along with Liu Xiang, that the Central States had produced.

49 The Xiongnu were a nomadic confederation on the northwestern frontiers of the Han realm.

50 *Huayang guozhi* (Ren Naiqiang ed.) 10A.533.

51 Huan Tan, cited in *Yilin* 3.9a.

52 See Nylan, forthcoming-b.

53 See below. In a letter ("Da Xie Minshi shu" 答謝民師書) Su Shi also criticized Yang Xiong's propensity to use unusual vocabulary (see Han and Zhao 2010, 262–66), whereas Han Yu, one of Zhu Xi's heroes, praised Yang warmly, saying that he and Xunzi were surpassed only by Kongzi and Mencius in terms of their ethical teachings and that Yang was equal to Sima Qian and Sima Xiangru as a historian and writer. See Han's "Yuan dao" 原道 essay; and "Song Meng Dongye xu" 送孟東野序.

54 *Fayan* 11.15.

55 For the Republican era roots of this propensity to allot each era one type of literary activity, see P. Kroll 2010.

56 Yang reserves the highest praise for two groups: those courageous enough to criticize the powers-that-be of their own eras and the real specialists in the classical texts (e.g., Wang Ji 王吉 [fl. 74–51 BCE] and Gong Yu 貢禹 [d. 44 BCE], called "shining stars" in *Fayan* 11.23). According to L'Haridon (2006, vol. 1, 58), this use of the Classics as a critical weapon constitutes an important new dimension of or stage in the emergence of a group of men of letters who distinguish themselves both from the emperor and from career classicists.

57 Wang Qicai 2009, 115ff. The Five Classics are the *Odes, Documents, Rites, Annals,* and *Changes*.

58 I owe this insight to L'Haridon 2006, vol. 1, 124.

59 Fukui 2005, passim, esp. 153.

60 See, e.g., *Fayan* 1.4.

61 *Fayan* 7.18.

62 *Fayan* 5.15, 1.21–24, 2.8, 1.8.

63 Knechtges 1982a, 50, citing *Hanshu* 87A.3570.

64 E.g., *Fayan* 7.16, 8.6.

65 *Fayan* 1.19.

66 *Fayan* 1.18, 3.21, 4.7, 4.16, 6.3, 6.7–8. Nearly all of chapter 6 relates to this.

67 Carruthers 2008, 180.

68 The *Shiji*, for example, spoke with pride of the empire in many passages; the "Fengshan shu" chapter throughout describes the "Great Han's charismatic power, which reaches everywhere to the four borders" (Da Han zhi de . . . pang bo si sai 漢之德, . . . 旁魄四塞). Similarly, Sima Xiangru praised the wealth and splendor, and sheer expanse, of the Han Empire. As Wang Qicai 2009, 108 comments, "It must have been the prevailing feeling at the time—a note of justifiable pride in the government."

69 Given the idea that "past and present were one" and the ascribed essential natures and motivating forces of human beings, it was reasonable to believe that historians could be seers as well and that one could draw upon the rich resources of history to resolve difficult issues. For early ideas about the historian's job (which serve equally well for China as for classical Greece), see Veyne 1988.

70 Surely the desire to display command of a set of technical skills accounts for the

form of *Exemplary Figures* and Yang's "philosophical" poems as much as Yang's desire to imitate the *Analects*, for in each work Yang artfully arranged dialogues masquerading as battles of wit like those that marked the Shiqu 石渠 court conference in 51 BCE. It was not at all unusual in Yang's era for masters to make such comparisons between oneself or others and the sages of antiquity. For example, a late Eastern Han stele from Shandong erected to Jing Yun 景雲 (dated 173 CE; discovered 2004) compares Jing to Confucius and Shun (two sages). See *Chongqing Zhongguo Sanxia bowuguan*, 98–99.

71 E.g., *Hanshu* 87A.3515, which often talks about the "right moment" and what to do if the moment is not propitious for action.

72 Cullen 2010.

73 Yang was listed as one of nine earlier experts on astronomy in "Lun Tian" 論天, in Yan Kejun, *Quan shanggu Sandai Qin Han Sanguo Liuchao wen*, "Quan Jin wen," 39.406.

74 Li Zehou 2000, passim, makes the point that this is true about Chinese thought in general and Han classicism in particular; see also Fingarette 1972, esp. chap. 2.

75 The same theme had preoccupied earlier self-described Confucian masters. See, e.g., *Mencius* 3A.4.

76 *Fayan* 5.26.

77 *Fayan* 2.1.

78 *Fayan* 4.8.

79 *Fayan* 9.7.

80 *Fayan* 7.7.

81 As one Six Dynasties writer, Xie Lingyun 謝靈運 (385–433), put it, "Ornament and structure together are what perfects the beauty [of the piece]" 文體宜兼，以成其美. See Yan Kejun, *Quan shanggu Sandai Qin Han Sanguo Liuchao wen*, "Quan Song wen," 31.299 ("Shanju" 山居 *fu*).

82 See Yan Kejun, *Quan shanggu Sandai Qin Han Sanguo Liuchao wen*, "Quan Liang wen," 27.283 ("Zhu zhi zhi" 注制旨).

83 *Fayan* 5.13. Contrast the reading given this passage in Gu 2005, 35–43, which provides a useful introduction to its import.

84 See *Shiqu baoji* 32.31b.

85 See Taniguchi 2010.

86 See Matsukawa 1994, esp. 23–40.

87 Yang may well have been mindful of the tradition whereby no fewer than three of Kongzi's inner circle of disciples (Zixia, Zizhang, and Ziyou) wanted to serve You Rou as if he were the Master himself because of his physical resemblance to the Master. See *Mencius* 3A.4.

88 See *Huayang guozhi* (Ren Naiqiang ed.) 10A.533.

89 See L'Haridon 2006, vol., 1, 78.

90 Knechtges 1968, 99 (trans. modified).

91 *Fayan* 12.9.

92 *Hanshu* 76.3239.

93 E.g., the Appraisals to *Hanshu* 57 and 65 (on Dong Fangshuo). Ban Gu openly imitated Yang Xiong in his writings, according to *Hanshu* 100B.4165. One also suspects that parts of these chapters reflect the prefaces that Yang wrote for thirty-eight *pian* of the *Han Records* (Hanji 漢記). See *Ershi wushi bubian* 1.1588.

94 For this insight, I am grateful to L'Haridon 2006.

95 *Hanshu* 62.2737–38; *Shiji* 20.1062. Yang Yun, son of the chancellor Yang Chang 敞, received five million cash in assets upon his father's death, as well as his stepmother's wealth, which he then increased several-fold by engaging in business. Both Yangs have biographies in *Hanshu* 66. Sima Qian's daughter was Yang Yun's mother, according to *Hanshu* 66.2885. (The characters *yang* 揚 and *yang* 楊 were

used interchangeably in old editions, and it is conceivable that the two Yangs, Yang Xiong and Yang Yun, were somehow related.) Loewe (2000, 640) says of Yang Yun that his "main service perhaps lay in rescuing Sima Qian's book from the obscurity into which it had fallen after the author's death and bringing it to attention during Xuandi's time." Yang enjoyed close relations with several distinguished men of letters; he himself was a man of talents with an interest in history, though his outspoken criticisms of others, extravagant lifestyle, and aggressive moneymaking greatly displeased Xuandi, who finally had him publicly executed for "gross immorality." See J. Kroll 2010.

96 See *ECT*, pp. 405–14.

97 A request made by Liu Yu 宇, King of Dongping (r. 52–20 BCE), to see a copy of "the Grand Archivists' writings" (*Taishi gong shu* 太史公書) was denied, but Wang Feng 王鳳, maternal uncle of Chengdi, had seen enough of the *Shiji* to give a scathing assessment of its content, proving that some privileged people were allowed to see the text. See *Hanshu* 80.3324, for the request. For Sima Qian's tomb and shrine, see *KGYWW* 1981.2, p. 108.

98 Yang Yun was able to restore Sima Qian's good name under Xuandi (r. 92–74 BCE), but his works seem not to have been in wide circulation following that. Yang Xiong praised Sima Qian in his *Exemplary Figures*. For Yang's own pronounced bias against Han Wudi, see the notes to *Fayan* 13.28, for example.

99 For the phrase 然自劉向揚雄,博極群書,皆稱遷有良史之才,服其善序事理,辯而不華, see Yan Kejun, *Quan shanggu Sandai Qin Han Sanguo Liuchao wen*, "Quan Song wen," *juan* 17, preface to the *Shiji jiejie* 史記集解; cf. *Sanguo zhi*, *juan* 13.

100 See Xu Fuguan 1979. One exception is L'Haridon 2005, 2006, forthcoming. L'Haridon suggests that one principal difference between Sima Qian and Yang is that Yang put more weight on loyalty than did Sima Qian. The issue is more complicated, however, and not only because Yang mentions loyalty in *Exemplary Figures* only twice (7.20, 10.15). (Ironically, one of the main accusations leveled by Yang's detractors was that he was disloyal, insofar as he served two dynasties.)

101 *Fayan* 10.30.

102 Finley 1975, passim.

103 *Fayan* 12.1.

104 *Fayan* 8.18.

105 It is probably significant that Yang's teacher, Yan Junping 嚴君平, was also purportedly a "historian" working in the style of Zuo Qiuming (see *Shitong*, chap. 2). In *Exemplary Figures*, about seventy-five Western Han figures are named, and a clear majority of these are figures whom the court suspected of crimes (e.g., Bing Ji, Dong Zhongshu, Dou Ying, Guan Ying, Han Yanshou, Jia Yi, Jia Juanzhi, Li Guangli, Luan Bu, Shen Pei, Master Yuangu, Shi Qing, Sima Qian, Wang Zun Wei Qing, Xiahou Sheng, and Zhi Buyi); who were executed by the court (e.g., Chao Cuo, Han Xin, Han Yanshou, Jing Fang, Liu An, Sang Hongyang, Shangguan Jie, Yuan Ang, and Zhao Guanghan); who were wrongly favored by the court (e.g., Chen Tang, Dongfang Shuo, and Gongsun Hong); or who played more ambiguous roles than they should have, given the trust invested in them by the Han court (e.g., Chen Ping, Zhou Bo, and Huo Guang). By my rough count, Yang considered only fourteen people to have been more or less correctly judged by the Han court: Fan Kuai, Feng Tang (possibly?), the Four Graybeards, Guan Fu, Juan Buyi, Lou Jing, Lu Jia, Su Wu, Xiahou Ying, Yin Wenggu, and Zhang Anshi. I say "rough count," because figures like the Four Graybeards implicitly criticize one ruler but honor and are honored by another. By means of one incident or another, *Exemplary Figures* portrays every single ruler from the Han founder down to Chengdi, Yang's own ruler, in an unflattering light. I have argued elsewhere, in forthcoming-b, that Yang Xiong also criticizes Wang Mang.

106 Smith et al. (1990, 227–28) identified this way of reading as a Song innovation, but it is certainly Han, if not pre-Han.

107 The *Gongyang* 公羊 commentaries to the *Annals*, for example, said that histories were written to elucidate the power of the Way by revealing the distinctive patterns (good and ill) forged through actions and events. See *Gongyang zhuan*, Lord Ai, year 14.

108 *Hanshu* 72.3057 says of Yang that he "truly knew men" (楊子雲誠知人).

109 Han moralists—in stark contrast to the adherents of the True Way Learning espoused by Zhu Xi—did not posit a strong contrast between moral purity and practical efficacy; they sought instead to cast practical wisdom and calls for efficacy as twin components of the admirable Way of the sages. However, Yang does not hesitate to condemn the Han rulers and regents for empowering greedy, unscrupulous, or sycophantish upstarts who harmed the ordinary subjects most grievously. It is hardly coincidental that most of the political figures whom Yang praises had been executed, exiled, or dismissed by the Han.

110 See, e.g., *Fayan* 3.16, 9.17: "True and false—that is the core. If the truth is not perceived as true, nor the false as false, then an administration lacks a moral core."

111 *Fayan* 1.3.

112 Because the Classics contained so many different characters and supplied rhetorical models, study of one or more of the Classics was often undertaken to learn reading and writing, and testing of characters and rhetorical forms was used for some posts in government. However, it would be wrong to ascribe to the Han anything like the full-blown examination culture of the Song period. For more on this, see Nylan 2008.

113 *Fayan* 2.11.

114 Ji An is usually identified as a Huang-Lao proponent, as if that should make him an enemy of all the classicists; see *Shiji* 120.3108, which says that Ji An often slandered the Ru. But Yang Xiong thought him a man of principle, which clearly indicates that the Ru were not a monolithic group—a fact confirmed in many early texts of the time.

115 *Fayan* 10.12.

116 *Fayan* 3.20.

117 *Fayan* 4.11.

118 *Fayan* 4.11.

119 *Fayan* 3.20.

120 *Fayan* 6.11.

121 "Of the many writers of Han times, Sima Qian and Yang Ziyun are like the Yellow River and the Han; the rest are like the Jing and the Wei Rivers" (quoted from *Lunheng juan* 29, *pian* 83, entitled "Anshu").

122 Few modern early scholars seem to have put the elementary facts about the derivation of the term Mystery Learning together, probably because Han historians and Six Dynasties historians too seldom read the basic texts from both time periods. See Wagner 2000; Nylan 2001b. Wang Baoxuan (2004) sometimes seems to recognize this link and sometimes to forget it.

123 For Qiao Zhou, see Farmer 2007. Qiao was the author not only of writings on history but also of a "Faxun" (Glosses on the Model 法訓) and "*Wujing lun*" (On the Five Classics 五經論), in altogether several hundred *pian*. For Pei Ziye, see Blitstein 2009; J. Chen, forthcoming; Cao 2002, 297.

124 For examples, see *Shitong*, "Preface" (Zixu 自敘), pp. 288–98. See also below.

125 Also, the *Zizhi tongjian* 64/27a says that Xun Yue's *Shenjian* in five *pian* (compiled ca. 205 CE) was described, at the time it was written, as being "somewhat like Yang Xiong's *Fayan*" (see *Shenjian*, p. 1). Some part of this loss is almost certainly due to the extremely negative pronouncements on Yang Xiong offered by Zhu Xi

(1130–1200) and other adherents of the True Way Learning movement (see below), whose writings became exceedingly influential guides to reading the Classics after the Southern Song.

126 Han Yu traces the transmission of the Way (Daotong) from Mencius to Xunzi to Yang Xiong. There are numerous examples of Han's praise of Yang, one being Han's collected works, *Han Changli quanji* 韓昌黎全集, 14.227, which insists that Yang Xiong, along with Mencius, "enabled people now and afterward to understand how [the sages' teachings] differed from heterodoxies." Nonetheless, Wilson (1995, 81) strongly doubts that Han Yu had the fully developed notion of the Daotong that Zhu, not to mention later scholars, have credited him with. Cf. Ouyang Xiu's praise for Yang's literary skills in *Ouyang Wenzhong quanji* 50.6b, 67.1b, 3.12a.

127 See Wilson 1995, 41. Cf. *Songshi* 105.2549; *Gujin tushu jicheng* 199.56a. Farmer 2000, 119, cites evidence for a shrine built to Yang Xiong in Chengdu.

128 See *Songshi* 336.10762. Yang Xiong was highly regarded in his own time as a classical master, but this was probably not the case with Dong Zhongshu. See Loewe 2011, which examines the place of Dong within early Chinese history. The names of Dong and Yang are still repeatedly linked in post-Han writings. See, e.g., *Shen Yue ji* 1.96/42 ("On Passing by Liu Huan's Tomb" 奉和竟陵王經劉瓛墓).

129 See *Wei shu* 22.1145, 1156 (Zhao Yi 趙逸 biography), 21.114.52; cf. *Yanshi jiaxun* 9.38.16. At the same time, Liu Xin's conduct was deemed far worse, as he was a member of the Han imperial house. See, e.g., *Taiping yulan* 599.

130 *Xin Tangshu* 168.5136.

131 See Yan 1993, 5.326. That commentary now exists only in fragments.

132 Liu Shi Shun 1979, "Da Xie Minshi shu" 答謝民師書. See Han and Zhao 2010, 262–66.

133 See *Huayang guozhi* (Ren Naiqiang ed.) 10A.543.

134 See Zhu Xi, in Chan 1967. Zhu Xi wrote, "Don't read Master Yang. There is nothing good in what he said, and there is nothing concrete in his theories. Although Xunzi made mistakes, what he said is really concrete." See *Zhuzi yulei* 137.2b (Chan 1967, 93). This diatribe occurs in a chapter devoted to revision of earlier theories about the Daotong, including the assessment of Yang Xiong as one of three Han figures whose "words and deeds are helpful to the education of the world and should be studied." Zhu Xi also said, "Yang Ziyun lost his integrity by serving Wang Mang." See Zhang Boxing, *Jinsilu jijie* 14.5b (Chan 1967, 95). Zhu ascribed to his teacher Cheng Yi the saying "Neither Xunzi nor Yang Xiong could have uttered exceedingly wise sayings" (Chan 1967, 297). Zhu also cited with approbation a criticism of Yang Xiong; trans., p. 298. Zhu believed, with his master Cheng Yi, that "after Mencius, the Learning of the Sage was no longer transmitted. From the Qin and Han dynasties on, none reached the [requisite] level of truth" (Chan 1967, 300).

135 Chan 1967, 98.

136 For a reception history of Dong demonstrating this very point, see Loewe 2011. Dong was held in high esteem in Southern Song (as earlier) by the very people who were condemning Yang Xiong, including the Cheng brothers and Zhu Xi. Lou Yue (1137–1213, *jinshi* 1163) wrote that Yang Xiong should have felt "ashamed" by Dong's statement (recorded in *Chunqiu fanlu* 6.17, p. 162) that "a victory won without reliance on Dao is of less value than a defeat by such reliance." Lou Yue's remarks are recorded in *Songshi* 宋史 395.12045; also in his *Gongkui ji* 77.1a. No reputable Han scholar today regards the *Chunqiu fanlu* 春秋繁露 (usually rendered as *Luxuriant Dew on the Annals*) ascribed to Dong as an authentic work by Dong.

137 *Mingshi* 明史 50.1297.

138 Wilson 1995, 55–56, citing, among other texts, Wang Qi, *Xu wenxian tongkao* 48.3230.

139 Thomas A. Wilson notes that debates recorded in the *Mingshi* suggest that he was

(re?)enshrined just before 1530, and he suspects that "some of the people who were memorializing the throne about his status thought Yang was still enshrined there" (personal communication, 26 July 2010).

140 The phrase "exclusionary logic" comes from Wilson 1995, 56.

141 Lu Xun (1958) not only emphasized the greater "vigor and force" of other Han writers, particularly Jia Yi 賈誼 and Chao Cuo 鼂錯, but also underscored the overly simplistic idea that each dynasty had one literary specialty. Lu also formed an analogy between the "dark ages" following the Mediterranean classical period and the Han following the Zhanguo period, whereby the Han thinkers were condemned as "unoriginal" "scholastics" intent upon merely classifying the "true philosophy" of the pre-imperial period.

142 For the best introduction to the condemnations of Confucian teaching, see Louie 1980. Joseph Needham, in his monumental *Science and Civilisation in China* (over twenty vols. to date), labored under the misapprehension that Confucians were "anti-science" and Daoists "pro-science." See his volume 2, where this is discussed.

143 On the Confucian Revival, see Nylan 2001a, chap. 7; and Nylan, with Wilson, 2010, chap. 7.

144 Arthur Danto, cited in *The Nation*, 14 May 2007, 50.

145 *Fayan* 8.11.

146 Jacob and Polignac 2000, 95.

Exemplary Figures / *Fayan*

卷第一

學行

天降生民。倥侗顓蒙。
恣乎情性。聰明不開。
訓諸理。譔學行。

1.1 學行之上也。言之次也。教人又其次也。[1] 咸無焉為眾人。

1 A similar ranking is given in *Zuozhuan*, Xiang 24.1, which lists "deeds" after "character" and "speeches" (立德立言立功). Both *yan* and *jiao* involve speaking about "what one has learned": *yan* implies formulating a tradition or "a way of thinking," while *jiao* can refer to the mechanical methods of transmitting knowledge typical of the uninspired student or teacher of the Classics.

Chapter 1

Learning and Practicing

VERSE SUMMARY

When heaven first came down to give birth to the people,[1] they were dense and dim-witted. As they gave free rein to their own instincts, their faculties of sight and hearing were quite undeveloped. In order to instruct them [the people] according to certain principles, I compiled chapter 1, "Learning and Practicing."[2]

....

To practice what one has learned is best; to articulate it is second best; 1.1
and to teach it to others, a distant third.[3] Those who fail in all of these are but ordinary men.

---

1 Cf. *Odes* 255/1, on heaven's giving birth to the masses (天生烝民). This citation often prompts a different conclusion; for example, *Mencius* 5B.6 uses this passage to argue for the existence of at least the "beginnings" of innate goodness in human beings.

2 All the verse summaries for the thirteen chapters of *Exemplary Figures* follow the translations of Knechtges 1982a, with minor modifications. Regarding the title of this chapter, readers should note that the word for both "study" and "learning" (the goal of study) in Chinese is *xue* 學, the goal not being distinguished graphically from the process. For that reason, sometimes *xue* is translated as "study" (to refer to the process) and sometimes as "learning" or "classical learning" (to refer to the final goal). Note the frequency with which authoritative texts (e.g., the *Analects* and the *Xunzi*) begin with treatises encouraging study (as the process leading to learning) and its application to conduct. Classical learning qualifies as the proper object of study, so I render *xue* in this meaning as "true learning." See *Analects* 1.7, 1.13, for definitions of "true learning" (which is not book learning but cultivation of one's character).

3 Cf. *Analects* 2.13; cf. *Liji*, "Zaji" (B.20): "There are three conditions that grieve [*huan* 患] the noble man: if there be a subject of which he has not heard, and he cannot get to hear of it; if he hears of it, but he has no opportunity to study it; and if he studies it, but he has no opportunity to put it into practice." See Legge 1967, vol. 2, 166. Cf. *Hanshi waizhuan* 1.18.

1.2 或曰人羨久生。將以學也。可謂好學已乎。曰未之好也。學不羨。[2]

1.3 天之道不在仲尼乎。仲尼, 駕說者也。[3] 不在茲儒乎。如將復駕其所說, 則莫若使諸儒金口而木舌。[4]

1.4 或曰學無益也，如質何。曰未之思矣。[5]

---

2 Cf. *Xinxu* 新序, cited in *Beitang shuchao* 83.3a; or *Taiping yulan* 607.4a, which has Mozi say that one should study, not to please others, but rather to improve oneself.

3 *Tuo* sometimes is a loan for *yue* 悦 (to delight in), as in *Shiji* 23.1170. But Han Jing (1992, 2n2) suggests reading *shuo* 說 as *tuo* 脱/挩/*shui* 稅 ("to get free of"; "to put down"; "to take off"; and, in this case, "to die"). L'Haridon (2006) ties this to *Odes* 50/3 ("Ding zhi fang zhong" 定之方中), where the characters 說+ 駕 appear together, and the metaphor of "abandoning one's carriage" signifies death. For *jia shuo* 駕說, see *Zhouli zhushu* (e-*SKQS*) 27.20b, 33.9a. Similarly, Wang Rongbao (1987, 1.6–8) defines the binomial expression *jia tuo* as *mei* 沒 (to die), and others read *shuo* as *tui* 蜕 ("to exuviate" or "to undergo transformation"). My translation seeks to retain the carriage metaphor. Christoph Harbsmeier (pers. comm.), an outlier here, would retain the *shuo*, so that the line reads "Kongzi is the one who steers the explanations . . ."

4 To Yang's comment, compare *Hanshu* 21A.978, which claims that those who are wearing Ru clothes are reciting words that are "not right." *Lunheng* 13/36/15–17 says, "The person with wisdom and ability could serve the court better with a tongue of three inches and a writing brush of one foot," meaning he should talk less and write more.

5 Contrast *Huainan zi* 20.220.28 ("Taizu xun" 泰族訓): "Every single person knows learning's utility to the self." The position that learning is of no use is ascribed to Xiang Yu 項羽 in *Shiji* 7.295, where the attitude is said to be the root cause of Xiang's downfall. The confusion of Kongzi's own disciple, Zilu, regarding the utility of classical learning is showcased in several *Shuoyuan* anecdotes, including 5.27 and 8.20.

Someone asked me,[4] "If a person covets long life, and he studies with this in mind, can we call that 'love of learning'?"[5] 1.2

"That hardly qualifies as love.[6] True learning does not covet a particular end."[7]

The Way of Heaven—was it not invested in Kongzi [i.e., Confucius]? But the reins of his carriage were set down [at his death]. Is the Way then not invested in these classicists?[8] If one were to try to take up again the reins that were laid down, then the best way of doing this would be to cause all the classicists to make their voices ring out loud and clear, like wooden tongues giving voice to bells of bronze.[9] 1.3

Someone asked me, "Learning confers no possible advantage![10] What does it have to do with matters of substance?" 1.4

---

4 One is sometimes tempted to translate *huo yue* 或曰 as "people say," since the arguments that typically follow this phrase, while not all that coherent or well constructed, are "common wisdom" and thus powerful nonetheless.

5 *Analects* 6.3 defines "love of [the process of] learning" in relation to Yan Hui, Kongzi's favorite disciple. Cf. *Analects* 6.20: "To know it [the Way] is less good than to love it, and to love it, less good than to take pleasure in it." See also *Analects* 1.14, which depicts love of learning as implicit in cultivating the truly good life. *Expounding the Canon*, included in the *Later Mohist Canon* (See Graham 1978, EC 10), equally states that "learning" must be disinterested (不為己之可學也).

6 Zach 1939, 1, prefers "He still does not love it yet."

7 I.e., "other than itself." Yang denounces the merely instrumental use of learning; one learns in order to cultivate oneself. Debates over the purpose of study and learning, and specifically whether it is done for others or for oneself, are frequent in the early texts. See *Analects* 8.12, which bemoans the modern tendency to study for the sake of reward; *Analects* 14.25, which has Kongzi remark, "In olden days men studied for the sake of self-improvement; nowadays men study in order to impress other people." But Christoph Harbsmeier (pers. comm.) prefers to translate "In studying, one is not coveting things." Learning is an end in itself; therefore, it does not covet a particular end. Cf. *Analects* 4.8 ("In the morning hear the Way; in the evening die [content]"). Furthermore, Kongzi, cited in *Liji* 32.11/144/6, claims that all forms of right conduct should be ends in themselves, not a means of fame in this life or after it. L'Haridon (2006) ties this saying to *Fayan* 12.20, 12.22, which discuss a proper death and misapprehensions about limits. Wang Rongbao (1987, 1.6) speaks of the questioner's failure to understand the proper limits of one's desires in general and, more specifically, to understand that it is wrong to covet longevity.

8 Mather 2003, 25n, reads this differently: "Was not the Way of Heaven implicit in Kongzi? Kongzi was its transmitter." Cf. *Analects* 9.5: "When King Wen died, did that mean that culture ceased to exist?" Alternatively, "Since the death of Kongzi, does not the Way lie with the Ru?" Here the term "Ru" refers to the subset of classicists who follow Kongzi. See Nylan 1999 for the three meanings of "Ru."

9 Literally, "then nothing would be as good as causing all the classicists to gild their mouths and make their tongues wooden." This phrase may hint at using "golden [i.e., effective] rhetoric but wooden tongues [less wagging]." However, the phrase "wooden striker" [lit., "tongue"] appears alone in *Analects* 3.24, which compares Kongzi to a wooden striker used for the signal bell to arouse the masses, usually for battle. The wooden striker creates the loudest possible sound; see Bagley 2000. Note that bronze bells look golden when first cast.

10 Significantly, the Kongzi of the *Analects* does not think human nature is "fixed" (i.e., impervious to training and acculturation), except for those operating at the very

夫有刀者礲諸。有玉者錯諸。不礲不錯，焉攸用。礲而錯諸，質在其中矣。否則輟。[6]

1.5 螟蛉之子，[7] 殪而逢蜾蠃。祝之曰類我，類我。久則肖之矣。速哉！七十子之肖仲尼也。

6 Cf. *Xunzi* 20/8/10: 儒無益於人之國. For Zheng Xuan's use of this line, see *Hou Hanshu* 35.1209–10.

7 *Maoshi zheng yi* 12/3/2a (p. 419). For a case where the same lines from *Odes* 196 became the basis for a legal judgment, see case 1 ("A had no son") of Dong Zhongshu's *Chunqiu jieyu*, quoted in Ma Guohan 1967, 2.1180–81.

"You certainly have not thought it through yet![11] Now, surely, those with knives grind them, and those with jades polish them. Unground and unpolished, of what possible use are knives and jades?[12] Certainly, there is something substantial in the grinding and polishing processes. Were that not so, then one would stop doing it."[13]

When the young of the corn worm were on the point of dying, they hap- 1.5
pened upon a wasp, who beseeched them, "Be like me; become worthy like me!"[14] And at long last the larvae did indeed come to resemble the wasp. How quick by comparison was the seventy disciples' successful emulation of Kongzi![15]

---

highest level of wisdom or the very lowest level of stupidity (惟上智與下愚不移).

11 Cf. *Analects* 9.30 for the phrase *wei zhi si ye* 未之思也.

12 The beauty of the jade comes more from the way it is polished and carved than from its material substance, as jade workers know; hence, it becomes the perfect analogy for cultivation. Also, the beauty of the substance is recovered or realized only through polishing, as in the modern proverb "Uncarved jade does not make a finished object; people without learning do not understand the basics" (玉不琢, 不成器; 人不學, 不知理). This association between social cultivation and learning and polishing jade is very old; see, e.g., *Odes* 55/1, 256/5; the opening lines to the "Record of Learning" (Xueji 學記) chapter in the *Liji*; and Xia 1983.

13 I.e., "were there no substance involved." The phrase "not stop" (*bu chuo* 不輟) recalls *Analects* 18.6. One does not stop "trying to improve things" is implied.

14 The original text repeats the phrase "be like me" or, alternatively, "become as worthy." *Xiao* 肖 usually indicates not only resemblance but comparable worth—hence, the overtranslation in an attempt to capture both senses. Cf. *Odes* 196/3 ("Xiao wan"), which includes the lines "The corn worm has its young / The wasp bears them off [rears them?] [*fu* 負]." The idea of education and training appears in the ode itself (教誨爾子, 式穀似之). The parasitic wasps called *guoluo* belong to the family Eumenidae, while the meal snout moth, or corn worm, belongs to the Pyralididae family. See *Tiandi kunchong tuce*, 15–16. According to this ode's commentaries, which reflect a basic misunderstanding of the parasitical process in nature, the solitary wasp or robber fly takes the corn worm larvae back to its nest, where it treats them as its own progeny, thereby inculcating in them the habits of wasps or robber flies.

Some of the *Odes* commentators—and Yang tends to follow the Lu tradition of the *Odes*—celebrate this as an image of the potential for complete transformation from one spirit to another and use it to "prove" that humans can transform themselves for the better, probably because the character *fu* 負 means "to bear on one's back," "to carry off," "to shoulder responsibility for," and "to rear." Others are doubtful, however, that the wasp's actions show kind intentions. Do the wasps "adopt and rear" ("setting a good example for them," so that they "advance every day, progress every month," as later lines in the ode suggest) or do they "feast upon and destroy" the larvae? (Apparently, the mistaken view of the process is the commentator's, not the poet's.) The passage raises interesting questions, among them: How does a parasite live on its host? What is the character of education? Does one digest a master's words and so become something else, thanks to the nourishment, or does learning happen in another way?

15 The result of the successful transformation of the larvae was that they did not die, according to Han belief (see below); adding the phrase "by comparison" for sense. The tone of Yang's remark is hard to judge. Christoph Harbsmeier (pers. comm.) thinks the joke is that the disciples did not wait until they were on the point of dying before they began to imitate Kongzi. The problem is that in most traditions only three of Kongzi's disciples (Yan Hui, Min Ziqian, and Ran Niu) ever came to resemble their master. So the point may be that it is exceedingly difficult to emulate a master. However, Yang Xiong, like Mencius and Xunzi before him, tried to make the case that he

1.6 學以治之。[8] 思以精之。朋友以磨之。[9] 名譽以崇之。不倦以終之。可謂好學也已矣。

1.7 孔子習周公者也。顏淵習孔子者也。羿逢蒙分其弓。良捨其策。般投其斧。而習諸，孰曰非也。或曰此名也。彼名也。處一焉而已矣。曰川有瀆。山有嶽。高而且大者，眾人所不能踰也。

1.8 或問世言鑄金。金可鑄與。曰吾聞覿君子者。問鑄人。不問鑄金。或曰人可鑄與。曰孔子鑄顏淵矣。或人踧爾曰旨哉。問鑄金。得鑄人。

---

8 Reading *zhi* 治 as "engage with," "govern," and even "treat [an illness]." Wang Rongbao (1987, 1.13) reads *zhi* 治 as *shi* 始 (to begin [the work of cultivation]). Note also that in this passage, it is not entirely clear to what the "it" (*zhi* 之) refers, let alone whether the pronoun refers to the same object. Christoph Harbsmeier (pers. comm.) prefers to understand *zhi* 之 as "things" (not just "it" or "one's own person").

9 Cf. the Guodian manuscript entitled "Yucong" 語叢 4: "If a man in service has friends who give him counsel, his oratory will not be strained" 士有 (悔 =)謀友, 則言談不刁(=約). Cf. the Guodian manuscript entitled "Xing zi ming chu" 性自命出, strips 10–12. See *Guodian Chu mu zhu jian*. On the utility of good behavior, cf. "Zhongyong" 32.14/144/31: 或安而行之, 或利而行之.

The purpose of classical learning is to govern oneself; of reflection, to refine oneself; of making friends, to polish oneself; and of a good name, to ennoble oneself. If a person exhibits unflagging determination, staying on course to the very end—this and only this is what I would call "love of learning."[16] 1.6

Kongzi emulated the Duke of Zhou; and Yan Hui, Kongzi.[17] Had Hou Yi and Peng Meng snapped their bows in two, or Wang Liang thrown away his horsewhip, or Gongshu Ban tossed aside his ax, so as to emulate one of those men,[18] who would say that they were wrong? 1.7

Someone remarked, "The one group is famous, but so is the other. It is just that each man occupies a unique place in a single specialty—that's all."[19]

"Among the waterways, there are the great rivers, and among the mountains, the mighty peaks. The elevated, the great—*that* the common run of men cannot surpass."[20]

Someone asked me, "In today's world, people are always talking about casting alchemical gold.[21] Can gold really be produced in this way?" 1.8

"From what I have heard, those who see a noble man ask about casting men, not about casting gold."

Someone asked me, "Can men really be cast like metal?"[22]

"Surely Kongzi, in a sense, cast Yan Hui."

Startled,[23] the interlocutor responds: "Well done! I asked about creating metal and I get an answer about transmuting a man's mettle."

---

measures up to the Master. Cf. *Mencius* 3A.4, which reports that because one of the disciples physically resembled Kongzi, after Kongzi's death they considered making him their master.

16 Christoph Harbsmeier (pers. comm.) reads this as "Friends contribute to a person's polish." *Analects* 1.14 gives a different, if related, definition for "love of learning." Cf. *Analects* 14.25 (cited above) and *Analects* 7.22: "Whenever I am walking with three men, I always find a model among them."

17 See *Analects* 9.11.

18 I.e., the Duke of Zhou, Kongzi, or Yan Hui.

19 This translation tries to capture both senses of the phrase *chu yi yan* (lit., "to live in one of them"), where "one" almost certainly refers to "techniques" or "specialties" that make a man famous for all time. *Mencius* 2A.7 hints that certain occupations can help or hurt one's moral state. Contrast the famous satirical comment in *Lüshi chunqiu* 11.4.1 ("Dangwu"), where the robber Zhi explains that thievery requires all the virtues, including sageliness, courage, dutifulness, wisdom, and benevolence (cf. Knoblock and Riegel 2000, 251; *Lüshi chunqiu jiaoshi*, 602.

20 Contrast *Daode jing*, section 66, which identifies greatness with the "ability to lower oneself." The idea is then that only the Way of Kongzi and the Duke of Zhou is truly extraordinary, unlike expertise in other arts or crafts. Mountains typically symbolize the noble in spirit, rulers, as opposed to their subjects, and the idea of "each attaining his or her proper place." See Zheng 2009, esp. 7–9, 12.

21 I have added the word "alchemical."

22 Or as a different metal (again, an alchemical model)?

23 Or, according to Ma Rong's commentary to the *Analects*, cited in Wang Rongbao 1987, 1.15–16, "with a reverent demeanor" (*gongjing mao* 恭敬貌). Christoph Harbsmeier (pers. comm.) follows Ma Rong.

1.9 學者所以修性也。視聽言貌思,性所有也。學則正。否則邪。

1.10 師哉師哉。桐子之命也。[10] 務學不如務求師。師者人之模範也。[11] 模不模,範不範,為不少矣。

1.11 一閧之市,不勝異意焉。[12] 一卷之書,不勝異說焉。一閧之市,必立之平。一卷之書,必立之師。[13]

1.12 習乎習。以習非之勝是。況習是之勝非乎。於戲。學者審其是而已矣。或曰焉知是而習之。曰視日月而知眾星之蔑也。[14] 仰聖人而知眾說之小也。

1.13 學之為王者事,其已久矣。堯舜禹湯文武汲汲。[15] 仲尼皇皇。[16] 其已久矣。

---

10 Following Wang Rongbao (1987, 1.19) in reading *tongzi* 桐子 as *tongzi* 童子 (uncapped youth). Wang Rongbao notes, however, that some traditions read *tong* as *rong* 榮 (full flowering), as *ying* 嫈 (faint of heart), or as *tong* 侗 (ignorant, crude, rustic)—hence C. Harbsmeier's (pers. comm.) preferred reading of "frail sapling."

11 See *Xunzi*, chap. 1; also Huan Tan, in *Taiping yulan* 404.8a, who cites a proverb: "To study for three years is not as good as spending one year choosing the right teacher." Cf. Heraclitus: "Much learning does not teach sense—otherwise, it would have taught Hesiod and Pythagoras."

12 Following Wang Rongbao (1987, 1.19) in reading *hong* 閧 (usually "din," "raucous," "shouting") as a form commonly mistaken for *hang* 巷.

13 The Li Shan commentary to *Wenxuan* 36.1a, in citing Ren Fang 任昉, "Xuan de huanghou ling" 宣德皇后令, cites this passage but with a slightly different wording.

14 In *Shiji* 84.2482 Sima Qian compared the poems of Qu Yuan to the brightness of the sun and moon; and a philologist compared Yang's own *Fangyan* to the same. See Knechtges 1977–78, esp. 317. Cf. *Taiping yulan* 613.4b, which employs the same metaphor, there attributed to Zouzi 鄒子 (i.e., Zou Zhan 湛). Alternatively, one could read this reference to "sun and moon" as an allusion to "Zhongyong," pars. 30–31, which twice likens Kongzi to the sun and moon, because he spread light and enlightenment over his own and succeeding ages.

15 *Zhuzi yulei* (121.4b, 137.22b) understands this reduplicative phrase to mean that the ruler cannot but study.

16 Reading *huang huang* 皇皇 (= 惶惶) as *mang mang lu lu* 忙忙碌碌, following Han Jing (1992, 12n3).

Learning is the means by which to cultivate one's nature.[24] Sight, hearing, 1.9
speech, bearing, and thought—the inborn nature possesses these capacities.[25] Through learning, these come to function correctly. Otherwise, they remain less than true.[26]

The model teacher; the model teacher—he it is who represents the very 1.10–11
fate of the ignorant stripling.[27] To work hard at study is less important than working hard at finding the right teacher, for the teacher is the very model and standard for people. In quite a few cases, of course, the model is no model, and the standard no standard at all.[28] Just as countless numbers of ideas exist in a single alleyway's market,[29] so, too, innumerable arguments may coexist in any single scroll of writing. And just as a balance must be set up for each little market, so, too, must a teacher be set up even for a text one scroll in length.[30]

Practice! Practice! If practicing what is wrong can overcome the right, 1.12
how much more can practicing the right overcome the wrong![31] Ah! True learning consists in nothing more than determining what is right in a given situation—that and nothing more.

Someone asked me, "But how is one ever to know what is right so that one may practice it?"

"When one sees the sun and moon, one knows the faintness of the light emitted by the stars. In looking up to the sages, one sees the pettiness of ordinary arguments."[32]

To make learning the very enterprise of a true king—surely this endeavor 1.13
has been going on for a long time by now! Yao, Shun, Yu, Tang, and Kings

---

24 *Xunzi* 4.15.13 says that humans are uniquely endowed with the capacity to make distinctions, so that even if they do not have these capacities fully developed at birth (*fei sheng er ju zhe* 非生而具者), each may train that potential and thereby become a sage.

25 The same list of five capacities appears in the "Hong fan" chapter of the *Documents* (Shangshu 尚書).

26 Using "true" in the sense of "true north," meaning that "they veer away from their original potential."

27 For the general message, cf. the *Shanghai bowuguan cang Zhanguo Chu zhushu* manuscript entitled "Junzi weili," vol. 1, 261 (strip 10), where one teacher is said to be enough to convey a sense of success and failure, wrong policies, etc.

28 As *Hanshu* 21.978 remarks, those who wear Ru clothes are "intoning and spouting words that are not right / [or] aligned with the right."

29 See Vankeerberghen 2006 for the metaphor of the balance in choosing values and weighing paths in life. The question here is clearly one of weighing disputed values. Note the metaphor of the book as a discursive space.

30 Note the practice in Qin and Han of having Academicians (*boshi*) specialize in one or more specific texts.

31 The implication is that what is wrong, by virtue of being widely practiced, can appear to be right, and what is right can be further validated through practice.

32 Note that the *conduct* of the sages is here compared to the *sayings/theories* of other thinkers, suggesting that Yang believes certain words to be transparent reflections of actions (hence, realities). If this passage does not imply a dichotomy between words and actions, Yang is simply contrasting the true teachings of the sages to petty arguments from other thinkers.

1.14 或問進。曰水。[17] 或曰為其不捨晝夜與。曰有是哉。滿而後漸者，其水乎。或問鴻漸。曰非其往不往。非其居不居。漸猶水乎。請問木漸。曰止於下而漸於上者，其木也哉。[18] 亦猶水而已矣。

17 Cf. *Xunzi* 103/28/26–29 for water as a metaphor for the Way and the virtues.

18 Cf. Huan Tan, cited in Pokora 1975, entry 92, p. 92, on people's need to imitate wood in their demeanor (in being slow to act) and water in their hearing (in being receptive).

Wen and Wu pursued it unflaggingly.[33] And Kongzi toiled on and on with great determination. Surely this has been going on for a long time now![34]

Someone asked me, "But what about advancement?" 1.14

"It's water."

Someone asked me, "Because it never stops, day or night?"[35]

"You've got it.[36] After filling up, gradually and inexorably it spills over.[37] Such is the nature of water."[38]

Someone asks about that of the wild geese.[39]

"They go only where it is right to go; they stay only where it is right to stay.[40] Their gradual yet inexorable advance resembles that of water!"

"May I be so bold as to ask about the gradual growth of trees?"[41]

"Well rooted below but with gradual growth above[42]—such is the nature of wood. Wood in its own way is surely much like water!"[43]

---

33 Compare Yang Xiong's own statement about the lure of learning versus career in his autobiography, "I do not scurry after wealth and honor" (*bu jiji yu fugui* 不汲汲於富貴).

34 Were it not that this phrase, *qi yi jiu yi* 其已久矣, repeats the earlier phrase, one might be tempted to understand the second phrase as referring to how long ago Kongzi lived, suggesting that the world was due for another sage. The commentators stress how easy it is for crowned kings to accomplish their aims and how difficult it was for Kongzi, an uncrowned king.

35 Cf. *Analects* 9.17, in which Kongzi uses this phrasing to speak of the river's flow as a metaphor for life's journey; and *Mencius* 4B.18 (不舍晝夜). What is interesting is that Kongzi, Mencius, and Yang Xiong are using the same metaphor for different ends. According to the commentators, "advance" refers to "career advancement" or to "advancement in the Way" in *Analects* 11.1.

36 For this whole paragraph, it is useful to compare *Changes*, Hexagram 53 (Gradual Progress), and its counterpart in the *Taixuan jing*, Tetragram 14, as each links advancement to gradual progress.

37 Li Gui comments, "Water fills the pit and then proceeds to spill out; men study broadly and later serve." Certainly "advance" calls to mind "career advancement."

38 In other words, a person should not act until he or she has achieved a measure of cultivation.

39 Probably this refers to Hexagram 53 of the *Changes* (as noted above), as it describes the migrations of the great geese. Otherwise, the line simple means "Someone asks about great advance."

40 Cf. *Analects* 10.6–7, in which Kongzi describes the noble man as doing nothing that is improper.

41 Given that many lines in *Exemplary Figures* show an interlocutor whose question is then converted to a different question (one that Yang is more prepared to answer), another possible translation of this line would have the unnamed interlocutor asking about Jianmu, a deity (lit., Gradual [or possibly Planted] Tree), named in the Baoshan manuscript divination strip 250 (group 22 of the strips). The divination for Shao Tuo mentions Jianmu as a god for whom rites can be performed in order to expel one of the illnesses of the *qi* that plagues Shao. See *Kaogu* 6 (2001), 68 (552).

42 There is a parallel with Mencius's water metaphor, as seen in *Mencius* 4B.18.

43 Comparison of these three metaphors is illuminating: the water metaphor implies ceaseless self-cultivation and biding one's time; the migrating geese, reliance on timing and selectivity; and the trees, their luxurious yet effortless growth (as distinct from the endeavor of self-cultivation) or their reliance on timing or the right conditions. Yang Xiong prefers the analogy with water, clearly, which emphasizes unflagging attention to social and self-cultivation and becoming a person of substance.

1.15 吾未見好斧藻其德若斧藻其楶者也。

1.16 鳥獸觸其情者也。眾人則異乎。賢人則異眾人矣。聖人則異賢人矣。禮義[19]之作，有以矣夫。人而不學, 雖無憂, 如禽何。[20]

1.17 學者所以求為君子也。求而不得者有矣。夫未有不求而得之者也。[21]

1.18 睎驥之馬, 亦驥之乘也。睎顏之人, 亦顏之徒也。或曰顏徒易乎。曰睎之則是。[22] 曰昔顏嘗睎夫子矣。正考甫嘗睎尹吉甫矣。公子奚斯嘗睎正考甫矣。[23]

19 Reading *yi* 義 as *yi* 儀; alternatively, *yi* 義 refers to "duties" and "a sense of duty."

20 For the formula *ru X he* 如X何, see *Analects* 3.3, 4.13.

21 *Taiping yulan* 613.4b, citing the *Zouzi* once again (see above), has a close parallel to this line. On the basis of several citations, Wang Rongbao (1987, 2.27–28) would change "there have been cases" (*you* 有) to "there have been few cases" (*xian* 鮮).

22 Following Li Gui in reading *xi* 希/睎 as *wang* 望 (to look at or up to).

23 See Wang Rongbao (1987, 2.30).

I have never seen anyone whose love for carving out and embellishing his 1.15
moral power matched in intensity the love he brought to having ornate patterns carved on the lintel struts of his home.[44]

Birds and beasts are moved by their own inclinations.[45] Is the common 1.16
run of men any different?[46] Certainly, the truly worthy differ from the common run of men, just as the sages differ from the worthy. The institutions of the rites and ceremonies by the sages[47] have their rationales, then, do they not? For although a person who fails to learn anything may be free of care,[48] he is virtually indistinguishable from an animal.[49]

By definition,[50] learning prompts and facilitates the search to become a 1.17
noble person. There have certainly been cases where seeking a goal did not bring attainment of it, but in no case has a goal ever been attained without seeking it.

A horse that aspires to be a legendary swift charger will be teamed up 1.18
with swift chargers.[51] And whoever, for his part, aspires to be a Yan Hui is in a class with Yan.

Someone asked me, "Is it so very easy, then, to be in a class with Yan Hui?"

"One has only to really aspire to be something or someone to become it.[52] They say that long, long ago Yan Hui once aspired to become another Kongzi. Zheng Kaofu aspired to be a Yin Jifu, and Meng Xizi, another Zheng Kaofu.[53] If a person has no such desires and aspirations, then

44 Cf. *Analects* 9.18, where the contrast is between love of sex and love of power and wealth. The carved lintels signify high office and conventional success.

45 *Shuo yuan* 18.40/171/16–20 ("Xiu wen" 修文) equates those who "are moved by their inclinations" and give way to their desires" with "birds and beasts."

46 Apparently, Li reads this sentence: "Ordinary persons are quite different, then!" Li Gui comments: "Men who follow the rites and the right contain their less-than-upright inclinations; therefore, they differ from birds and beasts." Li Wai-yee (pers. comm.) concurs. However, Han Jing (1992, 14) believes the *hu* makes this a question, and his interpretation gains support from the last line of the passage.

47 Adding "by the sages" as implied.

48 *Daode jing*, section 20.

49 Literally, "a bird," as synecdoche for "birds and beasts." Cf. *Xunzi* 2/1/28: "He who acts of behalf of it [duty] is a real man, whereas he who abandons it is a bird or beast."

50 Adding, "by definition," as implied. *Suoyi qiu* 所以求 means "it is the means by which to search" and "the tool that makes us seek."

51 Or, more literally, "will likewise draw a great charger's chariot." According to *Analects* 14.33, "The horse Ji was famed not for its strength but for its inner qualities [*de* 德]." Ji was said to be one of the four horses driven by the renowned charioteer Zaofu 造父 for King Miu of Zhou 周繆王 (*Shiji* 5.175); supposedly, these horses could traverse one thousand *li* in a day. Metaphors that use fast horses to stand for human talents are quite common in early China. Cf. *Han Feizi* 34/11; also Guodian 郭店 "Qiong da yishi" 窮達以時 manuscript, section 3, which claims that only if an excellent horse is paired with an excellent charioteer like Zaofu will it manage to go a thousand *li*.

52 It is the act of desiring that makes the difference.

53 According to the Mao commentary, cited in *Maoshi zheng yi* 20.3.352b, Zheng Kaofu arranged the Shang Hymns; Yin Jifu composed two of the Zhou Hymns ("Song gao" 崧高 and "Zheng min" 蒸民); and Meng Xizi composed the Lu Hymns on the model

不欲睎則已矣。如欲睎，孰禦焉。

1.19 或曰書與經同而世不尚，治之可乎。曰可。或人啞爾笑曰須以發策決科。曰大人之學也為道。小人之學也為利。子為道乎。為利乎。或曰耕不穫，獵不饗，耕獵乎。曰耕道而得道。獵德而得德。是穫饗已。吾不覩参辰之相比也。[24] 是以君子貴遷善。遷善者，聖

24 See the poem attributed to Li Ling 李陵 (d. 74 BC), in Lu Qinli 1983, 338 (今為参與辰); and Xu Gan 徐幹 (171–218), Poem 5 of "Bedchamber Thoughts 室思詩 (in Six Stanzas)," in Lu Qinli 1983, 377 (故如比目魚,今隔如参辰). Fu Xuan 傅玄 (3rd cent.) plays off this metaphor as well. See ibid., 556.

there's nothing more to be said or done.[54] But so long as a person *has* such desires and aspirations, then who can really stand in his way?"[55]

Someone asked me, "If a given piece of writing were to agree with the Classics in form, style, and quality, but the age did not value it, would it be right to study it?" [56] 1.19

"It would be right to do so."

An interlocutor remarks with a laugh, "But one had better wait for the topics to be set in the exams for office!"[57]

"For the great man, the Way is the goal of learning, whereas the object for the petty person is profit.[58] Are you for the Way or for profit?"

Someone asked me, "Yet to plow but not to harvest, or to hunt but not to feast[59]—surely *that* is not plowing and hunting!"

> A person who plows the Way gets it.
> A person who hunts for virtue gets it.[60]
> That is quite a harvest and a feast!
> Never do we see Orion and Antares together in the sky.[61]

For this reason, the noble man places a high value on advancing in goodness.[62] Are not those who would advance in goodness in the same

---

of those of Shang. In a variant "old" tradition (the Lu commentary to the *Odes* followed by Yang but not by Zheng Xuan), Zheng Kaofu got the twelve Shang Hymns from the Zhou music master rather than composing the hymns himself.

54 Or "there is nothing more to talk about." Cf. *Analects* 1.14 or, also on the subject of learning, 5.27.

55 Cf. *Mencius* 1A.6. *Fayan* 1.18 implies that so long as one has the drive to emulate a sage, one will become a sage; obviously, the drive to emulate a world-class athlete will not ensure that one becomes a world-class athlete, but there are no material barriers to becoming a sage.

56 Adding "in form, style, and quality" to aid the reader. Possibly, Yang here refers to his own writings or to obscure writings handed down from the past that he claims expertise in; otherwise, he may refer to those of Mencius. To become well versed in a text by "working on it" (*zhi shu* 治書) requires a great expenditure of effort, which could be devoted to some other course of learning—hence, the inquiry.

57 Topics were set for an individual by his shooting of an arrow. Unfortunately, we do not know the content of the curriculum that those exams tested.

58 Cf. *Analects* 4.16.

59 To put out the meats and wine for sacrifice or the feast (i.e., for the dead and the living). Hunting and wading through deep waters will become standard metaphors for careful reading by Eastern Han times, as in *Dongguan Hanji* 19.22 (biog. Huang Xiang 黃香): 記群書無不涉獵.

60 Cf. *Analects* 7.15: "They sought *ren* 仁 [humaneness] and they got *ren*, so what is there to complain about?"

61 As Shen (Orion) appears in the west and Chen (Antares or Scorpio) in the east, these two constellations are common figures for the highest degree of separation. Polar opposites cannot be combined; one can study either to advance in the Way or to advance in profit. Cf. *Mencius* 1A.1. Note also that Shen and Chen are the two constellations whose settings mark the time when the weary traveler should rise to resume his journey, and Chen 辰, as part of the Heart constellation, supposedly controlled the passage of the seasons and hence hunting.

62 *Changes*, Hexagram 42 (Increase), the "Image," for the phrase *qian shan* 遷善 (lit., "to

人之徒與。百川學海而至于海。丘陵學山而不至于山。是故惡夫畫也。

1.20 頻頻之黨甚於鸒斯。亦賊夫糧食而已矣。朋而不心,面朋也。友而不心,面友也。

1.21 或謂子之治產不如丹圭之富。曰吾聞先生相與言則以仁與義。市井相與言則以財與利。如其富。如其富。或曰先生生無以養也。死無以葬也。如之何。曰以其所以養,養之至也。[25] 以其所以葬,葬之至也。

1.22 或曰猗頓之富以為孝,不亦至乎。顏其餧矣。曰彼以其粗。顏以其

25 The interlocutor here reproduces the argument made in *Shiji* 129.3258 regarding Zigong, Kongzi's richest disciple.

class as the sages?[63] The hundred rivers that would emulate the sea make their way to it.[64] There's a reason why the hills and knolls may try to emulate mountains, but they never measure up to them: they act like the despicable fellows who draw lines in the sand beyond which they refuse to budge."[65]

Those who flock together are worse than crows, for surely they, too, steal the other fellows' grain.[66] Companions who are not of one mind are boon companions only to one's face, and friends not of one mind are dear friends only to one's face.[67] 1.20

Someone remarks, "The assets that you have managed to amass cannot compare with Cinnabar Gui's wealth."[68] 1.21

"I have heard that gentlemen, in conversing with one another, talk of humaneness and a sense of duty, while merchants talk of wealth and profit. So much for riches! So much for riches!"[69]

Someone asked me, "But if you are poor,[70] in life you have nothing to live on, and when you die, there will be nothing to bury you with. What about that?"

"To have whatever is appropriate to nourish oneself—that's the very best sort of nourishment. To use whatever is appropriate for burial—that's the finest sort of burial.[71]

Someone objected: "But if you took Yidun's wealth and used it to fulfill your filial duty, would that not be the very best kind of filiality?[72] Surely Yan Hui often went hungry!" 1.22

---

advance toward the good").

63 Adding "in goodness," to help the reader.

64 Cf. *Huainan zi* 13.121.8 ("Fanlun xun" 氾論訓), which says, "The Hundred Rivers have different sources, but all return to the sea. The Hundred Experts have different trades, but all work hard at governing." Then see *Analects* 6.12, which also talks about limits (惡夫畫也) in relation to setting limits for oneself and then claiming one has no real strength. By a pun, this may also poke fun at the person who is "the perfect picture of a bad fellow" (*efu hua* 惡夫畫).

65 Adding "beyond which they refuse to budge." Sima Guang, cited in Wang Rongbao (1987), says, "The hundred streams move ceaselessly and so they come to the sea; the mounds and hills store and do not advance, and so they do not reach the mountains."

66 *Fu* is probably not an empty particle, as some commentators suggest; most probably it means either "a fellow's" *or* is the demonstrative adjective *fu* that generalizes the following noun along the lines of "any kind of . . ." See Graham 1972. I thank William G. Boltz for this citation. For *dang* 黨, see *Analects* 15.22. The bird *yu si* (here "crow") is mentioned in *Odes* 197; however, some commentators think the bird's name is *yu* and *si* is a particle.

67 Cf. *Zuozhuan*, Xiang 31.12: "Men's minds are different, even as their faces are. How would I dare say that your face is like my face?"

68 A legendary moneymaker.

69 Alternatively, "Such is their wealth! Such is their wealth!" (but Yang, like the *Analects*, employs repetition of a phrase to indicate a sigh or distaste).

70 Adding "if poor."

71 Cf. *Analects* 2.5. The Wu Mi commentary says: "The rites need not be lavish; . . . the mode of burial need not be extravagant." Some editions omit the second instrumental *yi* 以.

72 Yidun 猗頓 was a legendary moneymaker; see the Glossary. Cf. *Analects* 6.11. Accord-

精。彼以其回。顏以其貞。顏其劣乎。顏其劣乎。

1.23 或曰使我紆朱懷金,[26] 其樂不可量已。[27] 曰紆朱懷金者之樂,不如顏氏子之樂。顏氏子之樂也內。紆朱懷金者之樂也外。或曰請問屢空之內。[28] 曰顏不孔,雖得天下不足以為樂。然亦有苦乎。曰顏苦孔之卓之至也。或人瞿然[29] 曰茲苦也,衹其所以為樂也與。

1.24 曰有教立道,無止[30] 仲尼。有學術業,無止顏淵。或曰立道,仲尼不可為思矣。術業,顏淵不可為力矣。曰未之思也。孰禦焉。

26 Han Jing (1992, 23n1) takes *huai jin* 懷金 (here "stores of gold") to mean "gold seals [of office]." This is plausible but unnecessary.

27 Han Jing (1992, 22) reads the last character as *yi* 已 rather than *ye* 也, which is in the Wang Rongbao (1987, 2.41) version. Li Waiyee (pers. comm.) suggests reading *ye* 也 as *ye* 邪, so that the line reads "wouldn't the pleasure be immeasurably great?" and better conveys the interlocutor's cupidity.

28 Cf. *Hanshu* 91.3684.

29 *Ju* 瞿 often describes "delight" rather than fear, but see Han Jing (1992, 24n8). *Ju* can mean "timid," and perhaps the interlocutor hazards this observation.

30 Most editions write *xin* 心, but that makes no sense, hence the change. Wang Rongbao (1987, 2.44) reads *wuxin* 無心 as *wuzhi* 無止.

"The former used his own crude methods, while Yan Hui used his refined sensibilities. The former employed a bent and partial way, in contrast to Yan, who used the most reliable, upright, and true method.[73] In what way was Yan Hui inferior? In what way, pray tell?"

Someone said to me, "Were I to have crimson sashes and stores of gold, the pleasure would be infinite!" 1.23

"Crimson sashes and stores of gold—the pleasures that come with those are inferior to those known by Yan Hui. For Yan Hui's pleasures were internal, whereas high rank and wealth are external."[74]

Someone asked me, "I beg to ask about the inner happiness that you think comes from 'repeatedly going hungry.'"[75]

"If Yan Hui could not become another Kongzi, he would not have thought even possession of the empire enough to make him happy."[76]

"But did he not, for all that, have his bitter sorrows?"

"Yan Hui was deeply troubled by the perfection of Kongzi."[77]

The interlocutor is startled:[78] "That particular form of trouble—was it not the very means by which Yan made himself truly happy?"

"They say of Kongzi that he was the one who had the moral teachings[79] and established the Way, never ceasing in his efforts. They say of Yan Hui that he was the one who acquired learning in order to transmit the tradition, also without ceasing." 1.24

Someone asked me, "To establish a Way, as Kongzi did, would be unthinkable, and to transmit[80] a tradition, as Yan Hui did, requires more strength than is possible."

"You still have not thought it through.[81] Who, pray tell, is stopping you?"[82]

---

ing to *Lunheng* 61.265.19 ("Yi wen" 佚文篇), Chengdi (r. 33–7 BCE) thought that having the books of Yang Xiong and his pupil Huan Tan made him "richer" than any Yidun.

73 *Zhen* 貞, which is often glossed as *ding* 鼎 (the [stable] tripod), refers to the best course of action that brings stability, since the tripod is stable. Rao Zongyi (2001) argues, against some commentators, that *zhen* always means *zheng* 正 (upright). With its homophone *zhen* 真 (true), it belongs to the same rhyme group as *shen* 神 (divine), which may account for the association of ideas in Yang's text. The answer Yang gives here recalls *Analects* 2.7.

74 And so liable to being taken away.

75 Reference to *Analects* 11.18. Given the rest of the question, the phrase *qing wen* 請問 (I beg to ask)—normally a polite expression—seems overly polite and to be questioning Yang Xiong's good sense.

76 Cf. *Analects* 1.15, on taking pleasure when poor.

77 Because Kongzi's very perfection made him all the more difficult to emulate.

78 My translation is tentative. Perhaps he was startled by his own insight.

79 See *Analects* 15.39 for the phrase *you jiao* 有教.

80 Following Yu Yue (1874), cited in Wang Rongbao 1987, 2.44, in reading *shu* 術 (technique, art) as *shu* 述 (transmit).

81 Cf. *Analects* 9.31.

82 Adding "pray tell" for emphasis. L'Haridon (2006, vol. 2, 124) interprets, "Is it because you have not enough aspiration, if it's not a question of an obstacle?" See *Fayan* 1.5 for lines about "being stopped" from attaining one's goal.

卷第二

吾子

降周迄孔。成于王道。
然(=終)後誕章乖離。
諸子圖徽。[1] 譔吾子。

....

2.1 或問吾子少而好賦。曰然。童子彫蟲篆刻。[2] 俄而曰壯夫不為也。或曰賦可以諷乎。曰諷乎。諷則已。不已, 吾恐不免於勸也。或曰霧縠之組麗。[3] 曰女工之蠹矣。劍客論[4] 曰劍可以愛身。曰狴犴[5] 使人多禮乎。

---

1 Following Wang Rongbao (1987, 20.567), who thinks it a mistake that many editions read *hui* 徽 (streamer, banner) instead of *wei* 微 ("subtle," as in *weiyan* 微言, "subtle teachings"). *Hui* in those editions is then understood to mean "fashioned their own distinctive banners [as if to lead armies into the fray]." Wang believes, however, that *tu* 圖 should be read as *bi* 鄙 (low, debased), meaning that the many philosophical masters thought little of the subtle teachings of Kongzi—hence, my slight modification of Knechtges' translation (1982a).

2 Li Gui says, "He regrets having done it," rather than seeing this as a general statement about all immature boys and their activities. However, Knechtges (1994, 530n1), generalizes the experience: "Yang Xiong is saying here that the writing of *fu* . . . is a puerile exercise comparable to the calligraphic exercises of young boys, who were expected to master six types of script, including the worm and seal script."

3 Cf. *Hanshu* 64B.2829, where Xuandi speaks approvingly of *fu* in comparable ways. The term *zu* is left out of the citation in *Taiping yulan*, *juan* 816.

4 The *Swordsman's Treatise* is also cited in *Yantie lun* 6.3/45/12, which likewise argues that a good swordsman is likely to be careless about life and death.

5 Wang Rongbao (1987, 3.45) reads *bi an* 狴犴 (prisons) as 批扞 (feints and parries [in the art of swordsmanship])—that is, "offense and defense." However, Chen Shou's *Sanguo zhi*, Wu Mi, and Sima Guang, cited in Wang Rongbao (1987, 3.49) think "prisons" is the right metaphor; just because men in prison are constrained in their actions does not mean one should celebrate imprisonment as the most efficient means to increase courtesy. Wang Rongbao (1987, 3.49) believes that *duo* 多 (increase) is a mistake for *wu* 無 (to be without).

Chapter 2

Our Masters

VERSE SUMMARY

In the period from the Duke of Zhou to Kongzi, they perfected themselves with respect to the Kingly Way. Afterward the great precepts were subverted, and the various masters held subtle teachings in contempt. Thus, I have compiled chapter 2, "Our Masters."[1]

Someone asked me, "When you, sir, were young, you liked composing *fu*." 2.1

"That is true. Young lads *will* carve insect and seal scripts."[2] A moment later, I added, "But grown men do not engage in such activities."[3]

Someone asked me, "Can the *fu* be used for indirect remonstrance?"

"Remonstrance! If it would serve for such, that would be all well and good. But it does not stop there. My fear is that it cannot avoid encouraging bad behavior."[4]

Someone said to me, "But the *fu* are as lovely as the filmiest of sheer gauzes!"

"Surely it is rather more like wood moths in women's work."[5]

"The *Swordsman's Treatise* says, 'Swords are the means we use to protect our persons.'"[6]

---

1 Knechtges (1982a) prefers "My Master" for the chapter title, but Yang describes many masters in the chapter, including himself.

2 During the Han period a knife was employed for engraving characters on wood or bamboo, as noted by Jia Gongyan 賈公彥 (fl. 650 CE) in *Zhouli zhushu* (Ruan Yuan ed.) 40.10a–b.

3 Xunzi reportedly said, "The sign of a decadent age is that its literary products are particularly gorgeously ornamented" (*luandai zhi zheng, wenzhang nicai* 亂代之徵, 文章匿綵), which is cited in Pei Ziye's account of the Daming (457–64) era, according to Mather 2003, 25n.

4 Adding "bad behavior," as implied.

5 I.e., a hole or a defect, rather than an achievement that bespeaks wholeness. "Women's work" refers to weaving cloth, just as "men's work" refers to agriculture.

6 And so deflect harm.

2.2 或問。景差唐勒宋玉枚乘之賦也，益乎。曰：必也淫。淫則柰何。曰詩人之賦麗以則。[6] 辭人之賦麗以淫。如孔氏之門用賦也，則賈誼升堂，相如入室矣。[7] 如其不用何。[8]

2.3 或問蒼蠅紅紫。[9] 曰明視。問鄭衛之似。[10] 曰聰聽。或曰朱曠不世，

---

6 One tradition, found in Guo 1979, 93–94n8, says that the first phrase describes the *fu* of the songwriters, including Qu Yuan, while the second phrase refers to Mei Cheng, Sima Xiangru, and other court poets. Knechtges (1976, 96) believes that *shi ren zhi fu* refers to Yang's poetic ideal, embodied in the *Odes*. The two understandings are not that far apart.

7 Wang Rongbao (1987, 3.45, 60). *Hanshu*, "Yi wen zhi," cites this, as does *Taiping yulan* 587.5b–6a, on *fu*. Li Gui, cited in Wang Rongbao (1987, 3.50), remarks in connection with the "what": *yan wu yi yu zheng* 言無益於正 (It is of no use in aligning [the self].). By Huan Tan's time, even Kongzi himself is said to have authored poetry or *fu*, as can be seen in *Xinlun*, cited in Pokora 1975, entry 141, p. 146, citing *Taiping yulan* 496.4b.

8 However, if we then read *nai . . . he* 乃 . . . 何 as *wu nai* 無奈 (What alternative do we have?), the *qi* can possibly refer either to Kongzi (in which case, Kongzi's *fu* are the *Odes*) or to the two poets Jia Yi and Sima Xiangru (in which case, one had better try to focus on using their *fu*). Support for this more positive reading of the line comes from *Hanshu* 87B.3583, which tells us that Yang Xiong modeled four of his *fu* upon those of Sima Xiangru, and from *Hanshu* 30.1756 and *Huayang guozhi* (Ren Naiqiang ed.) 10A.533, which give unambiguous praise of these two figures. Then the line should mean that if the very greatest *fu* writers nonetheless failed to persuade emperors to reform their conduct, the *fu* is not the right vehicle for reformist arguments. Han Jing (1992, 29n6,) writes: "What alternative would there have been for the Ru if they did not write *fu*?" Similarly, Yuan Jixi (2000, 50), reads the line as "Since Jia Yi and Sima Xiangru imitated the *Odes* in writing *fu*, reverently maintaining charismatic virtue and power, and the [proper] systems, their works have aesthetic value." For a review of the *fu* writers, see Gong 1997.

9 In antiquity, *zhu* 朱 or *chi* 赤 denoted the primary color red. *Hong* 紅, here translated as "reddish," was considered a mixed color (and so inferior); probably it required less expensive mineral colors to produce. In later times, clear red was equated with the good and purple with the bad, as in *Jinshu* 44.1251. For a later allusion to "greenfly" as "slanderers at court who mislead their rulers," see *Wenxuan* 51.11b (Wang Ziyuan's 王子淵, "Four Master Discoursing on Virtue" 四子講德論).

10 Cf. *Taiping yulan* 565.5b.

"By that logic you would say that feints and parries make men all the more courteous!"

Someone asked me, "Is there anything to be gained from the *fu* of Jing Chai, Tang Le, Song Yu, and Mei Cheng?"[7] 2.2–3

"They always go too far!"

"Well, if they go too far, what is to be done?"

"The rhymed compositions by the authors of the *Odes* are both beautifully balanced[8] and properly regulated, while the compositions of the court poets are stunningly beautiful but excessive. Had Kongzi's followers employed the *fu* form, then Jia Yi would have ascended to the hall and Sima Xiangru would have entered the inner sanctum, to be sure.[9] But what are we to deduce from the fact that they *did not* use the *fu*?"[10]

Someone asks about the greenfly and the "reddish and purple."[11]

"Sharpen your sight!"[12]

---

7 The first three *fu* writers were natives of the state of Chu during the Zhanguo period. The fourth writer, Mei Cheng, is the author of several extant works, including the *Seven Stimuli* (Qifa 七發), which extols the therapeutic power of fine rhetoric by classical masters.

8 Or "beautiful and balanced." *Li* 麗 probably refers here to parallelism in poetry, but since it also refers to reticulated light and to densely interlaced horizontal and vertical patterns, as in *Changes*, Hexagram 30 (also Li), I have used "beautifully balanced" as a translation that attempts to capture all senses of the word.

9 Cf. *Analects* 11.15, 19, for the same analogy of spatial to moral progression. Based on the *Analects*, we would tend to assume that this is high praise for Sima Xiangru (179–118 BCE), at least, but a "lost line" (*yi wen* 遺文) from *Exemplary Figures* quoted in *Wenxuan* 50.2218 (Li Shan commentary) is extremely critical of Sima Xiangru; as is *Huayang guozhi* (Ren Naiqiang ed.) 10A.533 (a variation on this passage, apparently). Still, Sima Xiangru was, like Yang, a native of Shu, and he compiled an expanded *Cang Jie pian*, a project that Yang himself continued. Later traditions, such as the early sixth-century *Xijing zaji*, entry 83 (p. 100), portray Yang as an unabashed admirer and imitator of Sima Xiangru's *fu*. See Greatrex 1994, esp. 102. Kern 2003, 390, prefers to stress Yang's ambivalence about Sima Xiangru: "While he [Yang] first regarded Sima's work as the foremost model to follow, he later used his forerunner's compositions as the prime example to illustrate the serious shortcomings and ultimate failure of the genre."

10 Tentative translation for *he* 何 (what?), taking it to mean "We cannot but conclude that *fu* writing is not a legitimate activity for the true followers of Kongzi." This reading follows Knechtges (1982a, 531), who translates this as a counterfactual, based on *Fayan* 2.1. Gao Guangfu (1990, 6n10) takes the *he* to mean that the true Ru teachings are at odds with the spirit of the *fu* makers; while it is true that in certain contexts Yang admired Sima Xiangru, he did not particularly admire him as a classicist. Of course, the real problem is that Jia Yi and Sima Xiangru *did* compose *fu*. All we can say with certainty is that "we are to deduce from this" that it is best not to write the grand-display *fu*.

11 The greenfly is the symbol of slanderers, as in *Odes* 219. Because the fly was thought to be capable of changing from black to white, it symbolized the sycophants and slanderers whose talk confounds right and wrong. For red and purple, see *Analects* 17.18: "I hate the manner in which purple takes away from vermilion; I hate the way in which the sound of Zheng confounds the truly refined [*ya*] music." See also *Analects* 10.4 for rules about colors of clothing.

12 So as to discern their true qualities.

如之何。曰亦精之而已矣。

2.4 或問交五聲，十二律也。或雅或鄭，何也。曰中正[11]則雅。多哇則鄭。[12]請問本。曰黃鍾以生之。中正以平之。確乎鄭衛不能入也。

2.5 或曰女有色。書亦有色乎。曰有。女惡華丹之亂窈窕也。書惡淫辭之淈法度也。

11 The term *zhong zheng* 中正 may mean "moderation and propriety" (as Knechtges 1994, 531, has it). However, Han Jing (1992, 31nn2–3) glosses *zhong zheng* 中正 as *zheng pai* 正派 (orthodox faction) and as *zheng da zhi xin xiong* 正大之心胸 (the proper and great attitude). As no orthodoxy existed during Western Han times, Han Jing is wrong.

12 Reading *duo* 多 as *chi* 侈, meaning "exaggerated," "excessive," "wasteful." Wang Rongbao (1987, 3.53–54) also suggests that *duo* 哆 implies *xie* 邪 (what is askew).

"And what about the likes of Zheng and Wei?"[13]

"Train your hearing so that it becomes more acute!"

Someone asked me, "But the exemplary Li Lou and Shi Kuang[14] do not live in our age, so what is to be done?"

"It is simply a matter of refining our senses and sensibilities—that's all."

Someone asked me, "How is it that the same Five Notes played on the same Twelve Pitch Pipes sometimes produce the classical *ya* sound[15] and sometimes the immoral sounds of Zheng and Wei?" 2.4

"When the sounds are moderate and proper,[16] that produces the classical mode, but when they are excessive and improper,[17] then you get the Zheng mode."

"I beg leave to ask about the basics."[18]

"The Yellow Bell[19] is used to generate them [the notes], and by moderation and propriety they are put in proper balance and harmony. If these are fixed and true, the sounds of Zheng and Wei cannot possibly intrude."

"Women have a certain allure. Do books also have this quality?"[20] 2.5

"They do.[21] With women, one hates it when paints interfere with their feminine graces.[22] And with writings, one hates it when overelaborate phrasing sullies or confounds[23] the model and measure."

---

13 Presumably, the Zheng and Wei musical modes are but "semblances" of the best music. *Hanshu* 64B.2829 has Xuandi (r. 79–48 BCE) characterizing the songs of Zheng and Wei as popular "entertainment" for the ears. Yang would agree that these modes are enticing, and therefore popular and entertaining, but he still deems them inferior to classical music.

14 Zhu 朱, the personal name of Li Lou 離婁, refers to the primary color red. Li Lou and Music Master Kuang were known for their extraordinary powers of seeing and hearing. The coupling of Li Lou and Master Kuang is standard in early works. See *Han Feizi* 14/25/5 for one example.

15 Wolfgang Behr (pers. comm., 25 June 2010) says that the similarities between the roughly 260 Zhou bronze rhyming inscriptions and the *Odes* in lexicon and rhyme schemes suggest the existence of a common ritual koine in the pre-Qin period.

16 But this phrase could also mean "When the [spirit at] center is proper, then . . ."

17 As *wa* 哇 also refers to cries, yells, or cacophony, it may well allude to the high-pitched variations of the licentious Zheng music, whose tempo tended to be much faster than that of the solemn court music. The *Zuozhuan*, Lord Zhao 10.1, describes Zheng music as "causing trouble with the fingering and sounding licentious" (*fan shou yin sheng* 煩手淫聲) and also "exceedingly fine" (*qi xi yi shen* 其細已甚). The term *wa* [or *ya*] *yin* 哇淫 appears in the *Yue shu* (Book of Music), 183/2a, a twelfth-century compilation supposedly based on an earlier *Songshi* 宋史 treatise on music.

18 The question is ambiguous. The questioner may well be asking Yang the basis for his remark.

19 The Yellow Bell is the fundamental pitch of the five-tone classical scale, which is generated by a mathematical formula.

20 Or, more simply, reading *you* 有 as "being abundant" or "having plenty": "Women are plenty sexy. Is this also true of books?"

21 Cf. *Analects* 9.17, 15.12, on "caring as much for virtue as for sex."

22 Cf. Lu Jia, *Xinyu*, *juan* 10: "Now true beauty cannot be achieved with cosmetics and powder, nor can the authority of awesome wrath be achieved through mere physical force" (Ku 1990, 121).

23 Or "overflows." The phrase *yin ci* 淫辭 appears repeatedly in *Mencius* 2A.2, and *yin*

2.6 或問屈原智乎。曰如玉如瑩。[13] 爰變丹青。如其智。如其智。

2.7 或問君子尚辭乎。曰君子事之為尚。事勝辭則伉。辭勝事則賦。事(事)辭稱則經。足言足容, 德之藻矣。[14]

2.8 或問公孫龍詭辭數萬以為法, 法與。曰斷木為棊, 梡革為鞠, 亦皆有法焉。不合乎先王之法者, 君子不法也。[15]

2.9 觀書者譬諸觀山及水, 升東岳而知眾山之峛崺也。[16] 況介丘乎。浮

---

13 Yang's "Fan Sao" (Contra the [Li] Sao) certainly criticized Qu Yuan. Accordingly, Han Jing (1992, 33n3) believes that this expresses Yang's disappointment or grieving (*wanxi* 惋惜) over Qu Yuan's lack of wisdom, since a pale "jade color" (*yu se* 玉色) is the external manifestation of inward sagacity, according to many early texts, including both the excavated Guodian and Mawangdui "Wuxing" (Five Conducts), strips C6.1–6.3 in the former and w9.3–w12.18 in the latter (see Csikszentmihalyi 2004, 285–86, 318). Cf. the fragment from an otherwise-lost poem by Cao Zhi entitled "Seven Pains" (Qi ai 七哀), which includes the couplet "With rouge and cosmetics, making up the visage, / [But] the bright mirror, once dimmed, cannot impose order."

Wang Rongbao (1987, 3.59) nonetheless prefers to read *danqing* as the "glow of jade" (*yu cai* 玉采), presumably because Qu Yuan's writings won him everlasting fame and Wang would like to save Yang Xiong from a misjudgment. Some support for Wang's view comes from *Yantie lun* 5.1/29/14, where "red and green" is the metaphor for the divine transformation by the ministers. In addition, *Wenxin diaolong* 1.5/9/1–3 also quotes an opinion ascribed to Yang Xiong that the style of the "Li Sao" is the same as that of the *Odes*. This quotation is not found in Yang's genuine works today, however.

14 *Zao* refers to silk threads of variegated colors with which jade ornaments were strung, also the silk threads that decorate other items, according to glosses to the "Yuzao" 玉藻 chapter of the *Liji* (chap. 13).

15 These lines also implicitly criticize Gongsun Hong, of whom the *Xijing zaji* (*juan* B, entry 8, p. 115) reports that he invited *shi* 士 from all around the empire, seeing that even those who commanded the smallest virtues and a single art or technique (*shu* 術) received an official lodging and a salary at the capital. Of course, the *Xijing zaji* is a much later text, but it certainly preserves some Han information. Gongsun Hong was meanwhile the man chiefly responsible for setting up some of the institutions of learning that Yang Xiong disapproved of. See *Fayan*, chap. 2 passim for more examples. Cf. the preface to "Danqi fu" 彈碁賦, cited in *Quan Jin wen* 45.462.

16 Later, Lu Ji's 陸機 (261–303) "*Fu* Responding to Praising Reclusion" ("Ying jia" 應嘉) would play on this theme. See *Lu Shiheng wenji jiaozhu*, vol. 1, 156.

Someone asked me whether Qu Yuan was wise.[24] 2.6

"He was once like jade or a lustrous polished white gem, but later he changed, so that he became more like gaudy paints.[25] So much for *his* wisdom; so much for *his* wisdom!"

Someone asked me, "Does the noble man place such great value on rhetoric?" 2.7

"What the noble man values is substance. If a person's substance outweighs his rhetorical powers,[26] the person will be too bold and blunt. But when his rhetoric outweighs the substance, then we have the *fu*. When the substance and the rhetoric are well balanced, then we have a classic and constant model.[27] Just enough talk; just enough pleasing appearance—that is the true adornment of character."[28]

Someone asked me, "Gongsun Long's paradoxes—numbering in the tens of thousands[29]—certainly have been taken as standards or models.[30] Are they good models?" 2.8

"Cutting down trees to make game boards or taking scraps of leather to make balls—even for such activities there are standard ways of doing them. The noble man does not take as a model anything that fails to conform to models of the former kings."[31]

Reading through the various writings is like contemplating mountains and rivers. After an ascent up the Eastern Peak,[32] one grasps how meandering are the slopes[33] of the lesser mountains, not to mention the small 2.9

---

shuo (licentious sayings) occurs in *Lüshi chunqiu* 16.897/24.

24 For the power of Qu's legend, see Schneider 1980.

25 Yang is probably referring to red and blue-green paints, possibly cinnabar and malachite, but certainly paints that not only obscure the underlying quality of the material that they cover but also fade in time. This implies that Yang believed that Qu's committing suicide was overly dramatic and also that Qu's work was not of lasting value—arguments that Yang elaborated in his famous "Contra Li sao" (Fan Li sao).

26 Or, possibly, here and below, *shi* refers to "deeds" (*shigong* 事功) versus words, as in Wang Rongbao (1987, 3.60).

27 Taking *jing* 經 to mean both a "constant" model for behavior and a model in writing.

28 Cf. *Fayan* 1.5; also *Analects* 6.18, where the substance and ornamentation must be balanced before we have the *junzi*.

29 Gongsun Long was a famous sophist of the Zhanguo period. Yang criticized the "various masters who used their knowledge to gallop off in different directions, . . . for the most part reviling the sages . . . [by] engaging in strange volutions, hairsplitting arguments, and paradoxical language that confused the affairs of the world" (*Hanshu* 87B.3580).

30 Knechtges (1982a, 531) retains Gongsun Long as subject: "Kung-sun Lung thought his ten thousand paradoxes could serve as standards. Are they standards?"

31 One wonders how Yang Xiong would have answered Gadamer's (1975) talk of structured play or the value of purposeless activities. One possible allusion behind this talk of leather balls: Liu Xiang supposedly persuaded Chengdi to switch from playing kickball to playing chess, believing the latter activity to be more dignified. See *Fayan* 7.10.

32 Mount Tai (Shandong). Cf. *Mencius* 7A.24, for Kongzi's climbing of Mount Tai.

33 The contrast is between the winding mountain slopes and the straight slopes of the taller mountain.

滄海而知江河之惡沱也，況枯澤乎。舍舟航而濟乎瀆者，末矣。舍五經而濟乎道者，末矣。棄常珍而嗜乎異饌者，惡覩其識味也。委大聖而好乎諸子者，惡覩其識道也。

2.10 山之蹊，不可勝由矣。向牆之戶，不可勝入矣。曰惡由入。曰孔氏。孔氏者，戶也。曰子戶乎。[17] 曰戶哉。戶哉。吾獨有不戶者矣。

2.11 或欲學蒼頡，史篇。[18] 曰史乎。史乎。愈於妄闕也。

2.12 或曰有人焉，（曰）〔自〕云姓孔，而字仲尼。入其門，升其堂，伏其

17 Wang Rongbao (1987, 4.68–69) believes this exchange should be read as "Do you consider Confucius a door?" "How could I fail to consider him a door!" Li Gui, followed by Knechtges (1982a, 532), takes this to mean "How could I not have entered his [Kongzi's] door [since there is no other door by which to enter]?" For earlier examples of Confucians comparing themselves to Kongzi, see *Xunzi* 110/32/33. Huan Tan, cited in *Taiping yulan* 68.4b, has someone calling Yang a "Kongzi of the Western Parts," despite his poverty, to which Huan replies, "Ziyun is also a Kongzi of the Eastern Parts. Was Zhongni only a sage of Lu? He was a sage of Qi and Chu as well!"

18 According to *Taiping yulan* 213.1a, 4a, 5a, citing *Han guan yi* 漢官儀, memorization of these two manuals qualified one for a supervisory office in the Lantai palace scriptorium. Probably the *Scribe's Manual* is identical with the *Scribe Zhou* 史籀篇, also called the *Fifteen Sections* ("Shiwu pian" 十五篇). Tradition ascribed that work to a scribe at the court of King Xuan of Zhou (9th cent. BCE), with characters in small or large seal script forms (the sources disagree); six *pian* of that work were lost at the beginning of Eastern Han, during Guangwu's reign (r. 25–57). See Wang Guowei 1983; Hsing I-t'ien 2009. Yang is described as an expert in the *Shi Zhou pian* in *Hanshu* 30.1721. For a study on lexicons, see Bottéro 2003. Yang evidently was included among the philological experts who convened at the court, by order of Wang Mang, in 4–5 CE; Yang expanded the *Cang Jie* in pre-Qin seal script in his *Glosses* ("Xunzuan pian" 訓纂篇) in eighty-nine parts, fragments of which are now in Ma Guohan 1967, vol. 4, 2228–29. Cf. Greatrex 1994.

hillocks. And after floating on the azure seas, one understands the turgid flow of the Yangzi and Yellow Rivers and even the dried-up marshes.[34] One can never set aside the boat if one intends to cross the river. Likewise, one can never set aside the Five Classics if one intends to cross over to the Way.[35] To discard the time-honored fare while developing a craving for unusual delicacies—how could such a person be deemed "a connoisseur of tastes"? To abandon the great sages and prefer the Masters—how could such a person be deemed "a connoisseur of the Way"?[36]

"As the saying goes, 'A trail through the mountains is too narrow a path to follow,' and 'a door facing the wall'[37] leaves too little space to enter." 2.10

"How is a person to go in, then?"

"Kongzi. Kongzi is the door."

"Are you, Master, a door?"

"A door! What a door! How could I possibly fail to be a door!"[38]

Someone was going to study the *Cang Jie* and the *Scribe's Manual*.[39] 2.11

"Ah, scribal learning! Scribal learning![40] Certainly, it is preferable to reckless assertions and omissions."[41]

Someone asked me, "Suppose a man were to take the surname of Kong 2.12–13
and the sobriquet of Zhongni [like Kongzi]. Were he then to enter Kong-

---

34 Cf. *Analects* 9.28, citing proverbial wisdom: "Only when the year grows cold do we see that the evergreens are the last to fade."

35 Contra *Zhuangzi*, chap. 14 ("Tianyun"), p. 513; trans., Watson, *Complete*, pp. 159–60: "Trying to practice the ways of Zhou in the state of Lu is like trying to push a boat overland—a great deal of work, no success, and certain danger to the person who tries it."

36 Contrast Guodian ms, *Yu cong* 語叢: "Stupid wives and their husbands cannot distinguish the noble man from the base, even in their own community; lacking wisdom, they eat leeks all their lives."

37 For the first saying, see *Mencius* 7.21; for the second, see *Analects* 10.10 (said of one who has not studied the Zhounan and Shaonan sections in the *Odes*) and *Analects* 17.8.

38 Literally, "Do you mean to say that I have/am something not [like a] door?" Cf. *Analects* 6.17: "Who expects to go out [of a house] except by the door?" But L'Haridon (2006, vol. 2, 18) reads this instead as "My only fear is of being a door that no one will find," citing *Analects* 6.25. Yang Xiong seems to claim equal status with Kongzi, a parity that would be unthinkable in late imperial China, but it was not unusual in the Tang and pre-Tang eras for thinkers to claim to be sages.

39 Two word lists that beginners used to study characters in the course of "elementary learning" (*xiao xue* 小學).

40 Here Yang imitates *Analects* 14.25, which writes, 使乎! 使乎! instead of 史乎! 史乎! The repetition here implies approbation, according to Wang Rongbao (1987, 4.71), citing the Lu commentary, although such repetition usually implies a criticism. Here, unlike Wang Rongbao, I presume that Yang thinks scribal learning a good start but hardly sufficient for true classical learning.

41 Strictly speaking, the last phrase means only "They surpass [*yu* 俞] [in either goodness or badness]." My reading is based on *Hanshu* 36.1971: "Do not the archaic script forms seem better to you than the nonstandard?" (*guwen bu you yu yu ye hu* 古文不猶愈於野乎). Cf. *Hanshu* 87B.3583: "Of the scribal writings, there is thought none better than the *Cang Jie*, and so he [Yang] wrote his own *Compilation of Annotations*."

几，襲其裳，則可謂仲尼乎。[19] 曰其文是也，其質非也。敢問質。曰羊質而虎皮，見草而說，見豺而戰，忘其皮之虎矣。[20]

2.13 聖人虎別，其文炳也。君子豹別，其文蔚也。辯人貍別，其文萃也。貍變則豹，豹變則虎。

2.14 好書而不要諸仲尼，書肆也。好說而不要諸仲尼，說鈴也。[21] 君子言也無擇。聽也無淫。擇則亂。淫則辟。述正道而稍邪哆者有矣。未有述邪哆而稍正也。

19 See also below, citing *Yantie lun* 5/7/36/3–4, which has the *wenxue* saying that those in the chancellor's party are not true Ru; and ibid., 5.8/36/23: "Let's say that the *wenxue* wear a full robe and broad belt, and they steal the Duke of Zhou's robe . . . and they steal Zhongni's countenance, whenever they discuss remarks or intone the proper phrases." Andrew Plaks (pers. comm.) reads this as "Would you really call him Kongzi?"

20 This may be a very indirect jab at the Qin dynasty, which was often compared to a wolf or other ferocious animal. See, e.g., *Jiaoshi yilin* 12/54/19 (Hexagram Pi 否:秦為虎狼).

21 Wang Rongbao (1987, 4.74) contrasts the tinkling sounds of this passage with the booming sound of the wooden clapper mentioned in *Fayan* 1.3.

zi's gate, ascend his hall, lean on his armrest, and wear his robes, could he be rightly called Kongzi?"[42]

"The surface pattern would be right, but the substance would be wrong."[43]

"May I inquire about substance?"

"A sheep in wolf's clothing will be delighted when it spies some grass, and it will shake with terror when it sees a fox, since it will have forgotten all about the pelt it wears."[44]

"The sage is as distinct as the tiger, with patterns bold and brilliant! The noble man is as distinct as a leopard, with patterns fine and elegant. The rhetorician is like the fox, its patterns dense and luxuriant enough to provide cover.[45] A single change of the fox and it can become a leopard, and a single change of the leopard and it can become a tiger!"[46]

To love books yet fail to see the centrality of Zhongni's writings[47] is to be 2.14
nothing more than a bookstall.[48] To love rhetoric yet fail to see the centrality of Zhongni's sayings is to make nothing more than tiny tinkling sounds.[49] In the noble man's speech, there is nothing to weary or sate[50] a person, and in what he hearkens to, there is nothing immoderate. When one is weary or sated, chaos results. With excess, bias results. Certainly, there have been cases when a person following the right way nonetheless gradually goes astray and degenerates.[51] But there has never been a single case where a person following a bypath[52] gradually puts himself to rights.[53]

---

42 Cf. *Analects* 6.15, 11.15, 11.19, and 19.23: "To wear Ru clothes and to wear Ru caps but not to be able to carry out the Ru Way—that is not what we mean by Ru. You are not card-carrying [canon-carrying] Ru who keep to the Way." Cf. *Mencius* 6B.2, which says that a person wearing the robes of Yao, acting like a Yao, and speaking like a Yao is a Yao. That this debate is about the degree to which habit remakes basic nature is indicated by the fact that it is raised once again in the "Cheng cai" 程材 chapter of the *Lunheng* in mid-Eastern Han.

43 Or "The surface could be called such, but not the substance."

44 Literally, a tiger skin rather than a wolf's pelt, but I have adopted the more common metaphor in English. In addition, both tiger and leopard are associated with advanced cultivation in the lines below, and the metaphor of the leopard "changing its spots" suits the sense of improvements in cultivation. Also, I have translated "fox," although the Chinese has "wild dog," or "dhole," or "raccoon dog" (*li* 狸).

45 *Changes,* Hexagram 49 (Shang) and image. Adding "enough to provide cover," as implied. Note that *li* again has become "fox," as this seems a good substitute in this context.

46 Cf. *Analects* 6.22: "A single change could bring Qi to the level of Lu, and a single change would bring Lu to the Way."

47 As Knechtges (1982a, 532) puts it, "but not seek the essentials in Kongzi." However, one could also treat *yao* 要 as a verb, meaning *qiu* 求 or *qu* 取, so that the phrase means "and not to partake from Kongzi."

48 To exercise no discrimination is, in effect, to be merely a collection of texts.

49 Kongzi's teachings are here labeled "persuasions" (i.e., "rhetoric").

50 Or "corrupt," as this is one of the meanings of 斁/擇.

51 Or is "profligate."

52 Or, possibly, "transmitted teachings that had strayed."

53 *Zheng* 正 here cannot refer to "following orthodoxy" as in later times.

2.15 孔子之道，其較且易也。[22] 或曰童而習之。白紛如也。何其較且易。曰謂其不姦姦不詐詐也。如姦姦而詐詐，雖有耳目，焉得而正諸。

2.16 多聞則守之以約。多見則守之以卓。寡聞則無約也。寡見則無卓也。[23]

2.17 綠衣三百，色(=炎)如之何矣。紵絮三千，[24] 寒如之何矣。

2.18 君子之道有四易。簡而易用也。要而易守也。炳而易見也。法而易言也。

2.19 震風陵雨。然後知夏[25] 屋之為帡幪也。虐政虐世。然後知聖人之為郛郭也。

2.20 古者揚墨塞路。孟子辭而闢之。廓如也。後之塞路者有矣。竊自比於孟子。

---

22 Reading *jiao* 較 as *jiao* 皎 (splendid, shining, clean), or *jiao* 皦 (dazzling). Cf. *Guangya*, which glosses *jiao* as *zhi* 直 (straightforward).

23 Many early texts make nearly the same points, for example, *Huainan zi* 9/68/10–70/17, 9/81/71–82/1. *Bo* 博 and *yue* 约 appear as antonyms in many early texts.

24 Or possibly "tattered hemp," following Wang Rongbao (1987, 4.79). L'Haridon (2006) and Han Jing (1992, 44n2) take *zhuxu* 紵絮 (sackcloth, coarse, hemp-refuse silk) to refer to "cloth that is torn or of poor quality." I read *zhu* as *yuxu* 紆繻 (silk cord, silk gauze), on analogy with the famous *Huainan zi* passage (7/61/1) that calls a "fan in winter and furs in summer" of "no use" in arguing the merits of "knowing what is enough" (i.e., limiting desires). I take this as a separate query to Yang about the utility of fine writings (i.e., Kongzi's teachings set down in writing), simply because it is too obvious that tatters can provide no protection against the piercing cold.

25 Reading *xia* 夏 as *da* 大 or possibly *ya* 雅. The commentary to "Summon the Soul" ("Zhaohun" 招魂) defines *xia* as *da*, as does the commentary to the *Huainan zi* (8/61/19, 8/63/19); "Benjing" 本經, and also *Zuozhuan*, in the phrase *neng xia bi da* 能夏必大.

"Kongzi's way is brilliantly clear and easy!" 2.15

Someone asked me, "One may practice it as a young boy, and even as an old man find it confusing, so in what sense is it both 'brilliantly clear and easy'?"

"I mean that it does not meet treachery with treachery or deceit with deceit.[54] Were it to do so, then how would a person even with good ears and eyes be able to correct himself by it?"

Those who hear much retain it by concentrating on the main points,[55] and 2.16
those who see a great deal retain it by attending to what is most outstanding. A person who hears only a little has no sense of the main points, and a person who sees but little has no sense of what is outstanding.

Even if one were to own three hundred sets of green clothes,[56] what pos- 2.17
sible good would those colored clothes be, since they may not be worn in the temple?[57] And even if one were to have three thousand robes of silk floss, of what possible good would that fabric be in the cold?[58]

The noble man's way has four kinds of ease: Being simple, it is easy to use. 2.18
Being focused on the essentials, it is easy to maintain. Being brilliant, it is easily revealed. Being a model, it is easily expressed and explained.[59]

Only after a raging thunderstorm or driving rain does a person fully 2.19–20
appreciate the shelter afforded by a great house. Similarly, only after an oppressive rule or a tyrannical reign does he fully appreciate the protection afforded by the sages' sheltering walls. Of old, Yang Zhu and Mo Di blocked the road, and Mencius spoke up in order to clear the road, in this displaying true greatness.[60] Later there came others who blocked the road. I compare myself to Mencius.[61]

---

54 Alternatively, following Knechtges (1982a, 533), "He did not treat the wicked as wicked and did not treat falsehood as falsehood." If I understand Knechtges correctly, this line would then refer to Kongzi's willingness to treat flawed persons as if they were without fault.

55 Cf. *Mencius* 2A.6.

56 See *Ode* 27 for the "green skirt," in the Mao and Lu versions. As green, unlike yellow, is not a primary color, skirts should not use that color, since they are reckoned to be more "fundamental." A green skirt with a yellow lining symbolizes a reversal of proper positions, and the ode supposedly criticizes the Wei royal house, in which a concubine usurped the place of the main consort.

57 Adding "since they may not be worn in the temple," as implied.

58 The criticism is of nonstandard and insubstantial teachings.

59 Andrew Plaks (pers. comm.) reads, "Simplicity that is easy to use. . . . Brilliance that is easy to see."

60 Knechtges (1982a, 533) prefers "so that all was clear and open again," preserving the road metaphor. Note that elsewhere, however, in his *fu* "On Hunting" (Jiao 校碏), Yang Xiong mentions Mozi as an early eminent thinker (in Yan Shigu's 顏師古 words, "*qu gu xian*" 取古賢).

61 Cf. *Analects* 7.11, where Kongzi compares himself to Pengzu, the Chinese Methuselah (竊比於我老彭).

2.21 或曰人各是其所是，而非其所非，將誰使正之。曰萬物紛錯則懸諸天。[26] 眾言淆亂則折諸聖。或曰惡覩乎聖而折諸。曰在則人，亡則書，其統一也。

26 Knechtges (1982a, 533) reads *xuan zhu tian* 懸諸天 (hangs it from/in heaven) as "their disposition depends upon Heaven"; similarly, Christoph Harbsmeier (pers. comm.) translates as "all depends upon Heaven." I adopt the metaphor of the carpenter's line or gnomon, which aligns things by the light of day, following Wang Rongbao (1987, 4.82).

Someone asked me, "People each have their own standards for right and wrong, so who can ever be employed to put them right?"[62] 2.21

"The myriad phenomena, howsoever diverse and entangled, can all be measured by the heavens. Just so, the multitude of sayings, however contradictory, may be judged aright by reference to the sages."[63]

Someone asked me, "But how is one to spot a sage, so as to judge him?"

"If he be alive, one takes the person as model, but if he be dead, one consults his writings.[64] The principle is one and the same."

62 Here the interlocutor comes close to repeating the main argument of *Zhuangzi*, chap. 2 ("Qiwu lun").

63 *Zhe* 折, literally, "cracks them open [to sort the mess out]."

64 Adding "as model," for sense.

第三

修身[1]

事有本真。陳施於意。
動不克。咸本諸身。譔修身。

3.1 修身以為弓。矯思以為矢。立義以為的。奠而後發。[2] 發必中矣。

3.2 人之性也。善惡混。修其善則為善人。修其惡則為惡人。氣 也者。所以適善惡之馬也與。[3]

1 Cf. Bartsch 2006 for the Roman Empire, and Henry Rosemont (unpublished) for early China.

2 Reading *dian* 奠 as *ding* 定 (to fix, to determine, to settle), by the standard gloss.

3 Li Gui says, "What drives or directs the *qi* is the person. If he drives the horse on the main thoroughfares, then he swiftly gains advantages [or "is in a good position to gain speed], but if he drives the horse on a poor road, then the horse is hobbled." Sima Guang, cited in Wang Rongbao (1987, 5.85), emphasizes that even the sage's nature has some less desirable aspects, and even the morally benighted are not completely lacking in admirable impulses. Cf., e.g., *Lüshi chunqiu jiaoshi*, 1281.

Chapter 3

Cultivating One's Person

VERSE SUMMARY

Affairs have a basic truth in them, which unfolds in an infinite number of forms. If one's deeds do not persuade others, one should seek the fundamental reason in one's own person. Thus, I have compiled chapter 3, "Cultivating One's Person."[1]

Cultivation of one's person can be likened to a bow. Straightening one's 3.1
thoughts can be likened to arrows. Fixing one's sights on one's duty can be likened to setting up a target. And letting the arrow fly only after aligning one's stance—that ensures that the arrow will always hit the target, certainly![2]

Human nature is a mixture of the admirable and deplorable. Practicing 3.2
the good makes a person good, while cultivating the deplorable makes a person deplorable. Is not the *qi* 氣 the steed by which one hastens to the good or ill?[3]

---

1 I do not use the term "self," since that term implies an undue focus on a more modern notion of the self. In early China, there is much greater emphasis on the *shen* 身, the physical person (whose synonym is *xing* 形, "form"), along with the *xin* 心 (heart).

2 *Analects* 15.7 compares Shi Yu 史魚, an upright official, to an arrow.

3 This is the only place in *Exemplary Figures* where Yang employs the word *qi* 氣 (a word regularly used in *Supreme Mystery*). *Qi* seems to function as the material carrier for development; it directs our energies to a task and thereby hastens the effect of our habitual activities upon our inclinations. Cf. *Mencius* 2A.2, which calls the "will" or the "commitments" the "commander of the *qi*" (*fu zhi, qi zhi shuai ye* 夫志,氣之帥也). Many early texts take a high-stepping steed as metaphor for life's swift passing and the concomitant desire to seize the moment, as in the fourth of the Nineteen Old Poems; many early texts would have the ruler direct the people just as the charioteer directs fine horses. Contrast *Phaedrus* 254C, which likens human nature to a chariot drawn by two horses, one white and one black, one standing for the *epithumêtikon* (roughly, "appetite for sensual satisfaction") and the other standing for the *thumoeides* (often translated "spirit" and closely connected to anger, ambition, and self-respect), with the charioteer standing for reason.

3.3 或曰孔子之事多矣。不用。則亦勤且憂乎。[4] 曰聖人樂天知命。樂天則不勤。知命則不憂。

3.4 或問銘。曰銘哉。銘哉。有意於慎也。

3.5 聖人之辭。可為也。使人信之。所不可為也。是以君子彊學而力行。[5]

3.6 珍其貨而後市。修其身而後交。善其謀而後動。 成道也。

3.7 君子之所慎：言,禮,書。

3.8 上交不諂。下交不驕。則可以有為矣。[6] 或曰君子自守。奚其交。曰天地交。萬物生。人道交。功勳成。奚其守。

---

4 The word *qin* 勤 implies both "long-suffering" and "diligence" or "industriousness," with both senses tied to "hard work." Han Jing (1992, 50), following Liu Shipei (1916), reads *qin* as *ku* 苦 as in *ku nao* 苦惱 (to be anxious about, to wear oneself out with worry).

5 See Wang Rongbao (1987, 5.89).

6 However, Wang Rongbao (1987, 5.90) argues that *you* 有 should be read as *you* 友 (to make friends and allies).

Someone asked me, "Kongzi had many activities,[4] to be sure. But since neither he nor his Way was employed, then did he really toil[5] and worry?" 3.3

"They say, 'The sage "takes pleasure in heaven and recognizes his fate."'[6] Since he takes his pleasure in heaven, he does not regard his life as toil, and since he knows his fate, he does not worry unduly."[7]

Someone asked me about inscriptions. 3.4

"Inscriptions! Inscriptions! They would have us be vigilant."[8]

The sages' teachings—those one can get easily enough. But it is far from easy to get someone to put his trust in them![9] That is why the noble man makes every effort to improve his learning, why he uses every ounce of his strength to put them into practice.[10] 3.5

Just as a person takes an object to market only after evaluating it, so, too, does the exemplary person interact with others only after cultivating his person,[11] or make his move only after he has prepared his plans well.[12] That is the very definition of "perfecting the Way."[13] 3.6

The noble man takes care about his speech, his performance of the rites, and his writings. If "he neither fawns on his superiors nor looks down on his subordinates,"[14] then he may really achieve something. 3.7

Someone asked me, "Since the noble man is to guard his integrity, why would he engage in social relations at all?"[15] 3.8

"Through the comingling of heaven and earth the myriad sorts of

---

4 Cf. *Analects* 9.6, where Kongzi sarcastically is described as a man of many talents (*duo neng* 多能). But the binome does not convey sarcasm in Kongzi's own reply.

5 "In his own time" is implied.

6 Cf. *Analects* 2.4, 20.3.

7 "He does not regard his life as toil" because "sagacity" develops a strong sense of duty (*yi* 義), according to the "Wuxing" texts excavated at Guodian (300 BCE) and Mawangdui (186 BCE).

8 Yang is probably *not* referring to stele inscriptions here, most of which date to after his era. Yang probably means inscriptions on bronze, durable records bearing witness to the deeds of members of the governing elite.

9 Presumably, because the person must come to an understanding that cannot be forced upon him or her. The person who would persuade another of the appropriateness of a certain way of behaving must cultivate his learning (to acquire arguments that he can use in person) and improve his conduct (so that others wish to emulate him).

10 That is, actions speak louder than words.

11 Inserting "exemplary" because it is implied. Cf. *Analects* 9.13, in which Kongzi urges that his Way be "sold" at court, just like a commodity in the market.

12 Or "improved or verified the good in plans or counsels." Christoph Harbsmeier (pers. comm.) prefers "after working on considered approval of one's plans."

13 Where "perfecting" implies "achieving success," according to Wang Rongbao (1987, 5.90).

14 *Changes*, "Wenyan" (2/1/言); cf. *Analects* 1.15: "poor without cadging; rich without arrogance." *Analects* 8.11 reinforces the ideal whereby the powerful show no trace of arrogance toward others.

15 Or "of what possible good are relations [with others]?"

3.9 好大而不為大，不大矣。好高而不為高，不高矣。[7]

3.10 仰天庭[8]而知天下之居卑也哉。

3.11 公儀子董仲舒之才之邵也。[9]使見善不明。用心不剛。儔克爾。[10]

3.12 或問仁，義，禮，智，信之用。曰仁，宅也。義，路也。禮，服也。智，燭也。信，符也。處宅。由路。正服。明燭。執符。君子不動。動斯得矣。[11]

3.13 有意哉。[12]孟子曰夫有意而不至者有矣。未有無意而至者也。

---

7 This punctuation differs from that given in Han Jing (1992), and one reason to follow Han Jing's punctuation is Yang's predilection for paradoxical phrases that take the form X *bu* X. Andew Plaks (pers. comm.) objects that a sentence should not end with *bu wei* 不為.

8 See *Zhongguo da baike quanshu* 中國大百科全書, "Tianwen xue," pp. 43–48, for the relevant star maps on the Three Walls 三垣 constellation.

9 Reading *shao* 邵 as *gao* 高.

10 Han Jing (1992, 55n2) prefers "How could they have achieved such a degree of excellence?" If *shi* 使 is read not as *ruguo* 如果 (if, supposing) but as "to cause [others to act]," the sentence could also mean "They caused others to see the good when it was unclear and to apply their hearts and minds to something not firmly fixed upon, so who could surpass them?" But I find this reading less likely.

11 Han Jing (1992, 56n4) translates instead "Unless the noble man chooses not to act, his actions attain success."

12 Wang Rongbao (1987, 5.93) believes that the initial placement suggests Yang's admiration, so it should be translated here as "How fine it is to have an intention!" Note that this saying does not appear in the extant *Mencius*, which derives from the version edited by Zhao Qi 趙歧 (d. 201).

creatures are born. Through human interactions great achievements may be realized.[16] What good is preservation if it threatens that?"[17]

"One who admires the great but does not emulate greatness is anything but great![18] One who admires nobility but fails to emulate the noble is anything but noble! Gazing up at Heaven's Court[19] one learns the lowliness of the world one resides in!" 3.9–10

The characters[20] of Gong Yizi and Dong Zhongshu[21] were very fine. Suppose there were a group of people who, upon seeing the good, remained unclear about it, or who were less determined to apply their whole hearts and minds to the tasks of deliberation and cultivation.[22] Who among such a group would be a match for them? 3.11

Someone asked me about the utility of the virtues of humaneness, commitment to duty, ritual decorum, wisdom, and trustworthiness. 3.12

"Humaneness is the dwelling; commitment to duty, the road; ritual decorum, the garments;[23] wisdom, the candle; and trustworthiness, the proper credentials.[24] One abides in a dwelling; travels by the road; straightens his garments; lights candles; and holds his credentials in his hands. The noble man does not act otherwise, so that he is successful when he acts."[25]

Of the phrase "to have an intention,"[26] Mencius says, "Surely there have 3.13

---

16 These lines about the "Ways" of heaven, earth, and man are cited as a quotation from *Changes* or one of its traditions mentioned in *Fengsu tongyi* 3.5a (*SKQS*). Cf. the similar line in editions of the "Shuo gua." Here the moral person is to imitate heaven-and-earth, for social contact between superior and inferior is the precondition for state and society. See *Changes*, Hexagram 12 (Duan 彖).

17 Or "What good is preservation?" Adding "if it threatens that [i.e., human contact]," as implied.

18 Literally, "will be greatly ungreat" (*da bu da* 大不大).

19 The term "Heaven's Court" refers to one of the three starry regions around the North Star (known in Chinese as the Great Pole), namely the Great Tenuity Wall (i.e., the constellations to the south of the Northern Dipper), but the commentators identify it as the four stars in the middle of Heaven's Market (Tianshi 天市), which form the seat of the Lord.

20 Cf. *Analects* 5.11. See Wang Rongbao (1987, 5.92).

21 Gong Yizi was a native of Lu noted for his incorruptibility. Dong Zhongshu was an expert in the *Gongyang* tradition. It may be important, as L'Haridon (forthcoming), ms. p. 2, says, that Dong is praised for his character rather than his scholarship. Dong is criticized in *Fayan* 11.18.

22 Adding "to the tasks of deliberation and cultivation," as implied.

23 More common is the Han equation of *li* 禮 (ritual) with *ti* 體 (physical form), where form—graphic and semantic—supplies the bridge. See Boodberg 1953, 326.

24 Cf. *Mencius* 6A.11, which gives nearly all these metaphors.

25 Or possibly, "seldom acts," by analogy with *Analects* 7.21 ("the Master [Kongzi] seldom spoke," *zi bu yu* 子不語). This phrase seems to encompass two ideas: (1) so long as a person is on the way to becoming a noble man by acting like one, his action(s) will be successful; (2) unless it is a situation in which the noble man should not act at all, his actions will be successful. My translation tries to capture both.

26 The binomial *you yi* 有意 can mean "to have had an intention [to do something]," "to put one's whole self [into a certain act]," or "to find it gratifying [to do something]." It also can mean "Now there's an idea!"

3.14 或問治己。曰治己以仲尼。或曰治己以仲尼。仲尼奚寡也。[13] 曰率馬以驥。不亦可乎。或曰田圃田者。莠喬喬。[14] 思遠人者。心忉忉。曰日有光。月有明。三年不目日。視必盲。三年不目月。精必矇。熒魂曠枯。糟 (=精)莩曠沈。[15] 擿埴索塗。冥行而已矣。

3.15 或問：何如斯謂之人。曰取四重。去四輕。則可謂之人。曰何謂四重。曰重言,重行,重貌,重好。言重則有法。行重則有德。貌重則有威。好重則有觀。[16] 敢問四輕。曰言輕則招憂。行輕則招辜。

---

13 Not following the punctuation in Wang Rongbao (1987, 5.93).

14 The variant reading is *fu tian* 甫田, meaning "[overly] large fields."

15 Han Jing (1992, 58n7) reads *zao* 糟 (dregs, spoiled materials) as *(mu) jing* 目精 (eyeballs), citing Liu Zongyuan's 柳宗元 explanation (apparently based on an old edition now lost), which reads *jingfu* 精莩 as *guang* 光 (the eye's "luster" or "sight"). My translation follows Li Gui, who takes *fu* 莩 to be the "outer covering" or "husk" of the eye (the sclera?). Wang Rongbao (1987, 5.94) reads *fu* 莩 as the color (of the eye), probably referring to the iris.

16 Given the brevity of the expression *you guan* 有觀, the binomial could mean that the person has either (1) something "worth showing" (*shi* 示) to others (who will then hasten to imitate it), as Li Gui suggests; or (2) something in his possession worth showing to himself. Han Jing (1992, 60n4) takes *you guan* to mean the former, and based on the sound glosses cited in Wang Rongbao (1987, 5.96), this is 去聲觀, "to show."

been cases where a person has a certain intention but it goes unfulfilled, but there has never once been a case where a person has no intention to do something, yet he succeeds at it."

Someone asked me about "self-mastery."[27] 3.14

"In self-mastery, one takes the model of Kongzi."

Someone asked me, "If Kongzi is such a wonderful model of self-mastery, then why are so few like Kongzi?"

"What is so wrong with making the lead horse a fabled racehorse like Ji?"[28]

Someone remarked, "'In the orchards and fields you tend,' 'the bristle grass weeds have grown far too high.'[29] In 'longing for that far-off man,' 'our hearts are sore aggrieved.'"[30]

"The sun has its rays; and the moon, its light. A person who never saw the sun for three years would certainly lose his capacity for sight. A person who never looked at the moon for three years would certainly find that his pupils grew dim. After a long period of disuse, the spark of life inside the pupil of the eye dries up, while the lens collapses inward.[31] Then the person can only feel his way around, like a blind man using his staff to locate the path or walking in the dark."

Someone asked me, "What is this that we call 'being human'?" 3.15

"To seize upon four things as important and to deem four things as inconsequential—that, then, is what is rightly called human."

What four things are of importance?"

"Placing importance on one's speech, deeds, appearance, and preferences.[32] If a person thinks speech important, he will acquire the proper models for emulation;[33] if deeds, he will acquire charismatic virtue; if appearances, he will acquire dignity; and if preferences, he will acquire vision and a bearing well worth contemplating."[34]

---

27 I.e., "self-control," juxtaposed with "control" or "mastery" over others.

28 Kongzi has fully developed humanity; he represents the attainment of the highest potential.

29 See *Odes* 102/1, which takes the bristle grass's (*Setaria viridis*) invasion of cultivated fields as a metaphor for the invasion of inferior and unproductive types at court.

30 Cf. *Odes* 102/1, 146/1, for *dao dao* 忉忉. The heart is aggrieved since it cannot secure the object of its longing; hence, the interlocutor's sarcastic implication is that a person can create trouble for himself if the object of longing is unattainable. In *Odes* 102 the lines begin with an injunction pointing to the dangers of "thinking of a distant man" or men.

31 Adding "inside the pupil of the eye," as implied. The main sense of the passage is clear: "Use it or lose it!" In any case, the rhetoric builds upon the comparison of Kongzi to the "sun and moon," which appears already in the *Analects*.

32 Cf. *Analects* 7.25, which lists Kongzi's four types of teachings, and *Analects* 8.4, which lists three things on which a superior man places much value: proper acts, proper demeanor, and proper speech.

33 Literally, "then he will have the proper models," and act on the same pattern below.

34 Pushing, possibly too far, the idea of *guan* (to contemplate) to both active senses ("vision," as the capacity to see) and passive (to be contemplated). One may compare this passage with *Analects* 1.8, on the importance of taking things seriously. The *Lunyu zhengyi* relates these two passages.

貌輕則招辱。好輕則招淫。

3.16 禮多儀。[17] 或曰日昃不食肉。肉必乾。日昃不飲酒。酒必酸。[18] 賓主百拜而酒三行。不已華乎。曰實無華則野。華無實則賈。[19] 華實副則禮。

3.17 山雌之肥。其意得乎。或曰回之簞瓢。臞如之何。曰明明在上。百官牛羊。亦山雌也。闇闇在上。簞瓢捽茹。亦山雌也。何其臞。千鈞之輕。烏獲力也。簞瓢之樂。顏氏德也。

3.18 或問：犁牛之鞹與玄騂之鞹有以異乎。[20] 曰同。然則何以不犁也。

17 For this complaint about Ru teachings, see *Shiji* 130.3290. However, Knechtges (1982a) thinks that *li* 禮 probably refers to a *Rites* classic (in Yang's time, almost certainly the *Yili*); in this, he follows subcommentaries to the "Zhongyong" 中庸 chapter of the *Liji*, cited in Wang Rongbao (1987, 5.97). Two passages in the *Zuo* clarify the relation of *li* to *yi*, and the distinction between them; see Lord Xiang 31.12, talking of *wei yi* 威義, and Lord Zhao 25.3a(2) (*shi yi ye, fei li ye* 是儀也, 非禮也).

18 Cf. *Huainan zi* 7/60/7, which denounces the Ru in the following terms: "They hasten forth in circles and formally scrape and bow, while the meat goes bad and becomes inedible / and the wine goes sour and becomes undrinkable." Arguing that none of these verbs are transitive, Knechtges (1982a) prefers "If by sunset one has not eaten the meat, it will surely be dried out, and if by sunset one has not drunk the wine, it will certainly turn sour." The sense of either version then would be that the rites are so elaborate that the meat and wine used in them will become spoiled long before the participants can enjoy them at the end of the ceremonies.

19 Li Gui and some later commentators read *gu* 賈 ("mercantile," referring to commercial transactions). I wonder whether *jia* 賈 does not mean here *jia* 假 (false, fake), as both received and excavated texts use the former character as a loanword. I thank William G. Boltz for confirming the possibility.

20 Commentaries to the *Lunyu* passage generally identify the *li niu* 犁牛 (plow ox) as brindled. However, Wang Yinzhi (1968, vol. 2, 754–55) makes a compelling case for the *li niu* being a sacrificial ox rather than a plow ox.

"And the four things deemed inconsequential?"

"To think speech of little consequence is to invite trouble; to have that view of deeds, is to invite wrongdoing; of appearances, is to invite humiliation; and of preferences, is to invite excessive, illicit, or extravagant behavior."

On the saying "The rites have many points of decorum." 3.16

Someone asked me, "'By sunset, the meat—still uneaten—has spoiled, and the wine—still undrunk—has soured.'[35] Is it not too elaborate a show for the guests and hosts to bow a hundred times and the wine to be passed three times?"[36]

"As the saying goes, 'Substance without decoration is crude. And decoration without substance is simply false.'[37] When the decoration and the substance are fitting and in balance, *then* we have ritual decorum."

The plumpness of the female mountain pheasant[38]—does it not epitomize attainment of the goal?[39] 3.17

Someone asked me, "Speaking of Yan Hui's bamboo basket of rice and single gourd of wine, did Yan really have any alternative to being so emaciated?"[40]

"When a clear and shining presence occupies the throne, 'the Hundred Offices and even the oxen and sheep serve him,'[41] so men like Yan become plump as the mountain pheasant. But when a blockhead is enthroned, and good people are then forced to subsist on the most meager fare,[42] in that case they are still mountain pheasants. How can you see Yan as emaciated? The strength of Wu Huo[43] was such that he looked upon a thousand heavy weights[44] as light. Yan Hui's character was such that he took real pleasure in a basket of rice and gourd of wine."

Someone asked me, "What's the difference between the hide of the plow ox and that of a pure black or red ox, once the hides are shorn?"[45] 3.18

---

35 Such mockery of the overelaborateness of the Ru ceremonials recalls *Mozi*, chaps. 38–39 ("Fei Ru" 非儒). But cf. *Analects* 10.6.

36 Or "this being endless, is it not too elaborate a show?" Han Jing (1992, 61n3) reads *yi* 已 = *tai* 太 (too much). The commentators note the exaggerations of the interlocutor, since guest and host bow to each other only once in many of the rituals.

37 Cf. *Analects* 6.18, which contrasts *ye* 野 and *shi* 史 ("scribalish"; i.e., "pettifogging").

38 Cf. *Analects* 10.21, where this is said to be the type of fowl that best understands timing; it also symbolizes high bureaucratic rank. Some *Changes* commentators read *fei* 肥 (fatness, plumpness) as *fei* 飛 (in flight). See Hexagram 33 (Dun 遯), *shang* 上, and *duan* 彖 (and below).

39 A return to the theme of determination and intentions as related to success.

40 Or, more literally, "What was he to do about such emaciation?" See *Analects* 6.9 and, for Kongzi's comparable attitude, *Analects* 7.16. *Lüshi chunqiu* 14.6/76/26–27 ("Shen ren") speaks of being happy whether one is "poor" or "successful" (窮亦樂, 達亦樂).

41 In *Mencius* 5A.1 and 5B.6 this is said of those in service to the sage-king Shun.

42 Adding "and good people are then forced to," as implied. The meager fare consists of wild greens and a basketful of rice.

43 Wu Huo was a legendary strong man from Qin during the Zhanguo period.

44 Each of the weights measured 30 *jin* 斤.

45 See *Analects* 6.6. The pure red or black oxen are used in sacrifice, and those of mixed color are used for plowing.

曰將致孝乎鬼神。不敢以其犁也。如刲羊刺豕。罷賓犒師。惡在犁不犁也。

3.19 有德者好問聖人。或曰魯人鮮德。奚其好問仲尼也。曰魯未能好問仲尼故也。如好問仲尼。則魯作東周矣。[21]

3.20 或問：人有倚孔子之牆。弦鄭,衛之聲。誦韓,莊之書。則引諸門乎。曰在夷貉則引之。倚門牆則麾之。惜乎衣未成而轉為裳也。[22]

3.21 聖人耳不順乎非。口不肄[23] 乎善。賢者耳擇,口擇。眾人無擇焉。或問眾人。曰富貴生。[24] 賢者。曰義。聖人。曰神。觀乎賢人。則見眾人。觀乎聖人。則見賢人。觀乎天地。則見聖人。天下有三

21 Cf. 如有用我者，吾其爲東周乎.

22 Another famous metaphor has a person exchanging "cap and coat" for his person: "If for the sake of the means of adornment you kill what they [cap and coat] adorn, you do not understand what they are for" (*Lüshi chunqiu* 21/4.1, "Shen wei" 審為: 殺所飾要所以飾, 則不知所為矣); cf. Knoblock, p. 557.

23 Following Wang Rongbao (1987, 5.105), who thinks *yi* 肄 a mistake for *wei* 違, which is similar in form.

24 Cf. *Shiji* 61.2127, on the different motivations driving men and women. However, Li Gui says, "It [their lack of discrimination] is driven by their lust for wealth and honor," taking *sheng* as a verb, "to give rise to."

"They are the same."

"But if that is so, why is the one not used in plowing?"

"To show the utmost filial reverence when serving the spirits, in sacrifices one does not dare to use the plow ox. But who cares whether the animals are brindled or not, if one is killing sheep and stabbing suckling pigs to entertain guests or to honor the troops' exertions with a feast?"

They say, "A man of virtue likes to pose questions of the sages." 3.19

Someone said to me, "Few of the men of Lu were virtuous, so how was it that so many liked to pose questions of Kongzi?"

"Because those in power in Lu never were able to pose the right questions of Kongzi! Had they been able to do so, then Lu surely would have become a second Zhou in the east."[46]

Someone asked me, "Suppose there was a person who leaned on Kongzi's 3.20
wall while strumming the sounds of Zheng and Wei or reciting the writings of Han Fei and Zhuangzi. Would such a man be brought into the house through the main door?"[47]

"If he dwelt among Yi and Mo to the east and south of the Central States, then he would be welcomed in that way, but he would be driven away if he were leaning on *our* doors and walls, with access to *our* cultural advantages.[48] What a pity that even before the upper garments are complete, that sort of person switches them for the lower ones."[49]

"The sages' ears are not accustomed to wrongdoing;[50] their mouths do 3.21
not offend the good. The worthies are selective in what they hear and say. The ordinary man has no such discrimination."

Someone asks about ordinary people.

"For them it's all about wealth, honor, and long life."

"And the worthies?"

"For them, it's about a sense of duty."

"And the sages?"

"Godlike qualities."

"A good look at worthy people and one sees the ordinary run of people clearly. A good look at the sages and one sees the worthy people clearly. And a good look at heaven-and-earth and one sees the sages clearly."

---

46 Cf. *Analects* 17.5.

47 The sounds of Zheng and Wei are licentious (see chap. 2, above), so liking them creates problems for the music lover. The writings of Han Fei and Zhuangzi, however alluring, are ultimately corrupt.

48 Adding the two phrases "east and south of the Central States" and "with access to *our* cultural advantages," as implied.

49 See *Odes* 100/1 for the metaphor of reversed upper and lower garments, which portends reversal of the proper sociopolitical hierarchies and subversion of the true Way transmitted from the sages.

50 Cf. *Analects* 2.4: "At the age of sixty, my ears were inclined to obey [heaven's will]."

好：眾人好己從。賢人好己正。聖人好己師。[25] 天下有三檢：眾人用家檢。賢人用國檢。聖人用天下檢。天下有三門：由於情欲。入自禽門。由於禮義。入自人門。由於獨智。入自聖門。

3.22 或問：士何如斯可以禔身。[26] 曰其為中也弘深。其為外也肅括。則可以禔身矣。

3.23 君子微慎厥德。悔吝不至。[27] 何元憞之有。

3.24 上士之耳訓乎德。下士之耳順乎己。

3.25 言不慚,行不恥者。孔子憚焉。[28]

25 But Sima Guang, cited in Wang Rongbao (1987, 5.105) has the sages becoming the teachers and models for all those who are like themselves.

26 Or if *ti* 提/禔 is read as *an* 安, more simply "secure the safety of his own person." Cf. "Xici, B" 君子安其身而後動 (66/83/19).

27 In *Changes*, the phrase *hui lin* 悔吝 refers to minor regrets and errors. *Dui* 憞 means "evil" (*e* 惡) or, following *Shuowen jiezi*, "resentment" (*yuan* 怨).

28 Two other lines in the *Analects* employ the phrase *bu chi* (not shameful): *Analects* 5.15 (where not being ashamed is good in certain circumstances) and 9.27 (where it is less ideal). The latter text is cited in the "Hereditary House of Kongzi" (*Kongzi shijia* 孔子世家) in the *Shiji* (*juan* 47). Cf. also *Fayan* 8.7; and *Chunqiu fanlu* 1.1: 君子不恥，內省不疚，何憂何懼，是已矣.

In the world we know "under heaven," there are three sorts of preferences:[51] Ordinary people like to follow their own whims. Worthy people like to correct their persons. Sages like to make themselves into proper teachers and models.[52]

In the world, there are three sorts of constraints: Ordinary people are bound by family concerns. The worthy are bound by those of their own countries. And the sages, only by larger concerns about the world.

In the known world, there are but three doors: To act according to one's own desires is in effect to enter the bestial realm. To act according to one's sense of ritual decorum and duty is to enter the human realm. And to act from singular wisdom is to enter the realm of the sages.[53]

Someone asked me how a man of breeding and cultivation, a *shi*, should 3.22
conduct himself, so as to secure good fortune for himself.

"He must make his innermost heart expansive and profound, and his visible attributes reverent and restrained. Then he can surely secure good fortune for himself."

The noble man, even in the most trivial matters, pays due attention to his 3.23–24
character. Since no occasion for the least regret or error arises, how could there ever be a cause for great enmity? The better sort of the man in service has his ears attuned to virtue, while the inferior sort is accustomed to hear what he wants.[54]

If there is nothing shameful in his words and nothing shameful in his 3.25
acts, even Kongzi would be impressed by him.[55]

51 Cf. *Analects* 16.7–8.

52 Or "to [get] teachers and models for themselves," if we think Yang recalls passages in *Fayan*, chaps. 1–2.

53 Something is higher than rites and duty, which Henry Rosemont (unpublished) suggests is practical wisdom leading to immersion in the writings of the sages.

54 I.e., sycophants, flatterers, and servile administrators.

55 I follow the earliest commentators, including Ma Rong and Wang Bi, and Wang Rongbao (1987, 5.108) in tying this line to *Analects* 11.23, which has even the Master impressed by a person who corrects his own sight, hearing, speech, and conduct. But later commentators, including Zhu Xi (Chan 1967), tend to read the line quite differently: "If his speech is shameless and his conduct also, then even Kongzi would have serious reservations [about him]," a possible allusion to *Analects* 14.20, which talks of the person whose boasts know no shame (其言之不怍，則為之也難).

卷第四

問道

芒芒天道。昔在聖考。
過則失中。不及則不至。
不可姦罔。譔問道。

4.1 或問道。曰道也者。通也。無不通也。[1] 或曰可以適它與。[2] 曰適堯舜文王者為正道。[3] 非堯舜文王者為它道。君子正而不它。

4.2 或問道。曰道若塗若川。車航混混。不捨晝夜。或曰焉得直道而由諸。曰塗雖曲而通諸夏則由諸。川雖曲而通諸海則由諸。或曰[4] 事雖曲而通諸聖。則由諸乎。

---

1 Possibly over-translating the single phrase *wu butong* 無不通, in order to suggest that *tong* denotes both "communication" and a "lack of impediment."

2 Or "go by another route," following Han Jing (1992, 72n2). Li Gui, cited in Wang Rongbao (1987, 6.109), says, "It means that just as a path can be used to get through to the Central States, as well as to go to the Yi and Di [non–Central States groups], so, too, can learning be used to unify the right standards [or "canons"?] and to grasp, as if in one hand, all the many masterworks."

3 This perhaps overtranslates *zheng* 正, which refers to what is "true" in the sense of "true north," as well as to the main route. Wang Rongbao (1987, 6.109), somewhat improbably, wants to tie the word *zheng* 正 (straight, right) to the binome *zheng yue* 正月 (first month), an expression that itself signifies the sovereignty of the Zhou royal house.

4 I take this to be a sarcastic retort by Yang's interlocutor. Some commentators, including Sima Guang and Han Jing, think that this comment represents the viewpoint not of the unnamed interlocutor but of Yang himself, however. See Han Jing (1992, 73–74n5).

Chapter 4

Asking about the Way

VERSE SUMMARY

Vast, vast is heaven's Way. In times past, the sages perfected it. "Going beyond it" means losing the Mean, while "failing to reach it" spells a failure to attain it. It cannot be defiled or maligned. Thus, I have compiled chapter 4, "Asking about the Way."[1]

Someone asked me about the Way. 4.1

"The Way is the unimpeded path that reaches everywhere."

Someone asked, "Can one use it to go elsewhere?"

"Whatever leads straight to Yao, Shun, and King Wen is the true and straight path. The paths that have nothing to do with Yao, Shun, and King Wen are bypaths. The noble man keeps to the straight path. He does not take a bypath."

Someone asked me about the Way. 4.2

"The Way is like a road or a river on which carts and boats do roll and flow, 'without ceasing, night and day.'"[2]

Someone asked me, "But how is a person to find the direct path to follow?"

"A road may wind around, but so long as it leads straight to the Xia,[3] it should be followed. And the river may wind around, but so long as it flows to the sea, it should be followed."

Someone said, "So even if certain actions and affairs are less than direct, we should follow through with them, so long as they allow unimpeded access to the sages?"

1 Here, as in some other chapters, the chapter title is taken from the opening lines of the chapter, as is generally true in the received *Analects* traditions.

2 *Analects* 9.17 uses this expression to mean that the noble man never leaves the Way for an instant. Cf. *Mencius* 4B.18.

3 This refers to the civilization and values of the Central States once allied with the Zhou royal house.

4.3 道德仁義禮。譬諸身乎。夫道以導之。德以得之。仁以人之。義以宜之。禮以體之。天也。[5] 合則渾。離則散。一人而兼統四體者。其身全.

4.4 或問德表。曰莫知作上作下。[6] 請問(禮)莫知。[7] 曰行禮於彼。而民得於此。奚其知。或曰孰若無禮而德。曰禮, 體也。人而無禮。焉以為德。

4.5 或問天。曰吾於天與。見無為之為矣。[8] 或問：彫刻眾形者匪天與。曰以其不彫刻也。如物。(物)刻而彫之。焉得力而給諸。[9]

---

5 Sima Guang, cited in Wang Rongbao (1987, 6.112) takes this phrase to mean "They cannot be added to or subtracted from." In a second, late reading cited in Wang Rongbao (1987, 6.111), *ren* is taken as the root for the other four virtues, here analogized to the four limbs.

6 Setting off *mo zhi* 莫知 with the four-character phrase *zuo shangzuo xia* 作上作下 as object, to keep the parallelism with the following line, even if it is the ruler who is most often mentioned in connection with displays of charismatic power. Li Gui says, "They do not [consciously] know the pleasures of acting as rulers or the pain of acting as subjects." Li Gui further explains that when the ritual regulations (especially the sumptuary regulations) have been set up, then high and low stations are fixed. However, Sima Guang punctuates after *zuo*, and CHANT follows him. Andrew Plaks (pers. comm.) prefers "One sees no distinction between one's actions toward superior and inferior."

7 Most editions supply *li* 禮 (ritual) here, even if some editions omit *li* 禮, thinking it an interpolation from the following sentence.

8 Wang Rongbao (1987, 6.114) says, "With respect to taking one's ease in matters, that is *wuwei*, but with respect to the labors of the Way, they are acting without explicit aim."

9 A similar argument appears first in chapters 6 and 13 of the *Zhuangzi* (where the word order is inverted: 刻彫眾形) and then in *Lunheng* 23/92/20. Andrew Plaks (pers. comm.) prefers, however, "If they are not created, then how would heaven get the strength to impart to them?"

The Way, its charismatic power, humaneness, sense of duty, and ritual decorum—why not discuss them by analogy to the physical person? Now, as we all know, the Way is what guides it. Moral power is what allows him to gain full possession of it.[4] Humaneness is what fully humanizes it. A sense of duty is what makes it fitting. And ritual decorum is what allows him to embody it. These make a person as powerful as heaven itself.[5] When conjoined in a single person, they constitute something akin to the primal unity. But if separated, their force dissipates. By analogy,[6] if a single person is in command of all his four limbs, he is "whole and intact" by definition, is he not? 4.3

Someone asked me about the display of charismatic powers. 4.4

"None will be conscious of it, with superiors acting this way and inferiors too."

"May I ask what in ritual decorum corresponds to your phrase 'none will be conscious of it'?"

"A person [of high rank] carries out the rituals at his place, and his men gain from him a sense of propriety in theirs. How would *that* be an instance of conscious action?"[7]

Someone asked me, "What if a superior were to lack ritual decorum, and yet possess charisma?"[8]

"Ritual decorum is the way to embody virtue.[9] If a man lacks ritual decorum, how can he ever establish his charisma?"

Someone asked me about heaven. 4.5

"I see it acting with no explicit aim."

Someone asked me, "But isn't it heaven that carves out the myriad forms?"[10]

"It is precisely because those were not carved out that we know it to be the work of heaven. For if each of the phenomena had to be carved and cut before it could exist, where would one get the strength to give to this sort of activity?"[11]

---

4 As is usual in many Han texts, Yang here defines the virtue words by a series of puns, so that *dao* = *dao*, *de* = *de*, *ren* = *ren*, *yi* = *yi*, and *li* = *ti*. The phrase *de* 德 = *de* 得, when not applied to the physical person, is best translated as "The charisma [associated with fine character] means to gain [one's ends, including conventional success]."

5 *Tian ye* 天也 can mean "These are heaven sent" or "innate," but as the phrase implies efficacy, I translate it as a lead-in to the next sentence.

6 I have added this phrase, as implied.

7 Cf. *Mencius* 7A.13: "Every day they move to do good without realizing who prompts them to do this" 民日遷善而不知為之者 ·

8 Cf. *Laozi*, chap. 38. More literally, "How does it compare to a ruler who possesses charismatic powers but lack ritual decorum?"

9 Note the paronomastic gloss (already used in 4.3) that ties *li* 禮 to *ti* 體, since ritual behavior embodies and communicates the authentic self. Another possible translation would stress the relation between "ritual" (*li*) and the "physical framework" of the body (*ti*), casting ritual as the appropriate framework for all human activity.

10 In other words, one could call "heaven" anything that did all that work in fashioning things.

11 Or "to impart to them?"

4.6 老子之言道德。[10] 吾有取焉耳。及搥提仁義。絕滅禮學。吾無取焉耳。[11]

4.7 吾焉開明哉。[12] 惟聖人為可以開明。他則苓。[13] 大哉。聖人言之至也。開之。廓然見四海。閉之。閛然不覩牆之裏。

4.8 聖人之言。似於水火。或問水火。曰水，測之而益深。窮之而益遠。火，用之而彌明。宿之而彌壯。

4.9 允治天下。不待禮文與五教。[14] 則吾以黃帝堯舜為疣贅。

4.10 或曰太上無法而治。法非所以為治也。曰鴻荒之世。[15] 聖人惡之。是以法始乎伏犧。而成乎堯。匪伏匪堯。禮義哨哨。[16] 聖人不取也。

4.11 或問：八荒之禮。禮也。樂也。孰是。曰殷之以中國。[17] 或曰孰為

---

10 Cf. Graham 1978, the "Great Takings" and the "Lesser Takings" ("Xiao qu" 小取). This phrasing also recalls that in *Mencius* 7B.3: "To completely trust the *Documents* would be worse than not having a *Documents* text at all" 盡信書則不如無書 (said of the "Wucheng" 武成 chapter of the *Documents*, now often assumed to be the "Shifu" 世俘 chapter of the *Yi Zhou shu*), where Mencius objects to that chapter's depiction of the bloodiness of the Zhou conquest.

11 The line *chuiti renyi* 搥提仁義 is associated with Laozi, *Daode jing*, sec. 18. See *Daode zhen jing zhu* 2.22b. The line "he rejects that but borrows this" comes from the *Laozi*, sec. 72. Wang Fu (*Qianfu lun*, *pian* 29 釋難) ascribes to Laozi the argument that agriculture is a better basis for the empire than learning.

12 Cf. *Shangshu*, "Yaodian," the same phrase is used as a gloss for the phrase *chi ming* 啟明. See *Shangshu* 01.0246. However, *kai* 開 and *ming* 明 may be two qualities rather than verb and object ("to open the light").

13 Yu Yue (1874), cited in Wang Rongbao (1987, 6.116) reads *ling* as referring to the "tinkling bells of the carriage," which emit small sounds that do not carry far. Some editions insert here *kai fa* 開發.

14 See *Zuozhuan*, Lord Wen 18.9, on the five types of ideal family relations.

15 Wang Rongbao (1987, 6.118) cites *Guangya* to support his reading of *hong huang* 鴻荒 as "greatly uncivilized," "verging on the bestial," adopting the same meaning for *huang* as in *Fayan* 4.11.

16 Contra Han Jing (1992, 81n3), who prefers to read *qiao qiao* as "not upright." Note the rhyme between Yao 堯 and *qiao* 哨.

17 Li Gui reads *yin* 殷 as *zheng* 正 (to correct, to deem correct)—hence this translation. See Wang Rongbao (1987, 6.119).

I have merely borrowed something from Laozi's talk about the Way and its Power.[12] But I reject every impulse "to chisel away at humaneness and a sense of duty" or "to extinguish ritual decorum and learning." 4.6

"How may I come to be open to enlightenment?"[13] 4.7–9

"It is precisely the sages who can open one to enlightenment. Others only obscure what's true.[14] The sages' ultimate articulations of the Way are truly great. If one is open to them, then all the vast space enclosed by the four seas becomes visible. Shut them off, and a person cannot even see clearly into a space confined within four walls."[15]

"The sages' teachings may be likened to water and fire."

Someone asked me, "What about water and fire?"

"With water, the more one plumbs it, the deeper it gets; the further one would pursue it, the farther one goes.[16] With fire, the more you feed it, the brighter it burns; the more you tend it, the stronger it gets. Were one to try to govern the realm without resort to rituals and refinements[17] or the Five Teachings[18]—well, that would be just like looking upon Huangdi, Yao, and Shun as mere excrescences or superfluities!"[19]

Someone said to me, "High antiquity had no such exemplary figures and models or laws,[20] yet it was still well ruled. That being the case, your exemplars and laws are hardly the way to bring about good rule!" 4.10

"The time of flooding and droughts before the dawn of civilization[21]—this the sages abhorred. That explains why the models were first instituted by Fuxi and then perfected by Yao. Without Fuxi and Yao, ritual decorum and a sense of duty would be so much senseless babble, from which sages could borrow nothing at all!"

Someone asked me, "The uncivilized peoples in the far-flung regions all have their rites and music. Which of them is right?" 4.11

---

12 Cf. *Mencius* 4B.21, where Kongzi borrows from other early histories when writing his *Chunqiu*.

13 *Odes* 254/6 compares heaven's enlightening the people to opening a window: "Heaven's enlightening the people [opening their windows, *Tian zhi you min* 天之牖民] / Is like the *xun* [ocarina] and the *chi* [bamboo flute], / Like grasping something and taking it away. / Taking it away with no more effort. / Enlightening the people is truly simple."

14 Translation tentative, as the commentaries devote much discussion to *ling* 苓.

15 Cf. *Fayan* 1.11, 3.15, which compares the Way to the "sun and moon."

16 See the earlier citation of *Xunzi*, chap. 28, for water as a metaphor for the virtues and the Way.

17 *Li wen* 禮文 (possibly, "liturgies" or "ritual patterns" or "rituals and writings")?

18 Perhaps the Five Constants, given variously as *ren* 仁, *yi* 義, *li* 禮, *zhi* 智, *xin* 信 or as father's duty, mother's love, friendliness by the elder brother, respect by the younger brother, and filial duty of the child (*fu yi* 父義, *mu ci* 母慈, *xiong pengyou* 兄朋友, *di gong* 弟恭, *zi xiao* 子孝).

19 Or "abscesses," "swellings," on the body politic.

20 All three are *fa* 法.

21 Adding "before the dawn of civilization," as implied.

中國。日五政之所加。七賦之所養。中於天地者。為中國。過此而往者。人也哉。

4.12 聖人之治天下也。礙[18]諸以禮樂。無則禽。異則貉。吾見諸子之小禮樂也。不見聖人之小禮樂也。孰有書不由筆。言不由舌。吾見天常為帝王之筆, 舌也。

4.13 智也者知也。夫智用不用。益不益。則不贅虧矣。[19]

4.14 深知器械舟車宮室之為。則禮由已。[20]

---

18 Reading *ai* 礙 as *xian* 限 (constraints). However Yu Xingwu 于省吾 thought *ai* was a misreading for *ni* 擬 (measuring, circumscribing). If Yu is right, it would mean that "the sages took the measure of it [the known world] using the rites and music," with the line then a possible reference to *Fayan* 13/21, the "Xiao zhi" 孝至 chap.: 君子動而擬諸事 and the "Xici" A.6 line about the sage: 擬諸其形容.

19 Sima Guang, cited in Wang Rongbao (1987, 6.123) believes the *bu* 不 (not) before "surplus or deficiency" is an interpolation to be excised. He glosses this phrase as "If one tries to use one's knowledge in cases where it cannot be used, or add to one's knowledge in cases where it cannot be added to, then, as with [adding or subtracting from] the human body, this creates superfluities and deficiencies." Wang Rongbao (ibid.) disagrees and retains the *bu*, reading instead "If one has some knowledge but fails to use it, then his knowledge seems superfluous; and if one lacks knowledge [of something] but fails to increase it, then his knowledge will surely be deficient." Yu Yue (1874) notes that since two editions do not gloss the phrase "surplus [or] deficiency," perhaps the entire final phrase should be deleted. However, Yu comments, "The wise man uses [his wisdom] by not using it, adds to [his wisdom] by not adding to it. To use by not using means that there will be no deficiencies, and to add to it by not adding means that there will be no superfluities." See Wang Rongbao (1987, 6.123). Han Jing (1992, 83–84nn1–2) is clearly puzzled, for he glosses this as "Human wisdom comes from factual knowledge. How much factual knowledge a person has determines the degree, high or low, to which he is wise. Thus, wisdom that undergoes training and continual use will increase."

20 Most early editions and commentators write *ji* 己 (self), but some later editions, e.g. Wang Rongbao (1987, 9.124) write *yi* 已 (end, finish, telos). Wang also reads *yi* as *ye* 也, which would make the phrase mean "With someone who understands . . . , then the rituals derive from this understanding that is complete." This means that if one truly understands the sages' intention, then ritual propriety can be realized easily everywhere. Han Jing (1992, 85n1) remarks that here Yang merges in a single system the material inventions of the sages and their invention of ritual.

"One judges or corrects them by the Central States."[22]

Someone asked me, "Then which are the Central States?"

"Wherever the Five Rules[23] are applied and the seven crops cultivated,[24] and the land is located at the center of heaven and earth—*this* is the Central States. Is anyone who goes beyond these boundaries fully human and humane?"[25]

The sages' rule of the known world "under heaven" is as follows: they 4.12
set up constraints in it, using rites and music. Without them, the people would be no better than birds and beasts, and had they[26] in any way differed and diverged from them, the people would have been as uncivilized as the Mo. I have seen the disparagement of rites and music by the various masters, but I have never seen the sages belittle the rites or music. Who can write without making use of the brush, or speak except with the tongue?[27] I see heaven's constants as the brushes and tongues of emperors and kings.

"Wisdom" means "to understand."[28] Now, as we all know, wisdom has 4.13–14
a special feature: though one may use it, it will never be used up, and though one may add to it, any addition is not a mere increase.[29] So long as a person has a thorough understanding of the reasoning behind the invention of such utensils, tools, and contraptions as boats and carts, houses and chambers, the rites may be issued by that person.[30]

---

22 Possibly the phrase represents a little pun relating to the Yin-Shang dynasty.

23 Perhaps the Five Constants; perhaps also the Five Planets (see the chapter "Hong fan," in which case, Yang is talking about maximizing the potential of the Way (*huang ji* 皇極).

24 The so-called five grains plus mulberry and hemp.

25 Translating *ren* 仁 as both "human and humane," since the contrast with "bestial" is implied here as in some other passages. Perhaps the implication is that many within the Central States "go too far or do not go far enough." Certainly, this centrality seems to be a metaphor rather than a physical location.

26 It is unclear to me whether the subject here is "the rites and music" or "the people." Possibly, it is both.

27 Cf. *Fayan* 8.19.

28 A visual and aural pun.

29 Translation tentative. L'Haridon (2006, vol. 2, 33) translates instead as "Wisdom uses what has not been used before and develops what has not been developed before." Contra most commentators, I take Yang to mean that the degree of wisdom the person commands does not correlate simply with the person's training or application; rather, it correlates with the models he emulates. Furthermore, additions to factual knowledge cannot add to one's wisdom, which concerns not "knowing that" (facts) but "knowing how" (practical wisdom).

30 Both senses of *wei* 為 (to make, to be done for a purpose) are reflected in this translation. An alternate rendering of "may be issued by that person" (which I take to mean that Kongzi had the right to devise new rites and music, as do men like Yang) would be "the rites derive from that person" (referring to emulation of exemplary figures) or "the rites are carried out according to the person's [understanding]." By this logic, if a person understands why the sages invented the tools of civilization, as well as the underlying patterns within them (the same patterns that inform the *Changes* hexagrams), then he can also understand the necessity for ritual decorum, another invention by the sages. As Wu Mi, the commentator, writes (in *Yangzi Fayan zhu*), "He understands the reason for the systems being what they are, so there is no aspect

4.15 或問大聲。曰非雷非霆。隱隱[21]耾耾。久而愈盈。尸諸聖。[22]

4.16 或問道有因無因乎。曰可則因。否則革。[23]

4.17 或問無為。曰奚為哉。在昔虞夏。襲堯之爵。行堯之道。法度彰。禮樂著。垂拱而視天下民之阜也。無為矣。紹桀之後。纂紂之餘。法度廢。禮樂虧。安坐而視天下民之死。無為乎。

4.18 或問太古塗民耳目。惟其見也,聞也。見則難蔽。聞則難塞。曰天

21 It is possible that *yin yin* 隱隱 (here understood by commentators to mean *zhong che sheng* 重車聲) refers instead to a sound just as it begins, or a muffled sound whose source is difficult to locate.

22 To act as ritual impersonator (*shi* 尸) is also to represent the sages on solemn occasions. By the formulation of Han Jing (1992, 85), *shi* means "to entrust it [one's view and way of life?] to the sages" (*ji tuo zhi yu sheng ren* 寄託之於聖人) and possibly "to attend to the matter," as in the phrase *shei qi shi zhi* 誰其尸之.

23 Cf. Sima Guang's commentary, as well as Xu Fuguan's (1979, 2.524–25) gloss: 法在內的治道. Yang's *Taixuan*, "Xuan ying" sec., uses four words, *yin* 因, *xun* 循, *ge* 革, and *hua* 化, to describe the various modes of activity of the Way, terms that are borrowed from the *Changes* (e.g., Hexagram 1, "Tuan"; Hexagram 49; "Xici" A.6, 11) and discussed in Sivin 1977. For *ge* 革, Andrew Plaks (pers. comm.) prefers the literal "strips it away." The notions attached to *yin* 因 and *ge* 革 are moreover discussed in Gu and Jiang 1990, 533–37. What underlines this discussion is the assumption, shared by those interested in Huang Lao and the *Changes*, that the only constant is change.

Someone asked me about an impressive sound.[31] 4.15

"It is not thunder nor a thunderclap. A distant rumbling followed by a booming sound, which resounds all the louder the longer it goes on—this stands in for the sages' wisdom."

Someone asked me whether in carrying out the Way a person relies on 4.16
anything or anyone else.[32]

"The person cleaves to the appropriate course of action and, if something is inappropriate, he changes course."[33]

Someone asked me about nonpurposive activity.[34] 4.17

"Why are we talking at all about purposive activities?[35] In olden days, Shun and Yu inherited their system of ranks from Yao, and they practiced the way of Yao. Their laws and measures were brilliantly set out for all to see;[36] their rites and music were clear. Sitting with their arms folded and robes flowing, they observed their subjects flourishing throughout the realm. Such was their sort of 'nonpurposive activity.' By contrast, with the successors to the last tyrannical rulers of Xia and Shang, laws and measures were abandoned and rites and music were in decline. If the founders of the succeeding dynasties had then sat at their ease and watched the people in the realm dying, would that really have been a form of nonpurposive activity?

Someone said to me, "They say that[37] in highest antiquity, they blocked 4.18
the people's ears and eyes, since this was thought to be true seeing and hearing.[38] But once people have seen anything, it is hard to hide anything from them, and once people have heard anything, it is hard to stop up their ears."

---

of ritual which does not lie within him," presumably because to invent these items, the sages had to understand the inherent patterns in the basic stuffs from which the inventions were made. Here Yang comes close to articulating a position like that of Aristotle, whose objects and inventions have an inherent function for their being. Perhaps that is why Christoph Harbsmeier (pers. comm.) reads these lines as "then ritual propriety will follow suit."

31 A double entendre, meaning "great reputation." The readings of all these reduplicatives are tentative and based on earlier guesses about what the passage must mean.

32 Or, more simply, "whether the Way depends on anything other than itself," following Christoph Harbsmeier's (pers. comm.) suggestion.

33 This is very close to several passages in the *Analects*, including *Analects* 15.5, but this line clearly also refers to *Analects* 18.8, where Kongzi distinguishes himself from other men by saying that he has no fixed rules (*wu ke wu bu ke* 無可無不可), as he aligns himself only with the Right.

34 See Graham 1983.

35 Christoph Harbsmeier (pers. comm.) prefers "What is it [*wuwei*] good for?"

36 Christoph Harbsmeier (pers. comm.) prefers "were fully public."

37 Adding "They say that" (here and below), as implied.

38 The particle *wei* means "to be precisely X" or "to regard it as precisely X." Given the ambiguity of the term, the line could also mean "thinking it precisely to be their seeing and hearing [that made for trouble]."

之肇降生民。使其目見耳聞。是以視之禮。聽之樂。如視不禮。聽不樂。雖有民。焉得而塗諸。

4.19 或問新敝。曰新則襲之。敝則益損之。

4.20 或問太古德懷不禮懷。嬰兒慕。駒犢從。焉以禮。曰嬰犢乎。嬰犢母懷不父懷。母懷, 愛也。父懷, 敬也。獨母而不父。未若父母之懿也。

4.21 狙詐之家曰 狙詐之計, 不戰而屈人兵。堯舜也。曰不戰而屈人兵。堯舜也。沾項漸襟。堯舜乎。衒玉而賈石者。其狙詐乎。或問：狙詐與亡。孰愈。曰亡愈。[24] 或曰子將六師。則誰使。曰御得其道。則天下狙詐咸作使。御失其道。則天下狙詐咸作敵。故有天

24 If the alternative reading is correct, that would change the previous sentence, too, making *wang* = *wu* (to be without).

"They also say that 'when heaven first bestowed life on the people, it caused them to have eyes to see and ears to hear.'"[39] For this reason, the ruler would have them observe ritual and listen to music. If the people do not observe ritual or listen to music,[40] then how is the ruler, even if he has subjects, ever to obtain their loyal services while blocking up their ears and eyes?"[41]

Someone asked me about the new versus the worn-out.[42] 4.19

"The new is continued and renewed, and the worn-out, suitably adjusted."

Someone asked me, "In high antiquity, charismatic virtue[43] was cherished 4.20
but not the rites. They were just infants attached to breasts, or colts or calves following their mothers, so of what use were rituals?"

"An infant or a calf cherishes the mother but not the father. One should feel love for one's mother and respect for one's father.[44] To have feelings for the mother only can never be as good as having proper feelings for them both."

The experts in deception say, "Anyone who can subdue another's armies 4.21
using deception without going to war is a veritable Yao and Shun!"

"I grant you that he who subdues another's armies without going to war is a Yao or a Shun. But is it really being another Yao or Shun if the people are up to their necks in blood, with their collars[45] steeped in it? Surely it is deceptive to boast of having jade while hawking rough stones!"

Someone asked me whether it's not better to use deception than to die.

"It is better to die."[46]

Someone asked me, "So if you were to lead the Six Armies, whom would *you* employ?"

"In carriage driving, as in ruling, so long as the driver gets on the right Way, then he can get all the masters of deception in the known world in his employ. By contrast, should a driver lose his way, then all the masters of deception in the known world become his peers and rivals. Therefore,

---

39 Cf. *Odes* 255/1, 260/1.

40 Or "something that offends ritual" and "something that offends music."

41 Adding "their loyal services" as implied. Or, as the anonymous reviewer of this translation suggests, "If [the ruler] does not let them observe ritual and listen to music, then even if he [as ruler] has [control over] his subjects, how can he be allowed to block up their ears and eyes?" I take this to mean that we as human beings have been given our faculties to use them in service of the state and its people; to try to prevent their use would be both impossible and counterproductive. Moreover, the interlocutor posits the existence of a state of primal unity before ritual music, but Yang argues that to posit this would contradict the very purpose of heaven's "giving birth to the people" (see above) and the idea of a functioning polity.

42 Or, more literally, "used" and so shabby.

43 "Grace" or "favors" is one meaning of *de* that may be relevant to a mother breast-feeding a child.

44 Literally, "To cherish the mother is to love her; to cherish the father is to respect him."

45 Literally, "lapels."

46 That is, it is better not to use stratagems.

下者。審其御而已矣。或問：威震諸侯。須於征與狙詐之力也。如其亡。曰威震諸侯。須於狙詐。可也。未若威震諸侯而不須狙詐也。或曰無狙詐。將何以征乎。曰縱不得不征。不有司馬法乎。何必狙詐乎。

4.22 申韓之術。不仁之至矣。若何牛羊之用人也。若牛羊用人。則狐狸螻螾不膢臘也與。[25] 或曰刀不利。筆不銛。而獨加諸砥。[26] 不亦可乎。曰人砥則秦尚矣。

4.23 或曰刑名[27] 非道邪。何自然也。曰何必刑名。圍棊擊劍反目[28] 眩形。亦皆自然也。由其大者作正道。由其小者作姦道。[29]

25 Note the visual and aural pun on *lou* 螻 (mole cricket, ant, or frog) and the Lou festival. Yu Yue (1874), cited in Wang Rongbao (1987, 6.131) suggests that if the laws of Shen Buhai and Han Fei are carried out, many will die, and these four creatures will then feast on the piled-up corpses, "just like the people who enjoy being drunk and sated during the Lou and La festivals."

26 Cf. *Taiping yulan* 346.4b.

27 *Xing* 形 is used often to refer to *xing* 刑.

28 The binome *fanmu* 反目 means "quarrels between husband and wife or between close friends," but most commentators, including Sima Guang, read *fanmu* as either *fan shen* 反身 or *fan zi* 反自, presuming a scribal error. Han Jing (1992, 94n2) glosses the binome as "somersaults" (*fan gen dou* 翻跟斗).

29 *Jiandao* 奸/姦道 for "treacherous byway." Ban Gu nearly quotes this passage in *Wenzhang bianti huixuan* 777.1b.

he who would possess all the known world had better pay heed only to the driver's way of driving."[47]

Someone asked me whether the ruler can ever manage without relying on punitive campaigns and deception to overawe his nobles.

"One may rely on stratagems and deception to impress the princes. But such a course of action can hardly compare with one that impresses the nobles without resorting to stratagems and deception."

Someone asked me, "But absent recourse to deception, what means can the ruler use to undertake punitive campaigns?"

"If there is really no alternative to launching a punitive attack, then don't we have a military manual by the title *Models for the Colonel*?[48] What need is there for stratagems?"

"The arts of Shen Buhai and Han Fei are the ultimate expression of man's inhumanity to man. Why treat people like animals to be driven and sacrificed?[49] If one treats the people this way, will we not soon have foxes and jackals, ants and worms, performing the solemn Lou and La festivals?"[50] 4.22

Someone said to me, "But if the knife has not been sharpened or the brush trimmed, surely it would be alright to apply the grindstone to criminals."[51]

"In grinding down the people, surely Qin was best!"[52]

Someone asked me, "Is the 'forms and titles' theory[53] not the true Way? How natural it is!" 4.23

"Why must we discuss 'forms and titles'? Games like chess and sword-play, acrobatic stunts and illusionistic tricks[54]—all these are 'natural' in some sense, but so what? He who follows what is great carves out a straight path for himself, but he who follows what is inferior sets out on a treacherous byway."[55]

---

47 Taking *yu* 御 to refer to both the driver and his way of driving—hence the possible overtranslation of the single graph. As stated above, the analogy between driving a chariot and ruling a state was very old by Yang's time.

48 *Sima (bing)fa* 司馬(兵)法 is a book of strategies mentioned in the *Shiji*. There the name "Colonel" is taken as the surname Sima.

49 Literally, oxen and sheep.

50 The Lou festival was a harvest festival observed in Chu, in which sacrifices were offered to the grain gods. The La festival was performed shortly after the winter solstice to honor all the gods. See Bodde 1975, chap. 3. It may or may not be relevant that during both the La and the Lou festivals sheep and oxen were sacrificed; clearly, the phrase "foxes and jackals, ants and worms," refers to rapacious creatures. Cf. *Fayan* 2.13.

51 Adding "to criminals," as implied.

52 This may be a general reference to Qin's harsh laws or a specific reference to the persecution of *fangshi* 方士 (often misconstrued as Ru, classicists, or Confucians).

53 For the definition of *xingming* 形名 (forms and names), see Creel 1970, chap. 5.

54 The illusionistic tricks recorded in early sources include swallowing swords, spitting fire, planting trees, and butchering men.

55 The game of *liubo* 六博 used a chessboard called "crooked ways" (*qudao* 曲道), as noted in Xu Rongsheng (p. 64), which may explain much of the play on words here.

4.24 或曰申韓之法非法與。曰法者，謂唐虞成周之法也。如申韓。如申韓。

4.25 莊周申韓不乖寡聖人而漸諸篇。則顏氏之子閔氏之孫。其如台。[30]

4.26 或曰莊周有取乎。[31] 曰少欲。鄒衍有取乎。曰自持。至周罔君臣之義。衍無知於天地之閒。雖鄰不覿也。[32]

---

30 The formula *ru qi X* 如其X or *ru X*, in accordance with its use in *Analects* 5.18, supposedly expresses Kongzi's sense of exasperation, disdain, or censure. See Wang Rongbao (1987, 6.134).

31 Laozi, sec.19, of course, advises the person "to have little self-interest and few desires." Notably, Yang described himself as one who had learned "to reduce his desires" (少嗜慾). Cf. Mohist talk of 小取, 大取 (take one thing rather than another 取此擇彼), where the "choosing" or "taking" refers to categories used in logic. See, e.g., *Mozi* 44–45, A95–96.

32 *Di* 覿 means "to see/meet face-to-face." However, Han Jing (1992, 97n5), following Tao Hongqing 陶鴻慶, takes this to mean that these thinkers (pretend to?) see what is far away but not what is near to hand, assuming an allusion to Zou Yan as that kind of expert "in things beyond the sea that people cannot see" (*ren zhi suo bu neng du* 人之所不能睹). See *Shiji* 74.2344–46.

Someone asked me, "Aren't the laws and standards of Shen Buhai and Han Fei true laws and standards?" 4.24

"The term 'standards' refers to the standards set by Yao, Shun, Cheng-Tang of Shang, and the rulers of the Zhou dynasty.[56] So much for those of Shen Buhai and Han Fei!"

As for Zhuang Zhou, Shen Buhai, and Han Fei,[57] if they had not opposed and disparaged the sages, but instead had steeped themselves in their writings, how would the followers of Yan Hui and Min Ziqian[58] ever have bettered them?![59] 4.25

Someone asked me whether to adopt anything from Zhuang Zhou.[60] 4.26

"His injunction to lessen desires."[61]

"And from Zou Yan?"[62]

"Self-reliance and self-restraint.[63] But Master Zhuang is less than adequate when it comes to the duties between rulers and subjects, and Master Zou seems to know nothing about the social world between heaven and earth. So in the case of these two masters, even 'if they were near neighbors,' I would not bother to pay them a visit."[64]

---

56 Taking *cheng* 成 to refer to Cheng-Tang, the founder of Shang, rather than to either King Cheng (the boy-king whom the Duke of Zhou served as regent) or Chengzhou (an early Zhou capital). Han Jing (1992, 95n2) disagrees. But the question then becomes, Why not mention Shang?

57 For the pairing of Zhuangzi and Han Feizi, see *Fayan* 3.20. The first pairing of Shen Buhai and Han Fei comes in the previous passage.

58 Kongzi's best disciples.

59 *Qi ru* 其如 *he/yi* 何/台 means *nai he* 奈何, according to Wang Rongbao (1987, 6.134), which the commentators take to mean "How could the followers ever have [bettered them]?" Some commentators take *yi* to mean "to us."

60 Or the question could be whether Yang has borrowed anything from Zhuangzi.

61 While Yang Xiong occasionally disparages the Zhanguo masters, he is much more laudatory about some (e.g., Zhuangzi) than about other classical masters (e.g., *Hanshi waizhuan* 4/22; Hightower, p. 146).

62 Zou Yan (d. ca. 240 BCE) was famous for his theories about the universe.

63 The term *zichi* 自持 means "getting a firm grip on the self, so that one is careful not to invite trouble." Thus, it refers both to "supporting the self" and to "restraining the self." L'Haridon (2006, vol. 2, 39) translates instead as "remaining true to oneself." The famous "tipping vessel" is described in similar terms because it is self-regulating in that it keeps itself from being overfull and tipping over. See *Fayan* 10.28. Knechtges (1982a) and Zach (1939) prefer "self-containment."

64 L'Haridon (2006) similarly reads this as "This is truly to remain blind to what is nearby."

卷第五

問神

神心忽恍。經緯萬方。
事繫諸道德仁義禮。
譔問神。

5.1 或問神。曰心。請問之。曰潛天而天。潛地而地。天地,神明而不
測者也。心之潛也。猶將測之。況於人乎。況於事倫乎。敢問

Chapter 5

Asking about Divine Insight

VERSE SUMMARY

The heart so divine may *seem* as vague and unknowable as the gods, yet it is the alpha and omega when it comes to governing the myriad regions.[1] Its workings are tied to the Way, to charismatic virtue, to humanity, to a sense of duty and propriety, and to ritual decorum. Thus, I have composed chapter 5, "Asking about Divine Insight."[2]

....

Someone asked me about the divine. 5.1

"It is the heart."[3]

"May I ask what you mean?"

"It immerses itself in heaven and so becomes heaven; it immerses itself into earthly things and so becomes earth. Heaven and earth are divinely illumined,[4] even if they cannot be completely fathomed.[5] Through these processes of immersion, the heart comes to seem almost on the point of

---

1 Both L'Haridon (2006) and Knechtges (1982a) translate this line quite differently.

2 Pfister (2006) discusses the history of the term *shenming* 神明, which in pre-Han and Han texts signifies not only the gods of heaven and earth but also the "divine spark," "daimonic illumination," or "god-like perspicacity" that comes to the adept, including the adept of sexual techniques, as well as to the expert in the Way. This use refers to "a controlled altered state of consciousness" where "the perceptual capacities are strengthened . . . and the concentration is strong but flowing" and is not focused on only a single object (187). The earliest occurrence of the term seems to be in the "Neiye" chapter of the *Guanzi*. Of course, the term in Han also refers to the "gods of heaven and earth." Since Yang Xiong constructs good government as the opposite of Wudi's policies, it may moreover be relevant that Wudi built a terrace called Shenming, which was supposedly some 50 *zhang* high, to use when worshiping the gods.

3 Andrew Plaks (pers. comm.) prefers "faculties," intellectual and emotional, as he points out that the word "heart" implies both sorts of faculties in the pre-Cartesian world.

4 See n. 2 for *shenming* 神明, literally, "divine light," but here "divine insight."

5 For the phrase *bu ce* 不測 (unfathomable), see "Xici" A.5, which describes the cosmos and the gods; see also the "Zhongyong" (32.23/146/9, 32.24/146/13) dictum "Since events are never duplicated, their proliferation is unfathomable [*bu ce*]."

潛心于聖。曰昔乎仲尼潛心於文王矣。達之。顏淵亦潛心於仲尼矣。未達[1]一間耳。神在所潛而已矣。

5.2 天神天明。[2]照知四方。天精天粹。萬物作類。

5.3 人心其神矣乎。操則存。舍則亡。能常操而存者。其惟聖人乎。

5.4 聖人存神索至。成天下之大順。致天下之大利。和同天人之際。使之無間也。[3]

5.5 龍蟠于泥。蚖[4]其肆矣。蚖哉。蚖哉。惡覩龍之志也與。或曰龍必欲飛天乎。曰時飛則飛。時潛則潛。既飛且潛。食其不妄。形其不可得而制也與。曰聖人不制。則何為乎羑里。曰龍以不制為

1 *Da* conveys the sense of having access to a person or principles. Cf. *Analects* 13.35.

2 See Han Jing (1992, 99n1).

3 *Jian* 間 can, of course, refer to the boundary between heaven and earth, but here I believe it refers to the human realm. This is perhaps a reference to *Huainan zi*, which talks about there being "no gap" between "heaven and man" for the one who has "self-possession" (*zide* 自得).

4 Han Jing (1992, 101n1) says this is an amphibious water lizard commonly called "Stone Dragon" (*shi long zi* 石龍子), a name that implies a contrast between higher and inferior creatures. Some commentators identify it as a venomous snake (*hui* 虺).

fathoming them.[6] How much more, then, can the heart fathom people, not to mention social affairs and relations!"

"I make bold to ask about immersing one's heart in the sages."

"Long ago, Kongzi certainly immersed himself, heart and soul, in King Wen, and he fully apprehended him.[7] Certainly Yan Hui, for his part, also immersed himself, heart and soul, in Kongzi, and he nearly apprehended all of him. Clearly, divine insight depends solely upon immersion!"

Heaven, being divine and bright,[8] shines forth upon and allows us to perceive the four quarters of the land. Heaven, being extraordinarily refined and subtle, engenders the myriad phenomena in their categories. The human heart—how divine it is! As the saying goes, "Grasp hold of it, and it is preserved. Let it go, and it is lost."[9] Yet it is only the sages who continually grasp hold of it so as to preserve it! The sages preserve their godlike insight and they seek perfection. They complete the great concord in All-under-heaven, confer great benefit upon All-under-heaven, and bring harmony and unity[10] to the space between heaven and human, so that no gap exists. 5.2–4

"The dragon coiled in the mud, awaiting the proper time to act."[11] The humble water lizard,[12] which emerges prematurely, has its way. Those lizards, lizards! How can they possibly discern the dragon's ultimate aim to take flight? 5.5

Someone asked me, "Does a dragon always want to fly up to the heavens?"

"If it is time to fly, then the dragon flies, and if it is time to hide, then it hides. No matter whether it takes wing or hides, since it battens on nothing wrong,[13] its bodily form cannot be constrained." [14]

---

6 Through intuitions and insights.

7 The translation "apprehended him" suggests both that Kongzi was able to emulate him completely, in effect becoming King Wen; and Kongzi fully apprehended him, since *da* 達 means both "to reach" and "to realize."

8 The term *tian* 天 here simply refers to the "whole cosmos," not to an anthropomorphic god (the existence of which Yang Xiong never affirms). If heaven were conceived of as an anthropomorphic god, the phrase would mean "So it shines forth upon and perceives the four quarters." But Yang most likely means that the heavens allow *us humans* to apprehend the four quarters of the realm. Support for the translation given here comes from *Changes*, Hexagram 30 (Xiang).

9 The *xin* 心 refers to intellectual and emotional capacities and inclinations. Most Zhanguo and Han texts agree that if the *xin* is not "kept" (*shou* 守), man's very life is in danger. See *Mencius* 6A.8, which attributes this saying to Kongzi.

10 Contrast *Analects* 13.23.

11 This metaphor comes from *Changes*, "Wenyan" 2/1/言 and "Xici" B.3. I added the phrase "awaiting the proper time to act," since it is implied.

12 One wonders if Yang is not pointing here also to the chameleon-like faces of the duplicitous.

13 Andrew Plaks (pers. comm.) prefers "its feeding is correct." Cf. Hexagram 1 of *Changes* and Tetragram 1 of *Taixuan jing*, as well. "To feed upon" in Chinese has the double meaning of "to take a salary for."

14 Han Jing (1992, 101n3) reads "Its bodily form cannot be restrained by others." This translation, in effect, ignores the particle *er* 而.

龍。聖人以不手為聖人。[5]

5.6 或曰經可損益與。曰易始八卦。而文王六十四。其益可知也。詩書禮春秋。或因或作。[6]而成於仲尼。[7]其益可知也。故夫道非天然。應時而造者。損益可知也。[8]

5.7 或曰易損其一也。雖惷,知闕焉。至書之不備過半矣。而習者不知。[9]惜乎。書序[10]之不如易也。曰彼數也。可數焉故也。如書序。雖孔子亦末如之何矣。

5.8 昔之說書者序以百。而酒誥之篇俄空焉。[11]今亡夫。[12]

5 Or "manipulated," if we follow Liu Shipei (1916), in Wang Rongbao (1987, 7.416). Cf. *Zuozhuan*, Ai 6/8. Similarly, *Xunzi* argues that the "sage is not a slave to things," as noted in Nylan 2001c.

6 Knechtges (1982a) believes *yin* 因 refers to "following" the old texts that had been transmitted, while *zuo* refers to creating texts anew (referring to the composition of the *Annals* by Kongzi). It also has the sense of "elaborating" something.

7 Wang Rongbao (1987, 7.146) writes that Kongzi made no substantive change in the rites and the music transmitted to him, drawing on the pseudo-Kong Preface to the *Documents* and its Kong subcommentary.

8 But Yang's formulation recalls lines in the "Great Commentary" in the *Liji* (16.2/91/25) (此其不得與民變革者也), and also in *Shiji* 47.1935–38, which make Kongzi's decision to fix the text of the Classics a highly self-conscious one.

9 See *Lunheng* 20.61 for details.

10 However, Wang Rongbao (1987, 7.154) certainly takes *xu* as "preface." I take *xu* in the second instance to refer to the "Xugua" 序卦 commentary to *Changes*. The current Preface to the *Documents* certainly postdates Yang Xiong, as it makes reference to the pseudo-Kong chapters inserted into the canonical text in the fourth century CE. My translation assumes that an earlier version of the Preface existed for the Modern Script *Documents*, as seems to be indicated by Fu Sheng's *Shangshu dazhuan*.

11 This statement seems to draw upon Liu Xiang's catalog, *Bie lu* 別錄 (finished ca. 8 BCE). Note, however, that Yang's statement does not refer to missing strips in the "Shaogao."

12 Originally, I read this as "Now these are [real] losses, are they not?" But if one thinks this passage rewrites *Analects* 15.26 and reads *fu* 夫 as *bu hu* 不呼, following Pulleyblank (1995), then it means "Is it not so that this is now not the case?" (i.e., the lacunae have been filled in). I thank David R. Knechtges for pointing this out to me; L'Haridon (2006) concurs. Andrew Plaks (pers. comm.) prefers "Now, even in our own day, these parts are missing, are they not?"

"But if you say that sages cannot be constrained, then how do you explain the imprisonment of King Wen at Youli?"[15]

"The dragon is a dragon by virtue of its being unconstrained. The sage is a sage by virtue of his not being led around by the nose."[16]

Someone asked me, "May one add to or subtract from the Classics?" 5.6

"The *Changes* began with the Eight Trigrams, from which King Wen produced the sixty-four Hexagrams. This is proof that the Classics can be added to. As for the *Odes*, *Documents*, *Rites*, and *Annals*, in some places they were transmitted writings, without additions, and in some cases new compositions. That they were completed[17] by Kongzi is proof that they could be added to.[18] Thus, we see that the Way is not 'spontaneously created'! Rather, it is fashioned in response to the times, which means that it can be added to or subtracted from."[19]

Someone said to me, "Were the *Changes* to lose even one part, even an idiot would be able to discern the omission in it. But surely over half the full complement of chapters in the *Documents* has gone missing, a fact even those well versed in the text are completely unaware of![20] What a pity that the Preface[21] for the *Documents* is not as good as the Hexagram Arrangement for the *Changes*." 5.7

"As the *Changes* is composed of numerical patterns, one can reckon the number of chapters in it.[22] But when it comes to the order of the *Documents* chapters, even a sage like Kongzi would not know what to do with it!"

"Those of long ago eras who explicated the *Documents* arranged it in one hundred chapters.[23] But then the 'Proclamation against Wine' chapter 5.8

15 I have inserted "King Wen" in the translation, for sense.

16 Some would prefer to replace the homely phrasing "being led around by the nose" by the more elevated "[his spirit] is unfettered," since this would work well with talk of imprisonment, but I suspect that Yang means to say that while physical constraints may be placed on the sage, there are no constraints on his way of thinking, and he is thus not liable to false arguments or allurements.

17 The verb *cheng* 成 implies both "put in their final form" and "perfected." This presumably refers to the so-called Modern Script order of the Classics (adopted in Yang's list), which puts the *Annals* last, making Kongzi the completer of the Classics.

18 Here Yang anticipates by two millennia the latest scholarly findings about the Classics; see, e.g., Vogelsang 2007; Steck 1998, 47–61.

19 Cf. *Analects* 2.23. This statement by Yang would have struck some as radical, since *jing* 經 is often glossed as *chang* 常 (i.e., unchanging).

20 This may well be a barbed comment, for Yang Xiong's ruler, Chengdi, allowed a forged version of the *Documents* in one hundred *pian* to circulate, knowing that it was a forgery. See n. 23 below.

21 *Xu* 序 (possibly "order," as below). This statement by the interlocutor may allude to a statement by Han Wudi, "We are very concerned [about lacunae]" (*zhen shen min yan* 朕甚閔焉), recorded in *Shiji* 26.1260.

22 *Shu* 數 refers not only to "numbers" and "numbering" but also to "numerical [i.e., regular] sequences" and to "the regular patterns of the cosmos"—hence the translation.

23 That the *Documents* once consisted of 100 or 120 chapters is a standard Han view. Shortly before Yang's time, the court official Zhang Ba 張霸 of Donglai had compiled

5.9 虞,夏之書渾渾爾。商 (=商)書灝灝爾。周書噩噩爾。下周者,其書譙乎。[13]

5.10 或問聖人之經不可使易知與。曰不可。天俄而可度。則其覆物也淺矣。地俄而可測。則其載物也薄矣。大哉。天地之為萬物郭。五經之為眾說郛。[14]

5.11 或問聖人之作事。不能昭若日月乎。何後世之訔訔也。曰瞽曠能默。[15] 瞽曠不能齊不齊之耳。狄牙能喊。狄牙不能齊不齊之口。

5.12 君子之言。幽必有驗乎明。遠必有驗乎近。大必有驗乎小。微必有驗乎著。無驗而言之謂妄。君子妄乎。不妄。

---

13 Reading *hao hao* 灝灝 (boundless, vast, deep) as *hao hao* 浩浩; and *e e* 噩噩 (a hapax used for the first time here) as *bu afu* 不阿附 (not to toady to someone), after the Shide Tang 世德堂 edition, assuming *e e* to be the same as *e e* 諤諤, often glossed as *zheng zhi mao* 正直貌 (straightforward). Wang Rongbao (1987, 7.156–57), following Li Gui, takes the phrase *xia Zhou* 下周 (either "in the latter days of Zhou," "Zhou's successor," or "after Zhou") to refer to the pre-imperial Qin state, and so he glosses the phrase as "harsh and punitive." Support for this comes from the *Yinyi* 音義, which glosses *qiao* 譙 as *sha* 殺 (to kill). *Qiao* can also mean "glib" or "superficial," displaying no refinement or grace. *Taiping yulan* 608.6a, in citing this line, glosses *qiao* as *qiao cui* 憔悴 (careworn, haggard), which means that the later chapters in the *Documents* reflect the severe decline of Zhou power and virtue. However, basing himself on the Song and Wu editions, Sima Guang, cited in Wang Rongbao (1987, 7.156), reads *shei* 誰 (who?) instead of *qiao*, in the belief that Yang here queries the authorship of these *Documents* chapters (and hence their reliability). Wang Rongbao (1987, 7.156) argues that Sima Guang's solution is unlikely to be right, since *qiao* seems of a piece with the earlier reduplicatives. Yang seems to have thought that the chapters about Shang were actually "writings of Shang" reflecting the era in which they were produced, so it follows that the writings of Qin reflect the harsh laws that Yang ascribes to them. For Yang's special excoriation of Qin, see Nylan 2013.

14 Rendering both 郭 and 郛 as "retaining walls."

15 Cf. *Xunzi* 27.518 ("Da lue"). Han Jing (1992, 109n2) takes this to mean that Music Master Kuang could not make people with a tin ear like the best sort of music, even if the *Documents* "Yaodian" chapter has Music Master Kui's performance delighting the birds and beasts, as well as all humans; see *Shangshu* 02.0705. In both instances, the idea is that even the most accomplished master cannot make regular (i.e., conforming to norms) an irregular or nonstandard sensibility. These lines suggest that the moral person must refine his own sensibilities before he will be able to understand anything that the sages would impart to him. Maintaining silence, according to Wang Rongbao (1987, 8.158), means that one says nothing but still understands something in his own heart; the sage is one who can rise above any din to understand the highest music contained in silence. Cf. Knechtges, 1982a, 50.

came to have unexpected gaps in it.[24] Now these lacunae are gone, are they not?[25]

The chapters on Yu-Shun and Xia are deep and potent,[26] while those on Shang are vast in scope. Those pertaining to Zhou do not flatter, while those on the latter part of Zhou are cutting. 5.9

Someone asked me why the sages' Classics[27] could not have been made easier to understand. 5.10

"That would not be possible. If the heavens could be measured in an instant without further ado, then the shelter it afforded things would be slight indeed! And if earth could be fathomed in an instant without further ado, then its support for things would be paltry indeed! True greatness we impute to heaven-and-earth[28] as retaining walls for the myriad sorts of things, and to the Five Classics as retaining walls for the masses of explications."[29]

Someone asked me why the sages' deeds cannot shine forth like the sun and moon.[30] "Why allow later generations to be mired in endless debates over their meaning?"[31] 5.11

"The legendary blind music master Kuang could maintain silence in order to mark the changing rhythms, but even he could not elicit the right response from a tin ear. The legendary chef Yi Ya knew how to season things, but even he could not impose a connoisseur's sense of taste on an unrefined palate."[32]

With the noble man's speech, obscure points can always be proven by what is clear as day, and far-reaching points, by what is close to hand. The major points can always be proven through the minor, and the less-than-apparent, through what is obvious to all. To have no proof at all for one's claims is the very definition of "recklessness."[33] Is the noble man ever reckless? I think not! 5.12

---

such a lengthy version by adding to the 29 Modern Script chapters transmitted by Fu Sheng a series of other pieces deemed to have merit (*Hanshu* 88.3607). Note that some scholars presume the 71 chapters of the *Yi Zhoushu* were part of the original *Documents* Classic of 100 chapters.

24 *Hanshu* 30.1706 confirms that the "Jiu gao" and "Shao gao" chapters are missing strips.

25 One implication is that Kongzi was content to transmit the incomplete.

26 Reading *hun hun* 渾渾 as referring to the primal unity of undifferentiated *qi*, which contains within itself all potentials.

27 But note that *jing* 經 refers as often to "norms" as to "Classics."

28 I.e., the cosmos.

29 The metaphor of the outer walls (i.e., defenses against invasion) appears to indicate that the Classics contain within them all the main ideas to be found in inferior works while rendering them invulnerable to attack.

30 E.g., cf. *Fayan* 1.12.

31 Adding "over their meaning" as implied.

32 Adding "to mark the changing rhythms" as implied. Kuang was a legendary blind musician who served Duke Ping 平 of Jin (r. 557–532 BCE) as music master. *Mencius* 6A.7, makes the palate of Yi Ya 易牙, a celebrated cook, the standard for good taste and then argues, by analogy, that the heart has a taste for reason and duty.

33 Or "baselessness," in the sense of "lacking proof" (here and below). My translation

5.13 言不能達其心。書不能達其言。難矣哉。惟聖人得言之解。得書之體。[16] 白日以照之。江河以滌之。灝灝乎其莫之禦也。面相之。辭相適。[17] 捈中心之所欲。[18] 通諸人之嚍嚍者。莫如言。彌綸[19] 天下之事。記久明遠。著古昔之㖧㖧。傳千里之忞忞者。[20] 莫如書。故言,心聲也。書,心畫也。[21] 聲畫形。君子小人見矣。聲畫者。君子小人之所以動情乎。[22]

5.14 聖人之辭。渾渾若川。順則便,逆則否者。其惟川乎。

---

16 Wang Rongbao (1987, 8.160) takes *ti* 體 to mean *ti cai* 體裁 (style, format), as does Han Jing (1992, 110n2). I instead take Yang to be playing (or expanding?) upon the standard Han definition that equates "ritual" (*li* 禮) with "body" (*ti*), insofar as he makes texts embodiments of the world, including the sages in it. The "words" may refer to speech (also *yan* 言), in contrast to writing.

17 Reading *tu* 捈 as *shu fa* 抒發 (pour out and express). "Elicit" implies "unburdening" the self of the emotions and desires.

18 Reading *jin jin* 嚍嚍 as *fen fen* 憤憤, following the Li Gui 李軌 commentary. Some editions read *hua hua* (嚍嚍), which refers to what is "perverse" or "at odds," in which case the sentence would mean that speech is best for "resolving differences between people who have been at odds with one another." *Yili* 8/53.27 ("Binli" 賓禮 chap.); Steele trans., pp. 284–85), speaks of the necessity for speeches to be "agreeable and persuasive" and "also to make their points."

19 *Mi lun* 彌綸 recalls "Xici" A.3: 彌綸天地之道.

20 *Hun hun* 㖧㖧 refers to whatever is not clearly seen or apprehended; *min min* 忞忞, in Li Gui's commentary, refers to what "the mind cannot understand" (*xin suo bu liao* 心所不了). Yu Yue (1874), cited in Wang Rongbao (1987, 8.163) suggests that *min min* is the same as *hun hun* 㖧㖧, with both reduplicatives referring to what is unclear—hence Andrew Plak's (pers. comm.) preferred reading "transmitting confusion that goes on forever." Knechtges (1982a) similarly speaks of "murky things" not well understood. Reference perhaps should also be made to *Shiji* 84.2486, in Qu Yuan's biography, where *min min* in the phrase *shouwu zhi minmin* 受物之汶汶 means defilement, but whether 忞忞 and 汶汶 conveyed the same idea during Han is hard to say. Certainly, these lines would apply to Sima Qian's "Letter to Ren An," recorded in *Hanshu* 62.2725–36. There is a slim possibility that *min min* refers, as in the *Shuowen jiezi*, to *zi mianqiang* 自勉強 (what one forces oneself to do). Note the rhyming of *yuan* and *min*.

21 Tying *hua* 畫 to "images," "designs," or "delineations" (*xiang* 象), as in the preface to the *Shuowen jiezi* and in *Changes* ("Xici" B.3 and "Shuo" 2). Han Jing (1992, 111n6) interprets *xiang* 象 (image) to refer to *chouhua yu neixin de tuhua* 籌畫於內心的圖畫 (the images designed in the inner heart or mind), by which he means thinking and visualizing. For further insight, see Lei 2000, 13–14; Thern 1966.

22 I translate the passage in light of the "Yueji" maxim in the *Liji*, sec. 1 (情動於中,故形於聲), and the famous Mao preface line 情動於中,而形於言,言之不足,故詠歌之.

They say, "Speech cannot fully express what is in the heart, nor can writing fully express speech."[34] What a difficulty![35] Only sages apprehend the true meaning of words and achieve the substantial embodiment of standards in their writing.[36] [Of Kongzi it was therefore said:] "The white sun shone down on him; the Yangzi and Yellow Rivers cleansed him. So powerfully does his example flow onward that 'none have been a match for him.'"[37] 5.13

Nothing is as good as speech for exchanging remarks during face-to-face meetings, expressing the heart's desire or communicating people's pent-up emotions. And nothing compares with writing for fully delineating the affairs of the whole realm, for recording events of the distant past or the remote, for clarifying what has been obscured by the mists of time, or for transmitting the difficult-to-comprehend over thousands of miles. Therefore, speech is the heart's sounds, and writing, its images.[38] When sounds and images assume form, then the noble and petty appear in high relief, for sounds and images are surely the means, with the noble and petty alike, to see what motivates them.[39]

The sages' eloquence flows on and on like a river. When one follows that current, things go easily and well. But travel against that flow makes for hard going. Is that not just like a river?[40] 5.14

---

focuses on his habitual mode of conduct rather than his temporary lack of proof.

34 Cf. "Xici" A.12.

35 Cf. *Analects* 15.17, the Zheng Xuan commentary, which implies the difficulty of accomplishing this. I thank David R. Knechtges for this reference.

36 One helpful introduction to such passages in Yang's work is Gu 2005, 35–43, though my translation departs from Gu's, except in agreeing that Yang's main focus is on the writing and reading of texts (37). The idea is that only the sages can formulate expressions that express the right intention, and only their writings sufficiently transcribe speech.

37 Cf. *Mencius* 3A.4. See *Mencius* 7A.16 for the phrase *mo zhi neng yu* 莫之能禦, where *yu* means "to resist."

38 Cf. Aristotle, *De interpretatione* (16a3–8): "Spoken sounds are symbols of affections in the soul, and written marks, symbols of spoken sounds." Ralph Waldo Emerson remarked to his daughter that letters were "a kind of picture of a voice." How the heart participates in creating representations or images of its own evaluative emotions is the subject of much Zhanguo and Han thinking. That oral and written sources are tied to speech and paintings has allowed this line to serve as comment on aesthetic choices down through the ages.

39 Wang Chong, an ardent admirer of Master Yang, spun off from this passage to write a comparison of writing and painting in *Lunheng* 38/184/8–9. In attempting to reconcile the views of Yang Xiong with those of Mencius, Gu Ming Dong (2005, 36) interprets the end of this lengthy discourse differently, allowing him to say that while Yang's statement initially seems to accept the position of the *Zhuangzi* and the "Xici," in the end it comes closer to the intentionalist position taken by Mencius. Gu's argument, while interesting, depends upon switching the meaning of terms midtranslation, and it ignores the longstanding convention by which speech = sounds and writing = images.

40 In classical Greek, there are two kinds of truth: accuracy in narrative and the sort of "truth" that may be inaccurate but that still represents time-tested solutions. Yang probably speaks here of the second sort of truth, but he mainly wants to emphasize

5.15 或曰仲尼聖者與。何不能居世也。[23] 曾范,蔡之不若。曰聖人者。范,蔡乎。若范,蔡。其如聖何。

5.16 或曰淮南太史公者。其多知與。曷其雜也。曰雜乎雜。[24] 人病以多知為雜。[25] 惟聖人為不雜。

5.17 書不經。非書也。言不經。非言也。言,書不經。多多贅矣。[26]

5.18 或曰述而不作。玄何以作。曰其事則述。[27] 其書則作。

5.19 育而不苗者。吾家之童烏乎。九齡而與我玄文。[28]

5.20 或曰玄何為。曰為仁義。曰孰不為仁。孰不為義。曰勿雜也而已矣。

---

23 Reading *ju shi* 居世 as *chu shi* 處世 (to be in the world) but taking it in the well-attested sense of "to get on in the world."

24 *Za* 雜 can refer either to texts that are unsystematically assembled from varied sources or to texts whose content is morally ambiguous or imperfect.

25 The *yi* 以 (using, on account of) is omitted in *Wenxuan* 11.531.

26 Reading *duo duo* 多多 as *ji yan qi duo* 極言其多. Han Jing (1992, 114n2) says, "The more they are, the more harmful they are."

27 The Li Gui commentary ties the word *shi* 事 (treatment, activities, carrying out tasks) to *Analects* 7.1, the origin of the line "transmitting and not creating"; Yang's treatment of the *Supreme Mystery* can be described by the phrase *xin er hao gu* 信而好古 (trusting and loving antiquity), taken from the same line.

28 The Li Gui commentary says that Yan Hui, even before he was capped, discussed the *Yijing* with Kongzi, and similarly, Yang's child Wu or Tongwu, at the age of nine, discoursed on the *Supreme Mystery*. *Huayang guozhi* (Ren Naiqiang ed.) 10.533n4 puts the child's death at age nine and his work on the *Supreme Mystery* at age seven. Liu Xiang's 劉向 *Bie lu* 別錄 (cited in *Taiping yulan* 385.5b as *Biezhuan* 別傳) says that Yang Wu was Yang Xiong's second son; two sons are definitely mentioned in *Taiping yulan* 556.1b. Liu Shipei (1916), thinking that writing the *Supreme Mystery* would be impossible even for a child prodigy, interprets *yu* 與 as *ju* 舉 (meaning here "formally reciting and recording/copying"). This is speculation, but perhaps the line refers to *Analects* 9.22.

Someone asked me, "Was Kongzi truly a sage? If so, why could he not get on in the world? He is not to be compared with Fan Ju and Cai Ze, surely!"[41] 5.15

"Is a sage just another Fan or Cai? In what sense are people like Fan and Cai sages?"

Someone asked me, "But weren't Master Huainan and the Senior Archivist Sima Qian both more erudite than Kongzi? How varied are their writings!"[42] 5.16

"Varied they are, but such an 'admixture'!"[43] The problem with such people is that they used great erudition to produce mixed bags.[44] Only the sages wrote in a manner that was pure in its quality and content."[45]

Writing that does not embody the classical principles is not proper writing, and speech that does not embody them is not true speech. Speeches and writings that do not embody the classical principles are absolutely superfluous. 5.17

Someone asked me, "Given the model of 'transmitting and not creating,'[46] how is it that you came to create the *Mystery*?" 5.18

"The traditions have been transmitted through the ages,[47] though the writing is newly done."

The phrase "raised but never sprouted"[48]—does this not apply to my own child, Tongwu? At the age of nine *sui*, he joined me in composing the *Mystery*.[49] 5.19

Someone asked me, "Why write the *Mystery*?" 5.20

"For the sake of humaneness and a sense of duty."

---

that the sages' words are true, powerful, and efficacious—so much so that to go against them is like swimming upstream in a strong current.

41 Both men served King Zhao of Qin (r. 306–251 BCE); Fan Ju was "rich as Croesus."

42 Yang Xiong had mixed feelings about Sima Qian's judgments and appraisals. Cf. *Hanshu* 87B.3580.

43 Andrew Plaks (pers. comm.) prefers "Varied they are, so various!" which would make the concessive begin with "But people . . ." Yang's idea is that these writings are undiscriminating catchalls, despite their displays of great erudition. While there was certainly no orthodoxy in Yang's time, Yang himself had a strong sense of what he deemed faithful to the sages' teachings; he therefore deplores works that send mixed messages to the reader.

44 Knechtges (1982a, n. 126) prefers, however, "People fault them because they consider great erudition to be eclecticism." I believe that Yang faults Sima Qian for lacking a unified principle or set of principles by which to evaluate historical figures and events.

45 Adding "in quality and content."

46 *Analects* 7.1. Cf. *Changes*, "Shuogua" 1, 2; "Xici" B.2.

47 Adding "through the ages," as implied. After all, Yang wrote a neoclassic, *Supreme Mystery*, whose propositional content and style was based on his understanding of the Five Classics. Yang claims here to reenact the sage's actions.

48 Cf. *Analects* 9.22, which depicts Kongzi's favorite disciple as one who "sprouted but never flowered," where *xiu* 修 is rendered as *xiu* 秀.

49 Yang's child was a byword for precocious erudition, as can be seen from the Zheng Gu stele, which claims that Zheng's oldest son had the talent of Yang Wu 揚烏 (Crow).

5.21 或問經之艱易。[29] 曰存亡。或人不諭。曰其人[30] 存則易。亡則艱。延陵季子之於樂也。其庶矣乎。如樂弛。雖札末如之何矣。如周之禮樂，庶事之備也。每可以為不難矣。如秦之禮樂，庶事之不備也。每可以為難矣。

5.22 衣而不裳。未知其可也。裳而不衣。未知其可也。衣，裳。其順矣乎。

5.23 或問文。曰訓。[31] 問武。曰克。未達。曰事得其序之謂訓。勝己之私之謂克。

5.24 為之而行，動之而光者。其德乎。或曰知德者鮮。何其光。曰我

---

29 See *Hanshu* 87B. 3573; Knechtges 1982a, *Hanshu* trans., p. 55.

30 A great many commentators, beginning with Sima Guang, Yu Yue (1874), and Han Jing (1992, 116n2) would change *ren* 人 (people) to *wen* 文 (writings, patterns). I do not, for two reasons: (1) Yang elsewhere writes of good books as substitutes for contact with the right people; (2) it is probably anachronistic to place more emphasis on textual transmission than on personal transmission. However, if those commentators (all late) are correct, the line would mean "When the tradition is preserved, then things go easily; and when it is not, they go hard [or go awry]."

31 Li Gui glosses *xun* 訓 as *shun* 順; Wang Rongbao (1987, 8.171–72) follows him, as does Gao Heng (1989, 138).

"But who *isn't* in favor of these two virtues? Who *isn't*?"
"The point is not to have other messages mixed in—that's all."[50]

Someone asked me about the difficulties or ease associated with the Clas- 5.21
sics.[51]
"It's a case of preservation and loss."
This the interlocutor fails to understand.
"When the model of the right people is preserved, then things go easily; and when it is lost, they go hard. For example,[52] Yanling Jizi's[53] grasp of music was nearly perfect. But were he to set down his musical instruments,[54] then even Jizi himself would have no way to proceed.[55] Now surely the rites and music of Zhou, being nearly perfect in every detail,[56] can be used in every instance to obviate difficulties. But the rites and music of Qin, being incomplete and imperfect in nearly every instance, always cause difficulties!"

I've never known it to be all right to have a top garment but not the bot- 5.22
tom. Nor would the reverse be right. Shouldn't the top and bottom both be in proper order?[57]

Someone asked me about the civil. 5.23
"It means following."
"What about the martial?"
"It means overcoming."
The interlocutor doesn't fully grasp the point.
"By 'following' I mean 'affairs attain the proper order,' and by 'overcoming' I mean 'overcoming one's own selfish impulses.'"[58]

To act knowingly on behalf of something or someone and carry it 5.24

---

50 Cf. *Fayan* 5.16.

51 Yang confronts a similar problem in his autobiography, when an unnamed interlocutor asks why the sages were so "fond of making things difficult." He answers, "Because of circumstances, they had no other choice!"

52 Adding " the model of" and " For example," as implied.

53 Yanling Jizi or Ji Zha 季札 was regarded as a connoisseur of music and an exemplary statesman.

54 Tentative reading. Yanling Jizha was not a performer himself but an observer and an astute critic of performances, so perhaps others set down their instruments.

55 There would be nothing he could do when confronted with this situation.

56 I take Yang to be echoing *Analects* 3.14 (周監於二代，郁郁乎文哉), which praises Zhou for preserving earlier traditions. Qin, by destroying traditions, created difficulties for later generations. However, Andrew Plaks (pers. comm.) prefers "covers nearly every possible situation," as he takes *bei* to mean "comprehensive."

57 "Xici" B.2 speaks of Huangdi, Yao, and Shun letting their upper and lower robes fall loose, "after which the realm was well-ordered." Yu Fan's commentary argues that "this is taken from the Qian and Kun hexagrams (Hexagrams 1 and 2, respectively). Hexagram 1 is associated with superiority and the top garments, while Hexagram 2 is associated with the lower position and the bottom garments." These metaphors often indicated high and low ranks in society (as above). The same metaphor of clothes reversed appears in *Taixuan jing*.

58 Contrast *Analects* 12.1. *Fayan* refines the language and rejects certain interpretations, including that associated with Ma Rong of Eastern Han; this passage suggests, therefore, that the content of Ma's gloss existed already in Yang's time. See Kieschnick 1992.

知。為之。不我知。亦為之。厥光大矣。必我知而為之。光亦小矣。

5.25 或曰君子病沒世而無名。盍勢諸名卿。可幾也。[32] 曰君子德名為幾。梁, 齊, 趙, 楚之君。非不富且貴也。惡乎成名。谷口鄭子真。不屈其志。而耕乎巖石之下。名震于京師。豈其卿。豈其卿。[33]

5.26 或問人。曰難知也。曰焉難。曰太山之與蛭垤。江河之與行潦。非難也。大聖之與大佞。難也。烏呼。能別似者為無難。

5.27 或問鄒莊有取乎。曰德則取。愆則否。何謂德, 愆。曰言天地人, 經德也。否愆也。[34] 愆語, 君子不出諸口。

---

32 Cf. *Daode jing*, sec. 33: 死而不亡者,壽, discussed in Erkes 1953. Following Yu Yue (1874), I punctuate before *ke*. Yu Yue suggests that "power" and "strategy" (*shi* 勢) are generally opposed to "name" (reputation) in Yang's works, so the line should read "Why not force it [the situation] and become a famous minister? That would be worth aspiring to!" See Wang Rongbao (1987, 8.174).

33 Cf. *Hou Hanshu* 72.3056.

34 Reading *jing* 經 in both senses, as (1) *chang* 常 (constants) and (2) *dian* 典 (canons, classics). See Wang Rongbao (1987, 8.177). However, Han Jing (1992, 122n2) punctuates differently, so that the sentence reads "It is the constants [i.e., morality] and the Classics that speak of heaven, earth, and man. They are virtue."

through, to take the initiative in something and obtain honor and glory thereby—now that is true "charisma"![59]

Someone asked me, "As 'those who recognize virtue are so few,' where's the glory and honor in acting *that* way?"[60]

"As the saying goes, 'Whether others recognize me or not,'[61] the glory is certainly great if I act properly. There would surely be very little glory in acting a certain way only after others recognized us!"

Someone remarked to me, "'But the noble man hates to die without a name!'[62] Why not use one's position[63] to get one? Surely it is right to aspire to a fine reputation and ministerial rank!"[64] 5.25

"The noble man aspires to a fine reputation for virtue. The lords of Liang, Qi, Zhao, and Zhu—every single one of them was rich and highly ranked, but not one of them perfected his own reputation.[65] Zheng Zizhen of Gukou[66] refused to bend his will, and so he plowed the fields below the rocky cliffs. But his name thundered throughout the capital. Surely this was not because he held ministerial office! Surely not!"

Someone asked me about men. 5.26

"They are hard to know."

"Why so hard?"

"It is hardly difficult to tell the difference between Mount Tai and an anthill or between the Yangzi and Yellow Rivers, on the one hand, and a rivulet, on the other. But the great sage and the hugely clever knave—those are very hard to tell apart. How sad! Those who can actually distinguish between seemingly similar things and people will surely experience no trouble."

Someone asked me whether Zou Yan and Zhuangzi have ideas worth borrowing.[67] 5.27

"One should borrow their virtuous points and reject those in error."

"But what do you deem 'virtuous' and 'in error'?"

"In speaking of heaven, earth, and man, it's the constants and the Classics that embody the true character and virtue of things. Speech opposed to them is 'in error.' The noble man never lets erroneous speech out of his mouth."

---

59 Charisma refers to the compelling quality associated with an admirable character.

60 *Analects* 15.4.

61 *Analects* 14.35, 39. Knechtges (1982a) notes that this can be punctuated 我知, 為之, so that the sentence reads "When I am recognized, I engage in something, and when I am not recognized, I also engage in it." In that reading, the lines recall *Hanshu* 62.2527, which avers that a man of breeding acts on behalf of the person who recognizes his good qualities, just as a woman will act on behalf of her lover. But Andrew Plaks (pers. comm.) prefers "so long as I am fully conscious of acting for its sake."

62 As Kongzi remarked in *Analects* 15.20. Contrast *Analects* 4.5, however.

63 *Shi* 勢 can also mean "situation" or "force of circumstances."

64 Recall here *Analects* 13.3, 16.11.

65 Cf. *Analects* 4.5.

66 Though Zheng never held public office, thanks to Yang he was renowned for his honesty. Gukou was in Zuopingyi, one of the three metropolitan districts.

67 Of course, *Fayan* 1–2, have talked often of borrowing from various models.

卷第六

問明

明哲煌煌。旁燭無疆。
遜于不虞。以保天命。譔問明。

6.1 或問明。曰微。[1] 或曰微。何如其明也。曰微而見之。明其誖乎。[2]

6.2 聰明。其至矣乎。不聰, 實無耳也。不明, 實無目也。敢問大聰明。曰眩眩乎。惟天為聰。惟天為明。夫能高其目而下其耳者, 匪

1 Li Gui, cited in Wang Rongbao (1987, 9.179), says this refers to "[unseen] acts," i.e., secret virtue.

2 L'Haridon (2006) prefers "then it is a particularly imposing light, is it not?" Cf. Wang Rongbao (1987, 9.176–77), who reads *bei* 誖 as *pengbo* 蓬勃 (flourishing, prospering), referring to the sage in high position. Wang Rongbao's reading gains some support from the *Analects* and the *Zuozhuan*, where the character *bo* describes something strong and possibly even "going against the grain."

Chapter 6

Asking about Illumination

VERSE SUMMARY

The man of illumined[1] wisdom, resplendent and bright, shines everywhere like a torch,[2] his influence without limits. Avoiding unforeseen dangers, he preserves the life that heaven conferred. Thus, I have composed chapter 6, "Asking about Illumination."

Someone asked me about light.[3] 6.1–2

"It is faint."

Someone asked me, "But in what respect is faint light comparable with bright light, then?"[4]

"When that faint light becomes visible, how is its inherent brilliance negated?"[5]

"To hear and see clearly—is that not of supreme value? If one does not hear or see well, then one really may as well have no ears or eyes."[6]

"I venture to ask about superior insight."

"It is dazzling indeed! Only heaven hears and sees *that* well. Now, a

1 In *Analects* 12.6, one of Kongzi's disciples asked the meaning of "illumination" or being "illumined." Kongzi described such a person in this way: "He who is influenced neither by being drenched with slander nor by an assault by denunciation may indeed be called 'illumined' [or 'perspicacious']."

2 More literally, a candle, but that does not convey a sense of strong light to Western readers.

3 The character *ming* 明 in Chinese, as in the English "bright," conveys the senses of "brightness," "perspicacity," and "enlightenment."

4 Meaning "How can the dim past possibly compare with present careerist impulses?"

5 An inherent brightness is indicated by the fact that something is visible even when faint.

6 Cf. the assessment of Yang's teacher in *Huayang guozhi* (Ren Naiqiang ed.) 10A.532–33: "If it was not right [to do so], he did not say anything. If it was not right, he did not act. If it was not right, he did not hear it."

天也夫?

6.3 或問小每知之。可謂師乎。曰是何師與。是何師與。天下小事為不少矣。每知之。是謂師乎。師之貴也。知大知也。小知之師。亦賤矣。

6.4 孟子疾過我門而不入我室。或曰亦有疾乎。曰摭我華而不食我實。[3]

6.5 或謂仲尼事彌其年。蓋天勞諸病矣夫。曰天非獨勞仲尼。亦自勞也。天病乎哉。天樂天。聖樂聖。[4]

6.6 或問鳥有鳳。獸有麟。鳥,獸皆可鳳,麟乎。曰群鳥之於鳳也。群

3 Li Gui comments: "The flowers refer to the exquisitely worked *fu*, while the fruits refer to *Exemplary Figures* and *Supreme Mystery*." As the *Analects* quotation is usually thought to refer to Yan Hui, a disciple of Kongzi who died young, the line may also hint at the early death of Yang's son, supposedly a prodigy, in which case the "my" may be "our," for Yang claimed that he wrote the *Supreme Mystery* with his son. Cf. *Yanshi jia xun* 11/50/5 (trans., Teng Ssu-yu, p. 59, 61).

4 Cf. *Lüshi chunqiu* 4/4.2 (C); *Lüshi chunqiu jiaoshi*, 223; Knoblock and Riegel 2000, 126, where the gloss reads, "The king takes pleasure in the reason why he is king; and he who loses a kingdom for his part also takes pleasure in the cause for the loss of his kingdom." Cf. "Zhongyong," *Shisanjing zhushu*, 53.7a, which first talks of heaven's reason or wherewithal to be heaven and then describes the way or reason or wherewithal by which King Wen became patterned (*wen* 文), emphasizing the impossibility of greatness being otherwise than great unceasingly, as the commentary by Zheng Xuan remarks. Su Shi also follows Yang and the "Zhongyong," writing, "It is the sage's *cheng* [integrity] to like virtue, as if it were sensual pleasure, while disliking vices, as if they were foul odors." *Su Shi wenji*, 2.61 ("Zhongyong lun") is taken straight from Yang Xiong. *Shanghai bowuguan cang Zhanguo Chu zhushu* (2001–8, 1.271) uses the phrase *le sheng* (which I have translated "take pleasure in acting as sages") but with different meanings ("the ear/hearing takes pleasure" 目之好色, 耳之樂聖), raising the question whether the phrase is older than *Exemplary Figures*.

person who has the capacity to raise his sights to see all and bend his ear to hear all is undeniably like heaven,[7] is he not?"[8]

Someone asked me whether a person who knows every small detail can 6.3
be called a master and teacher.

"What sort of a teacher would *that* be? What sort, indeed? There are an awful lot of minor matters in the world. Would it be right to call the person who knew every last one of them a real teacher? A teacher's value depends upon his knowing what is important to know. A teacher with paltry bits of erudition is certainly not to be valued!"[9]

Mencius took it ill that some "went past his gates without entering his 6.4
house."[10] Someone said to me, "Do you, for your part, have something that irritates you?"

"Yes, when they pluck my flowers but never eat my fruit."[11]

Someone asked me, "Kongzi's labors continued throughout his lifetime. 6.5
It figures that heaven worked him hard, and so he was sorely afflicted!"[12]

"Heaven was not the only one that worked Kongzi hard.[13] Kongzi also worked himself hard! Did heaven really afflict him? Heaven takes pleasure in acting as heaven, and the sages take pleasure in acting as sages."[14]

Someone asked me, "The phoenix is a type of bird and the unicorn a 6.6

---

7 Adding "to see all" and "to hear all." But Andrew Plaks (pers. comm.) prefers "endowed by heaven with qualities."

8 Meaning "Is he not infallible, like heaven?" Cf. "Xici" A2, where those who act this way are sages and culture heroes.

9 Perhaps Yang Xiong here is covertly defending Kongzi, who was credited with having a vast store of erudition. Certainly, the *Shiji* biography of Kongzi (*Shiji* 47) has him identifying the origin of a strange hermaphroditic creature, of a large dinosaur bone, and of a strangely marked arrow; at the same time, he is incapable of obtaining and keeping an important advisory position.

10 Cf. *Mencius* 7B.37, where Kongzi criticizes someone for "going past my gates but not entering my door."

11 *Analects* 9.22: "There are indeed seedlings that do not flower, and there are flowers that do not fruit." Cf. *Laozi* 38: "Therefore, the great man . . . dwells in the fruit and does not dwell in the flower." Later, erudite men like Yan Zhitui develop this metaphor, comparing the studying of books to the planting of trees and making personal cultivation and beneficial deeds the fruits of reading.

12 Cf. *Analects* 13.1, 7.2, 7.34. Alternatively, "Surely it [heaven] found him to be flawed!" This line may also tie up with "Zhongyong," par. 26, which says, "Perfect integrity knows no cessation" (*zhicheng wusi* 至誠無息), a line that could be (mis)construed as "Perfect integrity has no rest!" "Zhongyong," par. 3, describes the sages' actions as something "the people all take pleasure in."

13 My reading echoes *Fayan* 3.3, which has Kongzi working himself very hard; also *Analects* 6.23, where the "wise take pleasure [in acting wisely?]." The "Xici zhuan" commentary to *Changes* in particular emphasizes the duty of the sages to work and worry on behalf of others, as noted in Nylan 2001a, chap. 6. But the subject of the phrase *yi zi lao ye* 亦自勞也 may still be heaven; in that case, in order to maintain parallelism, one must adopt the alternate reading of "heaven works itself hard," which presumably alludes to the fact that the heavenly bodies tirelessly follow their daily, monthly, and annual circuits.

14 Cf. *Analects* 4.2: "The humane person abides in humaneness." See also *Analects* 6.11, 6.20, 6.23, 7.16, on sages feeling pleasure.

獸之於麟也。形性。[5] 豈群人之於聖乎。

6.7 或曰甚矣。聖道無益於庸也。聖讀而庸行。盍去諸。曰甚矣。子之不達也。聖讀而庸行。猶有聞焉。去之。抏也。[6] 抏秦者。非斯乎。投諸火。[7]

6.8 或問人何尚。曰尚智。曰多以智殺身者。何其尚。曰昔乎。皋陶以其智為帝謨。殺身者遠矣。箕子以其智為武王陳洪範。殺身者遠矣。[8]

5 I take *xing xing* 形性 as verb-object. Wang Rongbao (1987, 9.183) takes *xing xing* to mean the visible forms given as part of their natures. Han Jing (1992, 126) equates *xing* 形 with *zhi* 質 (material substance). Li Gui takes *xing xing* as the two separate parts of each human being, the corporeal form and the inborn nature, as does L'Haridon (2006).

6 Reading *wan* 抏 as *wan* 刓 (cutting) and as *wan* 頑, as per Wang Rongbao (1987, 9.185).

7 Fukui (2005) argues that it was only late in Western Han that a full-scale attack on Qin was launched by classicists, especially Yang himself.

8 Wang Rongbao (1987, 9.187–88) argues that Yang Xiong may be analogizing himself and his era to these two sages and their times.

type of beast. Can all birds and beasts become phoenixes and unicorns then?"[15]

"The relation of ordinary birds and beasts to phoenixes and unicorns, the most marvelous sorts of birds and beasts[16]—that's a matter of their natures being realized in their forms.[17] How could this possibly be the relation that ordinary people bear to the sages?"[18]

Someone asked me, "It's really too bad that the Way of the sages is of no benefit at all in ordinary life. One may recite the sages' words and still act like a very ordinary person, so why not dispense with them altogether?" 6.7

"What's really too bad is your own failure to understand anything at all![19] When one recites the sage's words but acts like an ordinary person, one still has learned *something* from them. To dispense with them altogether would be sheer folly, in effect to cut oneself off from them entirely![20] Was it not Li Si who caused the Qin to engage in such follies, cutting them off? After all, he had them tossed into the fire!"[21]

Someone asked me what humans are to value. 6.8

"They should value wisdom."

"But many have gotten themselves killed on account of their wisdom. What's so valuable about *it*?"[22]

"Long ago, Gao Yao used his wisdom to compose the 'Counsels' for his lord, Yu. He was a long way from getting himself killed, certainly![23] And Jizi used his wisdom to lay out the 'Great Plan' for King Wu.[24] He was a long way from getting himself killed, certainly!"

---

15 The question posed is whether there is an inherent deficiency in lesser men, in their forms or their natures, or whether they become inferior (and possibly acquire deficient capacities) as a result of successive decisions. Cf. Cao Zhi's "Dew on the Oniongrass" (Xie luxing 薤露行): "Among scaly and shelled creatures we honor the divine dragon. / Among beasts that run we revere the unicorn. / If we recognize virtue even among beasts and cold-blooded creatures, / How much more so among gentlemen?" (*Cao Zijian ji* 6.4a).

16 Adding "the most marvelous sorts of the birds and beasts" as implied.

17 Or, more simply, "[a matter of their] natures and forms." Interestingly, the commentators cited in Wang Rongbao (1987, 9.183) cannot agree on the nature of the differences that separate the ideal and the ordinary. Yang most likely had in mind *Mencius* 2A.2, where Mengzi cites an authority who says that the sages belong to the same genus as ordinary people, and so all people can become Yaos and Shuns (i.e., sages).

18 The sages look just like ordinary people.

19 The reply clearly mocks the interlocutor by using the same formulaic language.

20 Trying to capture both the sense of "idiocy" (*wan* 頑) and "to cut" (*wan* 刓).

21 Or "Was it not Li Si who cut Qin off [from the sages' words]?" "Them" refers to the "private [i.e., anti-Qin] writings [inherited from tradition]." Yang refers here to the alleged Burning of the Books (213 BCE), whose apparent goal was to rid the state of "private learning" that could be cited against the state's interests; he perhaps also refers to throwing the classicists (Ru) into the fire or to Li Si's casting the entire Qin dynasty into the flames. My translation seeks to preserve something of the original's ambiguity. This passage alerts readers to the importance of historical evaluation and reassessment, the main topic of *Fayan*, chaps. 10–11.

22 Cf. *Mencius* 7A.29.

23 Adding "Yu" to identify Gao Yao's lord.

24 Jizi is credited with being the author of the "Great Plan" chapter of the *Documents*, the

6.9 仲尼,聖人也。或者劣諸子貢。子貢辭而精之。然後廓如也。於戲。觀書者違子貢。雖多。亦何以為。

6.10 盛哉。[9] 成湯丕承也。文王淵懿也。或問丕承。曰由小致大。不亦丕乎。革夏以天。不亦承乎。淵懿。曰重易六爻。不亦淵乎。浸以光大。不亦懿乎。

6.11 或問命。曰命者,天之命也。非人為也。人為不為命。請問人為。曰可以存亡。可以死生。非命也。命不可避也。或曰顏氏之子。冉氏之孫。曰以其無避也。若立巖牆之下。動而徵病。行而招死。命乎。命乎。

6.12 吉人凶其吉。凶人吉其凶。[10]

9 Wu Mi (Song) 吳 reads *shen* 慎 (to be cautious) instead of *sheng* 盛.

10 Cf., e.g., *Xunzi* 95/26/35; *Taixuan jing,* Tetragram 72, Appraisal 8, trans. in Nylan 1994, 394); or *Zuozhuan*, Lord Xiang 11.5, where the four-character phrase *ju an si wei* 居安思危 is ascribed to a *Documents,* thought it does not appear in the received text. However, cf. *Shangshu* 40.0404, for a close parallel.

Kongzi was a sage, yet some thought him inferior to Zigong.[25] Zigong declined the compliment and ascribed the very finest of qualities to Kongzi, thereby attaining true breadth of vision.[26] Ah, what a pity! If those perusing the texts contradict Zigong, then of what possible use are texts, no matter how numerous?[27] 6.9

"How flourishing they were—victorious Tang, who 'carried on so magnificently,' and King Wen, who was 'profound and good.'" 6.10

Someone asked me about the phrase "carried on magnificently."

"He went from a minor position to a great one. Is that not the very definition of magnificence? And in taking up heaven's Mandate, he took the place of the Xia line. Is that not the very definition of 'carrying on'?"

"And 'profound and good'?"

"He doubled up the six lines of the *Changes*, making trigrams into hexagrams—was that not 'profound'?[28] And he steeped himself in tradition until he became a leading light[29]—was that not 'good'?"

Someone asked me about the Decree.[30] 6.11

"By 'Decree,' I mean heaven's decrees, whatever is *not* due to human efforts. Whatever is achieved through human effort is not the 'Decree.'"

"I beg to ask about human effort?"

"Through effort one may preserve something or let it go, and determine who lives or dies. That is not the 'Decree.' The word 'Decree' refers to whatever cannot be avoided."

Someone asked me, "But what of the Yan Huis and Ran Bonius?"[31]

"Their untimely deaths were due to something unavoidable. But 'if a person stands beneath a collapsing wall,'[32] where any movement may bring injury and any step invite death, in what sense is *that* decreed? In what possible sense?"

As the saying goes, "The people who are truly fortunate see their good 6.12

---

subject of Nylan 1992; 2001a, chap. 3.

25 See *Analects* 19.22–25 (esp. 19.23) and 13.29, which describe Zigong's 子貢 defense of his master to many detractors. *Analects* 9.6 has Zigong saying, "Since humans were first born, there has never been such a splendid example as Kongzi" (cf. *Mencius* 2A.2). Cf. *Xunzi* 16/6/16–20. Zigong became a successful businessman who supposedly spent his money promoting Kongzi's reputation.

26 The single character *ci* 辭 can mean both "declined" and "explained." This could mean that Zigong's explanation (about Kongzi's superiority) was so finely wrought that "it gave broad application to the sage's Way." See *Xunzi*, n. 180.

27 Cf. *Analects* 13.5, where Kongzi asks, "Though they be many, of what use are they?"

28 Adding "making trigrams into hexagrams," in explanation.

29 L'Haridon (2006) reads this instead as "And his light gradually become ever greater."

30 I.e., the Mandate of heaven, fate, and one's lifespan.

31 Literally, "sons of the Yan clan and grandsons of the Ran clan" but more likely meaning "people like Yan Hui and Ran Geng," as both men died young. See *Analects* 6.2, 6.8.

32 Cf. *Mencius* 7A.2. The same proverb exists in Hebrew texts.

6.13 辰乎辰。[11] 曷來之遲。去之速也。君子競諸。

6.14 譐(=謣?)言[12] 敗俗。譐(=謣?)好敗則。姑息敗德。君子謹於言。慎於好。亟於時。

6.15 吾不見震風之能動聾瞶也。

6.16 或問君子在治。曰若鳳。在亂。曰若鳳。或人不諭。曰未之思矣。[13] 曰治則見。亂則隱。鴻飛冥冥。弋人何慕焉。鷦明遴集。食其絜者矣。鳳鳥蹌蹌。[14] 匪[15] 堯之庭。

---

11 The Yan Shigu commentary to *Hanshu* 62 (Sima Qian biography) suggests that the phrase *chen hu chen* may mean simply "Oh, time! Time!" (Wang Rongbao (1987, 9.193). Cf., e.g., *Taixuan jing*, Tetragram 26, Appraisals 6–7.

12 Reading *ning* 譐 ("sotto voce" or "in a small voice") as *yu* 謣 (reckless talk), following Sima Guang, cited in Wang Rongbao (1987, 9.193) and Han Jing (1992, 134n1). Han Jing defines *gu xi zhe* 姑息者 as "self-indulgent," "easygoing." Probably *Exemplary Figures* refers to *Liji* 3.18/12/30, "Tangong," which contrasts the noble man, who loves others for their virtue, with the petty man (*xi ren* 細人), whose fondness depends on the others' easygoing characters.

13 For the phrase *wei qi wei ye* 為其未也, see *Lüshi chunqiu* 3/2.6; cf. *Lüshi chunqiu jiaoshi*, 140.

14 *Qiangqiang* 蹌蹌 as a reduplicative describes rapid movement. Cf. *Han Feizi*, "Yu Lao" (*fei bi chong tian* 飛必沖天), for the bird (symbolizing the ruler) who soars off to heaven. However, Li Gui, cited in Wang Rongbao (1987, 9.194), uses the "foot" radical to gloss the phrase, which is odd, since the subject is flying off. Li Gui takes the phrase to mean, apparently, that the legendary phoenix will not perform its stately dance in any place but Yao's court.

15 Reading *fei* 匪 as *fei* 飛.

fortune as bad luck."[33] The truly unfortunate are those who mistake their bad luck for good!"[34]

Conjunctions! Conjunctions![35] How is it that opportune moments are so slow in coming and so quickly gone? The noble man spares no effort to seize the right time to act.[36] 6.13

Just as reckless talk ruins a person's habits, so, too, do reckless preferences ruin his principles and indulgence or complacency ruin his character.[37] The noble man is cautious in his speech and careful in his preferences, and he feels a sense of urgency about timing." 6.14

As the proverb goes, "I have never seen a thunderstorm that could move a deaf man."[38] 6.15

Someone asked me about the noble man. 6.16

"In times of good rule, he is like a phoenix. And in times of misrule, he is like a phoenix."[39]

The interlocutor does not understand.

"You certainly have not yet thought it through! I mean that in times of good rule, he reveals himself, and during times of misrule, he hides himself away. Like a bird, he soars on high, into the lofty realms beyond the heavens, so that the archer[40] with his arrow on the string has no hope whatsoever of snaring him! Like the Fire Bird,[41] the sages are very choosy about where they settle,[42] and they eat only the purest of foods.[43] But

---

33 Since good luck may make people incautious, the best and ultimately most fortunate people prefer to continue examining their consciences and redoubling their efforts. Of course, this theme threads through the *Changes*.

34 The histories in early China provide many examples of heaven's conferring favors on those who are actually doomed; victories can portend defeat, as indicated by the expression *ying er fa zhi* 盈而罰之 (lit., "to fill up and punish him").

35 *Chen* 辰 refers most often to either the constellations or to a single two-hour period of the day (7–9 a.m.), but it also refers more generally to "timing" and to "luck."

36 Cf. "Zhongyong," 52.3b: "That the Way has not been practiced—that I know certainly. The wise go past it and the stupid do not come up to it" (meaning that the wise tend to overprepare for all eventualities, while the stupid do not prepare enough).

37 Both "character" and "good behavior" are implied by the single *de* 德.

38 Yang reiterates an observation made earlier, in *Fayan* 5.11. Cf. *Mencius* 2A.2 on *dong xin* 動心 (moving the *xin*). Hence, I decided to add "As the proverb goes" to suggest the proverbial nature of the saying.

39 L'Haridon (2006) punctuates differently, but the sense is much the same.

40 Possibly a fowler. An arrow with a string attached is depicted in the Sichuan tomb tiles.

41 According to *Shuowen jiezi*, the *jiaoming* is a genus of marvelous birds of the south or west. See Knechtges 1982b, 1.414n615; Knechtges translated it as "blazing fire bird." Here it may be a type of phoenix, given the context.

42 *Ji* means both "flock together" and "stop" (i.e., alight).

43 Cf. *Fayan* 5.5. By contrast, the petty person in office "eats" his salary because he is ambitious, while failing to deserve his salary, since he is not loyal to his ruler's best interests.

6.17 亨龍潛升。其貞[16] 利乎。或曰龍何如可以貞利而亨。曰時未可而潛。不亦貞乎。時可而升。不亦利乎。潛升在己。用之以時。不亦亨乎。

6.18 或問活身。曰明哲。或曰童蒙則活。何乃明哲乎。曰君子所貴。亦越[17] 用[18] 明保慎其身也。如庸行翳路。[19] 衝衝而活。君子不貴也。

6.19 楚兩龔之絜。其清矣乎。蜀莊[20] 沈冥。蜀莊之才之珍也。不作苟見。不治苟得。[21] 久幽而不改其操。雖隨和何以加諸。舉茲以旃。不亦寶乎。[22] 吾珍莊也。居[23] 難為也。不慕由。即夷矣。何毚欲之有。[24]

---

16 The most common Han gloss for *zhen* 貞 is *ding* 鼎 (the tripod, symbol of stability and security because it rests on three legs). However, Han Jing (1992, 137n1) defines *heng* not as "constant" but as "to succeed," "to attain," or "to apprehend" (*tong da* 通達).

17 Alternately, following Li Gui, cited in Wang Rongbao (1987, 9.198) and Han Jing (1992, 138n3), "lies in using clarity" (if reading *yue* 越 as *yu* 於).

18 Yu Yue, cited in Wang Rongbao (1987, 9.199) says that *yong* 庸 should be read here as *rong* 容 ("demeanor," in contrast to "activity"). I do not follow Yu Yue.

19 Reading *yi lu* 翳路 as *zhe dang* 遮擋 (impeded, obstructed), "a dead end," "an obstructed path," or even "a roadblock." However, Wang Rongbao (1987, 9.199) takes *yi lu* to refer to a "hidden road," as in Yang's "Sweet Springs *fu*." Combining the two ideas, *yi lu* would mean "coming to an unexpected obstacle." The reduplicative *chong chong* 衝衝 means "crashing or ramming through," signifying "not fixed or unstable" (*bu ding* 不定) activities that are "directionless" (*meiyou dingxiang* 沒有定向).

20 Zhuang Zun, also known as Yan Junping, has a biography in *Huayang guozhi* (Ren Naiqiang ed.) 10A.532–33, where he is said to be the author of a work entitled *Guide to the True Classic of the Way and Its Power* (Daode zhenjing zhigui 道德真經指歸). A work by that title is included in the *Daoist Canon*, although it is unclear whether the attribution is correct. See *Zhengtong Daozang*, vol. 20, 651–734.

21 See Wang Rongbao (1987, 9.204) on refusals to serve in office. See *Hanshu* 72.3056. Knechtges (pers. comm.) prefers "He did not engage in obtaining undeserved celebrity, and he did not engage in obtaining undeserved gain."

22 Cf. *Lüshi chunqiu* 10/4.1 ("Yibao" 異寶; Knoblock and Riegel 2000, 235), which identifies one of the "other treasures" as moral worth; see also *Liji* 38/6 ("Ru xing" 儒行); Legge 1967, vol. 2, 404: "The scholar does not regard gold and jade as treasures, but rather loyalty and trustworthiness."

23 Following Han Jing (1992, 142n6), I take *ju* 居 as a full verb, meaning "to dwell [in]," but several commentators, including Wang Rongbao (1987, 9.201–7, esp. 204), argue that *ju* is a particle without meaning.

24 Alternatively, following Wang Rongbao (1987, 9.204), "He was one with whom the slanderers could not make their slander stick, and one who could not be moved by desires for profit" (讒賊之所不能加, 利欲之所不能動也).

when the phoenix takes flight, its wings all aflutter,[44] it flies straightway to Yao's court."[45]

"The Constant Dragon, whether hiding or taking flight, is secure[46] and advantageous, is it not?" 6.17

Someone asked me, "How can the dragon be secure, advantageous, and constant all at once?"

"When the time is not yet right, it is in hiding. Is it not then secure? And when the time is right, it rises up. Is it not advantageous? It hides or takes flight as it chooses, and it acts in accord with the times. Is it not then likewise constant?"

Someone asked me about keeping oneself alive.[47] 6.18

"It's a matter of clarity and practical wisdom."[48]

Someone asked me, "But if an unschooled child epitomizes life and liveliness,[49] what has staying alive to do with clarity and wisdom?"

"What the noble man values is surpassing others in his employment of clear-sightedness, as this preserves his own person. The ordinary way of conducting oneself is like this: the person somehow crashes through a roadblock[50] just to stay alive. *That* way of doing things the noble man does *not* value."

The purity of the two Gongs from Chu:[51] how incorruptible they were! 6.19
And then there was Yan Junping[52] of Shu, he of the hidden depths! So rare a talent was Yan of Shu that he would not act improperly just to increase his visibility or take up an office merely for gain. Long years he spent in obscurity, yet he never changed his principles. How could even Marquis Sui's pearl and He Bian's jade be of greater value than this? We should uphold such examples as standards. Are they not rare treasures also? My sense of Yan as a treasure stems from the way he dwelt in adversity.[53]

---

44 See *Fayan* 7.9 for a parallel.

45 For the sage-ruler Yao, see *Fayan* 1.13. This trope recalls that found in *Fayan* 3.17, which also concerns birds flying.

46 Adopting the most usual translation for *heng* 亨 as given in commentaries to the *Changes*, "Xugua" 1, and "Wenyan" 1.

47 See *Zhuangzi*, "Zhi le" chapter, and the various writings attributed to Yang Zhu.

48 A reference to the Mao Ode 260: 既明且哲, 以保其身.

49 For the young child as the epitome of liveliness, see *Changes*, Hexagram 4. Andrew Plaks (pers. comm.) prefers "an unself-conscious child."

50 Cf. *Fayan* 8.6.

51 This is a reference to two contemporaries of Yang Xiong—Gong Sheng 勝 and Gong She 舍—who were famous for their remonstrations and who later became recluses. There is a Sichuan connection with the two Gongs, according to *Huayang guozhi* 10A.

52 Yang Xiong's teacher in Chengdu. See Vervoorn 1998–99.

53 Cf. *Analects* 15.2, for "steadfastness in adversity," a theme that threads through *Changes* as well. Yan Junping is Yang's teacher.

6.20 或問堯將讓天下於許由。由恥。有諸。曰好大者為之也。顧由無求於世而已矣。允哲堯儃舜之重。則不輕於由矣。好大累克。巢父洗耳。不亦宜乎。靈場之威。宜夜矣乎。[25]

6.21 朱鳥翾翾。[26]歸其肆矣。或曰奚取於朱鳥哉。曰時來則來。時往則往。能來能往者。朱鳥之謂與。

6.22 或問韓非作說難之書。而卒死乎說(難)。敢問何反也。[27]曰說難。蓋其所以死乎。曰何也。曰君子以禮動。以義止。合則進。否則

25 See Wang Rongbao (1987, 9.207–8). In any case, *wei* 威 refers either to "might and prestige" or to "authority on display." Wang Rongbao argues that the phrase *yi hu* 矣乎 (that's for sure!) in most, if not all, instances in *Exemplary Figures* expresses Yang's admiration—hence Wang's belief that Yang's remark is by no means negative.

26 The reduplicative *xuanxuan* 翾翾 describes "short flights" akin to hops, so these lines may be ironic, depending on the meaning one ascribes to the Red Bird.

27 Han Jing (1992, 145n1) takes this to say, "How is it that the subjective viewpoint and the objective were, in fact, so at odds with one another?"

Certainly, he never thought to emulate Xu You or Bo Yi.[54] In what respect could he be said to have any greedy desires at all?[55]

Someone asked me, "When Yao was just about to cede all-under-heaven to Xu You, they say Xu You felt ashamed.[56] Did this actually happen?" 6.20

"This is a fabrication by those prone to exaggeration. The story simply gives a nod to[57] the tradition that Xu You sought nothing from his world. Whoever truly understands the gravity with which Yao ceded the realm to Shun can be sure that Yao never would have ceded it so lightly to Xu You.[58] Yet those prone to exaggeration pile it on until one tale outdoes another. Is it not fitting that Father Nest[59] washed out his ears to get rid of all the lies?[60] But the majestic authority displayed at the Spirit Altar—was *that* really more suited to the night?"[61]

The Red Bird[62] makes little forays, only to return when it pleases. 6.21

Someone asked me, "What should we take away from this example of the Red Bird?"

"Come when it is time to come, and go when it is time to go. Do they not all deserve to be called Red Birds who can manage to come and go as they should?"

Someone said to me, "Han Fei composed a piece of writing entitled 'The Difficulties of Persuasion,' yet in the end his death was due to these very difficulties of persuasion. What a paradox, I say!" 6.22

"Speaking about the difficulties of persuasion—probably *that* was his undoing."

---

54 These were ostentatious recluses. Alternatively, "Not emulating Xu You, he must be like Bo Yi." But neither Xu You nor Bo Yi are unproblematic exemplars. The lines praising Yan Junping are repeated in *Huayang guozhi* 10A.

55 The expected answer: "In none."

56 To be thought to be someone who might want the throne.

57 Literally, "It [the story?] looks back to [or 'alludes to']." Andrew Plaks (pers. comm.) prefers "he was mindful of . . ." If *gu* is not a verb here but rather a particle, the line means "It is only that Xu You sought nothing from the world." Alan Berkowitz (pers. comm., 18 December 2010) reads this in a way that leaves Xu's reputation intact: "The way I see it, Xu You simply sought nothing from his age." But see the preceding line.

58 A similar argument appears in *Shiji* 130 and 61, on Bo Yi and Shu Qi.

59 Caofu (Father Nest) was a recluse at the time of Yao.

60 The phrase "all the lies" is implied, and so I have added it.

61 Translation is tentative. Given Zheng Xuan's commentary on the *Shangshu dazhuan*, both Liu Shipei (1916) and Yu Yue (1874) thought that the abdication by Yao, as an example of a most solemn affair of state, must have taken place at a Spirit Altar outside the capital. However, the Spirit Altar may refer more generally to the performance of state sacrifices by cult masters. Until late in Western Han, imperial offerings were made at night, but shortly before Yang's *Fayan* was composed, brigands had set upon the imperial entourage, with the result that an administrative decision was taken not to worship at the imperial altars at night. Note, meanwhile, that Yang clearly regarded many cult masters' activities as mere superstition. There was something both "shady" and "baseless" (meaning "unprovable") about the claims made for the efficacy of these imperial offerings by night.

62 One name for the swallow. Swallows, of course, are birds that migrate, flying north and then south, according to the seasons. "Red Bird" is also an epithet for the sun in its daily course, and it could also signify the phoenix.

退。確乎不憂其不合也。夫說人而憂其不合。則亦無所不至矣。[28] 或曰說之不合。非憂耶。曰說不由道。憂也。由道而不合。非憂也。

6.23 或問哲。曰旁明厥思。問行。曰旁通厥德。

28 Here the single phrase *wu suo bu zhi* 無所不至 clearly refers to the gentleman being defined by what he refuses to do. L'Haridon (2006) takes this to mean simply "will meet grave difficulties."

"Huh? How so?"

"The noble man is motivated by the rites to take action, but his sense of what is right tells him when to stop.[63] When a given action is in accord with the rites and the right, then he advances. When it is not, he retreats. Such a man really does not worry whether he has secured his ruler's assent or not. As we all know, rhetoricians who worry about their rulers' disapproval[64] will certainly go to any lengths to win the favor of their rulers."[65]

Someone asked me, "But when a persuasion piece does not meet with approval, should this *not* be a matter of grave concern?"

"If a persuasion piece is not in accord with the Way, *that* is a matter of grave concern. But if the ruler disagrees with a rhetorical piece that is in accord with the Way, *that* hardly qualifies as cause for concern."

Someone asked me about wisdom. 6.23

"It means 'everywhere making one's thoughts and desires clear.'"[66]

And conduct?

"It means 'everywhere communicating one's virtue.'"[67]

---

63 Cf. *Mencius* 5A.8.

64 Or "disagreements" on the subject; literally, the ruler "not being in tune or harmony" with the adviser.

65 Adding "to win the favor of their rulers," as implied.

66 *Si* 思 refers to what one longs for, as well as what one thinks of.

67 The relation between the illumined inner state and one's conduct is the subject of the excavated manuscript "Wu xing," versions of which were found at both Guodian (ca. 300 BCE) and Mawangdui (ca. 186 BCE). This line recalls the "Xici" slogan "the broad application of unitary principles" (*yi zhi er bo lü* 一致而百慮).

卷第七

寡見

遐言周于天地。贊于神明。
幽弘(撗)(横)廣。絕于邇言。譔寡見。

7.1 吾寡見人之好假[1] 者也。邇文之視。邇言之聽。假則偭[2] 焉。或曰曷若兹之甚也。先王之道滿門。曰不得已也。得已則已矣。得已而不已者。寡哉。

1 Reading *xia* 遐 for *jia* 假, following Sima Guang, cited in Wang Rongbao (1987, 213–14). The single character *xia* 遐 means "distant," "far-reaching," and also "long lasting" (e.g., the Classics). Cf. *Zuozhuan*, Lord Xiang 31.12: "I have heard that a noble man applies himself to understanding what is important and far-reaching, while a petty man applies himself to understand what is petty and close at hand." Cao Pi (187–226) in his "Lunwen" flatly contradicts Yang's opinion about preferences and values, saying, "Ordinary people value what is far away and feel contempt for what is close at hand." See *Quan Wei wen* 8.82–84.

2 *Mian* 偭 can mean either "to turn toward" or "to turn their backs," according to Han Jing (1992, 147n1).

Chapter 7

Things Rarely Seen

VERSE SUMMARY

Far-ranging words from remote eras encompass heaven and earth, giving aid to divine insight. Profound and great, vast and broad, such words far surpass those of recent times and narrow scope.[1] Thus, I have compiled chapter 7, "Rarely Seen."

....

"Rarely have I seen people prefer what is remote.[2] Recent writings they 7.1
look at. Recent sayings they hearken to. But they turn their backs on those from distant eras."[3]

Someone said to me, "How can you say that the situation is so very dire? Students of the Way[4] of the former kings fill the gates of officialdom!"[5]

"Candidates for office cannot help themselves.[6] Were they free to do as they liked, they would stop.[7] Only a few who have that option refuse to stop!"[8]

---

1 Giving both possible meanings for the binome *er yan* 邇言.

2 See also *Analects* 15.11: "He who will not worry about something far off will soon find something worse than worry close at hand."

3 This line may well provide a gloss on the various meanings of *er* 邇 (close by, recent, something easily accessible).

4 Adding "students of" for sense. Below supplying "candidates for office" for sense.

5 Adding "of officialdom," as implied; one might supply "palace" before "gates," to the same end.

6 Meaning, they are forced to study old texts, including the Classics, to pass the tests to qualify for government office.

7 Cf. *Analects* 14.24: "Students in olden days used to learn for the sake of learning; students today study for the sake of other people" (古之學者為己，今之學者為人). Note the pun on the word *yi* 已, meaning "they have no other choice" or "they cannot help it." Knechtges 1968, p. 100, translates this as "They have no other choice. If they had their choice, they would give them up. Few indeed are those who would not give them up if they had their choice." Helmutt Wilhelm claimed that Yang tried to justify and rationalize contemporary institutions, according to Knechtges (pers. comm.); this seems doubtful.

8 Adding "have that option," as implied. These few are wise enough to recognize the

7.2 好盡其心於聖人之道者。君子也。人亦有好盡其心矣。未必聖人之道也。

7.3 多聞見而識乎正道者。至識也。多聞見而識乎邪道者。迷識也。

7.4 如賢人謀之美也。[3] 詘人而從道。如小人謀之不美也。詘道而從人。

7.5 或問五經有辯乎。曰惟五經為辯。說天者莫辯乎易。說事者[4] 莫辯乎書。說體者[5] 莫辯乎禮。說志者[6] 莫辯乎詩。說理者[7] 莫辯乎春秋。捨斯。辯亦小矣。

---

3 My reading follows Wang Rongbao (1987, 10.215); and Yu Yue 1874. Sima Guang, cited in Wang Rongbao 1987, however, reads *ru* 如 (to be like) as *wang* 往 (to go toward): "To go to worthy men for their counsels. . . . To go to petty people for their counsels." The two readings necessitate different punctuation.

4 I.e., *shi* 事, but *Yilin* 意林 in citing this passage wrote *di* 地 (land), presumably a nod to the "Tribute of Yu" chapter of the *Documents*, but hardly an adequate description of the entire *Documents*.

5 The most common Han gloss for *li* 禮 (rites) is *ti* 體 (embodiment). See the *Shi ming* 釋名 gloss.

6 Andrew Plaks (pers. comm.) ties these lines to an etymology offered by Chen Shixiang (1974) when describing poetic theory, which has the phrase that means "stop and go" relate to dancing.

7 For *li* 理 as "innate" or "inherent pattern," see *Wenxin diaolong* 1.3/6/6, which talks of the *hanwen* 含文 (pattern contained) in the Classics.

The noble man is defined by his desire to apply his whole heart and mind to the Way of the sages. Others, for their parts, may want to apply themselves wholeheartedly to something—but not necessarily to the Way of the sages.[9] 7.2

"Great discernment" means "acquiring considerable knowledge and experience and so ascertaining the straight path."[10] "Delusion" means "despite considerable knowledge and experience, choosing the bypaths."[11] 7.3

With excellence[12] like that in the counsels of worthy men, one impresses upon others the need to follow the Way.[13] With the gross flaws found in the counsels of petty people, one subverts[14] the Way so as to slavishly follow the lead of others. 7.4

Someone asked me whether the Five Classics contain any disputations.[15] 7.5

"Only the Five Classics are truly eloquent and discerning rhetoric! For explicating Heaven, there is no finer rhetoric than that of the *Changes*.[16] For explicating the affairs of state, there is no finer rhetoric than that of the *Documents*. For explicating bodily decorum, there is no finer rhetoric than that of the *Rites*. For explicating the heart's affects,[17] there is no finer rhetoric than that of the *Odes*. And for explicating the inherent patterns in events, there is no finer rhetoric than that of the *Annals*. If we discard these texts, all rhetoric becomes paltry and puny!"[18]

---

great rewards that will come from such study.

9 In other words, seeking office and emolument is the crassest form of *weiren* 為人 (being and acting as a humane, mature person).

10 "Ascertaining" here means "to single out," in the sense of "distinguishing and choosing one among many."

11 Andrew Plaks (pers. comm.) prefers "deviance," "heterodox" for "[divergent] bypaths," but I reject the notion that an orthodoxy existed in early China.

12 *Mei* 美 refers to the beautiful and the good.

13 Andrew Plaks (pers. comm.) prefers "to suppress one's own personal predilections and follow the Way."

14 Or "bends."

15 The single character *bian* 辯 refers to "rhetoric," "disputation," "discerning language," or even "eloquence." *Analects* 14.5 insists, "He who has accumulated moral power will certainly also possess eloquence." Here, as elsewhere, it is conceivable that the interlocutor's question is willfully misconstrued by Yang, who answers a slightly different question—hence this translation. This argument of Yang's counters Laozi's dictum "Good men do not engage in disputations; those who do engage are not good."

16 The *Changes* "Wenyan" 文言 commentary (3/1/言) speaks of the *Changes* being in sync with the four seasons and the cosmic order.

17 The character *zhi* 志 covers everything felt in the heart. By "affects" is meant "the affections," "commitments," and "aspirations." The "Yaodian" cites the phrase 詩言志, as does the *Odes*, in order to describe the affective power of music. See *Shangshu tongjian* 020681.

18 Or, as Knechtges (1982a) suggests, "Aside from these [the Five Classics], the discerning language [provided in other works] is, for its part, small." Some commentators, including Li Zehou, 153, tie these lines to *Analects* 6.16, which speaks of beauty and excellence in rhetoric. *Analects* 3.8, 6.25, and 16.13 also presume the importance of *Odes* rhetoric in cultivation.

7.6 春木之芚兮。援我手之鶉兮。[8] 去之五百歲。其人若存兮。或曰譊譊者天下皆說也。[9] 奚其存。曰曼是為也。[10] 天下之亡聖也久矣。呱呱之子。各識其親。譊譊之學。各習其師。[11] 精而精之。是在其中矣。[12]

7.7 或曰良玉不彫。美言不文。何謂也。曰玉不彫。璵璠不作器。言不文。典謨不作經。

8 Wang Rongbao (1987 10.217–19) reads *chun* 鶉 (usually "quail") as *da* 大, meaning "great." That would make *chun* a loan character for *chun* (純), "pure," "unpolluted," according to *Shuowen jiezi*.

9 Some editions write *song* 訟 (lawsuits, contention) for *shuo* 說 (explications), but Sima Guang, cited in Wang Rongbao (1987, 10.218) believes that is a scribal error. Others prefer to read *shuo* 說 as *yue* 悅 ([objects of] "delight"), thinking Yang would not repeat the same idea by using *nao nao* and *shuo*.

10 Both meanings are implied by the single four-character phrase *man shi wei ye* 曼是為也. Cf. *Analects* 19.24 (*wu yi wei ye* 無以為也).

11 If "each of those armed with competing theories emulates a teacher" (Wang Rongbao's reading), in that case, the sense of *shi zai qi zhong* 是在其中 would be "And what is right lies within them," which is more or less Wang Rongbao's (1987) reading (but see below). Often this line is read as a critique of the *zhangju* 章句 (commentaries by chapter and verse), given Yang's disparagement of *zhangju*, as recorded in *Hanshu* 87B.3568: "Chapter and verse commentators/May sit together and protect it [the empire when there are no crises]." I take the comment to be of broader application, however. Han Jing (1992, 152n7) assumes that Yang refers here only to the Ru 儒, but this is far from certain.

12 Wang Rongbao (1987, 10.220) says that this *shi* 是 is certainly not the *shi* of *shifei* 是非 (rights and wrongs); rather, it is the *shi* that refers to "the right way of the sages" (*sheng dao zhi zheng* 聖道之正). Cf. *Hanshu* 67.3620–21, which talks of the various traditions that under Pingdi were augmented by Archaic Script teachers, "in order to catch as in a net all the omissions and faults, in order to hold them together and preserve them, so that they [the best and truest readings] would be in their midst" 是在其中. Much has been written on the definitions of *shifa* 師法 and *jiafa* 家法, but usage was not consistent, so far as I can tell.

He, fresh as "the first sprouts of spring," 7.6
"Leads me by the hand to greatness." [19]
It was five hundred years ago,
And yet that man still seems to live.[20]

Someone said to me, "But given all the contentiousness in the realm filled with competing theories, how can you possibly say that he still lives on?"

"Don't say that! Not true! Indeed, for a very long time the realm has been without a sage. But every mewling infant knows his or her own parents; and each of those armed with competing theories emulates a teacher. If we would only refine and refine them, then certainly the right Way would be in their midst."[21]

Someone said to me, "There's a saying,[22] 'Good jade should not be carved, 7.7
nor should fine words be embellished.' What does this mean?"

"If jade was never meant to be carved, then the precious *yufan* ornament[23] would never have been fashioned into a ritual object. And if words were never meant to be embellished, then neither the Canons nor the Counsels[24] would ever have become part of the Classic."[25]

---

19 The first quotation cites the hexagram Tun/Zhun 屯, which describes the difficulty (*nan* 難) with which things are born, but the hexagram clearly also celebrates nascent growth and development (reading *nan* as *nuo*, in the sense of "flourishing," "leafing out"). The reference to temporality may be important here, for it implies that Kongzi was the founder of a tradition or the originator of the Classics. The second citation (which rhymes with the first) refers to the care with which heaven and/or Kongzi guide the person to greatness.

20 That the presence of Kongzi continues to inspire men in Yang's world suggests that Yang envisions himself as a second Kongzi and latter-day sage whose Way and writings can save the world. Note that some five hundred years had elapsed between the birth of Kongzi and the birth of Yang Xiong. Given the expectation that a sage will arise every five hundred years or so, Yang may be drawing attention to himself. See *Mencius* 7B.15 for the theory.

21 Presumably meaning "in the midst of the court."

22 Adding "There's a saying," as implied.

23 A jade ornament worn on the girdle or hat. The *Shuowen jiezi* defines it as a "precious jade in Lu."

24 The names of two types of sections in the *Documents*.

25 The implied debate here concerns the function of *wen* (embellishment, ornament), as some thought the "best talk" was unembellished, while others thought that embellishment was what allowed talk to be persuasive—a debate summarized in two four-character phrases: 至言不文 and 言以文遠.

7.8 或問司馬子長有言曰五經不如老子之約也。當年不能極其變。終身不能究其業。曰若是。則周公惑。孔子賊。古者之學耕且養。三年通一(經)。[13] 今之學也。非獨為之華藻也。[14] 又從而繡其(其)鞶帨。[15] 惡在老不老也。[16] 或曰學者之說可約邪。曰可約解科。[17]

7.9 或曰君子[18] 聽聲乎。曰君子惟正之聽。荒乎淫。拂乎正。沈而樂者。君子不聽也。

---

13 Cf. *Hanshu* 30.1723, citing Liu Xin.

14 Li Waiyee (pers. comm.) takes the phrase in much the same manner as Knechtges (1982a), following Ban Gu (*Hanshu* 30.1723: 便辭巧說) and Fan Ye (*Hou Hanshu* 79B.2588: 繁其章條): "Learning at present is such that not only is it decked out in fine form, but it is obsessed with superfluous ornament, such as adorning belts and girdle clothes." Pei Ziye in his "Diao chong lun" 雕蟲論 certainly followed this reading. But my reading takes account of the rich associations of the *zao* plant with lusciousness and moistness, two highly desirable qualities. See Zheng 2009, esp. 5, 21ff.

15 Han Jing (1992, 153n4) believes the compound *pan shui* 鞶帨 ought to refer to a kerchief and the bag for it. Li Gui, cited in Wang Rongbao (1987, 10.222) says that just as clothes have decorative embroidery on them, so texts have added to them over time commentaries, glosses, and explications, making learning more difficult as time goes on, which, as Han Jing mentions, seems to miss the point of Yang's argument.

16 Han Jing (1992, 155n5) reads the sentence as "How is this [false] following of Laozi not what makes one old?" pointing to Sima's implied comparison between the *Laozi* and the Classics ascribed to Kongzi as author or editor.

17 Reading *jie* 解 as "to let go." Andrew Plaks (pers. comm.) prefers "divide [the exams] into narrow topics." Cf. Han Jing (1992, 155n7), which glosses *jie* as *pan bie* 判別 (divide into parts). Yang's preoccupation with examination topics prompts my translation; cf. the well-attested reading of *ke* 科 to refer to the categories of learning tested in the state examinations (as in the phrase *jia ke* 甲科).

18 Or "ruler." Han Jing (1992, 156–57) seems to understand *junzi* as "noble man," not "ruler."

Someone asked me, "Sima Qian had a saying to the effect that the Five Classics are less concise than the *Laozi*. 'In all one's years, a person could not thoroughly grasp all their variations and permutations. To the end of one's life, a person could never fully realize the project set out therein.'"[26] 7.8

"Were this true, the Duke of Zhou would be deluded and Kongzi a fraud![27] They say that learning in the olden days was such that one could plow and support one's parents while mastering a single Classic within three years' time.[28] Learning at present is not merely for the sake of ornamenting one's character.[29] It is also spurred by the desire to have embroidered belts and girdle cloths.[30] What does being like or unlike Laozi have to do with it then?"[31]

Someone asked me, "But really now, can't the scholars' explications be made more concise?"

"One can shorten them, so long as one frees oneself from a preoccupation with the examination topics!"

Someone asked me, "Does the noble man listen to music?" 7.9

"The noble man listens only to music that is proper. Music that is wild with excess, that rejects propriety, or that wallows in sensual pleasure—that sort of music the noble man refuses to listen to."

---

26 These remarks are now ascribed to Sima Tan in *Shiji* 130.3288. Both "variations" and "permutations" are implied by the single character *bian* 變 (lit., "changes"). The sense of this passage might also be that "a person could never fully realize the magnitude of the cultural legacy therein."

27 *Zei* 賊 could also mean that Kongzi is a "thief of time," since study of the Classics is time-consuming.

28 Because this account of learning seems proverbial, the translation adds "They say that." In later texts the same phrase is often extended to mean "plowing through books." It is, in fact, told of Yang Xiong that he "tilled and farmed [books]" with all his might, seeking suitable classical allusions; see *Wenxin diaolong*, *juan* 38. For the phrase *neng yang* 能養, see *Analects* 2.7.

29 I take the phrase *hua zao* 華澡 to refer to "providing ornament to one's person" through social cultivation. Knechtges (1982a), however, reads *hua zao* as "providing ornament for the Classics," then translates the second line as "It also goes on [lit., "follows"] to embroider the belt and girdle cloth," meaning "to overelaborate [many points]." In that case, it is learning itself at present that tries "to be all decked out in fine form." Another possibility would, like Knechtges, not posit a contrast between *wei zhi hua zao* 為之華藻 and *xiu qi pan shui* 繡其鞶帨, but rather cast the latter as the intensification of the former: "learning at present is such that it is not only decked out in fine form, but also obsessed with superfluous ornaments, such as those adorning belts and girdle clothes."

30 In the compound *pan shui* 鞶帨, *shui* refers to a girdle cloth, and *pan* has two meanings: "a great leather belt worn by males" (as in *Changes*) or "a silk purse," following Zheng Xuan's gloss, cited in Wang Rongbao (1987.222). Such finery signifies high rank and wealth.

31 My translation is tentative. Or "In what respect do you say that Laozi is not like Laozi [or an old man]?" (meaning "He's just as convoluted as everybody else!"). Or "How can you say that Laozi doesn't grow old [after one has read him a few times]?" Apparently, the problem with the explication of the Classics does not lie in the length of those texts but in the convolutions and useless elaborations devised in the exegetical scholarship.

7.10 或問侍君子以博乎。曰侍坐則聽言。有酒則觀禮。焉事博乎。或曰不有博弈者乎。[19] 曰為之猶賢於已耳。[20] 侍君子者賢於已乎。君子不可得而侍也。侍君子晦斯光。窒斯通。亡斯有。辱斯榮。敗斯成。如之何賢於已也。

7.11 鷦明[21] 沖天。不在六翮乎。拔而傅尸鳩。其累矣夫。

7.12 雷震乎天。風薄乎山。雲徂乎方。雨流乎淵。其事矣乎。[22]

19 *Hanshu* 64.2829 suggests that this justification is improper, as it relates to a Han emperor.

20 Following the suggestion of Tao Hongqing 陶鴻慶 (1859–1918), cited in Han Jing (1992, 157n4).

21 Cf. *Han Feizi* 21/45/17 (*fei bi chong tian* 飛必沖天) for the bird (symbolizing the ruler) who soars off to the heavens.

22 Li Gui says, "The phrases in each case refer to heaven's affairs; as for humans, they cannot be without their own tasks and affairs" (*ren bu de wu shi ye* 人不得無事也), which Li Gui defines as "working at the Classics."

Someone asked me, "Can a person faithfully attend his ruler by chess playing?"[32] 7.10

"When attending the ruler, one listens to what he says,[33] and when wine is served, one observes the ceremonies. So what, pray tell, does playing chess have to do with it?"

Someone asked me, "But didn't *he* once talk of playing chess?"[34]

"Well, as *he* says, 'to do *that* seems better than doing nothing at all!'[35] But is attending the ruler in this way really 'better than doing nothing'?"[36] The ruler is not well served by this sort of attendance![37] True service to the ruler means hiding one's own light; blocking one's own understanding; losing sight of one's own good points; denigrating one's own glory; and regarding one's own successes as failures. In what sense would chess playing be 'better than doing nothing' then?"[38]

The blazing fire bird soars off to Heaven.[39] Does that not depend on its six pinfeathers? But were a person to pluck them and then attach them to a cuckoo,[40] what an encumbrance they would be![41] 7.11

When thunder shakes the heavens, and the wind bears down on the mountains, and clouds scud off in every direction, and the rain pours into the deep pools—can we really term this a matter of agency?[42] 7.12

---

32 For *yi* (chess), see *Analects* 17.22 ("Or is one not to play chess?" 不有博奕? 為之猶賢乎); cf. *Fayan* 4.23; *Mencius* 6A.9. By mid-Han times, we know there were several different kinds of chess. See Ma Rong's 馬融 (79–166 CE) "*Fu* on Encirclement Chess," included in *Yiwen leiju* (74.1271). See also Lien 2006, which provides a detailed discussion of all the early words for chess. That some moralists and strategists disparaged chess playing is clear from the discussion of Linzi city in the *Shiji* biography of Su Qin.

33 Or "listens and talks" (i.e., "engages in conversation").

34 Because *Analects* 17.22 has Kongzi himself mentioning chess, the interlocutor says it must be proper.

35 Adding "Well, as *he* says," to supply what a classical reader would have known.

36 Since chess playing is for amusement or for playing at strategizing.

37 The anonymous reader who evaluated this translation suggests instead, "It is hard to come by a noble man that one can serve!" Given the Han citation, however, I feel certain that (*a*) the ruler and (*b*) the definition of official service are involved.

38 For another possible allusion, see the commentary to *Fayan* 2.8, on Chengdi's playing chess.

39 For the bird, see *Fayan* 6.16.

40 *Jiu* 鳩 refers to the pigeon, dove, or cuckoo (*bugu niao* 布穀鳥), birds normally known for their predatory habits and for their inability to fly high for long distances. On the bird in question, see Lai 1998. However, *Xunzi* 2/1/23, in his "Encouraging Learning" (Quan xue) chapter, cites a line from *Odes* (152/1–3) that makes tying the cuckoo or ring dove to its nest of chicks in a mulberry tree a metaphor for the noble man's "constant bearing / As though his mind were tied."

41 This metaphor plays off the "popular" theme of birds "flying wing to wing, / spreading pinions to rise, soaring on high," which symbolizes perfect friends troubled by an imminent parting, as in Cao Zhi's second poem, "Sending Off Mr. Ying" (Song Yingshi er shou 送應氏二首), in *Cao Zijian ji*. It may also simply mean that a petty person will never accomplish much, even in a high position, and a petty scholar cannot become great simply by building grand theories.

42 Meaning, these are heaven's doing (not intentional human acts or affairs), even if considerable activity and energy are expressed. Yang Xiong perhaps alludes here to the

7.13 魏武侯與吳起[23]浮於西河。寶河山之固。起曰在德不在固。曰美哉言乎。使起之固兵每如斯。則太公何以加諸。

7.14 或問周寶九鼎。[24]寶乎。曰器寶也。器寶。待人而後寶。

7.15 齊桓晉文以下。至於秦兼。其無觀已。[25]或曰秦無觀。奚其兼。曰所謂觀。觀德也。如觀兵。開闢以來。未有秦也。

23 *Shiji* 65.2166. The Pei Yin commentary to the *Shiji* biography of Wu Qi reads *yong bing* 用兵 (using troops) instead of *gu bing* 固兵 (strengthening or securing troops), but the difference is not great. Cf. *Zuozhuan*, Lord Zhao 4.

24 See *Zhanguo ce* 1/1/15, 44/17–25–18/8. Cf. *Shiji* 40.1700, 70.2282; also Marsili 2005.

25 Note the use of *guan* 觀 to mean "what one observes intently" or "with rapt admiration." *Guan* suggests that efficacious action and virtue can be observed and then emulated, as in the *Zuozhuan* phrase, Lord Zhuang 23: 書而不法，後嗣何觀. Charismatic power and military force are also often used in opposition, as in *Guoyu*, "Zhou yu" 1: 先王耀德不觀兵. Recall, for example, that the controversial figure of Fan Ju (or Sui) led the Qin to "attack nearby states while maintaining ties with remote states" (*yuanjiao jingong* 遠交近攻), as shown in the so-called Bamboo Annals from Yunmeng Shuihudi, as reported in Mittag 2003, esp. 551.

Marquis Wu of Wei and Wu Qi were floating in a boat on West River when the marquis remarked that he valued the security afforded by the rivers and mountains in his domain. Wu Qi said, "But security lies in charismatic virtue, not in such security defenses!"[43] I say, "How fine were his words! Had Wu Qi been cognizant of this every time he was securing his troops, then how would even Taigong[44] have surpassed him?" 7.13

Someone asked me whether the Nine Tripods, the treasures of the Zhou house,[45] "were really such fabulous treasures." 7.14

"Those vessels *were* treasures. But their value as treasures depended upon having the right men recognize them as treasures."[46]

"From the time of the two [first] hegemons, Lord Huan of Qi and Lord Wen of Jin, on down to unification under Qin,[47] there was really nothing worth contemplating with admiration, really nothing at all!"[48] 7.15

Someone asked me, "Well, if you really think there was actually nothing worth contemplating in the case of Qin, then how was it that it was Qin that came to unify the states?"

"When I use the word 'contemplate,' I speak only of 'contemplating virtue.' But if we're talking instead of reviewing troops with intense admiration, then there never has been a state as impressive as Qin!"[49]

Han definition of *shen* 神 as an unseen force that moves or transforms things on a large scale.

43 Wu Qi was a general in Wei.

44 The comment is surely sarcastic, since Wu Qi, generally portrayed as a ruthless figure, was hardly an exemplary figure. Cf. the various meanings of *zha* 詐 (deception) in earlier passages (e.g., 4.21).

45 For the Nine Tripods supposedly cast by Yu the Great, see *Zuozhuan*, Lord Xuan 3, which records an event when the ruler of Chu asked about the tripods' size and weight. In response, he was told that the value of the tripods lay in the charismatic virtue they symbolized, "not in the tripods themselves" [i.e., not in their value as bronze vessels], since (*a*) the decoration of the tripods signified the tribute offered by the loyal Shepherds (i.e., provincial governors) in all parts of the realm; and (*b*) the tripods facilitated communication between "above and below" (here not only social superiors and inferiors but cosmic agents and earthly rulers), "thereby carrying on heaven's blessings" (*yi cheng tian xiu* 以承天休). Their value was talismanic, then, as well as economic and political. Supposedly, the Nine Tripods magically grew heavier or lighter, in response to the virtues of the reigning Zhou king. As long as the virtue associated with the Zhou dynastic legacy had not run its course, "the weight of the tripods cannot be asked," because it would vary according to the present ruler's virtue.

46 Cf. *Fayan* 6.19. The meaning here is that the Nine Tripods, symbols of charismatic virtue, were nonetheless inferior to charismatic virtue, whose excellence does not depend upon others' evaluation.

47 The two first hegemons are Lord Huan of Qi (r. 685–643 BCE) and Lord Wen of Jin (r. 636–628 BCE). Unification occurred in 221 BCE.

48 Han Jing (1992, 162n3) says, "There was nearly not a single edifying act."

49 Note the puns on *guan*, *guande* 觀德 (contemplating virtue), and *guanbing* 觀兵 (contemplating military might, as well as "reviewing the troops"). Unfortunately, English does not allow us to speak of "contemplating the troops" in this sense.

7.16 或問魯用儒而削。何也。曰魯不用儒也。昔在姬公用於周。而四海皇皇。奠枕于京。[26]孔子用於魯。齊人[27]章章。[28]歸其侵疆。[29]魯不用真儒故也。如用真儒。無敵於天下。安得削。

7.17 灝灝之海。濟。樓航之力也。[30]航人無楫。如航何。

7.18 或曰奔壘之車。[31]沈流之航。可乎。曰否。或曰焉用智。曰用智於未奔沈。大寒而後索衣裘。不亦晚乎。

---

26 Wang Rongbao (1987, 10.236) reads *dian* 奠 as the old form of *ting* 停 (stop, park) on the basis of *Shuowen jiezi*. The character *zhen* 軫, referring to the backboard of a carriage, is synecdoche for "carriage." At this time, the Western Zhou capital was Hao 鎬. The meaning here is that every lord in the realm rushed to the capital to submit tribute as a way of showing their allegiance to the duke and the new dynasty under his rule, since the duke had instituted suburban sacrifices to Hou Ji as coadjutor to heaven (*can* 參 or possibly "Triune Mediator"), as well as the clan sacrifice to King Wen in the Spirit Hall (Mingtang 明堂), naming the latter exemplar as coadjutor to the High Lord, Shangdi. (For this, see *Xiaojing*, 聖治 section.)

27 Yang's use of the phrase "men of Qi" (rather than "ruler of Qi" or named ministers) has interesting connotations if we follow *Gongyang zhuan* 6.14/12/69/7.

28 Or they "ran pell-mell, in no fixed order," following Wang Rongbao (1987, 10.236); as Li Gui notes, the binomial phrase elsewhere in Yang's works means "hesitating," but that makes little sense here. Wang Rongbao (1987, 11.236), following *Erya*, reads *zhang zhang* 章章 as *chong chong xing* 衝衝行, meaning "aggressive behavior or advance," "pushing every which way." Cf. Han Jing (1992, 163n3). Another possible reading would make *zhang zhang* = *zhang zhang* 傽傽 (terror-stricken, scared out of their wits).

29 There are slightly different accounts in *Guliang zhuan* 11.10.2/141/16–17 and in *Shiji* 47.

30 This line is cited in *Taiping yulan* 771.3b. Li Gui compares the big boat to the system of rites and music.

31 The phrase literally means "overturned carts at the earthen embankments or ramparts," following Yu Yue's (1874) glosses, which Wang Rongbao (1987, 10.239) approves. Han Jing (1992, 165n1) takes this to mean that when the carriage has already fallen into the enemy's hands and the boat already sunk in the sea, can they still be saved? *Ben* 奔 should be read as *fen* 賁 (i.e., "defeated" or "overturned"). Cf. *Taiping yulan* 769.3b, citing *Xinyan* 新言.

Someone asked me, "Why was the territory of Lu whittled away even though it employed classicists?"[50] 7.16

"Lu never really employed the classicists.[51] Long ago, at the time when the Duke of Zhou[52] was employed by Zhou, each and every vassal lord within the four seas rushed so as not to be the last to park his chariot in the capital. And when Kongzi was employed by Lu, the men of Qi[53] were so terror-stricken that they returned the border territories that they had occupied.[54] The reason for Lu's decline was that Lu did not really employ true classicists.[55] Had it done this, it would have had no peer or rival in the empire, let alone had[56] territory whittled away."

Crossing a vast ocean depends on the strength and power of multistoried boats. But when even the oarsmen lack oars, how can one possibly cross the sea?[57] 7.17

Someone asked me, "But is there no way to rescue the situation once the carts have crashed and the boats sunk?" 7.18

"None."

Someone asked me, "Then what good is wisdom?"

"Wisdom is to be used *before* the conveyance overturns or sinks! Isn't it already too late in midwinter to start looking for warm clothes and furs?"[58]

---

50 See *Yantie lun* 8.6/61/11 for the comment that Duke Ai of Lu "favored the Ru but [his territory] was pared." The state of Lu was utterly annihilated in 249 BCE by the neighboring state of Chu, after having its territory whittled away for centuries; see the *Annals* for details of what happened from the eighth to the fifth century BCE.

51 As several commentators note, the state of Lu, under Duke Mu, employed many Ru, including Gong Yizi as chancellor and Ziliu and Ziyuan as ministers. But Yang apparently focuses on Duke Mu's failure to employ Zisi, grandson of Kongzi. Certainly, Kongzi was never given much of a chance to use his talents in Lu. Here Yang's comment echoes *Mencius* 5B.6.

52 Called here "the Ji duke" (Ji gong 姬公), where "Ji" is the clan name. The duke was founder of the state of Lu and regent for King Cheng. Supposedly, the Duke of Zhou was so eager to gather worthy men around him that upon hearing that a guest had arrived, he would spit out his food if eating, or wring out his hair if washing, to greet the guest as quickly as possible.

53 The ruling line of the state of Qi was supposedly descended from Taigong (see the Glossary). It was formally overthrown in 279 BCE by a leading member of the Tian 田, a hereditary ministerial family, who then launched a "restored Qi" in the area corresponding to present-day Shandong. In 221 BCE the state was extinguished by Qin.

54 This refers to the famous meeting between Qi and Lu at Jiagu 夾谷, when three major tracts of land were returned to Lu at Kongzi's instigation, according to *Zuozhuan*, Lord Ding 10.

55 Adding "for Lu's decline," as implied. From the time of Xunzi onward, we have the sharp distinction between "true classicists" (*jen Ru* 真儒) and "vulgar classicists" (*su Ru* 俗儒).

56 More literally, "how would it ever have had . . .?"

57 Sailing is a metaphor for keeping the ship of state afloat, as the commentators suggest, but also for self-cultivation, since the Classics are seen as the tools one needs to float on the sea of learning, as in Su Shi's Preface to Su's matching of Tao's Poem 42 ("Drinking") and *Fayan* 2.9.

58 Cf. *Huainan zi* 7, "Jingshen" (cited above), which speaks of bad timing in terms of

7.19 乘國者。其如乘航乎。航安。則人斯安矣。

7.20 惠以厚下。民忘其死。忠以衛上。君念其賞。自後者。人先之。自下者。人高之。誠哉。是言也。

7.21 或曰弘羊榷利而國用足。盍榷諸。曰譬諸父子。為其父而榷其子。縱利。如子何。卜式之云。不亦匡乎。

7.22 或曰因秦之法。清而行之。亦可以致平乎。曰譬諸琴瑟。鄭衛調。俾夔因之。[32] 亦不可以致簫韶矣。[33]

7.23 或問處秦之世。抱周之書。益乎。曰舉世寒。貂，狐不亦燠乎。或

32 See the "Shundian" (Canon of Shun) chapter of the *Documents*, *Shangshu* 02.0713, where Kui's music sets the Hundred Beasts to dancing. Cf. *Shiji* 24.1197.

33 Huan Tan (Pokora 1975, 118–19) says that Yang chided him for his love of "modern tunes" (i.e., those of Zheng), saying, "It is very easy to be pleased by shallow things, but the profound can be understood only with difficulty."

Is not steering the ship of state just like steering a regular boat?[59] Certainly only when the boat is stable do the people in it feel secure. 7.19

If the ruler bestows favors generously on those below, the people will defend him to the death, and if the people protect him loyally, he in turn is to think hard about the proper rewards for them.[60] As the saying goes, "He who considers himself last will be put first, and he who keeps himself humble will be raised high by others."[61] How true are these words![62] 7.20

Someone asked me, "The expenses for administering the realm were met[63] when Sang Hongyang instituted monopolies for profit, so what are the arguments *against* instituting monopolies?" 7.21

"Let's draw an analogy to the father-son relation. If fathers were, for their own benefit, to impose monopolies on their children, how could this ever be construed as acting for the sake of the children, even if it unleashed a flood of profits? Was Bu Shi's[64] assessment of the policy not the correct one?"

Someone asked me, "If one were to adopt the laws of Qin but see that they are carried out with perfect fairness,[65] would this not bring about peace and security?" 7.22

"Let's use the analogy of playing on the *qin* and *se* lutes. Were Music Master Kui to try playing the Zheng and Wei tunes on his lutes,[66] even he would find it impossible to get the sublime music of the Xiao and Shao from his instruments!"[67]

Someone asked me, "But if you live under Qin while holding the Zhou writings dear to your heart, of what possible good is *that*?" 7.23

"When the whole world is cold, do not fine sable and fox furs keep you warm?"

---

wearing furs in summertime.

59 The ship of state is a common metaphor in early China, with the people usually described as the water that bears the ship. See *Analects* 15.26 for a similar metaphor: 有馬者借人乘之.

60 Cf. *Zuozhuan*, Lord Xiang 21, citing the *Xia Writings* 夏書.

61 This saying recalls lines in the *Laozi*, section 77, which speak of the low being raised and the high brought low.

62 Cf. *Analects* 13.11 for the four-character phrase *cheng zai shi yan* 誠哉是言. Here Yang quotes proverbial wisdom about the utility of "keeping to the low [position]."

63 Or "the income was sufficient [for its needs]."

64 Bu Shi criticized the monopolies and Sang Hongyang, their promoter.

65 Literally, "with no corruption."

66 Kui was said to have been Music Master under Shun.

67 The Xiao and Shao represent the sublime music of the sage-kings.

曰炎之以火。沃之以湯。燠亦燠矣。曰燠哉。燠哉。時亦有寒者矣。

7.24 非其時而望之。非其道而行之。亦不可以至矣。

7.25 秦之有司負秦之法度。秦之法度負聖人之法度。秦弘違天地之道。而天地違秦亦弘矣。

Someone said, "Well, Qin consigned them to the flames or doused them with boiling water.[68] Surely *that* warmed them up!"

"Oh, it warmed them alright. It fired them up! But the times were nonetheless deemed cold as ice!"

One has not a prayer of success if one looks for a good result when it is not the right time, or if one practices something that is not the right way. 7.24

Some of Qin's own officials betrayed Qin's laws and institutions, just as Qin's laws and institutions betrayed those of the sages. Since the Qin had contravened the Way of heaven and earth to such a great extent,[69] the cosmic powers' rejection of Qin was likewise great.[70] 7.25

---

68 According to legend, tyrannical Qin burned books and buried the Ru alive. Here both activities may refer more broadly to executing men. Yang is one of the most influential thinkers to demonize Qin. See Nylan 2013 on the revisionist Han views of Qin.

69 I.e., the patterns of phenomenal existence.

70 Cf. *Analects* 14.44: "So long as the ruler loves ritual, the people will be easy to handle."

卷第八

五百

聖人聰明淵懿。繼天測靈。
冠乎群倫。經諸範。譔五百。

8.1 或問五百歲而聖人出。有諸。曰堯舜禹。君臣也。而竝。文武周公。父子也。而處。湯孔子。數百歲而生。因往以推來。雖千一不可知也。[1]

8.2 聖人有以擬天地[2] 而參[3] 諸身乎。

1 My translation tries to capture both senses of *qian yi* 千一, following Li Gui, as cited in Wang Rongbao (1987, 248). In short, there is no discernible pattern in the appearance of sages.

2 Li Gui believes that the human parts are modeled on aspects of the cosmos (e.g., the four limbs correspond to the Four Seasons), but this observation probably does not correspond to Yang's observation that the sages model themselves as patterns worthy of emulation in cosmic processes or phenomenal existence ("heaven and earth"); that explains why the sages were to be coadjutors of heaven-and-earth in important sacrifices (see above).

3 Cf. *Liji* 32.20/145/29. For the sages as third partner in the sacred triad, see *Liji* 30.4/138/22: 三王之德, 參於天地. Andrew Plaks (pers. comm.) takes this not as an emphatic remark but as a rhetorical question: "Do sages have the capacity to imitate heaven-and-earth and make themselves their equal?" (The implied answer is "No.") However, the statement seems affirmative: to reach the highest level of cultivation is to become a full partner to heaven-and-earth.

Chapter 8

Every Five Hundred Years

VERSE SUMMARY

The sage, with senses keen and profoundly good, succeeds to heaven and fathoms the divine. Superior to the common herd, he it is who sets down all the norms. Thus, I have composed chapter 8, "Every Five Hundred Years."

Someone asked me, "Is it true that a sage appears every five hundred 8.1
years?"

"In the case of Yao, Shun, and Yu, the rulers and ministers were contemporaries. And with Kings Wen and Wu and the Duke of Zhou, we have a father and his two sons together at the same time.[1] King Tang, the Shang founder, and Kongzi were born many hundreds of years apart, however. Were one to try to use the past to predict the future, there would be no way to tell whether there would be a thousand sages every single year or a single sage every thousand years."

But the sages have what it takes to embody the patterns of heaven-and- 8.2
earth and to make of their persons the Third in the trinity of sacred powers.[2]

1 Adding, "at the same time," as implied.

2 Legge used "ternion" when translating the term *can* 參 in the "Zhongyong." I use the term "Third" to draw attention to the magnitude and religious connotations of the claim. I agree with Ames (2011, 243), that humans co-create the world in this vision.

8.3 或問聖人有詘乎。[4] 曰有。曰焉詘乎。曰仲尼於南子。所不欲見也。陽虎,所不欲敬也。見所不見。敬所不敬。不詘如何。曰衛靈公問陳。則何以不詘。曰詘身。將以信道也。如詘道而信身。[5] 雖天下。不為也。

8.4 聖人重其道而輕其祿。眾人重其祿而輕其道。聖人曰於道行與。眾人曰於祿殖與。

8.5 昔者齊[6] 魯有大臣。史失其名。曰何如其大也。曰叔孫通欲制君臣之儀。徵先生於齊,魯。所不能致者二人。曰若是。則仲尼之開跡諸侯也。[7] 非邪。曰仲尼開迹。將以自用也。如委己而從人。雖有

---

4 The single character 詘 means "constrained," "bent," "humbled." Literally, we are talking about a sage having to "bend his will" against his own desires and preferences due to the exigencies of the time.

5 Reading *xin* 信 as *shen* 申 (extend, propagate), as in *Taixuan jing*, Tetragram 1.

6 Commentary in the *Zizhi tongjian* entry for Gaozi, year 7, does not have "Qi"; then this quotation would only be about events in Lu.

7 Some commentators equate *kai ji* 開迹 with *chuang ye* 創業, referring to Kongzi's compilation of the *Annals*, but this seems unlikely.

Someone asked me whether the sages ever find themselves constrained. 8.3

"They do."

"How so?"

"When Kongzi paid a visit to Nanzi,[3] he didn't *want* to have an audience with her. And when he was visited by Yang Hu,[4] he didn't *want* to pay his respects to him. To see someone who should not be seen and to pay one's respects to someone unworthy of respect—if *that's* not being constrained, then what is?"

"Then when Duke Ling of Wei asked about troop deployments, why was Kongzi so heedless of such constraints?"[5]

"One may constrain oneself in order to expound the Way. But to constrain the Way in order to improve one's own situation[6]—*that* Kongzi would never have done, even if he could have gained the whole world by that sort of ploy."[7]

The sage places great value on the Way and little on rank and salary.[8] The ordinary person places great value on rank and salary but thinks little of the Way. The sage asks, "Will this further the Way?" The ordinary person says, "Will this increase my salary?" 8.4

"Long ago, Qi and Lu had their great officers, yet their scribes omitted their names."[9] 8.5

"In what way were they great, then?"

"When Shusun Tong[10] wanted to regulate matters of decorum between ruler and minister, he summoned learned masters from Qi and Lu, all but two of whom he was able to lure to court."

"If that is so, then was it so wrong for Kongzi to make the rounds of all the lords?"[11]

"Kongzi made the rounds with the intention of being of some use.[12] But if a person has to humiliate himself in order to submit to others, then

---

3 Nanzi, consort to Duke Ling of Wei, was a byword for licentious behavior.

4 Yang Hu was steward and power broker for the powerful Jisun 季孫 clan in Lu.

5 In *Analects* 15.1, Kongzi refuses to discuss the topic with him, preferring other topics. The *Analects* emphasizes Kongzi's refusal to speak (or to speak often) about certain topics, whereas this *Fayan* passage emphasizes Kongzi's refusal to accede to the request for information, since that would be to concede the Way.

6 This means to rely on schemes rather than follow the Way. For a statement about "bending," see *Mencius* 3B.1, which discusses bending and straightening while pursuing the Way.

7 Cf. *Mencius* 2A.24, 7B.13, said of Yi Yin, Bo Yi, and Kongzi.

8 Or "career."

9 According to *Gongyang zhuan* the names of bad officials and rulers were suppressed from the record. See Gentz 2005.

10 Shusun Tong is typically identified as the "ancestor/founder of the [Han] Ru."

11 Remember that Kongzi was notably less successful than Shusun Tong in securing court favors.

12 Or "being employed himself." Either he or his policies could implement his vision. Contrast *Daode jing*, sec. 48, where learning is associated first with "increase" but finally with "lack of worth."

規矩準繩。焉得而用之。

8.6 或問孔子之時。諸侯有知其聖者與。曰知之。知之則曷為不用。曰不能。曰知聖而不能用也。可得聞乎。曰用之。則宜從之。從之。則棄其所習。逆其所順。強其所劣。捐其所能。衝衝如也。[8] 非天下之至。孰能用之。

8.7 或問孔子知其道之不用也。則載[9] 而惡乎之。[10] 曰之後世[11] 君子。曰賈如是。不亦鈍乎。曰眾人愈利而後鈍。聖人愈鈍而後利。關(=貫?)百聖而不慚。蔽天地而不耻。[12] 能言之類。[13] 莫能加也。貴無

8 Han Jing (1992, 177n5) emphasizes that it would have created a great sense of uneasiness because it would no longer be a case of "business as usual." *Taiping yulan* 401.8b-9a, in citing this passage, omits these four characters, *chong chong ru ye* 衝衝如也.

9 *Zai* 載 can mean "to record" (i.e., make an entry on a register); "to load" (on a cart); and "to set to work." However, Li Gui takes *zai* to mean *zai song* 載送 ("to transport in a cart," meaning "to carry forward" his principles). Li Gui then talks of merchants biding their time and husbanding their goods to sell at a later date and of Kongzi "husbanding" or "tending" the Way to await future generations. Han Jing (1992, 177n1) therefore reads the phrase *ze zai er wu hu zhi* 则載而惡乎之 as *zai dao* (載道), so that it would mean "carrying forth his teachings, going where?"

10 Cf. the characterization of Bo Yi and Shu Qi in *Analects* 5.23, 7.15, 16.2, and 18.8, which is discussed in *Shiji* 61.

11 Cf. *Gongyang zhuan* 14.14.1/158/15 (Lord Ai): 所以俟後聖 (awaiting sages of later times).

12 Reading *bi* 弊/蔽 as *zhong* 終, following Wang Rongbao (1987, 11.257). The phrase "his name" has been supplied on the basis of a parallel in *Lüshi chunqiu* 2/4.2 ("Dang ran" 當染; Knoblock and Riegel 2000, 87): 功名蔽天地.

13 Sima Guang, cited in Wang Rongbao (1987, 11.255–56) says that the phrase "those who can talk" refers to humans, and Han Jing follows him. Han Jing (1992, 178n5) takes this description to refer to Kongzi, which means that it must be good; Han Jing reads *guan* 關 as referring to time and *bi* 蔽 as referring to space. However, the description uses characters whose connotations are not always so good, including *guan* 關 (to shut out); *zhe* 遮 (to interrupt, to fence off, to check). The passage may thus be a covert swipe at the "able speakers" at the pre-Qin courts, including Deng Xizi of Zheng. Note, meanwhile, that Han Jing (1992, 178n5), following Wang Rongbao (1987, 11.256), takes *guan* 關 as a loan for *guan* 貫, referring to "passing through time."

how could he be of any use whatsoever, even if he had all the right tools, the compass and square, the ruler and carpenter's line?"

Someone asked me whether, during Kongzi's lifetime, any of the lords understood the fact that he was a sage.[13] 8.6

"They knew it."[14]

"If they knew it, then why did they not employ him?"

"They were unable to."

"Please tell me why, if they knew him to be a sage, they couldn't find a way to use him."

"Because to use him properly, they would have had to follow him.[15] And had they followed him, they would then have had to abandon their customary ways, go against what they had acceded to, strengthen themselves where they were deficient, and downplayed[16] their own abilities. It would have caused a great ruckus![17] Who except for the very best in heaven's realm would ever have been able to employ him?"

Someone asked me, "If Kongzi, in the full knowledge that his Way was not going to be employed in his own age, still carried on the Way,[18] where did he think he was going with it?"[19] 8.7

"As it says, 'Going toward noble men of future generations.'"

"But if a merchant ever acted like this, wouldn't we consider him way too dull?"[20]

"The sharper the drive for profit with the middling sort of men, the duller they become. By contrast, the duller the sage, the more striking his example becomes.[21] A sage pierces through to the hundred sages, and he has no cause for regret. His name extends to the very ends of heaven and earth, and he has no reason to be ashamed. Among 'those who can really

---

13 Andrew Plaks (pers. comm.) prefers "appreciated his sagehood."

14 *Analects* 9.5 has a Lu official asking if the Master is himself a sage (夫子聖者與?).

15 Meaning "followed his advice." Cf. *Analects* 5.7, where Kongzi talks of floating off on a raft to the sea, since the Way is not followed, and only You (i.e., Zigong) is willing to follow him.

16 Or "give up on their own abilities" (meaning "limit what they could do"). I.e., they would have had to have exercised some moral restraint on their conduct.

17 Meaning that the members of the governing elite would then have had to renounce their former skills and goals and follow Kongzi. Cf. *Fayan* 6.18, which refers to petty people's conduct, which "has no fixed direction."

18 Certainly, the account told in *Shiji* 47, the biography of Kongzi, says that it was only late in life that Kongzi put things down in writing, so my own inclination would be to understand *zai* as "set it down in writing."

19 Alternate reading: "Where did he put/place his teachings?" If this relates to his saying that "the Way is not practiced, so I will take a raft and float away to sea" or "go to live among the Nine Yi," then the former reading may be correct.

20 Or "impractical." This whole passage plays on the senses of *li* as "profit" or "benefit" and as "sharp" (said of knives and weapons), and the antonyms for those senses of the word; wordplay is quite common in classical Chinese. Cf. *Zuozhuan*, Lord Xiang 31.12.

21 "Striking" represents an attempt to convey the idea of a sharp knife that is easily employed. The passages means either that "time will tell," or "the less mindful a person is of immediate practical gain, the more impressive his reputation will eventually become." Time is a factor, but not even the sage's contemporaries may be aware of this.

敵。富無倫。利孰大焉。

8.8 或曰孔子之道不可小與。曰小則敗聖。如何。曰若是。則何為去乎。曰愛日。曰愛日而去。何也。曰由群(謀)〔婢〕之故也。[14] 不聽正, 諫而不用,[15] 噫者吾於觀庸邪。[16] 無為飽食安坐而厭觀也。由此觀之。夫子之日亦愛矣。或曰君子愛日乎。曰君子仕則欲行其義。居則欲彰其道。事不厭。教不倦。焉得日。

---

14 Another reading would replace *mou* 謀 with *bi* 婢 (consorts, maids-in-waiting), so that the line reads "On account of the bevy of maids-in-waiting," recalling *Analects* 18.4, where it is said that such women distracted Ji Huanzi 季桓子 and Lord Ding 定 of Lu from affairs of state.

15 Punctuating according to the Li Gui commentary.

16 Following Han Jing (1992, 180n8), who reads *yong* 庸 as *yong* 慵, meaning *juan* 倦 (weary) or *xiedai* 懈怠 (sluggish, listless). Yu Yue (1874) says that *guanyong* 觀庸 means "to watch the crowd." Although Wang Rongbao (1987, 11.260) disagrees, the same usage of *yong* can be found elsewhere in the *Fayan*.

talk,'[22] no one can possibly outdo him![23] And which is really of greater benefit, to be peerless in honor or unrivaled in wealth?"

Someone asked me whether the Way of Kongzi could be shortened somehow. 8.8

"Were it to be shortened or simplified, that would represent a defeat[24] for the sages."

"Why? In what way? And if it's as you say, why on earth did he ever leave Lu?"[25]

"He wanted to save time."

"Why begrudge the time and leave?"[26]

"On account of the many plans he had.[27] If a ruler did not hold court or heed any remonstrances,[28] then Kongzi said, 'Ugh! Am I to be reduced to being a mere spectator? Am I to do nothing productive but eat my fill, sit at my ease, and watch on the sidelines until I'm sick of it?' From this we see that the Master, for his part, thought time exceedingly precious."

Someone asked me, "Does the noble man really begrudge the time?"

"When the noble man is in service, he wants to fulfill his duties, and when he is at home, he wants to make his Way a shining model to others. He is unstinting of himself in service and unflagging in teaching morality,[29] so how would he ever have any leisure time?"

---

22 Either the phrase "that can talk" includes the species of parrots and humans or it indicates those great talkers, the Hundred Masters. Two commentators suggest the following alternative reading: "Kongzi's teachings have passed through the time of the hundred sages [i.e., are time-tested] and they have nothing to be ashamed about [in them]; they cover heaven and earth and have nothing to be ashamed about [in that respect] also. Among those who 'can talk,' none would be able to surpass him." I thank David R. Knechtges for bringing the merits of this alternative reading to my attention.

23 Cf. *Mencius* 2A.2 (24): "From the time when men were first born until now, there has never been another Kongzi."

24 Or "betrayal," as in the sense of *baihuai* 敗壞 (here and below).

25 See above for "leaving." The Lu court was led by a ruler and ministers who had ignored him. Han Jing (1992, 179n3) takes this as a question: "Why did Kongzi leave the state of Lu?"

26 The phrase "begrudge the time" is associated as much with service to parents (and how much to remonstrate with them) as it is with service to the ruler because of *Analects* 4.21 and Zhu Xi's commentary on it.

27 Translation tentative. By an alternative reading, this refers to an incident where the Duke of Qi gave several female entertainers to the King of Lu, a very effective stratagem for distracting the king. In either case, the leaders in Lu did not heed good counsel and ignored Kongzi's remonstrance. Andrew Plaks (pers. comm.) suggests that this refers to the many other strategists/advisers or "fawners" at the various courts.

28 The King of Lu failed to hold court or listen to remonstrances after the neighboring state of Qi gave him some female entertainers.

29 *Analects* 7.2, 33, shows Kongzi describing himself as "unflagging" or "untiring" in his efforts to propagate the Way (學而不厭, 誨人不倦). By this formulation, a good teacher makes an important contribution to social order, even if he finds no place at court.

8.9 或問其有繼周者。雖百世可知也。秦已繼周矣。[17] 不待夏禮而治者。其不驗乎。曰聖人之言,天也。天妄乎。繼周者未欲太平也。如欲太平也。捨之而用他道。亦無由至矣。

8.10 赫赫乎日之光。群目之用也。渾渾乎聖人之道。群心之用也。

8.11 或問天地簡易。[18] 而聖人法之。何五經之支離。曰支離。[19] 蓋其所以

17 For some explanation of the Xia-Shang-Zhou cycle, see, e.g., Sima Qian's appraisal at the end of *Shiji* 7 ("Gaozu benji").

18 Referring, via an implicit "Xici" quotation (乾以易之, 坤以簡能), to the "cosmos and cosmic processes" or "phenomenal existence." Cf. texts like *Lüshi chunqiu*, which speak of the sages "modeling themselves on heaven-and-earth" (Knoblock and Riegel 2000, 2.3, 情欲).

19 The phrase *zhi li* 支離 today means "irrelevant," but here it refers to something being at odds with or contradictory to something else. Sima Guang, cited in Wang Rongbao (1987, 11.263), attributes the convolutedness and hairsplitting to the *explanations* attached to the Classics; once understood, the lessons of the Classics themselves appear "simple and easy." Han Jing (1992, 183n1) reads *zhi li* 支離 as *fensan posui* 分散破碎 (dispersed and broken/ruined), taking the phrase to criticize the failings of the Ru.

Someone asked me whether the successors to Zhou,[30] "even a hundred generations hence, can be known," as Kongzi claimed.[31] 8.9

"It is true that Qin already succeeded to the throne after Zhou, but Qin's decision not to use the Xia rituals in ruling is proof enough, is it not?"[32]

"The sage's words are like heaven.[33] Can heaven deceive us? Zhou's successor[34] never truly wanted to achieve the Great Peace in governing. And had it truly wanted this, to reject the one Way[35] and opt for another would hardly have been the right way to bring it about!"

The brilliant light of day—that is of use to everyone's eyes. And the vast mystery that is the sages' Way—that is of use to everyone's hearts and minds![36] 8.10

Someone asked me, "Heaven and earth are simple and easy,[37] and the sages took them as model.[38] So whence the convolutedness and hairsplitting[39] that we see in the Five Classics?" 8.11

---

30 Or possibly "what follows upon Zhou."

31 Adding the implied "as Kongzi claimed," as the passage alludes to *Analects* 2.23, concerning what can be known or predicted about cultural transmission and change in history. Notably, the sense of what can be known "a hundred generations" hence in the *Analects* has nothing to do with predicting dynastic cycles, a favorite (if extremely dangerous) late Western Han pastime for some advisers to the court. Note that arguments tying the simplicity of the early Western Han ritual system to the Xia dynasty may be relevant here.

32 Presumably the Xia rituals are Central States rituals. Yang may be making one or two points here: (*a*) that historical cycles cannot be so easily predicted, contra Kongzi's claim; or (*b*) that Qin, in failing to model itself upon Xia, forfeited the right to be called Zhou's true successor. Yang's idea, apparently, is that Han, unlike Qin, understands this cycle, and so early Han policies were indeed a return to the simplicity of Xia. However, readers should note that *Analects* 2.23 makes no reference to the presumed cycle of Xia-Shang-Zhou models, and thus the original meaning of the *Analects* phrase "[events and patterns] even a hundred generations hence can be known" (雖百世可知也) may well have differed from the later Han readings of it.

33 Lords over subjects and husbands over wives are said to be "like heaven" (to the inferior parties). While the phrase "Tian ye" (It is heaven) sometimes indicates doubt ("God only knows!"), here it refers to something like Tillich's "ultimate concern."

34 I.e., Qin.

35 The subject here ("it") could be either "the Way of Kongzi" or the "Xia rituals," neither of which Qin used.

36 The contrast between light and dark—and the attribution of both to aspects of the Way—is characteristic of Yang's work.

37 For the insistence that "enlightening the people . . . is truly simple," see *Odes* 254/6. For the Way of heaven being "simple and easy," see "Xici" A.2–4.

38 *Lüshi chunqiu* 2.3/9/8 ("Qing yu" 情欲) is but one of many Qin and Western Han texts to insist that the sages "take the model of heaven-and-earth" (*fa tiandi* 法天地), that is, the cosmos. Cf. 3.5/16/3.

39 Literally, "spreading and splitting," which refers to "disjointedness," "contortions," and "contradictions." However, the same compound could conceivably applaud the excellence of the Ru tradition, which can be divided and applied in diverse ways to diverse problems.

為簡易也。已簡已易。焉支焉離。

8.12 或曰聖人無益於庸也。[20] 曰世人之益者。倉廩也。取之如單。[21] 仲尼,神明也。[22] 小以成小。大以成大。雖山川丘陵草木鳥獸。裕如也。[23] 如不用也。神明亦末如之何矣。[24]

8.13 或問聖人占天乎。曰占天地。若此。則史也何異。曰史以天占人。聖人以人占天。

8.14 或問星有甘石。何如。曰在德不在星。[25] 德隆則晷星。[26] 星隆則晷德也。[27]

---

20 The "uselessness" of the Ru to the state is a topic that had been broached before Yang. See *Xunzi* 20/8/10 (儒效篇), where Xunzi supposedly talks with the (bad) King Zhao of Qin; cf. *Xunxi* 5.10/26/24 for 儒無益於人之國.

21 Reading *dan* 單/簞 (a small basketful) as *dan* 殫 (exhausted, used up), and *ru* 如 as *er* 而.

22 Sima Guang, cited in Wang Rongbao (1987, 263), takes *shenming* to refer to the creative powers of heaven-and-earth. If the binome does refer to the gods, the sentence would mean, as Han Jing (1992, 184n3) suggests, that "Kongzi is on a par with heaven-and-earth," since he is a sage, and sages represent a force equal to that of the cosmic powers.

23 One might cite here the lines from the "Yao dian" ("Shun dian"), in which Shun puts high officials in charge of "grasses and trees, birds and beasts." See *Shangshu* 02.0577.

24 Punctuating after *mo* 末. Alternatively, "But if his Way was not like this, then even his godlike perspicacity would be of no avail!" (taking *mo* 末 as *wuke naihe* 無可奈何). Because the passage seems more about employing the Way than its fundamental character, my rendering is different.

25 Cf. *Han Feizi* 19/32–4/5, which disparages any mention of astral and calendrical spirits along with their astromantic functions. Cf. *Zhuzi jicheng*, 88–89.

26 Sima Guang, cited in Wang Rongbao (1987, 265–66) also takes the gnomon to refer to the shadow, saying that the stars, like a person's shadow, assume an auspicious aspect. Zhu Xi, cited in Wing-tsit Chan 1967, reads this line in a similar way.

27 This follows Han Jing (1992, 185n3), who takes the word for "sundial" to mean "shadow," and hence "influence."

"This very quality of heaven and earth[40] is the reason why the corpus could be made simple and easy. And if it is already both simple and easy, then how can one possibly call it convoluted or hairsplitting?"[41]

Someone remarked to me that the sages are of no benefit to the ordinary person.[42] 8.12

"The men of this age see a granary as useful, but the more you take from it, the more it is depleted. Kongzi[43] had a godlike insight.[44] Small men can use him to perfect themselves in small things, and the great in great. Even mountains and rivers, hills and mounds, grasses and trees, birds and beasts, flourish under his influence.[45] But if his Way is *not* employed, then of what possible use is even his godlike insight?"

Someone asked me whether the sages divine the heavens. 8.13–14

"They divine heaven."

"If that is so, how do they differ from court diviners?"

"The diviner uses the heavens to divine about human affairs. The sage uses human affairs to divine the heavenly signs."[46]

Someone asked me, "For the stars, there are the experts Gan De and Shi Shen.[47] What about them?"

"A life depends upon the person's character and virtue,[48] not upon the stars. If a person's character is truly imposing, then the stars shadow

---

40 Adding "of heaven and earth" as implied.

41 The logic is that a Classic cannot be made unduly simple, lest an overly simple text prove of no use to the people who seek wisdom from it in so many different situations. Later commentators, including Sima Guang, cited in Wang Rongbao (1987, 11.262–3), explain this differently, arguing that the penchant for convolutedness and hairsplitting distinctions arose with the exegetical traditions used to explicate the Classics down through the ages, but once a person has truly achieved the Way, it is revealed as simple and easy to the beholder.

42 This theme of the uselessness of classical learning comes up repeatedly in *Fayan* 1–2.

43 Here called by his courtesy name of Zhongni.

44 Alternatively, *shen ming* 神明 refers to "the gods of heaven-and-earth," "divine illumination," or "godlike insight," the theme of chapter 6. This passage ascribes to Kongzi divine or semidivine religious powers, even if the general tenor of the *Fayan* is skeptical about most religious claims. See, e.g., *Fayan* 8.13–14.

45 *Yuru* 裕如 describes a situation of "abundance." Adding "under his influence," as implied.

46 This passage seems to play off of *Analects* 11.12, where Kongzi tells his disciple that he had better learn more about how to live well before inquiring further about the ghosts and spirits.

47 Two experts on the heavens.

48 Both are implied by the single word *de* (德), along with charismatic power.

8.15 或問大人。曰無事於小為大人。請問小。曰事非禮義為小。

8.16 聖人之言遠如天。賢人之言近如地。

8.17 瓏瓏[28] 其聲者。其質玉乎。

8.18 聖人矢口而成言。肆[29] 筆而成書。言可聞而不可殫。書可觀而不可盡。

8.19 周之人多行。秦之人多病。[30] 行,有之也。病,曼之也。周之士也貴。秦之士也賤。周之士也肆。秦之士也拘。

28 The compound *longling* is simply a variant of the more familiar *linglong* 玲瓏, frequently used to describe jade.

29 Reading *si* 肆 as "let fly," since Wu Mi glosses *si* as *fang* 放. Han Jing (1992, 187n1) agrees. If that reading is adopted, *shi* 矢 would refer to the arrow, known for the speed of its flight when the power with which it is loosed is great. However, Li Gui defines *si* as *zheng* 正 (to make correct, to properly align), which would make the sentence mean "The sages say the proper things, and so perfect their speech; they correct their brushes, and so perfect their writings." In both cases, the parallelism suggests that the verb should express the typical quality of engagement in the activity. Han Jing clearly recalls the way *shi* 矢 was used in *Fayan* 8.19.

30 Wang Rongbao (1987, 11.268) cites the *Hanshi waizhuan* maxim "To learn something but to be incapable of practicing it is what we call *bing* 病, an affliction or failing." Han Jing (1992, 188n1) takes *bing* to mean "a [source of] worry" (*youhuan* 憂患).

him.[49] But when the stars are deemed the more imposing of the two, this casts a shadow over his character."[50]

Someone asked me about the great man.[51] 8.15

"He's someone who never engages in petty matters."

"I beg to ask your definition of 'petty.'"

"Anything *not* about ritual decorum or the performance of one's duty."

The sage's words are as far-reaching as the heavens; the worthy man's, as close as the earth. 8.16

When the tinkling sound is *longling*, crystal clear, how can the substance be anything but jade?[52] 8.17

The sages talk straight and so perfect their speech. They let their brushes fly and so perfect their writings.[53] Their speeches are fit to be heard, and their excellence is inexhaustible.[54] Their writings are fit to be perused, and their excellence is inexhaustible. 8.18

Most men of Zhou practiced it, while most men of Qin deemed it an affliction.[55] To practice it is to have a way to go forward. But to deem it a mere affliction is to lack any way to proceed. Thus, the Zhou men in service were honored, while those of Qin were debased. And the Zhou officers could act as they chose,[56] so upright were they in their desires, while those of Qin had to be held in check.[57] 8.19

---

49 Translation tentative, following Yu Yue (1874) in taking the gnomon, or sundial, as a standard, meaning that the stars (i.e., fate) follow a person of truly imposing character and that person will have a good fate. (By implication, woe betide the evildoer.) However, it is just conceivable that the line means that the man of imposing character outshines the stars, leaving them in shadow. One is tempted to replace the metaphor of the sundial with that of the "eclipse," so that this line reads "When the stars are deemed more imposing, then the person's character and deeds are eclipsed."

50 Meaning that (*a*) one will pay correspondingly less attention to them, since the bright light of one's character will put the stars in shadow, and (*b*) the influence will be registered. The Mawangdui silk manuscript entitled "Yao" 要 has Kongzi saying of himself, "I have the same ultimate aim as the shamans and diviners but walk a different path," where presumably the "ultimate aim" is to align oneself with heaven's patterns. See Li Zehou 2004, 168, for further details.

51 This passage plays with the very different meanings and status implications assigned the term "great man" in moralizing works (e.g., the *Mencius*) and in the epideictic *fu* composed for and by Han Wudi, where greatness correlates with imperial or high bureaucratic rank.

52 Cf. *Fayan* 1.4, on jade and its properties.

53 Cf. *Analects* 2.4: "At seventy, I [Kongzi] could follow what my heart desired, without transgressing the right standards" (從心所欲而不踰矩). Vervoorn (1996, 57) translates this *Fayan* passage as "The sage corrects his thoughts and then speaks, disciplines his brush and then writes. Though his words can be heard, their meaning cannot be exhausted."

54 I.e., of use in every situation. Cf. *Fayan* 8.12.

55 "It" presumably refers to the Way. I take "men" here to refer to the "king's men" (members of the court), but it could equally well refer to men in general.

56 See n. 29 to 8.18 for the two senses of *si* that the translation tries to capture.

57 I.e., constrained by harsh laws. Adding the phrase "so upright were they in their desires."

8.20 月未望則載魄于西。既望則終魄于東。[31] 其遡於日乎。

8.21 彤弓盧矢。[32] 不為有矣。

8.22 聆聽前世。清視在下。鑑莫近於斯矣。[33]

8.23 或問何如動而見畏。曰畏人。[34] 何如動而見侮。曰侮人。夫見畏之與見侮。無不由己。

8.24 或問禮難以強世。曰難, 故強世。如夷俟倨肆。羈角之哺果而啗之。[35] 奚其強。或性或強。及其名一也。[36]

31 See Wang Guowei's essay "Sheng ba si ba kao" 生霸死霸, in *Guantang jilin*, vol. 1, 1/1a-4b.

32 Li Gui takes this to mean that there is a true ruler, but he has no true ministers (see Wang Rongbao 1987, 11.273). Since these items were conferred upon Wang Mang in 5 CE (*Hanshu* 99.4075), commentators assume that these lines must either criticize Wang (as per most traditional commentators) or celebrate him, following Han Jing (1992, 190n2). (Wang Mang essentially gave himself the Nine Conferrals.)

33 The phrase *zai xia* (as in *zai Xia hou zhi shi* 在下后之世) refers to what is happening now, what is "later" in relation to earlier generations.

34 Cf. "Xici" A.6, where good deeds or bad "issue from one's own person."

35 *Dan* 啗 can mean not simply *chi* 吃, as Han Jing (1992, 191n3) suggests, but "entice to eat."

36 Han Jing (1992, 192n4) glosses *ming* 名 (name) as *cheng* 成 (achievements), following Wang Niansun's gloss.

Before the moon is full, its first light appears in the West. After the full moon, its waning light is in the east.[58] Is this not because the moon faces the sun?[59] 8.20

The crimson lacquer bow with black lacquer arrows—these things do not count for much![60] 8.21

Certainly no mirror could give a closer and more accurate reflection than listening attentively to earlier generations and seeing clearly what happened afterward.[61] 8.22

Someone asked me how to act so as to be regarded with awe. 8.23

"Regard others with awe."

"And to be reviled?"

"Revile others. As we all know, awesome authority and insults in all cases stem from one's own actions."[62]

Someone asked me whether it is not too hard to impose ritual on society. 8.24

"It is because it's so hard that one imposes it on society.[63] Consider someone squatting on his heels, lolling about while taking his ease.[64] Or consider a young child with braids or topknot sucking on a piece of fruit and then swallowing it. What's so forced and unnatural about that?[65] Attainments are called by one and the same name, whether they are due to nature[66] or imposed upon a person's nature."[67]

---

58 Liu Xin had a different theory, however, which is followed in the pseudo-Kong Archaic Script chapters of the *Documents*, where *bo* refers to the moon's substance (i.e., the dark portion of the moon).

59 These are standard metaphors for relations between the ruler (sun) and minister or subject (moon), but it is not clear to me that this is Yang's subject here.

60 L'Haridon (2006) translates "signify much." Following *Analects* 19.2, which lists two of the Nine Conferrals given by ideal rulers to their highest ministers, they symbolize those officials' authority to wage war on their own initiative. Cf. *Odes* 175 ("Tong gong" 彤弓), which associates such items with "fine guests." If one follows Han Jing (1992), the line means "[These precious items] do not appear to be too much [to reward him with]!" More likely, it means "The outer trappings of power alone do not ensure an abundance of authority."

61 I.e., now. This makes of history a mirror. "Below" could refer to those in lower positions or to "what is to come" (as in my translation).

62 Cf. *Mencius* 4A.9, which notes that respect (*jing* 敬) and insults (*wu* 侮) are brought on by one's conduct to others. Xunzi (105/29/29–31) defines *ren* 仁 (consummate humanity) as *zi ai* 自愛 (love of self), again erasing the boundary between self and other.

63 Translation tentative.

64 Cf. *Analects* 14.43 for the phrase *yisi* 夷俟.

65 Translation tentative. Yang seems to regard the non-Xia peoples as virtual children, with each person a cultural tabula rasa.

66 The same character, *xing* 性, can refer to one's original endowment and one's second nature (what one becomes habituated to later on) in texts from the *Xunzi* on.

67 This passage echoes *Analects* 7.20 and 16.9 and their distinction between what is "understood at birth" (or "as a living creature") (生而知之) and "what is understood [only] through study and emulation" (學而知之).

8.25 見弓之張兮。弛而不失其良兮。或曰何謂也。曰檠之而已矣。

8.26 川有防。器有範。見禮教之至也。

8.27 經營。然後知幹, 楨之克立也。

8.28 莊揚(= 楊?) 蕩而不法。墨晏儉而廢禮。申韓險[37] 而無化。鄒衍迂而不信。[38]

8.29 聖人之材, 天地也。次。山陵川泉也。次。鳥獸草木也。[39]

---

37 *Xian* 險 often refers to "dangers" and so legal entrapments that endanger oneself (hence my translation of "too clever for one's own good"). But *xian* here may be read as *xian ke* 險克, 刻 (harsh, ruthless). Then the line would mean that Shen and Han were unduly harsh, denying the powers of moral transformation. Because Shen died of natural causes (unlike Han Fei), while serving as chancellor to Lord Zhao of Han, the second reading is arguably stronger. But Yang clearly means to show the deleterious effect of character failings, and the promotion of harsh laws thus seems the more unlikely interpretation.

38 This criticism of Zou Yan 鄒衍 echoes that found in his biography in *Shiji* 74.2344–45, where he is criticized for his unorthodox theories. This whole critique recalls the *Xunzi* chapter "Fei shi er" 非十二.

39 Li Gui explains, "in that each of the various types has what it excels in."

"One sees that a bow stretched taut for some time[68] does not lose its tautness!" 8.25–26

"What do you mean?"

"You're merely putting it in its own bow case, surely![69] From the fact that rivers have their dikes and utensils their molds, we see the ultimate utility of instruction in the rites."

One knows whether the railing and posts will stand upright only if the length and circumference have been carefully measured before. 8.27

Zhuangzi and Yang Zhu[70] exhibited a complete lack of control, and they upheld no models. Mozi and Yanzi[71] urged frugality, but they rejected ritual. Shen Buhai and Han Fei were too clever for their own good and not particularly edifying. And with Zou Yan, you have fantastic accounts that are simply not credible. 8.28

The resources of the sages are as vast as heaven and earth,[72] and the worthies in the next category are most like the mountains and rivers that are home to the gods,[73] while those in the third category are like the birds and beasts, the grasses and trees.[74] 8.29

---

68 Adding "for some time," as implied.

69 When you act according to ritual. This means that ritual activities not only do no harm to the basic substance of human nature but also help humans to perform their intended function, in the same way that the bow case helps the bow to retain its proper shape.

70 Yang Zhu was an influential thinker who argued for self-preservation as the supreme value.

71 For Mozi, see *Fayan* 2.20. Yanzi (Yan Ying) was minister in Qi when Kongzi lived.

72 "As vast as" is the implication.

73 Adding "that are home to the gods," since the major mountains and rivers were thought to be the dwellings of the gods. Cao Cao perhaps explains these lines best at the end of his "Short Song" 短歌行: "Mountains do not tire of being high. / The seas do not tire of being deep. / The Duke of Zhou spat out what he chewed [in the rush to meet good men]. / And all the world gave him their allegiance."

74 Cf. *Fayan* 8.12.

卷第九

先知

立政鼓眾。動化天下。莫尚於中和。
中和之發。在於哲民情。譔先知。

9.1 先知[1]其幾於神乎。敢問先知。曰不知。[2]知其道者。其如視忽眇緜[3]作昞。

9.2 先甲一日易。後甲一日難。

9.3 或問何以治國。曰立政。[4]曰何以立政。曰政之本。身也。身立則

1 The same phrase is used in two related senses in the "Kongzi at His Ease" (Kongzi xianju) chapter of the *Liji*: (1) to know in advance how events will evolve and (2) to have such good instincts or intuition about the underlying patterns of things that one can predict the future course of events well in advance. Neither of those senses of the word necessarily involves a nearly "divine"—because infallible—"prescience."

2 Contrast "Zhongyong" 32.22 (至誠之道，可以前知).

3 *Hu* 忽 refers to the smallest part of something, whatever is extremely fine, a light that blinks on and off, or to something blurry and indistinct. Li Gui takes *miao mian* 眇緜 as a compound referring to "far-sightedness." However, Wang Rongbao (1987, 12.283) indicates by punctuation that it is not a compound, both the second and third adjectives referring to something small and indistinct.

4 Because a line by Zheng Xuan cited in the subcommentary to the Gu 蠱 hexagram says that it was on the *jiazi* day that the imperial government promulgated new edicts, several commentators, including Wang Rongbao (1987, 12.286) and Han Jing (1992, 196n1), assume that Yang's pronouncement concerns legal prohibitions and the government's duty to carefully think through edicts before issuing them, since they are not easily emended once they have been made public, and also to use the laws to avert the commission of crimes.

Chapter 9

Foresight

VERSE SUMMARY

In establishing policies, rousing the masses, and influencing the empire, nothing is superior to putting the Mean at Center. To begin this requires knowledge of the people's predilections. Thus, I have composed chapter 9, "Foresight."[1]

"To know something in advance—how near to the gods that is!"[2] 9.1

"I make bold to ask about prescience."[3]

"I wouldn't know anything about *that*.[4] But for the person who recognizes the Way, foresight functions just like the faculty of sight, rendering even the faintest, most minute, or most indistinct thing brilliantly clear."

Things that are easy to do even one day before the start of a cycle become 9.2
difficult even one day after the cycle has begun.[5]

Someone asked me the method for ruling a state well. 9.3

1 Yang is very careful not to confuse "foresight" with "the ability to know things in advance." "Knowing in advance" (*xianzhi* 先知) is a phrase that can describe the ordinary ability of learned men to predict future events based on past patterns (foresight); sometimes, however, it refers to quasi-divine powers to predict the future. Most likely here it refers to the sense in which it is used in *Analects* 2.23, 7.19, and 7.27 (where Kongzi twice denies having innate knowledge). See two works by Jane Geaney (2002, 2010), which argue that the term usually refers, not to "god-like prescience," but to "prudent calculations about the connection between present actions and future consequences," with the latter a rational and nonmagical attribute of the sages' godlike wisdom, despite the quasi-mystical "Xici" B language: 知幾其神乎.

2 Cf. "Xici" B, cited in n. 1.

3 The same phrase in Chinese can mean "prescience" or "foreknowledge," with the former indicating quasi-divine powers.

4 Cf. *Analects* 19.3, where Kongzi denies having quasi-divine powers.

5 Yang's simple statement likely means no more than "the earlier one tackles a problem, the better," which is certainly Li Gui's reading.

政立矣。

9.4 或問為政有幾。曰思斁。[5] 或問思斁。曰昔在周公。征于東方。四國是王。召伯述職。蔽芾甘棠。其思矣夫。齊桓欲徑陳。陳不果內。執轅濤塗。其斁矣夫。於戲。[6] 從政者審其思斁而已矣。或問何思。何斁。曰老人老。孤人孤。病者養。死者葬。男子畝。婦人桑之謂思。若污人老。屈人孤。病者獨。死者逋。田畝荒。杼軸空之謂斁。

9.5 為政[7] 日新。或人敢問日新。曰使之利其仁。樂其義。厲之以名。

---

5 *Si* 思 means to "think of yearning about something"; *yi* 斁 means "to be weary or sated" with something, "to be thoroughly sick of it." As *yi* is the antonym of *si* 思, I have used "repulsion" to translate it. Yang's phrasing probably derives from *yi si* 繹思, which occurs twice in *Odes* 295 ("Lai") and from *si wu yi* 思無繹, which occurs in *Odes* 297 ("Si"), an ode supposedly sung during the ceremony of the great enfeoffment in the temple. In the Mao reading, the first poem describes the way that King Wen's mighty labors spread "abundance" everywhere. If we follow the Han commentators, the *si* functions *either* as a final particle or as the verb "to think [admiringly or longingly]" (as the enfeoffed ministers are to "think of expanding" the good results of the labors of King Wen [and his sons?]). While the Han commentators generally take *yi* as "ampleness" or "abundance," Zhu Xi was not the only later commentator to object, preferring to read *yi* as "to investigate." At this remove, all we can say is that if Yang here means to cite the "Lai" ode, he possibly attaches quite a different meaning to the phrase *yi si*, one that posits unity ("settling" the realm) in terms of extending to the whole realm an improved standard for feelings of longing and repulsion.

6 For *yu xi* 於戲, most would read "Alas!" "Ah!" One wonders if there is not a faint trace retained of the original meaning of *xi*, as in the bitter expressions "What a joke!" or "What sport [they have with me]!"

7 Li Gui, cited in Wang Rongbao (1987, 12.291), identifies *zheng* 政 as *ren jun* 人君 (the ruler of men).

"Set up a proper government."[6]

"But how is one to do that?"

"The basis of the government is the person in power. When the person is upright, the administration is upright, surely!"[7]

Someone asked me whether there are any keys to good rule. 9.4

"Longing and revulsion."

"What does that phrase mean?"

"It refers to the time long ago,[8] when the Duke of Zhou launched a punitive attack in the east, and 'Him the Four States took as king';[9] also to the time when the Lord of Shao faithfully carried out his duties, and he was said to be 'Lush and verdant, a sweet pear.'[10] Those certainly had the effect of making others yearn for them, did they not? But when Lord Huan of Qi wanted his army to cross through Chen, and Chen was adamant in its refusal to let him enter, the duke detained Chen's envoy, Yuan Taotu.[11] That certainly had the effect of making others feel repulsed, did it not? Ah! Those in power had better look to longing and revulsion—that and nothing more!"

Someone asked me what creates longing or revulsion.

"We speak of a ruler being the object of 'longing' if he treats the aged and the orphans as they should be treated, if he tends the sick and buries the dead, if he puts the males to fieldwork and the women to silk production. But we label the person in power 'repulsive' if he mistreats the aged, humiliates orphans, neglects the sick, exposes the corpses of the dead, or lets the fields become wasteland while the looms[12] lie empty."

Ruling well means "daily renewal."[13] 9.5

"I beg to ask you the meaning of that phrase."

"With incentives, the people can be made to see the benefits of humane action,[14] so that they take real pleasure in carrying out their duties. If the ruler encourages them with fame,[15] and leads them on with praise,[16] the

---

6 "Li zheng" (Setting Up Government) is the name of a chapter in the *Documents* ascribed the Duke of Zhou.

7 Cf. *Analects* 12.17, which defines "good governance" in terms of a homonym meaning "upright" (*Mencius* 7A.20). *Analects* 11.1 insists that those in office know the rites and music well.

8 Olivier Venture (2005) notes that in the bronze inscriptions, the term "long ago" (*xi* 昔) never refers to the pre-Zhou past. For Yang, there are several "pasts," including the more distant past of the sage-kings.

9 *Odes* 157/1–3 says, "The Duke of Zhou went east on a punitive expedition, and the Four States took him as sovereign [*huang* 皇]." The Four States are Guan, Cai, Shang, and Yan 奄.

10 *Odes* 16, a praise-song, describes the sweet pear tree below which Shaogong sat while administering justice.

11 Cf. *Fayan* 7.15. Yuan Taotu was counselor in Chen.

12 Literally, the *shu* 杼 (shuttle) and *zhu* 軸 (bolt); metonymy.

13 Cf. *Liji*, "Da Xue," sec. 43 (苟日新，日日新). Cf. *Analects* 7.3.

14 Cf. *Analects* 4.2, which says, 智者利仁.

15 *Ming* means not only "reputations" or "fame" but also "titles of offices," as in the phrase *xing ming* 形名.

16 *Mei* 美 refers to both reputations and praise.

引之以美。使之陶陶然之謂日新。

9.6 或問民所勤。曰民有三勤。曰何哉所謂三勤。曰政善而吏惡。一勤也。吏善而政惡。二勤也。政,吏駢惡。三勤也。禽獸食人之食。土木衣人之帛。[8] 穀人不足於晝, 絲人不足於夜, 之謂惡政。

9.7 聖人, 文質者也。[9] 車服以彰之。[10] 藻色以明之。聲音以揚之。詩, 書以光之。籩豆不陳。玉帛不分。琴瑟不鏗。鍾鼓不抎。則吾無以見聖人矣。

9.8 或曰以往聖人之法治將來。譬猶膠柱而調瑟。有諸。[11] 曰有之。曰聖君少而庸君多。如獨守仲尼之道。是漆也。曰聖人之法。未嘗

8 Han Jing (1992, 201n5) takes "earth and wood" to mean "architecture," but it could well refer to figurines made for tombs, as in my translation.

9 Following Li Gui for this reading. Wang Rongbao (1987, 12.291) refers to a variant reading, seen in Li Xiang's commentary to *Hou Hanshu* 30.3663, which ends in *bei ye* 備也; Li regards this as a copyist's mistake. *Yanti lun* 4 (18 "Duanxue") says that *li* (ritual propriety) thereby brings pattern to bear on substance.

10 According to Li Gui, cited in Wang Rongbao (1987, 12.291), "it" refers here to distinctions in rank (and, by implication, merit).

11 See also the use of the metaphor in *Shiji* 81.2440 (膠柱而鼓瑟); *Wenzi* 5/27/7; and *Huainan zi* 11 ("Qi su shuo").

people will become cheerful and easy, and that is what is meant by the phrase 'daily renewal.'"

Someone asked me what troubles the people. 9.6

"The people have three types of troubles."

"And they are?"

"If the administration[17] is good, but the officers[18] are bad—that is one sort of trouble. If the officers are good, but the administration is bad—that is a second sort. And if both the administration and its officers are working in tandem[19] in evildoing—that is yet a third. When animals eat the provisions meant for people and when earthen and wooden figurines[20] wear the silks meant for people, then the daytime will never be long enough for farmers, nor the nighttime, for weavers[21]—and that we call 'bad rule.'"

The sages are those who added ornamentation to the basic substance: 9.7

> Carriages and robes they use to display it.[22]
> Brilliant colors, to make it bright.
> Sonorous tones, to elevate and propagate[23] it, and
> The *Odes* and *Documents*, to imbue it with glory.[24]
>
> If platters and stands are not set out,
> Nor jades and silks distributed,
> Nor lutes and zithers played,
> Nor bells and drums struck,

then we would have no way at all to catch a glimpse of the sages, surely!

Someone said to me, "To apply the models used by past sages to control what is yet to come would be like applying glue to the fret before tuning the zither. Have there been such cases in history?"[25] 9.8

"There have."

"But since there are so few sage rulers and so many mediocre rulers, if one were only to keep to the Way of Kongzi, wouldn't this gum up the system like lacquer?"[26]

"In every case in the past, the models of the sages had a direct bear-

---

17 Or possibly "ruling power."

18 Not necessarily "petty officers" in Han, as it would be in late imperial China.

19 Literally, "harnessed together."

20 For the first case, we have Jester Meng's sarcastic remonstrance against a funeral service for a beloved dead horse of King Zhuang of Chu (r. 613–559 BCE), recorded in *Shiji* 126.3200.

21 Literally, "the grain-men" and "silk-[wo]men" (producers of grain and silk).

22 The rhyming poem in two stanzas (*A-A-A-A*, *B-B-B-B*) describes the system of sumptuary regulations promoted by Xunzi and implemented during Han times.

23 Two meanings of *yang* 揚.

24 Appropriate "ornament" refers always to ritual, music, and the Classics.

25 This argument reproduces one from the *Han Feizi* (25/57/13).

26 I.e., an inappropriate cleaving to the past.

不關盛衰焉。昔者堯有天下。舉大綱。命舜禹。夏殷周屬其子。不膠者卓矣。唐虞象刑惟明。[12] 夏后肉辟三千。不膠者卓矣。堯親九族。協和萬國。湯武桓桓。征伐四克。由是言之。不膠者卓矣。禮樂,征伐自天子所出。春秋之時。齊,晉實予不膠者卓矣。[13]

9.9 或曰人君不可不學律令。曰君子為國。張其綱紀。議其教化。導之以仁。則下不相賊。莅之以廉。則下不相盜。臨之以正。則下不相詐。修(=循?)之以禮義。則下多德讓。此君子所當學也。如有犯法。則司獄在。

9.10 或苦亂。曰綱紀。曰惡在於綱紀。曰大作綱。小作紀。如綱不

12 See *Shangshu dazhuan* 1.1/5/1–4; *Bohu tong* 24/49/1.

13 For the phrase *shiyu*, see *Gongyang zhuan* (e.g., 85/Xi 1/2 Gong; 87/Xi 2/1 Gong; 436/Ding 1/2 Gong): "They had the substance given them but not the written acknowledgment." Li Gui says, "[The sage] in effect acknowledges their merit, although the wording negates it." The *Gongyang*, in explaining the word ascribed to Kongzi, implies that he is the subject of the sentence rather than Qi and Jin. Li Gui concurs: "[The sages] in effect acknowledge their merit although the wording negates it." Wang Rongbao (1987, 12.295) would make this also refer to Kongzi as uncrowned king.

ing upon the flourishing or decline of the realm. Long ago, when Yao ruled over the world, he put in place the main institutions by which the Mandate was conferred upon Shun and then Yu. Xia, Yin, and Zhou [by contrast] assigned the throne to their sons. It is obvious that they did not stick to precedent, as to glue.[27] Yao and Shun made the images of the mutilating punishments manifest,[28] while the Xia rulers had 3,000 mutilating punishments. It is obvious that they did not stick to precedent, as to glue. Yao drew the Nine Clans to him, and he brought peace and harmony to the myriad states. Tang and King Wu, on the other hand, displayed their awesome powers in punitive attacks that led to the conquest of all the territories in the four quarters.[29] From this one may conclude the obvious: that they did not stick to precedent, like glue. They say that 'rites and music, as well as punitive campaigns, are all to be issued by the Son of Heaven.'[30] But during the Chunqiu period, Kongzi in effect acknowledged the merit of Qi and Jin in issuing these.[31] It is obvious that they did not stick to precedent, as to glue."

Someone said, "The ruler of men should never neglect to study the statutes and ordinances." 9.9–10

"The ruler, when making policy on behalf of the realm, sets forth the main and the secondary institutions and he makes every effort at moral suasion. If he leads them with humaneness, then his subjects will not do violence to one another. If he treats them with honesty and fairness, refusing to take bribes, then his subjects will not steal from one another.[32] If he deals with them in an upright manner, then his subjects will not cheat one another. And if he cultivates them with the rites and duties, then his subjects will generally respond with decorous self-abnegation. This is what the ruler ought to learn. Should there be those who break the law, then the superintendent of prisons is there [to handle that]."[33]

Someone frets about chaos.

---

27 The historicity of the Xia dynasty (traditionally 2140–1711 BCE) is still in doubt; the Shang-Yin, according to tradition, succeeded the Xia, until they were conquered by the Zhou ca. 1050 BCE. "Yin" refers to the period when the Shang rulers resided at their last capital.

28 This use of "image punishments" is explained in the *Documents*, "Yao dian" chapter, pt. 2 (in some editions called "Shundian"). See *Shangshu tongjian* 020268. According to the Han commentators, in an era of great peace, no mutilating punishments were needed as a deterrent; the mere threat of being compelled to wear images of the mutilating punishments was enough to prevent criminal activity.

29 Adding "all the territories in," as implied.

30 Cf. *Analects* 16.2.

31 In an unpublished paper Hans van Ess casts doubts on whether the full-blown notion of Kongzi as uncrowned king can be found before the Tang era except in a few apocryphal traditions (pers. comm., June 2010).

32 Cf. *Analects* 12.18–19. *Lian* describes honesty, fairness, and incorruptibility (i.e., the refusal to take bribes)—hence the translation.

33 One of the most famous prison superintendants was Zhang Tang, whose biography appears in the *kuli* 苦吏 (cruel officials) chapter of *Shiji* (122). See below for further information. Yang Xiong himself mentions Zhang Tang mainly as a cruel official, and he criticizes this sort of official in *Fayan* 11.18.

綱。紀不紀。雖有羅網。[14] 惡得一目而正諸。

9.11 或曰齊得夷吾而霸。仲尼曰小器。請問大器。曰大器其猶規矩準繩乎。先自治而後治人[15] 之謂大器。

9.12 或曰正國何先。曰躬工人績。[16]

9.13 或曰為政先殺後教。曰於乎。天先秋而後春乎。將先春而後秋乎。

9.14 吾見玄駒之步(=走), [17] 雉之晨 (=震?)[18] 雊也。化其可以已矣哉。[19]

9.15 民可使覿德。不可使覿刑。覿德則純。覿刑則亂。

9.16 象龍之致雨也。難矣哉。曰龍乎。龍乎。

---

14 This passage probably plays upon the sense, recorded in the *Shuowen jiezi*, that the root meaning of *zhi* 直 (upright [administrator]) is one component part of the character for "eye" (*mu* 目). While the "net of laws" is oppressive and ultimately ineffectual, the ordering of threads (*gang* and *ji*) builds moral rule and strengthens support for the ruling house.

15 Cf. the "Daxue" chapter of the *Liji* (section 2), which lays out a lengthy sequence of steps in cultivation of the self and others, beginning with perfecting one's own integrity and ending with making policy and pacifying the realm (誠意 . . . 正心 . . . 修身. . . . 齊家 . . . 治國 . . . 平天下).

16 Han Jing (1992, 210n2) defines *gong* 工 as *shan* 善 or *qiao* 巧 (to improve, to refine). Liu Shipei (1916) equates *gong* with *guan* 官 (to hold or put in office). Andrew Plaks (pers. comm.) prefers "The ruler must be personally involved in determining the others' levels of merit."

17 According to the "Xia Little Calendar" chapter of the *Da Dai Liji* and *Taiping yulan* 947.4b, cited in Han Jing (1992, 211n1), the ants march out from the earth in spring, "knowing that the rain which is to come will stop up [i.e., inundate] their nest."

18 But Wang Rongbao (1987, 12.300) would read *chen* 晨 as *zhen* 震 (lit., "thunderous"), a description in the "Xia Little Calendar" that is applied to the bird's flapping its wings (*gu qi yi* 鼓其翼). How this line relates to the preceding and succeeding lines is not clear to me, unless it means that there is more to be done if the ruler is to imitate the ceaseless round of activities ascribed to heaven's operations.

19 Sima Guang, cited in Wang Rongbao (1987, 12.303) would moralize the "transformation," seeing it as "moral transformation." Liu Shipei (1916) takes this further, casting the ants as metaphor for the right relations between ruler and subject and the pheasant as metaphor for the right relations between husband and wife. More to the point, the ant in the "Xueji" 學記 chapter of the *Liji* symbolizes "the continual exercise of the art [of amassing things or learning]," as do moths in *Liji* 18.2 (蛾子時術之). According to Han Jing (1992, 211n3), Yang Xiong, in pointing out the ceaseless change that things undergo, laments the people's failure to change themselves and others for the better.

"For that, we have the major and secondary institutions."
"Why does it rest on those?"
"For the great matters, the major institutions have been devised, and for lesser matters, the secondary. If the major institutions are not used for the great matters nor the secondary for the lesser, then how can you possibly set things straight, even if you have plenty of snares and nets in the form of the laws?"[34]

Someone said to me, "Qi obtained the services of Guan Zhong and went on to become hegemon.[35] But Zhongni disparaged Guan, calling him but 'a minor tool or functionary.'[36] May I ask, then, who qualifies as a major tool?" 9.11–13

"Great tools are those like the compass and the square, the level and the carpenter's line. First master thyself and later master others. That's how to define a 'major tool.'"

Someone asked me, "What takes priority when ordering a domain?"
"Work hard yourself, and let others take the credit for any merit."[37]
Someone asked me, "In ruling, does one kill first and instruct later?"
"Ah! Does heaven put autumn first and spring later, or the reverse?"[38]

"I have noted the march of the Black Colt ants [in spring] and the pheas- 9.14
ant's call at daybreak. Surely the transformations are not at an end?"

"The people may be allowed to look upon virtue, but they may not be 9.15
allowed to look at the mutilating punishments. Seeing virtue will purify them, but looking at chastisements will only make them disorderly."

"It is really hard for a dragon's image to bring rain." 9.16
"So much for dragons! So much for them!"[39]

34 Adding the phrase "in the form of the laws," since the equation of "snares and nets" with the "laws" is taken for granted by Yang's time. The sense of the passage relies on contrasting metaphors, all of which have to do with weaving (*gang* 綱, *ji* 紀, and *wang* 網).

35 The main outline of the story of Duke Huan of Qi is told in *Zuozhuan*, Lord Zhao 13. The list of Duke Huan's aides does not include Guan Zhong, since Guan originally favored another contender for power. But the *Zuo* says relatively little about Duke Huan or Guan Zhong, though they were the focus of an extensive body of legends.

36 *Analects* 5.4, 3.22. But note that Kongzi sometimes praises Guan Zhong in the *Analects*.

37 I believe that this passage celebrates the so-called secret virtue (*yin de* 隱德) associated with the Duke of Zhou in the "Metal Coffer" chapter of the *Documents* and also emphasized in the *Taixuan jing*. Several alternative readings are possible, however, including that by Li Gui ("Work hard oneself, and then determine the merit of others") and by Wang Rongbao (1987, 12.299) ("Work hard oneself, and others will follow suit"). See also the hard work and self-forgetting associated with Yu the flood-queller in *Analects* 8.21.

38 This understanding of heaven's priorities is usually ascribed to Dong Zhongshu, as it appears in his memorials addressed to the throne (see Dong's *Han Shu* biography). However, it appears in some form in many texts that predate Dong's era.

39 Repetitions in the *Analects* usually signal a negative attitude toward an object or phenomenon: thus, "Is this [really] a dragon? How can it count as a dragon?" Then there follows a discussion about "true" and "false."

9.17 或問政核。曰真偽。真偽則政核。如真不真。偽不偽。則政不核。

9.18 鼓舞萬物者。雷風乎。鼓舞萬民者。號令乎。雷不一。風不再。[20]

9.19 聖人樂陶成天下之化。使人有士君子之器者也。[21] 故不遁于世。不離于群。遁離者,是聖人乎。

9.20 雌之不才。其卵毈矣。君之不才。其民野矣。

9.21 或問曰載使子草律。曰吾不如弘恭。草奏。曰吾不如陳湯。曰何為。曰必也律不犯。奏不剡。[22]

9.22 甄陶天下者。其在和乎。剛則甈。柔則坏。[23]

20 Many Han memorials compare the wind to statutes and ordinances; see the Mao preface to the *Odes*, which describes a superior influencing those below in terms of the wind blowing (上以風化下). The Han scholar Yi Feng 翼奉, an expert in both the *Odes* and the *Changes*, noted that the Qi version of the *Odes* had thunder giving birth to and nourishing the myriad things, while the wind represents a warning. That may explain why the thunder comes more than once, but wind only once. If the wind symbolizes the ruler's authority, the ruler should never be of two minds. The question is whether his punishments should be swift and certain or not.

21 More literally, "vessels capable of becoming fit men of service and noble men." The commentators tie this passage to *Chunqiu fanlu*, *juan* 6.4, *pian* 17 ("Yuxu" 俞序), but as I believe that that work ascribed to Dong Zhongshu dates to the Six Dynasties, I am not sure of the relevance of their comments. The idea is clear, however: as a result of *taohua* 陶化, men are turned into noble men.

22 *Yan* 剡 refers to what is "sharp" and "pointed," such as a dart or arrow.

23 *Kongzi jiayu* 41 has Kongzi advising this (寬猛相濟), though the compilation of that text probably postdates the *Fayan*.

Someone asked about the core of good rule. 9.17

"True and false—that is the core. If the truth is not perceived as true, nor the false as false, then an administration lacks a moral core."

"Thunder and wind arouse the myriad things and set them to dancing. 9.18
Ordinances and decrees likewise arouse the masses and set *them* to dancing."

"Thunder does not sound only once, nor the wind twice."[40]

The sages take pleasure in perfecting the moral transformation of the 9.19–20
realm, as on a potter's wheel. They turn the officers into vessels having the right mettle. Therefore, they neither flee the world, nor detach themselves from the crowds.[41] Are those who take flight and detach themselves really sages?" ["No!"] After all, if the female does not conduct herself properly, her eggs will rot before they ever hatch. Similarly, if the ruler lacks men of the right mettle, his people will remain uncivilized.[42]

Someone asked me, "What if I were to employ *you* to draft statutes?" 9.21

"I would not be as good as Hong Gong."[43]

"What about drafting memorials?"

"I would not be as good as Chen Tang."[44]

"What *can* you do?"

"Make sure that the statutes are not disobeyed, and the memorials not so cutting."[45]

"To form and fashion the realm like pottery—doesn't that depend upon 9.22

---

40 Translation tentative. The meaning might be that the wind does not blow from two directions at once or, following Andrew Plaks (pers. comm.), "twice from the same direction."

41 A striking contribution to conversations that are typically believed to belong to the post-Han era.

42 Adding "before they ever hatch," for sense. The argument means that the ruler must tend to his subjects as a mother hen tends to her chicks.

43 Hong Gong was a powerful eunuch at the courts of Han Xuandi and Yuandi. Yang Xiong models his answer on that given by Kongzi in *Analects* 3.18, where Kongzi chastises the "Duke of She" (i.e., Chen Juliang, who took the title of "duke" for himself), arguing that it would be better not to take pride in subjects who abide by the laws if abiding by the laws means that they fail to observe filial piety, the basis of all moral obligation.

44 Chen Tang was a general during Chengdi's reign (r. 33–7 BCE) and was famous for forging an imperial decree and for arranging a real-estate development deal in connection with a second mausoleum complex. The comment drips with sarcasm, for Chen was an opportunist who was sometimes successful but always unprincipled. Kuang Heng's influence on Chengdi's religious observances may also underlie Yang's remarks, for in 32 BCE, Kuang Heng persuaded Chengdi to move the old altars to heaven-and-earth outside the capital, to the southern suburbs, and also to abandon the worship of the Five Lords that had been instituted by Han Wudi.

45 Cf. *Analects* 12.13, where Kongzi says he would prefer that there were no more lawsuits; also *Daxue*, par. 4, to the same effect. If the ruler had fewer faults, there would be no need for reproofs.

9.23 龍之潛亢。不獲其中矣。是以過中則惕。不及中則躍。其近於中乎。

9.24 聖人之道。譬猶日之中矣。不及則未。過則昃。

9.25 什一,天下之〔中〕正也。多則桀。寡則貉。

9.26 井田之田。田也。肉刑之刑。刑也。田也者與眾田之。刑也者與眾棄之。[24]

9.27 法無限。則庶人田侯田。處侯宅。食侯食。服侯服。人亦多不足矣。

9.28 為國不迪其法。而望其效。譬諸筭乎。

24 Another reading might be "The very best kind of fields are those plowed by the people, and the very worst kind of punishments are those abandoned [or rejected] by the people." Unfortunately, the superlative here can mean either "best" or "worst." And while Yang in an earlier passage praised the Xia's mutilating punishments (肉辟三千), there are many passages where Yang criticizes what he deems an overreliance on punishment.

having proper balance? Too hard a clay, and it will break. Too soft, and it will be as fragile as unfired clay."[46]

A dragon, if immersed in the deeps or flying too high, fails to attain the Mean.[47] That is why if people exceed it [the Mean], they become extremely cautious, and when they fall short, they then race to catch up.[48] That way they approach the Mean! The Way of the Sages is like the sun at noon. Before that point is reached, it is not yet at its apex, but once that point is past, it is all decline. 9.23–24

One in ten is the truest and best ratio in the realm. If taxes are heavier than that, the ruler becomes the cruelest of tyrants. But if the taxes are lighter, the ruler is no better than a barbarian![49] The very best field system[50] is that where fields are given to the masses to work. And the best sort of punishments are those meted out to those whom the masses reject![51] 9.25–26

If the laws make no provisions for a sumptuary system,[52] then some commoners will have fields[53] fit for a lord, live in houses fit for a lord, eat meals fit for a lord, and wear clothes fit for a lord. Meanwhile many others will lack even a bare sufficiency! 9.27–28

And if policy makers who fail to follow the proper models nevertheless look for results, then they are no better than those who idly manipulate the bamboo calculating rods before learning to calculate sums.[54]

---

46 The political implication is that the ruler must be neither too severe nor too lenient.

47 Adding "in the deeps," as implied, by reference to Hexagram 1 (Qian), where the dragon's flight is compared to the development and decline of things (潛龍勿用). Line 6, the highest point for the dragon, is thought to be inauspicious, as it represents a surfeit of *yang qi* and arrogance (亢龍有悔).

48 Or "leap to it" to close the gap.

49 Dong Zhongshu was one of several advisers to the throne to argue for setting agricultural taxes at either 1/10 (or, in some texts, 1/30) of the crop, with the larger ratio also associated with Fan Li's advice to King Goujian of Yue during the Zhanguo. See *Hanshu* 56.2111, 2520; 24A.1137. Yang thought that the Mo 貊, a seminomadic people to the north of the Central States, were highly uncivilized because they lacked a sense of the vital importance of the rites. Their leaders' decision to tax them so lightly meant that they paid no heed to the sort of expenses that should be incurred when encouraging performance of the rites and creation of the institutions associated with true civilization.

50 See *Mencius* 3A.3; and Dubs 1938, 3.506–36. Wang Mang, in the name of restoring antiquity, instituted the so-called King's Field System, which won him some support initially from the commoners, who lacked sufficient land to feed their families.

51 Translation tentative, based on *Liji*, "Wang zhi," which says, "If people are punished in the marketplace, they will be rejected by the masses" (刑人於市，與眾棄之). Cf. *Fayan* 13.24, 9.8. Wang Mang, of course, reinstituted the mutilating punishments.

52 Literally, "have no constraints." The reasoning may be that without the constraints of the sumptuary system, rich commoners could live like kings. However, another possible reading would applaud the built-in constraints in the penal code whereby the laws do not "reach to the nobility," lest so many of the nobility lose their estates and titles that commoners acquire them for their own.

53 Literally, "till fields," with the emphasis on hard work rather than vast possessions.

54 Literally, "are just like those . . ." Adding, "before learning to calculate sums," as implied.

卷第十

重黎

仲尼以來。國君將相卿士名臣參差不齊。
一概諸聖。譔重黎。

10.1 或問南正重司天。[1] 北正黎司地。今何僚也。曰近羲。近和。孰重。孰黎。曰羲近重。和近黎。

1 See the "Yaodian" in *Shangshu* 010116; cf. *Guoyu* 5.1/97/24, 6.10/106/4; *Shiji* 40.689–91. *Hanshu* 25A.1190 takes this to mean that Chong was in charge of the spirits whereas Li was in charge of the people. Cf. Yang's (ascribed, but possibly by Cui Yuan 崔瑗?) "Admonitions for the Taishi ling" (Zhen Taishi ling 太史令箴), which can be found in Zhang Zhenze 1993, 348–39: 重黎是司.

Chapter 10

Chong and Li

VERSE SUMMARY

Since the time of Zhongni, rulers, generals, chancellors, ministers, men in service, and famous officers have been judged by disparate standards. I judge them by a single standard, that of the sages. Thus, I have composed chapter 10, "Chong and Li."

....

Someone asked me, "If Chong, the Regulator of the South, was in charge 10.1
of the heavens, and Li, the Regulator of the North,[1] was in charge of earth, then what offices would correspond to theirs today?"[2]

"Theirs would be close to the offices of Xi and He."[3]

"Which would be Chong, and which Li?"

"Xi would be like Chong and He like Li."[4]

---

1 In antiquity, these officials supposedly calculated the path of the sun and of the Heart constellation to figure out the length of the agricultural seasons. In any case, as L'Haridon (2006, 89) remarks, this passage, expanding on *Shiji* 130.3285 (the autobiography of Sima Qian), immediately plunges us into the realm of the scribe-archivist and historian.

2 Li Gui explains, "True and false, beautiful and ugly [or "good and evildoing"], success and failure, preservation and loss—these are the means by which the ruler controls those below and the official serves his ruler." The commentary goes on to suggest that Yao is the ruler here, and Shun, the official.

3 One tradition identifies Xi and He as charioteers driving the horses that pull the sun across the sky. In 1 CE, Wang Mang urged Pingdi to set up the office of Xihe guan 羲和官, to which Liu Xin was appointed, with duties corresponding to those of the old Senior Archivist (*taishi ling*), who was in charge of astronomical and calendrical matters, and to those of the former minister of agriculture. Liu Xin was given another post in 5 CE, so he may or may not have continued as Xihe. In 14 CE, Wang Mang, as emperor, set up four assistants, all of whose titles referred to either Xi or He, since the "Yaodian" chapter of the *Documents* mentioned four aides to Xi and He, called the Four Marchmounts. See *Shangshu* 01.0062–77, 0347–0363. Apparently, Yang thought the phrase *xihe* referred to two separate offices, but see Needham 1954, 187–89.

4 Yang recalls an old legend in which Yao's two officers punished the San Miao 三苗 because they had tried to maintain regular communication between heaven and

10.2 或問黃帝終始。[2] 曰託也。昔者姒氏治水土。而巫步多禹。扁鵲盧人也。而醫多盧。夫欲讎[3] 偽者必假真。禹乎盧乎。終始乎。

10.3 或問渾天。曰落下閎營之。鮮于妄人度之。耿中丞象之。幾乎幾乎。莫之能違也。請問蓋(天)。[4] 曰蓋哉蓋哉。應難。未幾也。[5]

---

2 Following Li Gui, cited in Wang Rongbao (1987, 13.317), in his belief that a book entitled *The Yellow Emperor* stipulated a heavenly cycle 3,500 years long. Reference is made to cyclical theories in the "Treatise of the Feng and Shan Sacrifices" describing the time of Qin Shihuang (*Shiji* 28.1366–77), as noted in Wang Rongbao (1987, 13.317).

3 However, Li Gui glosses the verb as *lei* 類 ("to make [oneself] be in the same category," i.e., "be a match for"). For the reading of *chou* 讎 as *shou* 售, see Sima Guang, cited in Wang Rongbao (1987, 13.319).

4 For Yang's initial support of the Gaitian theory and later adoption of the Huntian, see *Taiping yulan* 2.6b–7a.

5 *Taiping yulan* 2.6–7a omits the phrase *ying nan* 應難; cf. *Xin lun*, "Zashi" 雜事 (Pokora 1975, entry 115, p. 116). Yu Yue (1874) theorizes that these two characters represent a gloss by Li Gui interpolated into the text.

Someone asked me about the cycles predicated in *The Yellow Emperor*.[5] 10.2

"That book just availed itself of his name.[6] Long ago, Yu ordered the water and the land, and now the shamans' paces mostly take Yu's name.[7] Bian Que was a native of Lu, and so physicians mostly claim to be from there too.[8] Invariably those who would peddle fakery pretend it is the real thing. Does that make each and every one of them another Yu? Does it make them from Lu? And does it make the book about cycles a work by the Yellow Emperor? [No!]"

Someone asked me about the Spherical-Heaven theory of celestial movements.[9] 10.3

"Luoxia Hong[10] laid it out [in 104 BCE]; Xianyu Wangren[11] performed the calculations to measure it. Geng Zhongcheng[12] drew a diagram for it. How close they came! How close! None could find a flaw in their work."

"Let me ask about the Cover-Heaven theory.[13]

"It covers, all right—it covers the truth![14] When difficult questions are posed of it, the answers do not even come close!"[15]

---

earth. See *Shangshu* 02.0319, 03.0674, 06.0644. The argument that this implies criticism of Wang Mang seems to read too much into this line.

5 Yang may be referring to *The Yellow Emperor's Succession Cycle*, one of the numerological treatises associated with Huangdi.

6 Or, as Andrew Plaks (pers. comm.) prefers, "It's an unwarranted attribution."

7 For the Pace of Yu, see Schafer 1977.

8 For Bian Que, see *Shiji* 105.2785–17. Li Gui identifies Lu as a place near the sacred Mount Tai.

9 For the Huntian, or Spherical-Heaven, theory, first described in full by Zhang Heng (a self-proclaimed disciple of Yang), see Cullen 2010. According to the Spherical-Heaven theory, heaven is a hollow sphere completely surrounding a flat earth, which extends wholly or partly across the sphere's horizontal diametral plane; earth is sometimes analogized to the yoke of an egg, with heaven the shell. The celestial sphere rotates daily about an axis inclined at 36 度 *du* above the northern horizon, or about 35 degrees (the latitude of the Yellow River basin), carrying the heavenly bodies with it. Day and night result from the sun rising and sinking over the edge of the earth, and the seasons result from its annual approach toward and recession from the north celestial pole, as it moves round the great circle of the ecliptic inclined at 24 *du* to the celestial equator.

10 Court astronomer during the reign of Han Wudi, ca. 104 BCE.

11 Court astronomer who flourished 78–75 BCE.

12 Geng may have been court astronomer during the reign of Han Xuandi.

13 This theory postulated an umbrella-like heaven rotating about a vertical (or, in some texts, tilted) axis passing through the center of a similarly shaped earth 80,000 *li* below it at the North Pole. The sun and other celestial bodies are attached to the underside of heaven and rotate with it once daily. According to the *Sui shu* treatise on astronomy, Yang composed eight (some editions say eighty-one, but that is almost certainly wrong) questions to "stump" (*nan* 難) the proponents of the Cover-Heaven (Gaitian) theory. See *Sui shu* 19.506.

14 Adding, "the truth."

15 Alternatively, with different punctuation, "Responses [to the Cover-Heaven theory] stump [the theorists]; they have not even come close!"

10.4 或問趙世多神。何也。曰神怪茫茫。若存若亡。聖人曼[6]云。

10.5 或問子胥種蠡。孰賢。曰胥也。俾吳作亂。破楚入郢。鞭尸藉館。皆不由德。謀越諫齊不式。不能去。卒眼之。種,蠡不強諫而山棲。俾其君詘社稷之靈而童僕。又終弊吳。賢皆不足邵也。至

6 Reading *man* 曼 as *bu* 不.

Someone asked me why so many spirits appeared during the reign of the Zhaos, rulers of Qin.[16] 10.4

"Spirits and prodigies are vague and indistinct. Sometimes they seem to exist and sometimes not. A sage does not speak of such matters."[17]

Someone asks who was more capable, Wu Zixu [the martial hero],[18] Wen Zhong, or Fan Li?[19] 10.5

"Wu Zixu engineered a coup in Wu,[20] broke Chu, and invaded the capital of Ying. He whipped the corpse of King Ping of Chu,[21] and he occupied the Chu official residences.[22] In no case did he follow the course of virtue. Wu Zixu's advice was ignored when he plotted against Yue and advised against attacking Qi. And since he found himself unable to leave Wu, in the end he "eyeballed" it.[23] As for Wen Zhong and Fan Li, they failed to remonstrate forcefully.[24] Instead, they perched high up on the mountainside.[25] They caused their lord to be humbled before the gods of the soil and grain[26] and reduced to the status of mere houseboy.[27] What was still worse: in the end, they destroyed Wu. As to being capable and wise, none of the three deserves high praise. And as for Fan Li's sending

16 As the ruling lines of Qin and Zhao 趙 derived from the same founder, "Zhao" often means the Qin. Certain Han texts refer to Qin Shihuang as Zhao Zheng 政. Therefore, this is perhaps an oblique criticism of the First Emperor, not to mention Zhao Jianzi 趙簡子, who was known to be credulous, and who claimed he had been to paradise in a dream or a delirious state during a grave illness. *Shiji* 43 ("Hereditary House of Zhao" 趙世家) mentions many prodigies, prophetic dreams, and the like. Similarly, the *Shiji* "Treatise on the Feng and Shan Sacrifices" describes the credulity of the First Emperor, along with that of Han Wudi (r. 141–87 BCE).

17 *Analects* 7.21 says that Kongzi "did not speak" of prodigies (*guai* 怪).

18 Adviser to King Helü of Wu, who helped plan Yue's defeat. For Wu Zixu in legend, see Johnson 1981.

19 Wen Zhong served the King of Yue, Goujian, until Goujian forced him to commit suicide.

20 This refers to the fact that Wu Zixu (d. 485 BCE) helped Helü kill the King of Wu and make himself king.

21 Adding "of King Ping of Chu," for sense. *Guliang zhuan* 11.4.13/138.7 (Lord Ding of Lu 4) speaks of "whipping the grave of King Ping."

22 Including the back palaces of those establishments, where women lived.

23 Wu Zixu requested that his eyeballs be nailed to the city gates of the Wu capital after his death so that he could witness the invasion of Wu with his own eyes. "It" refers to Yue's invasion of Wu, which Wu Zixu not only predicted but, by the time of his death, welcomed, since the Wu ruler had mistreated him and ordered his execution.

24 I.e., they failed to remonstrate against King Goujian of Yue (r. 497–465 BCE), though they knew Goujian's attack on Wu would be unsuccessful.

25 Here "to perch" (on a branch like a bird) means "to be recluses." Their perch was in the city of Kuaiji 會稽, which was high up on a hill. Clearly, they were intent mostly upon keeping themselves safe. The Yue king Goujian was defeated by the troops of Wu, at which point Wu's troops surrounded Kuaiji and besieged it.

26 I.e., the legitimating gods of his ruling line. Kings and rulers typically report major undertakings, especially war, to the local gods of the soil and grain in the hope of securing their blessings. They are also supposed to report their failings to the gods.

27 In Fuchai's establishment.

蠡策種而遁。肥矣哉。[7]

10.6 或問陳勝吳廣。曰亂。[8] 曰不若是則秦不亡。曰亡秦乎。恐秦未亡而先亡矣。

10.7 或問六國並。其已久矣。一病一瘳。迄始皇。三載而咸。[9] 時激。地保。人事乎。曰具。請問事。曰孝公以下。強兵力農以蠶食六國。事也。保。曰東溝大河。南阻高山。西采雍梁。[10] 北鹵涇垠。

---

7 According to one essay, Fan Li wrote to Wen Zhong, another official of King Goujian, saying, "The birds in flight have been exhausted, the good bows packed away; the crafty rabbits are dead, and the running dogs boiled for soup. You had better go, certainly!" See Su Shi, "On Fan Li," in Liu Shi Shun 1979: "He did escape and enjoy prosperity!" Han Jing (1992, 230n6) ties the *fei* to transcending convention.

8 See *Hanshu* 31.1786.

9 Reading *xian* 咸 as *he* 和 or *fa* 法. According to Wang Rongbao (1987, 13.340), Sima Guang, cited in Wang Rongbao (1987, 13.345), reads *xian* as *tong* (unified), however; and Yu Yue (1874), also cited in Wang Rongbao 1987, reads it as *jue* 絕 ([before] "being cut off"), noting the similarity in form between *xian* and another loan character and the *Yi Zhoushu*'s language in describing the "cutting off" of the Shang tyrant Zhou 紂 by King Wu of Zhou (ca. 1050 BCE). Wang Rongbao (1987, 13.339), however, thought that the statement "three years" refers either to three decades (roughly the time the First Emperor spent on the throne), or to the "three years" Wang Mang served as regent after the death of Pingdi. David R. Knechtges follows the former solution. In Wang Rongbao's view, every severe critique of Qin represents a jab at Wang Mang, which I doubt.

10 Sima Guang takes "Liang" to mean Liangzhou or Sichuan; see Wang Rongbao (1987, 13.344). But it is far more probable that Yang here points to the "land within the passes."

a letter to Wen Zhong urging him to go into hiding like Fan—that was certainly rich!"[28]

Someone asked me about Chen Sheng and Wu Guang. 10.6

"Bywords for rebels."[29]

"But had they not acted like this, Qin would not have fallen."

"Was it they who brought Qin down? I fear Qin was lost a long time before the end."

Someone asked me about the Six Kingdoms' close rivalry, which went 10.7
on for quite a while, with one state ailing as another healed.[30] Yet "when it came down to the First Emperor, within three years, the realm was at peace."[31] Was this because the time was ripe,[32] its land was more defensible, or was this due to human agency?"[33]

"It was due to all these factors."

"I beg to ask about human agency."

"From the time of Duke Xiao[34] on, they strengthened their troops and they put their efforts into agriculture, so that they might nibble away at the Six Kingdoms like greedy silkworms—that was human agency."

"And the defenses?"

"In the east, Qin had the Yellow River for a moat. To the south, it was impenetrable due to the high mountains.[35] In the west it reaped the fertile Yong and Liang River valleys.[36] In the north, it annexed the banks of the

28 Or "They were too fat" (i.e., living it up). Alternatively, "[that was a case of urging him] to fly off," since Fei 肥 in hexagram "Dun" 遯 (Flight), "Ninth Line at the Top," is glossed by most commentators, including Liu Shipei (1916), as *fei* 飛 (flight).

29 Or, "those who would confound [the truth]," since Chen She, who believed he should be emperor, put silk documents into the bellies of fish that he knew soldiers would buy; these were regarded as omens indicating that his rebellion was mandated by heaven.

30 The Six Kingdoms are Han, Zhao, Wei (successor states to Jin, which was partitioned), Yan, Qi, and Chu. Wu and Yue were considered too far south to be included among the Central Plains states, and both Wu and Yue had troubled histories.

31 It is clearly an exaggeration to say that the unification process took only three years, but about three years elapsed between the First Emperor's death and the rise of Liu Bang, founder of the Han dynasty. Most premodern commentators suggest that Yang wrote "three cycles" (i.e., "nine years") rather than "three years," for within nine years (230–221 BCE), all the Six Kingdoms were destroyed. As no solution seems entirely satisfactory, my translation preserves the original wording.

32 Andrew Plaks (pers. comm.) prefers "The timing hastened [unification]."

33 The question does not credit heaven's intervention on Qin's behalf as a factor in Qin's rise to power.

34 Reigned 361–338 BCE.

35 Of the Qinling range.

36 Adding "fertile," which is implied. "Reaped," according to Wang Rongbao (1987, 13.345), means "reaped the benefit of taxing." These lands to the west of the Qin capital of Xianyang eventually became part of the Youfufeng metropolitan district during Han, where the sacred altars were built. Though the acquisition by Qin in 316 of Sichuan was even more crucial to its eventual success over its major rivals, the river valleys associated with the Yong and Liang Rivers were extremely fertile.

便則申。否則蟠。保也。激。曰始皇方[11]斧。將相方刀。六國方木。將相方肉。激也。

10.8 或問秦伯列為侯衛。卒吞天下。而赧曾無以制乎。曰天子制公侯伯子男也。庸節。節莫差於僭。僭莫重於祭。祭莫重於地。地莫重於天。則襄文宣靈。其兆也。昔者襄公始僭。西畤以祭白帝。文宣靈宗[12]興鄜, 密, 上, 下。用事四帝。而天王不匡。反致文武

11 Wang Rongbao (1987, 13.345), paraphrase of Sima Guang. Wang also cites Zheng Xuan's commentary to the *Odes*, which reads *fang* 方 as *deng* 等 (to be equal to or of the same type), to explain Li Gui's gloss, which he does not accept.

12 However, Li Gui takes *zong* 宗 to mean *zun* 尊 (to honor), here presumably in an adverbial sense modifying *xing* 興 (to set up or establish).

Jing River. When it suited its purposes,[37] it extended itself. When it didn't, it curled up tight as a coiled snake.[38] Such were its defenses."

"And the time being ripe?"

"Right at that juncture, the First Emperor was an ax, and his generals and ministers were sharp knives. Right at that juncture, the Six Kingdoms were soft as wood, and their generals and ministers, as soft as meat under the blade. The timing was right."

Someone asked me, "The lords of Qin were ranked as 'Lord Protectors' for the Zhou overlords,[39] yet in the end they swallowed up its entire realm. Did King Nan[40] of Zhou really have no way to control them?" 10.8

"The Son of Heaven keeps the five noble ranks in order, so that the usages might be regulated.[41] With regulations, the worst infringement is usurpation, and of usurpations, the most serious concerns the sacrifices. With sacrifices, nothing is more serious than the sacrifices to the land,[42] and with land, nothing is more serious than that dedicated to heaven.[43] Thus, the Qin kings Xiang, Wen, Xuan, and Ling were already the first signs of usurpation.[44]

Long ago, Duke Xiang began the usurpation by offering sacrifices at the Western Altar to the White Lord.[45] Dukes Wen, Xuan, and Ling were the ancestral founders in setting up altars at Li, Mi, Upper, and Lower, in service to the Four Lords.[46] Not only did heaven's kings, the Zhou overlords, not correct them; they twice sent them the sacrificial meats that had been offered to their own Kings Wen and Wu![47] That explains

---

37 Or "When the circumstances were favorable. . . . When they were not favorable, . . ."

38 The language of extension and coiling up or retreating is applied not only to the snake but also to the dragon, portrayed as the most marvelous of snakes and the emblem of the noble man. See *Fayan* 5.5.

39 Adding "for the Zhou overlords," as implied. The Zhou overlords were kings.

40 King Nan (r. 314–256 BCE) was the last Zhou king.

41 Here "usages" probably refers to sumptuary privileges (e.g., ceremonial carriages and robes), graded prerogatives that differ by rank.

42 I.e., those offered to the gods of grain and soil (signifying political legitimacy over the area).

43 Han Jing (1992, 234n3) takes "earth" to mean "the land dedicated to sacrifices," and heaven to refer to the "land where sacrifices are offered to heaven."

44 Adding "of usurpation," as implied. The decline of a dynasty happens over many generations, as "Xici" insists. Each of the Qin kings mentioned whittled away at Zhou power.

45 In 770 BCE. Only the Son of Heaven should sacrifice to heaven, earth, and the deities of the four directions and center. Note that Yang does not call the rulers "kings."

46 The White Lord was the first to receive worship, followed by the Four Lords. In 756 BCE, Duke Wen of Qin instituted the Li Altar (located at Li) to worship the White Lord. In 672 BCE Duke Xuan of Qin built the Mi Altar south of the Wei River to worship the Green Lord. In 422 BCE Duke Ling of Qin built the Shang Altar to worship Huangdi and the Xia Altar to worship Yandi, the Red Lord. Missing during Qin rule is any altar to a Black Lord. Later commentators, including Zheng Xuan and Sun Yirang (cited in Wang Rongbao 1987), presuming a Five Phases system, try to insert that sacrifice into the narrative to tie the Qin, and especially the First Emperor, to worship of the Black Lord.

47 The sacrificial meats offered to Kings Wen and Wu were to be shared only with the Central States scions who had the same family name as the Zhou house or with the

胙。是以四疆之內各以其力來侵。攘肌及骨。而赧獨何以制秦乎。[13]

10.9 或問嬴政二十六載。天下擅秦。[14] 秦十五載而楚。楚五載而漢。五十載之際。而天下三擅。天邪人邪。[15] 曰具。周建子弟。列名城。[16] 班五爵。流之十二。當時雖欲漢。得乎。六國蚩蚩。[17] 為嬴弱姬。卒之[18] 屏營。[19] 嬴擅其政。故天下擅秦。秦失其猷。罷侯置守。守失其微 (=徽?)。天下孤睽。[20] 項氏暴強。[21] 改宰侯王。故天下擅楚。擅楚之月。有漢創業山南。發迹三秦。追項山東。故天下擅漢。

13 See Han Jing (1992, 236n8). Wang Rongbao (1987, 14.347) cites *Lunheng* 26.115/26–116/3 for the story.

14 Han Jing (1992, 237n1) reads *shan* 擅 merely as "handed over" (*chuan di* 傳遞), but *shan* always carries the whiff of unlawful arrogation of powers to oneself, hence my translation.

15 Cf. the preface to the *Shiji* "Table on the Transitional Period, Qin-Chu" (*Shiji* 16.760).

16 Reading *lie* 列 (set up) as *lie* 裂 (split up).

17 The reduplicative *chi chi* 蚩蚩 suggests their actions were "wormlike," hence, my translation. Liu Shipei (1916) reads *chi* as *bo* 驳 (refractory), on the basis of the *Fangyan*, but probably that gives these rulers too much credit.

18 Or, following *Guangya* and Wang Niansun, cited in Wang Rongbao (1987, 14.357): "In the end, they were fearful and weakened."

19 On the basis of a parallel passage ascribed to Yang, Wang Rongbao (1987, 14.357) takes *ping ying* 屏營 instead to mean "made them incapable of rising up" (i.e., weakened them). Following a gloss in the *Guangya*, Han Jing (1992, 238n4) argues that the Six Kingdoms in their weakness failed to rise up, and they kept close to their own camps. Otherwise, *ping ying* 屏營 probably means "it [Qin] they screened [or shielded] and built up [or made camp]," implying that the Six Kingdoms did Qin's dirty work for it. Li Gui reads *zhi* 之 as *zhi* 至, meaning "it came to the point where . . . ," but this change is probably unnecessary.

20 Reading *gu kui* 孤睽 as "felt isolated and stared at each other."

21 Or, reading *bao* 暴 as *turan* 突然 (quickly): "Xiang Yu quickly waxed strong."

why each of the local lords within the four borders of Zhou deployed his forces to invade its lands, relying on his own strength to pick the meat clean, down to the very bones. So why single out King Nan for his failure to discipline Qin?"[48]

Someone asked me, "For the twenty-six years Ying Zheng was on the throne,[49] power in the realm was arrogated by Qin. The Qin Empire lasted a mere fifteen years before Xiang Yu of Chu came along, and Chu lasted for a mere five years before it was Han's turn. Within the space of fifty years, then, the realm had changed hands no fewer than three times. Was this Heaven's doing or that of humans?" 10.9

"Both. Zhou set up sons and younger brothers as vassals. It parceled out the famous walled cities and distributed the Five Noble Ranks,[50] conferring them on twelve great noble houses.[51] At the time even if someone *had* wanted to be another Han, would it have been possible? [No!]

> The Six Kingdoms were so incredibly stupid and servile[52]
> that they, on Ying's behalf, weakened the Ji ruling line of Zhou.[53]
> And in the end, they dithered so
> that the Ying line could take over their administrations.
> Thus, power in the realm came to be handed over to Qin.
> But the Qin lost its way so badly that it
> dismissed the local lords, setting up governors in their place.
> Its governors were mired in minutiae,[54]
> and everyone eyed each other with deep suspicion.
> Xiang Yu was a tyrant and a bully,
> but he converted his chancellors into nobles and kings, and so
> power in the realm was handed over to Chu.
> But in the first month when Chu gained sway over the entire realm,
> the Han ruling house[55] began to build its legitimate base

---

descendants of the Two Kings (i.e., the founders of Xia and Shang). No ritual meats should ever have been sent to the Qin ruling house, which did not qualify for the honor. Nonetheless, twice, in 360 and in 334 BCE, King Xian of Zhou (r. 368–320 BCE) sent Duke Xiao and King Hui 惠 of Qin a portion of the sacrificial meats just offered to Kings Wen and Wu. The translation inserts "twice" into the text.

48 Alternatively, "So how could King Nan on his own [or relying on his own power] discipline Qin?" Or, more literally, "What means could King Nan, as an exception, have employed to control Qin?" King Nan ceded to Qin thirty-six walled cities with a population of thirty thousand people, which is why he was sometimes singled out for blame.

49 I.e., the First Emperor of Qin.

50 See the preceding passage for the Five Ranks.

51 The commentators cannot agree on the identity of all twelve on the list.

52 These lines about Qin and Xiang Yu rhyme—hence the format here.

53 Adding "ruling line of Zhou," as implied.

54 Alternatively "constrained," if *wei* 微 is read as *hui* 徽, following Wang Rongbao (1987, 14.358). Another possible translation is "The governors lost control over all the rules," so many were they.

55 The phrase *you Han* 有漢 refers to Liu Bang, who "had Han" for his territorial base.

天也。人。曰兼才尚拳。[22] 右計左數。動謹於時。人也。天不人不因。人不天不成。[23]

10.10 或問楚敗垓下。方死。曰天也。諒乎。[24] 曰漢屈群策。[25] 群策屈群力。楚憞群策而自屈其力。[26] 屈人者克。自屈者負。天曷故焉。[27]

10.11 或問秦楚既為天典命矣。秦縊灞上。楚分江西。興廢何速乎。曰天胙光德。而隕明忒。昔在有熊高陽高辛唐虞三代。咸有顯懿。故天(因而)胙之。為神明主。且著在天庭。是生民之願也。厥饗國

22 Reading radical 75 instead of 64. Han Jing (1992, 238n9) prefers "valuing strongmen" or the "powerful interests" (*quan* 權).

23 See commentary to the "Jin Teng" (Metal Coffer) chapter in *Shangshu quanji* 26.38a.

24 However, Li Gui and Han Jing (1992, 240n1) read *liang* 諒 as "true," so the sentence means "Was it true?" or "Were his words true?" In that case, *liang* would function as an adjective rather than a noun.

25 Alternatively, reading *qu* 屈 as *jin* 盡 (exhausted, depleted, used to the full), following Wang Rongbao (1987, 14.362). This entry hinges on the various associations of the character *qu*.

26 If one reads *dao* 刀 (knife) instead of *li* 力 (strength), this passage refers to Xiang Yu's suicide: "and so he himself submitted to the knife."

27 Yu Xingwu 1940, *ce* 冊 4, 1/4a, suggests that the *gu* 故 (cause) be read as *gu* 辜 (crime), since the two characters were cognate in early times. In that case, the sentence would read "As for heaven, what crime did it commit in this case?"

south of the Qinling Mountains,[56]
making tracks[57] in the San-Qin area[58] and
pursuing Xiang Yu to the area east of the mountains, and so
power in the realm came to be handed over to Han.
That was Heaven's doing."[59]

"And human agency?"

"That lay in bringing together talented men and valuing[60] expediency. Han Gaozu's right-hand men made plans while those on his left calculated the probable outcomes of a given policy. That, plus their attention to proper timing when they acted, was human agency. As the saying goes, 'If Heaven had no men, it would have nothing to rely upon, and if men had no Heaven, they would be unable to complete their plans.'"[61]

Someone asked me, "When Xiang Yu of Chu was defeated at Gaixia,[62] 10.10
and he was on the point of death, he said it was all Heaven's doing. Was this an excuse?"

"Liu Bang, King of Han, exploited every trick in the book, and his many stratagems bent every strong man to his use. Xiang Yu of Chu exhausted himself. Abjuring his many strategists, he would have others submit to *his* force.[63] Exploiting others always means victory, while exhausting oneself always means defeat. In what way, then, was *that* Heaven's doing?"

Someone asked me about Qin and Chu: "Their rulers had already received 10.11
the Mandates decreed by Heaven, but the last Qin ruler was strangled at Bashang[64] and Xiang Yu of Chu was dismembered on the west bank of the Wu River.[65] How quickly did they rise and fall!"

"Heaven blesses[66] those who exemplify virtue, and 'strikes down those with obvious faults.' Long, long ago, there was Youxiong, the Yellow Emperor, Gaoyang, Gaoxin, Yao, and Shun, and the three dynasties of Xia, Shang, and Zhou. Each rule was renowned for its virtue, and so Heaven blessed them. They became the chief officiants in sacrifices to the gods. Moreover, they became illustrious in Heaven's Court and thus

56 The phrase "south of the Qinling Mountains" means "south of Mount Zhong" 終山, in Hanzhong 漢中, near Xianyang. If one controlled Mount Zhong, one could control the territories of Ba and Shu to the southwest.

57 Andrew Plaks (pers. comm.) prefers "to score successes in the San-Qin." "San-Qin" refers to Henei, Hedong, and Henan.

58 I.e., Yong 雍, Sai 塞, and Zhai 翟.

59 Or, emphasizing the inexplicability of the transfer of power to the Han, "Heaven only knows!" (as in *Shiji*).

60 Or "attending to."

61 The phrase "their plans" is added, because it is implied in a Han proverbial saying.

62 In present-day Anhwei, Lingbi 靈璧 County.

63 The extant *Xunzi* contains a description of a suspicious lord who failed because he "made his own plans, thinking that none would compare with his own" (*mo jiruo* 莫己若). Throughout this paragraph, the language recalls that in *Mencius* 3A.2, on not bowing before the high and mighty (威武不屈).

64 A location east of Chang'an (in present-day Shaanxi, near Xi'an).

65 For parallelism, I have identified the river where Xiang Yu was dismembered.

66 Or "magnifies," "makes great."

久長。若秦,楚強閱震撲。胎藉三正。[28] 播其虐於黎苗。子弟且欲喪之。況於民乎。況於鬼神乎。廢未速也。

10.12 或問仲尼大聖。則天曷不胙。曰無土。[29] 然則舜禹有土乎。曰舜以堯作土。禹以舜作土。

10.13 或問聖人表裏。曰威儀文辭,表也。德行忠信,裏也。

10.14 或問義帝初矯。劉龕南陽。項救河北。二方分崩。一離一合。設秦得人。如何。曰人無為秦也。喪其靈久矣。

10.15 韓信黥布皆劍立。[30] 南面稱孤。卒窮時戮。[31] 無乃勿乎。或曰勿則

28 However, Han Jing (1992, 243n4) argues that the *sanzheng* originally referred to the great officers, ministers, and leaders of allied groups (not to a superstitious theory of dynastic turnover). Han reads *tai jie* 胎藉 (lit., "at birth availed themselves" or "tread upon and disordered") as *daiqi* 怠棄 (neglected and abandoned), emending the text on the basis of the received "Ganshi" chapter in the *Documents* (*Shangshu* 05.0029) It is even possible that *jie* 藉 = *ji* 籍, so that the phrase refers to the "registry of births."

29 Li Gui defines "bless" as "make him ruler" (i.e., put him on the throne). Contrast *Shiji* 17.760. *Bohu tong* (now cited in *Shiji* 16 *suoyin* 索引): "The sage without land does not become a king" (*sheng ren wu tu bu wang* 聖人無土不王), which directly contradicts *Zhanguo ce*, Zhao 2.1. The prevailing theory that those who had no land could not become emperors is noted in the concluding Appraisal to *Shiji* 16. *Xunzi* 52/14/9–10; (Riegel, II, 207) translates, "If there is no territory, then the people will have no secure households (*anju* 安居). If there are no [loyal] people, then the territory will not be guarded. If there is no Way and no model, then the people will not come."

30 However, Wang Rongbao (1987, 14.368) reads *jian* 劍 (sword) as *jian* 撿, which he then glosses as *gong* 拱 (to support), based on *Shuowen jiezi*. Han Jing (1992, 246n1) says this explanation is farfetched.

31 Following Wang Rongbao (1987, 14.368), for the four-character phrase *zu qiong shi lu* 卒窮時戮. Yu Yue (1874), cited approvingly in Wang Rongbao (1987, 14.369), would read into these lines a warning to Wang Mang, whose imprisonment and torture(?) of Chunyu Zhang 淳于張 (d. 8 BCE) and demotion of Chengdi's consort, Zhao Feiyan 趙飛燕, from the rank of dowager empress in 1 BCE initially won Wang a reputation for virtue. This reading is highly speculative, but another Chunyu *is* mentioned immediately below.

the object of adulation by all the living. They enjoyed possession of the realm for a very long time indeed.[67] As for Qin and Chu, given their fierce battles and violent strikes and their intrusion into the Three Rules,[68] they cast their oppression over the common people. Even their own sons and younger brothers wanted them dead, and this was all the more true among the people and the spirits! Their demise was not quick enough!"

Someone asked me about Kongzi, "If he was such a great sage, why did Heaven not bless him?" 10.12

"He had no land to use as a base."[69]

"If that was so, then did Shun and Yu have land?"

"Shun had land to rule on account of Yao; and Yu, on account of Shun."

Someone asked me about the exterior and the interior[70] of the sage. 10.13

"Impressive decorum[71] and exquisitely patterned phrasing—those are the visible expressions of the sage. And compelling conduct combined with faithful duty to superiors and peers—those are the inner qualities."[72]

Someone asked me about the time when the Righteous Emperor[73] was set up.[74] "Liu Bang had just taken Nanyang commandery, and Xiang Yu had saved the area north of the Yellow River. The two sides had divided the collapsing Qin Empire between them, acting sometimes as allies and sometimes as opponents. Supposing that Qin at that point had acquired some real men in its service,[75] how would that have changed the situation?" 10.14

"No man of substance would have acted on behalf of Qin.[76] It had lost its vitality a long time before that surely!"

"Han Xin and Qing Bu[77] both rose to power by the sword and each faced 10.15

---

67 Not only did the rulers themselves possess the empire; through their descendants and succeeding dynasties, they continued to be worshiped.

68 See the "Oath at Gan" ("Ganshi") chapter of the *Documents* for the term Sanzheng 三正 (*Shangshu* 07.0031), where Zheng Xuan's commentary defines the Three Rules as the three modes of equilibrium among heaven, earth, and humans. I suspect that the accusation means something like "they intruded themselves into the major dynastic cycles ordained by Heaven."

69 The translation adds "to use as a base." *Mencius* 5A.6 says, "Heaven puts aside the ruler only if he is like Jie or Zhou and, if he is a commoner, he has the recommendation of an emperor. That is why Kongzi, . . . Yi, Yi Yin, and the Duke of Zhou never possessed the empire."

70 I.e., the visible expressions and the internal proclivities.

71 Or "bearing."

72 The phrase rendered as "faithful duty to superiors and peers" means loyalty and trustworthiness (*zhong xin* 忠信). The commentators say that this passage shows that the inside and outside are of one and the same stuff or tenor.

73 A puppet emperor.

74 Usually, *jiao* 矯 means (1) set things right or (2) arrogate power to oneself. The second meaning probably colors its main meaning here, which is *ju* 舉 (to raise up).

75 I.e., to enter its service at that point.

76 Andrew Plaks (pers. comm.) prefers "No one would have been willing to give his life for Qin."

77 Two of Liu Bang's allies, who were eventually removed from office.

無名。如何。曰名者謂令名也。忠不終而躬逆。焉攸令。

10.16 或問淳于越。曰伎曲。[32] 請問。曰始皇方虎挒而梟磔。[33] 噬士猶腊肉也。越與亢眉。[34] 終無橈辭。[35] 可謂伎矣。仕无妄之國。[36] 食无妄之粟。分无妄之橈。[37] 自令之閒[38] 而不違。可謂曲矣。

10.17 或問茅焦歷井幹之死。[39] 使始皇奉虛左之乘。蔡生欲安項咸陽。不

32 Traditional commentaries take *ji* 伎 to mean "strong man" or entertainer. See Wang Rongbao (1987, 14.370); Han Jing (1992, 247n1) glosses *ji* 伎 as *zhi* 支吾 = 抵拒 (to hold firm [being ready to resist]) and also as 駊 "strong as a horse." *Jiji* refers to "boxers," "pugilists." But *ji* more generally refers to experts with marketable skills, including entertainers.

33 This characterization of Qin (not the First Emperor) appears also in *Zhanguo ce* (Shanghai ed.), 869.

34 Following Wang Rongbao (1987, 14.370), in reading *kang mei* 亢眉 as *yang mei* 揚眉 (to raise the eyebrows); Han Jing (1992, 247n3) follows Wang. But since *kang* often implies opposition between equals (*kang* 伉), one could also translate this as "was every bit a match for him," as this implies "looked him straight in the eye and operated on the same level."

35 Reading nao 橈 as *nao* 撓, "to bend," "to flinch."

36 The phrase *buwang* comes from *Changes*, "Xu gua" 1; also from the "Wuzi zhi ge" 五子之歌, a late chapter from the pseudo-Kong "Old Text" chapters. However, there is an alternative reading whereby *wuwang* means *buyu* 不虞 ("unexpected" and, by extension, "undeserved"); the second reading is offered in Wang Rongbao (1987, 14.371). I follow Li Gui, who reads *nao* 橈 as *ce* 策 ("tally" for an official appointed temporarily).

37 Wang Rongbao (1987, 14.369) reads *nao* 橈 as *rao* 饒 (plenty). However, Zhu Junsheng 朱駿聲 reads *nao* as *yao* 燿 = *rong* 榮 (glory), so that the phrase means "shared in its [Qin's] glory" or "took his portion of the glory." Han Jing (1992, 248n4) prefers Zhu's gloss, on the grounds that Wang's reading would introduce a repetition into Yang's description.

38 Reading *zi ling zhi* (自令之) not as *shan shi* 善是 (approving this [Qin's policy), following Liu Shipei 1916, but as a mistake for "[Bao]bo Lingzhi," an officer at the Qin court who reprimanded the future First Emperor. A third possibility, following Han Jing (1992, 248n4), reads "that he [Yue] so valued his own person/body that he did not resist." A fourth possibility is to read the character *ling* as "local prefect": "that he did not resist [the worst policies of Qin] from the time he entered the lowest ranks of government service."

39 Note, however, that both Sima Guang, cited in Wang Rongbao (1987, 14.373), and Wang Rongbao himself (in ibid.) argue that the severed limbs of the dead were piled up like well railings.

south, declaring himself a sovereign ruler. In the end each was sentenced to the harshest possible punishment under the law:[78] execution with all his family members. Was this not the height of idiocy?"

Someone said to me, "Had they been so very stupid, they would never have made their reputations, so how can you say that?!"

"The word 'reputation' means 'a good name.' When loyalty does not persist to the end, and a person foments a rebellion, what basis is there for a good name?"[79]

Someone asked me about Chunyu Yue.[80] 10.16

"A professional strong man[81] who bent."[82]

"Please explain."

"The First Emperor, just at that juncture, was fierce as a tiger tearing limb from limb or a savage bird[83] dismembering its prey. He was chewing up the men who served him as if they were dried meat. Chunyu Yue was brave enough to raise an eyebrow at such conduct,[84] and to the end, Yue never flinched in his speeches, which made him fit to be pronounced a strong man, certainly. But Chunyu Yue loyally served a country without hope;[85] he lived on a salary from a dynastic house without hope; and he accepted a charge and tally as representative of a ruler for whom there was no hope.[86] That Chunyu Yue offered no resistance to the First Emperor's policies from the time of Baobo Lingzhi—that could well be called 'being bent.'"[87]

Someone asked me about Mao Jiao and Master Cai.[88] "Mao had to make 10.17
his way through the piles of corpses flung every which way in wells and under railings in order to convince the First Emperor to offer his mother the empty place to his left in the royal carriage.[89] Master Cai wanted to persuade Xiang Yu to make his capital at Xianyang, but not only did Cai

78 Both were accused of treason, and Han Xin was cut in two at the waist by order of Dowager Empress Lü.

79 Or "How does this contribute to a good name?" Note the pun between "loyalty" and "end," both *zhong*.

80 An Academician and adviser of the First Emperor of Qin.

81 This translation tries to convey the sense that he was strong enough to oppose Zhou Qingchen but not strong enough to enter into a real fight with his emperor over the most important question facing the new dynasty.

82 Or "was forced to back down." *Mencius* 3B.2 plainly equates greatness with "not bending to power and military might."

83 Probably an owl.

84 Adding "at such conduct," as implied.

85 A country, dynastic line, or ruler is "without hope" when he or it is immoral.

86 The ruler holds one half of the tally, while his obedient servant as his representative takes the other half, so that he may carry out the ruler's orders in the ruler's name.

87 All these attitudes can be described as "bent" (*qu* 曲), meaning "bending to an illegitimate power or corrupt idea."

88 Mao Jiao remonstrated with the future First Emperor of Qin; and Master Cai, with Xiang Yu.

89 Or "in the empty carriage on his left." After making this offer, the First Emperor personally escorted his mother back to Xianyang and reinstalled her in the palace, ending her temporary exile.

能移。又亨之。其者未辯與。[40] 曰生捨其木侯而謂人木侯。亨不亦宜乎。焦逆訐而順守之。[41] 雖辯。劘虎牙矣。[42]

10.18 或問甘羅之悟呂不韋。張辟強之覺平勃。皆以十二齡。戊, 良乎。曰才也。戊良。不必父祖。

10.19 或問酈食其說陳留。下敖倉。說齊。罷歷下軍。何辯也。韓信襲齊。以身脂鼎。[43] 何訥也。曰夫辯也者。自辯也。如辯人。幾矣。

---

40 Han Jing (1992, 249n2) says, "Probably it was because his rhetoric was not skillful enough."

41 The reading implicitly contrasts *jie* 訐 (= *ni* 逆?) with *shun* 順, "going against and with the current," but *shun shou* 順守 can mean simply "defended it in compliance with the norms." Sima Guang, cited in Wang Rongbao (1987, 14.373), takes the phrase *shun shou* to mean "to exhort" the ruler to adopt the virtuous course of action.

42 Cf. *Han Feizi* 12/23/1–2 for 批其逆鱗; the later idiom *luo hu xu* 捋虎鬚 means something like "to beard the lion in his den."

43 See *Shiji* 97.2705, which casts Li Yiji as a loyal classicist intent upon offering his formidable powers of persuasion to good causes (i.e., the Han founder).

fail to sway him, but Xiang had him boiled alive. Was his an inept persuasion?"

"Master Cai, forgetting that he himself was no better than a monkey, then called the other person a monkey.[90] Was it not fit and proper that he was boiled alive? Mao Jiao, face-to-face with the emperor, went on the attack, and so brought him into compliance.[91] This may have been a fine piece of persuasion, but surely it was rubbing up against the tiger's muzzle!"

Someone asked me about Gan Luo's enlightening Lü Buwei,[92] and Zhang 10.18
Biqiang's alerting Chen Ping[93] and Zhou Bo, each at the age of twelve. "Was this remarkable insight possible because they were, respectively, Gan Mao's grandson and Zhang Liang's[94] son?"

"They were talented, but not because they had Gao Mao and Zhang Liang as grandfather and father."[95]

Someone asked me, "Li Yiji[96] persuaded Liu Bang to attack Chenliu, and 10.19
[later] he persuaded the Ao Granary commander to surrender. He then persuaded Qi to disband its army at Lixia.[97] Now those were some persuasions! But when Han Xin came to attack Qi, they used Li's body fat as tallow to grease a bronze tripod.[98] How was it that his powers of persuasion proved so inept then?"

"Now, as we all know, the phrase 'powers of persuasion' refers to persuading yourself to undertake the right course of action.[99] Persuading others of something—that's really quite dangerous!"[100]

90 The other person is Xiang Yu.

91 The probable implication: his defiance finally made the First Emperor comply with his duty. However, the phrase could conceivably allude to Mao's complicity in *it* (Qin rule), which preserved Qin's good reputation (for the moment), even as it preserved Mao's own life.

92 Gan Luo, at the age of twelve *sui*, finally managed to persuade Lü, a senior minister, about several others' misconduct.

93 Chen Ping reportedly devised the "six schemes" that allowed Liu Bang to secure the empire; then he served Liu Bang, his wife, and his son as senior adviser.

94 Zhang Liang, a loyal ally of Liu Bang, served as chancellor under Huidi and Dowager Empress Lü. Gan Mao was an official serving Qi and Chu in the late Zhanguo period.

95 Literally, "Gan Mao and Zhang Liang were talented, [but] it did not have to be because of their fathers and grandfathers." Here, Yang Xiong asks what heredity has to do with talent (and, by implication, perhaps, virtue).

96 Li Yiji was a famous persuader in service to Liu Bang.

97 Qi was the last of the "revived" kingdoms after the collapse of Qin power to resist the Han under Liu Bang, and was controlled by General Tian Guang and his chancellor Tian Gou. Lixia is west of present-day Jinan in Shandong.

98 Tian Guang punished Li Yiqi for what he mistook to be Li's act of treachery, but it was actually Han Xin who committed the act of treachery, since Han did not want Li Yiqi to secure a victory without committing troops.

99 I have added "to undertake the right course of action."

100 Or "Persuading others of something—that's just a rough approximation of a good piece of persuasion!"

10.20 或問蒯通抵[44] 韓信。不能下。又狂之。[45] 曰方遭信閉。[46] 如其抵。曰巇可抵乎。曰賢者司禮。小人司巇。[47] 況拊鍵乎。

10.21 或問李斯盡忠。胡亥極刑。忠乎。[48] 曰斯以留客至作相。用狂人之言。[49] 從浮大海。立趙高之邪說。廢沙丘之正。阿意督責。焉用

---

44 This reading accepts the *Erya* gloss that equates *ji* with *wei* (dangerous). Another reading of this verb is offered by Wang Rongbao (1987, 14.380), who writes instead of "trying to move Han Xin with innuendos and grand schemes" (以奇策感動, 謂不以直言正諫, 而迂迴其辭以觸發之, 正側擊之謂).

45 And abandoned him, according to Wang Rongbao (1987, 14.379).

46 However, Han Jing (1992, 253n2) reads this as "This, then, was the result of the dissension."

47 See, e.g., Tao Hongjing's 陶弘景 commentary to this passage, cited in Wang Rongbao (1987, 14.380).

48 Playing off the passage recorded in the letter sent by Zou Yang to King Xiao of Liang: 李斯盡忠, 胡亥極刑.

49 See Li Gui, cited in Wang Rongbao (1987, 14.382). However, Han Jing (1992, 254n3) thinks the "wild talk" was Li Si's own, when he compared the First Emperor to the sage-kings of antiquity. Thus, Han thinks the line *cong fu da hai* 從浮大海 (allow float great sea) is merely a poetic description of his travels on land as he accompanied the First Emperor on his tours of inspection throughout the realm.

Someone asked me about Kuai Tong's[101] badgering[102] of Han Xin: "He not only could not make him submit to his reasoning, but he also feigned madness."[103] 10.20

"He came up against Han Xin's intransigence, just as if he had had the door slammed in his face. So much for that sort of badgering!"[104]

"Had there been the slightest opening, would he have found a way to pry it open?"

"The worthy man looks to ritual, while the petty man looks for breaches in the wall and openings. How much worse is it to break down a bolted gate by force!"

Someone noted Li Si's[105] reputation for absolute loyalty. 10.21

"The Qin ruler Huhai[106] sent him off to be executed. Does that suggest loyalty? Li Si used a speech about foreigners residing in Qin as a stepping-stone to the chancellorship.[107] He then made use of the madmen's speeches[108] to allow those silly people to float off to sea.[109] He let Zhao Gao's perverse logic stand.[110] And at Shaqiu he set aside the imperial orders about the rightful heir.[111] In a sycophantic manner, he urged 'oversight and punishments'[112]—so in what way, pray tell, was he so very loyal?"[113]

"And Huo Guang?"[114]

---

101 Kuai Tong was a strategist famed for his ability to lay out the advantages and disadvantages of pursuing a given course of action.

102 Or "butting heads with."

103 Han Xin was a fool to trust Liu Bang, as Peng Tong tried to warn him.

104 Or possibly "How could he have caused the rift?"

105 Li Si rose to the post of chancellor under the First Emperor of Qin.

106 Calling the Second Emperor by his personal name is disrespectful.

107 Ironically, Li Si was himself an alien. An alternative translation is "Li Si, as the foreigner retained in Qin, became chancellor." But this translation does not convey the irony of the situation.

108 The phrase "madmen's speeches" almost certainly refers to the wild exaggerations about the First Emperor's virtue and potential for immortality made by the *fangshi* magicians, whose wild schemes he did not condemn. Those wild schemes included sending young boys to sea to search for the fabled islands of immortality.

109 In some traditions, not only "boys and girls" were sent off to search for the immortal islands but the First Emperor himself set off as well.

110 Twice Li Si let stand Zhao Gao's lies: first, when Zhao Gao changed the succession and later, under the Second Emperor, when Zhao Gao tested the level to which the Qin courtiers' sycophancy would rise when he called a sheep a deer and asked them to confirm his statement. Zhao Gao eventually found a pretext to execute Li Si, after which he assumed the title of chancellor.

111 *Zheng* 正 could refer either to the rightful heir, as in my translation, or to the real last will and testament, which Li Si and Zhao Gao destroyed.

112 A letter urging even harsher oversight, punishment, and taxation went to the Second Emperor, and it was crafted to appeal to his worst instincts.

113 Literally, "how did he use loyalty?" This may also imply "So what did his vaunted loyalty get him or Qin?"

114 In 87 BCE, at the death of Han Wudi, Huo Guang became coregent, with Jin Midi (a Xiongnu prince), for Han Wudi's heir, and when Jin Midi died soon afterward, Huo took almost all power into his own hands, over the objections of other high-ranking

忠。霍。曰始六〔世〕之詔。[50] 擁少帝之微。摧燕上官之鋒。處廢興之分。堂堂[51] 乎忠。難矣哉。至顯。不終矣。

10.22 或問馮唐面文帝得廉頗,李牧不能用也。諒乎。曰彼將有激也。親屈帝尊。信亞夫之軍。至頗牧。曷不用哉。德。曰罪不孥。宮不女。館不新。陵不墳。

50 Different editions here write *Shiyuan zhi chu* 始元之初 (beginning of the Shiyuan reign period) or *Shi liu zhi zhao* 始六之詔 (edict of the First Six [Emperors]), and the commentators cannot agree which reading is correct. Shiyuan 始元 was the first full year of Zhaodi's reign, 94 BCE. *Shiliu* 始六 may refer to the six emperors of Han who preceded Zhaodi, from Liu Bang to Wudi. Sima Guang, cited in Wang Rongbao (1987, 15.382), believes the character *liu* is correct; Wang Rongbao, however, is equally certain that *liu* is a mistranscribed character, and the passage refers to the first year of Zhaodi's reign. Liu Shipei (1916) argues for the second reading, however, by a logic that Han Jing (1992, 256n8) pronounces to be "too circuitous."

51 The phrase *tang tang* 堂堂 almost certainly alludes to *Analects* 15.16, 19.16: "When a circle of people can spend the whole day together without their conversation ever touching upon duty, and they like to employ petty cleverness, it is difficult indeed [to instruct them in the Way]. If they eat their fill the whole day, without ever once employing their hearts and minds, it is difficult indeed. . . . How impressive Zhang is [堂堂乎張也], but it is difficult to practice humaneness with him." (Cf. *Analects* 17.22.) My translation seeks to capture several aspects of the difficulties associated with Huo Guang.

"At the beginning of the Shiyuan reign period, he supported the child emperor Zhaodi in his youth and weakness. He mowed down powerful opponents, such as King Dan of Yan and Shangguan Jie.[115] He himself was in a position to determine the success or failure of the ruling house. Imposing was his loyalty! That was indeed difficult, but he certainly created difficulties for himself![116] And with respect to Huo Xian, he certainly failed to 'guard his virtue to the end.'"[117]

Someone asked me about Feng Tang's face-off with Wendi, in which Feng remarked that even had Wendi been able to get another general like Lian Po or Li Mu,[118] he would have been incapable of using him. "Was it true?" 10.22

"Feng meant to be provocative. The emperor personally humbled himself by not assuming the imperial prerogatives, and he showed confidence in Zhou Yafu's army.[119] So how could Feng say that a Lian Po or Li Mu would not have been used properly by him?"[120]

"And what about his charismatic virtue?"[121]

"He did not implicate the dependents of criminals in their crimes. He did not sequester[122] females permanently in the palace.[123] He did not constantly refurbish the official and palace residences. He did not have a high mound built at his imperial mausoleum."[124]

---

members of the court.

115 Supposedly, in 80 BCE, Huo Guang discovered a plot that involved several of the Shangguan family, including Sang Hongyang, the Shangguan princess, and the King of Yan. All were executed, along with their clan members (*zongzu* 宗族) and supporters.

116 Possible overtranslation of the three characters meaning "difficult indeed!" I take the line differently than Han Jing (1992, 257n13), who applies it to loyalty to the throne: "And that was no easy thing!" I suspect that Yang wants to use this single brief phrase to bestow both praise and blame on Huo Guang, for Huo Guang certainly brought ruin to his line when he failed to rein in his wife's ambitions.

117 The line *bu zhong yi* 不終矣 (lit., "did not end it, certainly!") could also mean "he did not exhibit such loyalty to the very end." My translation implies both that he did not put a stop to Huo Xian's machinations and that he did not persist in virtue to the very end of his own life. Following this logic, as the commentators point out, the Wang clan would have done better to kill ("put an end to") Wang Mang.

118 Two famous generals during the late Zhanguo period. Feng Tang reproved Wendi for his handling of military matters and punishments.

119 In the sixth year of the Houyuan period under Wendi, the Xiongnu invaded the north. Wendi, to encourage the troops, personally traveled to Bashang and other camps, and he dismounted from his horse to meet and greet the troops. At several places, he allowed himself to be subjected to the rules of the military encampments. L'Haridon (2006) suggests that the question of virtue is raised here in connection with Wendi.

120 Or "So with these virtual Lian Bos and Li Mus (i.e., generals of Wendi's own time in Zhou Yafu's army), how were they not used?"

121 I.e., of Wendi.

122 According to Michael Loewe, both *gong* 宮 and *yin* 陰 can refer to "arrest and confinement within the palace"; there was also, according to Zheng Xuan's commentary to the *Zhouli*, a form of "castration" for females in which the women's sexual organs were sewn up. See Loewe 2005; Liu Xingjun 2001, 143–45.

123 Wendi sent his ladies out of the palace and allowed them to marry, if they had had no sexual relations with an emperor.

124 Wendi (and his deathbed instructions) specified that these things not be done. Although there was considerable debate over Wendi's role in history, these lines indi-

10.23 或問交。曰仁。問餘，耳。曰光初。竇，灌。曰凶終。

10.24 或問信。曰不食其言。[52] 請人。曰晉荀息。趙程嬰公孫杵臼。秦大夫鑿穆公之側。[53] 問義。曰事得其宜之謂義。[54]

10.25 或問季布忍焉。可為也。曰能者為之。明哲不為也。或曰當布之急。雖明哲。如之何。曰明哲不終項仕。如終項仕。焉攸避。

10.26 或問賢。曰為人所不能。請人。曰顏淵黔婁四皓韋玄。問長者。

52 Wang Rongbao (1987, 15.397) shows that the various explanations tying the phrase *shi yan* to ordinary "lies" (*wei yan* 偽言) are wrong; rather, the phrase refers to "saying something and not doing [it]" (*yan er bu xing* 言而不行).

53 Wang Rongbao (1987, 15.395) notes that these courtiers were praised in one of the *Odes* exegetical traditions, that of Lu, which Yang tended to favor. Cf. *Hanshu* 81.335–36 for Kuang Heng's praise of the three.

54 Cf. "Zhongyong," sec. 14: 義者宜也，尊尊爲大. Li Gui, cited in Wang Rongbao (1987, 15.395), believes that *yi* refers to "attaining due measure or what is appropriate in life and death" (*de si sheng zhi yi* 得死生之宜).

Someone asked me about human relations. 10.23

"The key is humaneness."

"What about Chen Yu and Zhang Er?"[125]

"They epitomize glorious beginnings."

"And Dou Ying and Guan Fu?"[126]

"Bad ends."

Someone asks for a definition of trustworthiness. 10.24

"When a person does not have to 'eat his words.'"[127]

"Some exemplars, please?"

"Xun Xi, in Jin; Cheng Ying and Gongsun Chujiu, in Zhao;[128] and in Qin, the counselors who 'accompanied Duke Mu in death.'"[129]

"And a sense of duty?"

"Attaining what is appropriate in any given situation—that we call 'a sense of duty.'"[130]

Someone asks whether it was right and proper for Ji Bu to bear the 10.25
insults.[131]

"Those capable of acting this way can do it, of course, but those who have clarity and practical wisdom would not act that way."[132]

Someone asked me, "Hard-pressed as he was, what alternatives did Ji Bu have, even if he was thinking clearly and practically?"

"Those with clarity and practical wisdom do not end up in the service of a Xiang Yu. If they do end up that way, how can they possibly avoid that sort of outcome?"

Someone asked me for a definition of "men of worth." 10.26

"They are men who have things they cannot bring themselves to do."[133]

"Some exemplars, please?"

---

cate Yang's profound respect for Wendi (if only as foil to Wudi). For the debate, see Nylan 1983, Appendix: "Translations, Chapter Two."

125 These two were friends originally, but Zhang was eventually defeated by troops led by Chen.

126 Likewise, these two were renowned friends, the first a chancellor early in Han Wudi's reign.

127 I.e., forget or ignore what he said. Xun Xi was an adviser in Jin during the Chunqiu period who eventually, out of loyalty to his duke, committed suicide. The question raised by the commentaries is this: does it matter whether the original promise was misguided?

128 These two men engaged in a complicated scheme to save a young heir from the enemy of the child's family.

129 *Odes* 131, entitled "Yellow Bird" (Huang niao), criticized the duke's (r. 659–621 BCE) request to three of his men to accompany him in death.

130 For this paranomastic gloss *yi* 義= *yi* 宜, which is common in Han texts, see *Fayan*, chap. 4.

131 Ji Bu, general under Xiang Yu, sold himself into slavery to escape the death penalty for enemy generals.

132 Cf. *Fayan* 6.18.

133 Meaning that they have standards and principles. Note the paradox: these men compel attention because of their incapacities. Alternatively, as an anonymous reader prefers, "They do what others cannot." But these are men who won fame for their refusals.

曰藺相如申秦而屈廉頗。欒布之不塗。[55] 朱家之不德。直不疑之不校。[56] 韓安國之通使。[57]

10.27 或問臣自得。曰石太僕之對。金將軍之謹。[58] 張衛將軍之慎。丙大夫之不伐善。[59] 請問臣自失。曰李貳師之執貳。田祁連之濫帥。[60]

55 Only one edition reads *bei* 倍 (to rebel against) instead of *tu* 塗 (smear, obfuscate, cover over), but Wang Rongbao (1987, 15.402) prefers that reading.

56 The language here recalls *Zuozhuan* (君父之命不校).

57 This reads *tong* 通 in two senses, as an adjective modifying "envoy" (i.e., "splendidly serving") and as a verb, "to communicate or broker negotiations."

58 Cf. *Hanshu* 68.2967.

59 Bing Ji's *Hanshu* biography contains lines that probably are the source here (吉為人深厚, 不伐善. . . . 不道前恩). *Fa* 伐 could mean "attack" or "boast of" or "presume on" his good deeds.

60 The phrase *lan shuai* 濫帥 could mean "injudicious behavior as commander" or even "salacious leadership," since Tian failed to make the rendezvous because he was dallying with a widow, but this same phrase points to his ill-treatment of the troops under his command.

"Yan Yuan, Qian Lou,[134] the Four Graybeards,[135] and Wei Xuancheng."[136]

"And the best examples?"

"Lin Xiangru standing up to Qin and humbling himself before Lian Po;[137] Luan Bu's refusal to turn against Peng Yue;[138] Zhu Jia's refusal to take credit for his own virtues;[139] Zhi Buyi's refusal to counteract slanders;[140] and Han Anguo's splendid service as negotiator and envoy."[141]

"Give examples of officials keeping their heads in a crisis."[142] 10.27

"Imperial Driver Shi Qing's prompt and proper response,[143] General Jin Midi's prudence,[144] Colonel Zhang's caution,[145] and Bing Ji's refusal to boast about his good points."[146]

"And how about examples of failures in this respect?"

"General Li Guangli's duplicity,[147] Tian Guangming's abuse of his com-

---

134 A recluse not afraid of poverty.

135 The Four Graybeards were exemplary recluses who were persuaded to leave their reclusion to offer their advice to Liu Bang on his choice of heir.

136 Wei Xuan[cheng], a younger son of Wei Xian, feigned madness so that his brother might inherit his father's noble title in his place.

137 Lin Xiangru, minister to Zhao, served Zhao loyally, and he even managed to get the Qin ruler to return the Zhao state treasure. Lian Bo, who was inclined to self-aggrandizement, often picked fights with Lin Xiangru, who always managed to avoid an open break. Eventually Lian, realizing the error of his ways, apologized to Lin, and the two became fast friends.

138 Luan Bu was a paragon of loyalty toward his friend and patron, Peng Yue, King of Liang.

139 Zhu Jia, a knight errant in early Western Han, refused to take credit for his good deeds.

140 Zhi Buyi, when falsely accused of stealing, undertook to repay the missing sum.

141 Han Anguo was Han imperial envoy to Liang when Liang's king was misbehaving. Han dissuaded the emperor from killing the king, even as he persuaded the king to amend his behavior. Surely Yang recalled the definition of "great officer" (所謂大臣, 以道事君, 不可則止) in *Analects* 11.24, which requires the good officer to be loyal to his ruler and even willing to leave the court if the ruler is unreceptive to the official's remonstrance.

142 Literally, "self-possession" in crises, whereby they managed not to do violence to their own natures, even as they secured the emperor's trust by their actions.

143 One time Shi Qing took over the reins when an accident was likely to result from several teams of horses pulling the imperial carriage.

144 Or "[ostensible] deference," expressed by his refusal to have his daughter entered into the back palace of the emperor (i.e., consort with the emperor).

145 Colonel Zhang (Zhang Anshi), son of Chancellor Zhang Tang, held many high posts himself, but he was famous for both his modesty and his frugal way of life.

146 Bing Ji saved the grandson of Han Wudi in 91 BCE when his father, the former heir to Wudi, was forced to commit suicide in a witchcraft affair. Later this grandson ruled as Xuandi.

147 Presumably, this refers to Li Guangli's duplicity in surrendering to the Xiongnu.

韓馮翊之愬蕭。趙京兆之犯魏。[61]

10.28 或問持滿。曰扼。[62]

10.29 揚王孫倮葬以矯世。曰矯世以禮。倮乎。如矯世。則葛溝尚矣。

61 Wei Xiang sent a memorial to the throne that was particularly opposed to an earlier memorial by Sang Hongyang. See Wang Qicai 2009, pp. 8–9.

62 Hence Wang Rongbao's gloss (1987, 15.411) as *chi qing* 持傾 (keep from overturning). See the woodblock edition (Zuantu huzhu ed.) of the *Xunzi* dating to the late Song, which was intended for students. Cf. *Hanshu waizhuan* (Hightower, 111–12).

mander's position,[148] Han Yanshou's[149] accusations about Xiao Wangzhi, and Overseer Zhao Guanghan's confrontation with Wei Xiang."[150]

Someone asked me about the phrase "maintaining fullness." 10.28
"It means to grasp the principle of the Tipping Vessel."[151]

"Yang Wangsun had himself buried naked, as a corrective for the customs of his age."[152] 10.29

"Does one correct one's contemporaries by following rituals or by going naked?[153] A person who thinks it acceptable to right the world in *that* way is even capable of throwing corpses bundled up in reeds into a ditch!"

---

148 Tian maintained good order only by using the most draconian methods; he also failed to make a previously arranged military rendezvous.

149 In 59 BCE, Han Yanshou heard that Xiao Wangzhi was about to investigate allegations about Han's conduct in an earlier post, so Han preemptively charged Xiao with misuse of funds while in office. Eventually, it was Han, rather than Xiao, who was charged with a crime and executed.

150 Zhao Guanghan, when acting overseer of the capital, tried to preempt an inquiry into his own conduct by falsely accusing the wife of his accuser of killing a slave, for which perjury he was executed.

Given Yang's feelings about Han-Xiongnu, relations, it is important to consider the court advisers' positions on the Xiongnu civil war of 58–54 BCE. Many ministers in Emperor Xuan's court urged him to attack the Xiongnu (then divided) so as to destroy them once and for all. Xiao Wangzhi (then imperial counselor) opposed the plan on both ethical and practical grounds: first, because Tushetang 屠耆堂, the Xiongnu ruler overthrown in 58 BCE, had already indicated his goodwill and submission to the Han Empire by asking to restore the old *heqin* 和親 relationship, thereby setting a good example for other groups outside the Han Empire, and second, because the Xiongnu would be bound to respond to the planned invasion by flight deep into the steppe lands.

151 The "Tipping Vessel" (Youzuo 宥坐) chapter of the *Xunzi* says that Kongzi went to see Duke Huan of Lu, who had a vessel of this sort, which Kongzi took to be an apt symbol of the gentleman, for the Tipping Vessel, no matter how much was poured into it, always righted or "stabilized" itself, by pouring out any excess liquid; thus, it symbolized the capacity "to maintain fullness" by "holding oneself back" and "curbing one's arrogance." This metaphor of the Tipping Vessel is used to describe rhetoric as well in two "Outer Chapters" of the *Zhuangzi* (chaps. 27, 33); there it stands for good talk, as well as upright action and self-correcting impulses. A. C. Graham (1989, 200, 230), translating the *Zhuangzi*, rendered the phrase that I have translated as "Tipping Vessel" as "spillover sayings," which are said to be effective "nine times out of ten."

152 A strict proponent of frugal burials.

153 More literally, "One corrects one's age by ritual propriety. How can one achieve this by going naked?" (I.e., nakedness is a greater ritual violation than lavish funerals.)

10.30 或問周官。曰立事。左氏。曰品藻。[63] 太史遷。曰實錄。[64]

63 Wang Rongbao (1987, 15.415)—to my mind anachronistically—makes a great deal of what he takes to be the "downgrading" in Yang's text of these two candidates for canonical status, reading this as "It [the *Zuo*] is rich with ornamentation" 多文采, following the *Shuowen*'s reading of "pin" as "numerous" 眾庶; Wang rejects Sima Guang's reading, cited in Wang Rongbao 1987, on the grounds that all three judgments involve an adjective-noun combination, in contrast to Sima Guang's reading, which makes *pin* and *zao* parallel. The real question is, What does it mean that Yang Xiong treats these three texts as equal? Clearly, the *Fayan* praises all three compilations as works that are true to historical events and people. Hence, Hsu Fu-kuan (1979, vol. 2, 249) takes this to refer to the "clarity" of moral lessons presented in the *Zuo*.

The "Pinzao" 品藻 chapter of *Shitong* uses the binome in the neutral sense of grading people into moral ranks, good and bad. See *Shitong*, *juan* 23, pp. 431–44. The association with ornamentation, according to *Shitong* (p. 433), comes from the decorated backs of mirrors, where mirrors are analogized to good histories. The phrase *pinzao* reoccurs in the preface to *Shitong*, chap. 11.

64 Liu Xiang and Yang Xiong promoted Sima Qian's work, according to Wang Su, cited in *Sanguo zhi* 13.418.

Someone asked me about the *Zhou Officers*.[154] 10.30

"It establishes the proper spheres of duties."

"What about Zuo Qiuming?"

"His ranking of people is extremely artful."[155]

"And Sima Qian?"

"His is a true record."[156]

---

154 The commentators are sure that Yang's reference to the *Zhou Officers* 周官 refers either to the text now known as the *Zhouli* 周禮 or to the "Zhou guan" chapter of the *Documents* (with not enough context to tell which), but *Shiji* 28.1357 seems to cite yet a third text by this same title. Zuo Qiuming is the putative author of the traditions known as the *Zuozhuan*. The third book mentioned here is the *Shiji*. These three texts were all elevated in status in late Western Han or during Wang Mang's Xin dynasty. As Yang's principal interest in this chapter lies in moral exemplars (rather than exemplary texts), I translate with reference to the compiler-authors rather than the histories themselves.

155 Following Sima Guang, cited in Wang Rongbao (1987, 15.414–15), who says, "It ranks the distinctions of good and bad, giving events proper elaboration."

156 Sima Qian is, of course, the author of the *Shiji*, widely regarded as the best history ever written in Chinese. The phrase *shilu* 實錄 (true record) became the title of the "Veritable Records" compiled for each dynasty in late imperial China, although the *Shiji* was a privately compiled comprehensive history of the known world rather than a state-sponsored dynastic history. See Nylan 2011, chap. 4, for Yang Xiong's role in promoting Sima Qian.

卷第十一

淵騫

仲尼之後。訖于漢道。
德行顏閔。股肱蕭曹。爰及名將。
尊卑之條。稱述品藻。譔淵騫。

11.1 或問淵騫之徒惡乎在。[1] 曰寢。[2] 或曰淵騫，曷不寢。曰攀龍鱗。附鳳翼。[3] (巽)以揚之。[4] 勃勃乎其不可及也。如其寢。如其寢。

11.2 七十子之於仲尼也。日聞所不聞。見所不見。文章亦不足為矣。

1 The phrase *e hu* 惡乎 means "at what place?" It is the Chinese equivalent of "ubi sunt," which constitutes a whole genre of Latin literature asking, Where are the culture heroes now, when we need them?

2 The Song and Wu editions write *zai qin* 在寢 (in the tomb) instead of simply *qin*, but most editors have believed the *zai* to be an interpolation. Clearly the first observation and the follow-up question represent wordplay, with both playing off the idea of underground tombs as places of final rest. Wang Rongbao (1987, 16.417) glosses *qin* as *yan mo bu zhang* 湮沒不彰. The phrase *wenzhang* 文彰 may refer to literary refinement (as most traditional sources have it) or more broadly to refinement of conduct.

3 Cf. *Shiji* 61.2127, where Sima Qian uses similar language to talk of men such as Bo Yi and Shu Qi, who enjoy some renown in history because they clung to the coattails of the truly famous (in Sima Qian's argument about them, Kongzi). The four-character phrase *pan long fu feng* has come into popular usage.

4 Wang Rongbao (1987, 16.417) says the "gentle wind" represents heaven; Wang reasons that heaven helped the disciples to become famous, although only a small group of them did so (an overinterpretation?). I take the "gentle wind" to refer to the civilizing influence of Kongzi himself, as does *Shiji suoyin* 索隱, cited in Wang Rongbao (ibid.).

Chapter 11

Yan Hui and Min Ziqian

VERSE SUMMARY

From the time of Zhongni, on down to the Han way, there have been the exemplary men of virtuous conduct, the Yan Huis and Min Ziqians, and exemplary right-hand men, the Xiao Hes and Cao Shens,[1] not to mention famous generals. Ranking their eminence, I weigh and relate their types and qualities. Thus, I have compiled chapter 11, "Yan Hui and Min Ziqian."

....

Someone asked me, "Where are the disciples of Yan Hui and Min Ziqian?" 11.1
"Sunk without a trace."[2]

Someone asked me, "So why have Yan and Min *not* been laid to rest?"[3]

"Because they climbed up on the dragon scales and clung to the wings of the phoenix Kongzi. With that 'gentle wind to lift them up,"[4] they soared higher and higher, until no one could reach them at such great heights.[5] So much for being laid to rest! So much for *that*!"[6]

The relation of the seventy disciples to Kongzi was this: every day they 11.2
heard and saw things that up to then had never been heard and seen, so remarkable were Kongzi's teachings[7]—so much so that they felt that

---

1 Yan Hui and Min Ziqian were disciples of Kongzi; Xiao He and Cao Shen were ministers of the Han founder.

2 Or "Dead and gone."

3 Meaning consigned to the dustbin of history.

4 The hexagram Xun 巽 is associated with gentle winds.

5 However, Andrew Plaks (pers. comm.) thinks that this means that the disciples did not reach Kongzi's level of perfection, for although the passage describes these two disciples' fame, the names of *their* disciples have sunk without a trace. In any case, the disciples of Kongzi could not hope to rival him in eminence.

6 Reduplication typically signals a level of disdain or exasperation in Yang's writing. In history they continue to enjoy renown. They have hardly been "laid to rest."

7 This last phrase has been supplied for sense.

11.3 君子絕德。小人絕力。或問絕德。曰舜以孝。禹以功。皋陶以謨。非絕德邪。力。秦悼武烏獲，任鄙扛鼎抃牛。非絕力邪。

11.4 或問勇。曰軻也。曰何軻也。曰軻也者，謂孟軻也。若荊軻。君子盜諸。請[問]孟軻之勇。曰勇於義而果於德。不以貧富貴賤死生動其心。於勇也。其庶乎。

11.5 魯仲連蕩而不制。[5] 藺相如制而不蕩。[6]

11.6 或問鄒陽。曰未信而分疑。[7] 忼辭免罿。幾矣哉。[8]

---

5 See Geng and Yang 2007, esp. 4–5. However, Li Gui takes *bu zhi* 不制 to mean "he did not receive the stipulated rewards," despite his achievements.

6 If Li is right (see note 5), then the following statement about Lin Xiangru should also be emended to read, "While Lin *did* receive the stipulated rewards. . ." Cf. *Shiji* 34.1559–60. For Lu, see J. Kroll 2010. .

7 Yu Xingwu 1933, citing Song Xian 宋咸, glosses *fen* as *fen jie* 分解 (to resolve). However, Han Jing (1992, 276n2) reads *fen* 分 as *fen ji* 分際.

8 Expressing both senses of the word *ji* 幾 (*wei* 危, "danger"; *shu* 庶, "nearly") One would translate "managed to avoid prison" (or "fetters"), following Li Gui's commentary, were it not that Zou Yang had to defend himself from prison, as Wang Rongbao (1987, 16.422) points out.

merely perfecting themselves in the visible displays of refinement, such as writing,[8] was not enough!

They say, "The noble man is the last word in virtue, and the petty person, in strength."[9] 11.3–4

Someone asked me, "What does being 'the last word in virtue' mean?"

"It means Shun for filial duty; Yu for hard work and achievements; and Gao Yao for wise counsels.[10] If these are not examples of superlative virtue, then what is?"

"And the last word in strength?"

"Wu Huo and Ren Bi under King Daowu of Qin.[11] They could shoulder tripods on a carrying pole and wrestle oxen with their bare hands.[12] If that's not superlative strength, what is?"

Someone asked me about courage.

"Ke is the exemplar."

"Which Ke?"

"When I speak of Ke, I mean Meng Ke, Mencius.[13] The noble man regards men like Jing Ke[14] as violent criminals."[15]

"May I ask about Mencius' courage?"

"He was brave with respect to his duties and steadfast in virtue; he did not let poverty or riches, honor or base position, life or death, disturb him.[16] In courage, he was well-nigh perfect!"

Lu Zhonglian[17] was free in his conduct, and he knew no restraint. Lin Xiangru was restrained and none too free in his conduct.[18] 11.5–6

Someone asked me about Zou Yang.[19]

"Before he gained his prince's trust, he resolved the prince's doubts. He used defiant words to somehow escape the net of the law. But it was a close call and far too dangerous a course!"

---

8 For the broader sense of the phrase *wen zhang*, see *Analects* 5.13, 8.19. But here *wen* also can be taken in a narrower sense as "writing," since this becomes Yang's explanation for why the direct disciples of Kongzi left no writings behind.

9 See *Analects* 14.33: 驥不稱其力, 稱其德也.

10 Gao Yao was a legendary minister under Emperor Shun.

11 King Daowu reigned from 310 to 307 BCE. Wu Huo and Ren Bi were two strong men who attained high office under King Wu.

12 These feats of strength epitomize the "Hundred Amusements" 百戲 of court culture.

13 The self-proclaimed Confucian and defender of Kongzi's teachings against rival theories.

14 A famous assassin-retainer.

15 Literally, a "thief," but here the term refers to any person who wreaks violence on another. Yang thinks Jing Ke had an undeserved reputation as an admirable man of courage.

16 Literally, "move his heart." In *Mencius* 2A.2, Mengzi boasted of his equanimity when deliberating on questions of right and wrong.

17 Known for his high principles and his refusal to hold office.

18 Lin Xiangru refused to treat General Lian Po as his archrival, thinking Lian had served their home state of Zhao well. See *Fayan* 10.26.

19 An itinerant adviser whose rhetoric failed to dissuade Liu Pi from revolting in 154 BCE.

11.7 或問信陵平原孟嘗春申益乎。[9] 曰上失其政。姦臣竊國命。何其益乎。

11.8 樗里子之知也。使知國如葬。則吾以疾為蓍龜。

11.9 周之順赧。以成周而西傾。[10] 秦之惠文,昭襄以西山而東并。孰愈。曰周也羊。秦也狼。然則狼愈與。曰羊狼一也。[11]

11.10 或問蒙恬忠而被誅。忠奚可為也。曰塹山堙谷。起臨洮。擊遼水。[12] 力不足而死有餘。忠不足相也。[13]

---

9 See *Shiji* 75–78. That the idea of these men exercised a powerful influence over later men's imaginations can be seen from Wang Anshi's "After Reading the Biography of Lord of Mengchang," trans. Liu Shi Shun 1979, which calls the Lord of Mengchang "a leader of those who crowed like cocks and stole like dogs."

10 Wang Rongbao (1987, 16.429) equates "the west" with Qin. Han Jing (1992, 278n1) says that the phrase *xi qing* (西倾) refers to the Zhou kings' attempts to flatter Qin by making the Qin their Western Protector, and it is unlikely to refer to the Zhou kings' loss of their heartlands in the west to Qin and other peripheral groups. Some might argue, however, that the phrase *xiqing* could refer to either (1) King Nan's forming a "vertical" alliance with the lords, in order to try to resist Qin (taking *qing* in the sense of "overturn"), or (2) King Nan's decision, after he failed in that attempt, to offer thirty-six settlements to Qin to sue for peace (taking *qing* in the sense of "falling" or "collapsing"). It is to the second possibility that Li Gui alludes when he says 過猶不及，兩不與也. If we believe that both parties attempted aggression, there is no contrast between "excess" and "inadequacy" of the sort envisioned by Li Gui.

11 For the sheep and wolf, cf. *Zhanguo ce* 168/86/8.

12 Reading *ji* 擊 as *xi* 繫, as Meng connected the Liao River valley with territories to the east via new roads.

13 Li Gui, however, reads *xiang* 相 as *zhu* 助 (help), and *xiang* could also mean *guan* 觀 (to examine closely with a view to emulating). If Li Gui's commentary is followed, the idea is that one man's integrity and hard work did not spare great numbers from going to their deaths. See Wang Rongbao (1987, 16.429).

Someone asked me whether the Lords of Xinling, Pingyuan, Mengchang, and Chunshen were of any use whatsoever.[20] 11.7–8

"When their superiors lost the reins of government, these traitorous ministers arrogated to themselves the powers and mandates of their realms. How would *they* have been of any use?"

As to Ying Shuli's[21] wisdom: "Had he known the affairs of state as well as he knew the location of his final burial place, then I would hasten to make him my milfoil and turtle!"[22]

"Kings Shenjing[23] and Nan of Zhou used Chengzhou,[24] their capital, to try to overturn the western power, Qin.[25] Kings Huiwen and Zhaoxiang of Qin used Qishan, the Western Mountains,[26] to annex the realms to the east.[27] Which was better and which worse?" 11.9

"Zhou was the sheep and Qin the wolf."

"Well, isn't it better to be the wolf?"

"It's equally dreadful being the sheep or the wolf."[28]

Someone asked me, "Since Meng Tian was executed despite his loyalty, why act loyally at all?" 11.10

"Meng had the mountains dug out to fill up the valleys;[29] he set up Lintao[30] and he connected the Liao River valley with the east. So his manpower was never enough, though more than enough men died in the process. His loyalty was not good enough to bear close scrutiny."[31]

---

20 Four of the most famous princes of the Zhanguo period (the "Four Princes"), each of whom supposedly attracted thousands of clients and retainers to his service.

21 Ying Shuli, who served Kings Wu and Zhao of Qin as chancellor, supposedly foretold the location of his tomb before his death.

22 Milfoil and turtles were primary tools for divination. The idea is: Ying would have been a perfectly reliable guide, had he been able to predict the outcome of the affairs of state as accurately as he foretold the location of his final resting place.

23 King Shenjiing ruled from 320 to 315 BCE, and King Nan, from 314 to 256 BCE.

24 I.e., Luoyang in present-day Henan. This was a secondary capital for the Zhou during the Western Zhou period, and their main capital during the Chunqiu period, after 771 BCE.

25 Adding "their capital," as implied.

26 Huiwen ruled from 337 to 311 BCE, and Zhaoxiang, from 306 to 251 BCE. Qishan 岐山 is in the present-day Longxi corridor. The ancestral homeland of the Zhou ruling line (with at least one of the Qin rulers, Duke Wen, buried there), Qishan eventually became the possession of Qin. These two sets of examples show rulers willing to give up their traditional bases and legacies to acquire short-term gains.

27 I.e., the Zhou realm and the Six Kingdoms.

28 This means that the first position is practically untenable, and the second, morally untenable.

29 General Meng Tian is most famous for building the Great Wall and the Straight Road that cut through mountains and for having the rightful heir to Qin Shihuang in his care.

30 Lintao was a prefecture in present-day Gansu, on the northern frontier.

31 Of course, Meng Tian did not find a way to see that the rightful heir was spared either.

11.11 或問呂不韋其智矣乎。以人易貨。曰誰謂不韋智者與。以國易宗。[14] 不韋之盜。穿窬之雄乎。穿窬也者。吾見擔石矣。未見雒陽也。

11.12 秦將白起不仁。奚用為也。長平之戰。四十萬人死。蚩尤之亂。不過於此矣。原野猒[15] 人之肉。川谷流人之血。將不仁奚用為。[16] 翦。曰始皇方獵六國而翦牙。欸。

14 I follow Sima Guang, cited in Wang Rongbao (1987, 16.433) in reading *guo* 國 as *guo chuan* 國權.

15 Reading *yan* as *yan* 猒 (to cover). Andrew Plaks (pers. comm.) prefers to read it as "being sick of X." Wang Rongbao (1987, 16.436) seems to say that *yan* means *bao* 飽 (filled up [with blood]).

16 Yang Xiong emphasizes their cruelty more than Sima Qian (*Shiji* 73.2342) does.

“As for Lü Buwei, was he not smart to take people as commodities to be traded?”[32] 11.11

“Who says Lü Buwei was smart to act in this way? He traded a child of his own line for a fief.”[33]

“But speaking of Lü Buwei’s theft of high rank and a good name—wasn’t he an extraordinary example of a thief who slips in through a chink in the wall or climbs over it?” [34]

“If we are talking about slipping in through a chink in the wall or climbing over, I can certainly see that a thief might bear away with him something as heavy as a load of rocks, but I still can’t see that Lü got himself another Luoyang [a capital of a long-lasting dynasty].[35]

“The Qin general Bo Qi[36] was inhumane. Of what possible use was he then? Some 400,000 men died at the battle of Changping. Surely even Chi You’s rebellion did not surpass this in bloodshed![37] The plains and the unpopulated areas in the wilds were covered[38] with men’s flesh, and the rivers and valleys awash with the blood of the fallen.[39] If a general is inhumane, of what possible use can he be?” 11.12

“What about Wang Jian, then?”[40]

---

32 Alternatively, “He traded commodities for people,” which would refer to Lü’s decision to use his wealth to become a “kingmaker.” According to legend, Lü’s own putative son inherited the Qin throne as King Zheng (the future First Emperor).

33 Adding “a child of,” as I take this to refer to Lü’s willingness to forgo a claim to the future First Emperor being his own son in return for planting that same son on the throne. Alternately, “He traded his line for power over the domain,” if we follow Sima Guang. Lü, once the most powerful man in the Qin state, eventually had to commit suicide.

34 Adding “of high rank and a good name,” as implied. Wu Mi’s commentary suggests that Lü Buwei is “the most noteworthy of thieves” because other thieves steal only a certain amount of goods (擔石), while Lü Buwei’s act of theft won him a fief at Luoyang. Lü may have been the most successful of thieves for a time, but ultimately he was no more than a common thief.

35 Luoyang, the capital city of Lü Buwei’s domain, was also the Zhou capital during the Chunqiu period. Although my translation is tentative, the idea is clear: Lü lost his fief and line in return for no secure advantage. The text refers to Luoyang as “barren [rocky] territory,” presumably since Lü was not able to use the area as the base for a long-ruling dynastic line like that of Zhou. Li Wai-yee (pers. comm.) speculates that the lines should read, “The reason I called him a [mere] thief is that I can see the honor and emolument [reading 擔石 as 擔/儋石之祿] [he gathered], but I cannot see another Luoyang [established by him as the capital of a long-lasting dynastic line founded by Lü].”

36 A Qin general during the late Zhanguo period, who in four separate campaigns over three decades reportedly killed over a million combatants and civilians.

37 Chi You fought a mighty battle against the Yellow Emperor (Huangdi) and, by some accounts, became the god of war.

38 Note that “the wilds” usually refers to areas outside the cities and suburbs, which are relatively unpopulated—hence, my translation.

39 Adding “of the fallen,” as implied.

40 Wang Jian was a famous general who destroyed the four states of Zhao, Wei, Chu, and Yan in 236–227 BCE. Both Bo and Wang are discussed in the same *Shiji* biographical chapter, which seems to be why they are discussed together in the *Fayan*.

11.13 或問要離非義者與。不以家辭國。曰離也。火妻灰子以求反於慶忌。實蛛蝥之靡(=靡?)也。焉可謂之義也。政。為嚴氏犯韓。刺相俠累。曼面為姊。實壯士之靡也。焉可謂之義也。軻。為丹奉於期之首,燕督亢之圖。入不測之秦。[17] 實刺客之靡也。焉可謂之義也。

11.14 或問儀秦學乎鬼谷術而習乎縱橫言。[18] 安中國者各十餘年。是夫。曰詐人也。聖人惡諸。曰孔子讀而儀秦行。何如也。曰甚矣。[19] 鳳鳴而鷙翰也。然則子貢不為與。曰亂而不解。子貢恥諸。說而不

17 The phrase *buce* 不測 in Yang's other writings often means "impenetrably deep," but here the expression suggests "unfathomably dangerous." Here Yang disputes the relatively complimentary appraisal by Sima Qian of Jing Ke, which praises Jing's exemplary devotion to his principles, despite the failure of the assassination attempt (此其義, 或成或不成, 然立意較然, 不欺其志).

18 However, see *Cambridge History of China*, vol. 1, 634, where Mark Lewis notes, "The symmetry suggested by the terms 'horizontal' and 'vertical' alliances is illusory. While the vertical alliances were formed between independent states, . . . the horizontal versions were relations of dominance [by Qin]."

19 The phrase *shen yi* 甚矣 is definitely extremely negative. It may describe either the subjects of the query or the person asking the question—hence, my attempt to capture both possible translations of the single phrase. Andrew Plaks (pers. comm.) prefers the less colloquial "That is too extreme [a statement]." This line may play off the pun between *zhen* 振 and *chen* 晨. The word *shen* is certainly a strong criticism, as in the line 不為已甚.

"While the First Emperor was hunting down the Six Kingdoms, Wang Jian acted as his bared teeth.[41] How awful!"

Someone asked me whether Yao Li was dutiful or not when he did not refuse to help his ruler, even when it would involve his own family."[42] 11.13

"Yao Li was willing to consign his wife to the flames and turn his children to ashes, in order to undo Qingji.[43] In truth, he cut a fine figure as a scorpion, but how can *that* be called dutiful?"

"And Nie Zheng?"[44]

"On behalf of Yan Sui, he bore down on Han and assassinated its minister Xia Kui. To protect his elder sister, he disfigured himself.[45] In truth, he cut a fine figure as a strong man, but how can *that* be called dutiful?"

"And Jing Ke?"[46]

"For the sake of Prince Dan, he offered the Qin general Fan Yuqi's severed head and a map of Yan's lands in Dukang.[47] And so he gained entry into the impenetrable and unfathomably dangerous court of Qin. In truth, he cut a fine figure as an assassin-retainer, but how can *that* be called dutiful?"

Someone asked me, "Zhang Yi and Su Qin learned the Ghost Valley Master's[48] arts, and they were well versed in the rhetoric of Multiple Alliances, horizontal and vertical.[49] Each of them brought peace to the Central States for more than a decade, no?"[50] 11.14

"They deceived others.[51] The sage despises them."

"But how would it be if a person were to recite Kongzi's writings while performing the deeds of Zhang Yi and Su Qin?"

---

41 I.e., Wang Jian ripped the Six Kingdoms apart.

42 Yao Li, a subject of Wu, had his ruler kill Yao's wife and children so that Qingqi might regard Yao (mistakenly) as a trustworthy ally. Yao then killed Qingji at the first opportunity, lest Qingji seize power in Wu.

43 Li Gui takes *fan* 反 to mean "turn his back on" Qingji, but the verb "seeking" suggests that a broader sense of *fan* is required.

44 A Zhanguo period assassin who killed the Han minister Han Lei (aka Xia Kui). When Jin was partitioned in the mid-fifth century BCE, the state of Han was formed, which lasted from 402 to 230 BCE.

45 Literally, "his face," but traditions have him applying lacquer to his body as well as his face.

46 Suggesting a pun here.

47 Rich agricultural lands in an area corresponding to present-day Hebei.

48 The Ghost Valley Master, Guigu zi, was the purported author of a book on strategy (not necessarily on rhetoric). Su Qin and Zhang Yi were brilliant strategists working for and against Qin. Both were "itinerant persuaders" (professional orators and strategists for hire).

49 Generally, the vertical alliances were those of states fighting against Qin, while the horizontal pacts were those formed by the allies of Qin.

50 This question is similar to that asked in *Mencius* 3B.2: "Were not Gongsun Yan and Zhang Yi truly great men? When they grew angry, all the feudal lords trembled, but when they remained at peace, then the fires of war were extinguished throughout the world." Each question confuses greatness with brute force, instead of equating it with cultivation and adherence to ritual. Note that Gongsun Yan, like Zhang Yi and Su Qin, was a professional strategist for hire.

51 Or simply, "[They were] deceivers."

富貴。儀秦恥諸。

11.15 或曰儀秦其才矣乎。跡不蹈已。曰昔在任人。[20] 帝曰難之。亦才矣。才乎才。非吾徒之才也。

11.16 美行: 園公綺里季, 夏黃公, 角(=用?)里先生。言辭: 婁敬陸賈。執正: 王陵申屠嘉。折節: 周昌汲黯。守儒: 轅固申公。菑異: 董相夏侯勝京房。

20 Han Jing (1992, 237n2) defines *ren* 任 (entrust, employ) as *ren* 壬 (= *ning* 佞, meaning "sycophants"). Cf. *Shangshu* 04.0072, "Gao Yao mo": 惟帝其難之.

"That's too much! How pernicious they were! Such a person may have the sweet calls of a phoenix and the powerful wings of a bird of prey!" 11.14–15

"That may be so, but didn't Zigong act in this way too?"[52]

"Zigong thought it a shame for a chaotic situation to continue unresolved. By contrast, Zhang Yi and Su Qin were only ashamed of any failures to enrich and enfeoff their own persons!"

Someone asked me, "Weren't Zhang Yi and Su Qin men of exceptional talents? They did not 'tread the paths already trodden.'"[53]

"Formerly, when appointing officials, even sage-kings commented on the difficulty of telling true talents from eloquent sycophants,[54] since eloquence too is a special talent. So much for talent! For talent! That is not *our* kind of talent!"[55]

For good conduct: the Four Graybeards, Dongyuan Gong, Qili Ji, Xiahuang Gong, and Master Jiaoli.[56] For phrase making: Lou Jing and Lu Jia.[57] For steadfast rectitude: Wang Ling, Shentu Jia.[58] For staunch principles: Zhou Chang and Ji An.[59] For adherence to the classical way: Masters Yuangu and Shen.[60] For special expertise in disasters and prodigies: Dong Zhongshu, Xiahou Sheng, and Jing Fang.[61] 11.16

---

52 Zigong was also known as Duanmu Ci and was Kongzi's own disciple. Early sources credit Zigong with making Kongzi's reputation. The sources record Zigong's travels to Qi, Wu, Yue, and Jin to spread Kongzi's teachings, which resulted in the preservation of Lu, the weakening of Qi, the destruction of Wu, and the hegemony of Yue.

53 Meaning that they acted in new and creative ways. Contrast L'Haridon 2006: "None was able to follow their traces."

54 This remark, attributed to the emperors Yao and Shun, meant that the emperors would not allow sycophants to become members of their inner circles.

55 Meaning that this is not the kind of talent that is needed.

56 Adding "the Four Graybeards," the collective name for these four men. "Gong" here is a courtesy title meaning "old man." Cf. *Fayan* 10.26.

57 It was Lou Jing who dissuaded the Han founder from making Luoyang his capital and who persuaded Liu Bang to undertake *heqin* 和親 (marriage alliances) with the Xiongnu. Among his many accomplishments, Lu Jia persuaded Zhao Tuo to ally himself with the Han, but he is also well known for persuading Chen Ping to destroy the Lü family after Dowager Empress Lü's death and for persuading Liu Bang that he could not rule an empire solely "on horseback" (i.e., through war).

58 Wang Ling was one of Liu Bang's most trusted allies as secondary chancellor under Huidi, from which post he resisted the efforts of Dowager Empress Lü and her family to seize the throne from Han. Shentu Jia, chancellor and imperial secretary during Han Wendi's reign, is famous for denouncing the influence of the emperor's male favorite, Deng Tong.

59 Zhou Chang argued against Liu Bang, who wanted to choose Lady Qi's son as heir instead of his son by his legal wife. Ji An, usually identified as a Huang-Lao proponent, was famous for his forthright remonstrations.

60 Master Yuangu was famous for his brave critique of the *Laozi*, which nearly cost him his life. Master Shen Pei also incurred the wrath of Dowager Empress Dou because of his advice about a proposed Spirit Hall (Mingtang 明堂).

61 Most of these exemplars were within the living memories of aged witnesses during Yang Xiong's own time, as they had lived within the last three generations. "Chancellor Dong" (as he is identified here) is Dong Zhongshu (see above). Xiahou Sheng was a famous omen interpreter and master of the *Documents*; he was also an early critic of Wudi's policies, for which criticism he was jailed for two years. Jing Fang was

11.17 或問蕭曹。曰蕭也規。曹也隨。[21] 滕灌樊酈。曰俠介。叔孫通。曰槧人也。[22] 爰盎。曰忠不足而談有餘。鼂錯。曰愚。[23] 酷吏。曰虎哉。虎哉。角而翼者也。貨殖。曰蚊。曰血國三千。使捋疎。飲水。褐博。[24] 沒齒無慭也。[25] 或問循吏。曰吏也。[26] 游俠。曰竊國靈

21 Cf. the four-character *chengyu*: 蕭規曹隨.

22 Li Gui, cited in Wang Rongbao (1987, 16.449), glosses this two-character phrase as "hastily adapting to [new] circumstances" (*jian shi min ji* 見事敏疾); Liu Shipei (1916), as *jian* 漸 (= *zha* 詐, "deceiver").

23 Employing both senses of the word *yu* 愚.

24 Han Jing (1992, 293n7) reads "forcing the people to live frugally" instead of "and if only they had had people live frugally!" That changes his translation of the end as well, so that he reads "How could they possibly to the end of their days been resentful?" Variant editions give slightly different renderings of this passage; mine follows Li Gui's.

25 Andrew Plaks (pers. comm.) reads this more literally as "even unto their toothless old age."

26 Han Jing (1992, 294n8) translates differently: "They were true officials." My translation presumes that by this point Yang has turned from describing the good guys to the bad. Possibly, the "accommodating officials" made too many compromises with local culture, in Yang's view, in order to curry favor with the locals.

Someone asked me about Xiao He and Cao Shen.[62] 11.17

"Xiao set the rules and Cao was a good follower."

"And Xiahou Ying,[63] Guan Ying, Fan Kuai, and Li Shang?[64]

"They were stalwart supports."

"And Shusun Tong?"[65]

"A wily deceiver."[66]

"And Yuan Ang?"[67]

"He was not loyal enough, and he talked too much."

"Chao Cuo?"

"He was morally obtuse."

"The cruel officials?"

"Tigers! Tigers! But tigers with horns and wings as well!"[68]

"The moneymakers?"

"Mere mosquitoes. I say they sucked the blood of thousands of states.[69] And if only they lived frugally, picking wild greens to eat, drinking plain water, and wearing the simplest clothes, they would have sparked no resentment to the end of their days."[70]

---

famous for criticizing some of the Five Phases theories, though he upheld yin-yang explanations in his readings of portents. A formula very similar to this is employed in *Analects* 11.3, which is unusual in that text, however.

62 Xiao He and Cao Shen both served as chancellors to Liu Bang and his dowager empress, respectively, with Cao Shen succeeding to the post of chancellor after Xiao He's death.

63 Xiahou Ying had many accomplishments, including recommending Han Xin for office and helping to secure a pardon for Ji Bu. He also, in a crisis, managed to save two of Liu Bang's children, whom Bang had been ready to abandon, including the future Huidi.

64 Guan Ying was a successful general under Han Gaozu, and he helped to install Wendi after the death of Dowager Empress Lü. Fan Kuai fought with considerable success against some of the Qin generals; perhaps more importantly, in a well-known incident in 206 when Xiang Yu was entertaining Liu Bang, it was only thanks to Fan Kuai that Liu Bang managed to escape with his life. Li Shang was a successful general. These four men share the same biographical chapter in the *Shiji*. In this, as in other instances (e.g., the consecutive chapters devoted to Xiao He and Cao Shen), Yang Xiong's choice and sequence of historical characters are designed as comments upon Sima Qian's historical evaluations. On this, see L'Haridon 2011.

65 See above.

66 Translation tentative.

67 Yuan Ang's repeated protests concerning various policy matters eventually lost him favor at Jingdi's court, but then, in 154 BCE, with the help of Dou Ying, Yuan Ang was able to obtain a private audience with Jingdi, in which he blamed the whole revolt on Chao Cuo's mishandling of the seven kings' grievances. Later another king, Liu Wu, King of Liang, had Yuan Ang executed because Yuan had blocked his appointment as Jingdi's heir.

68 Meaning that they were more harmful than mere tigers, which lack horns and wings. Many stories says that tyrannical administrations do more harm than an influx of tigers (苛政猛於虎), including the "Tangong" chapter of the *Liji* (*xia*), sec. 56.

69 Yang specifies "three thousand."

70 Yang Xiong here overturns the conventional positive assessment of the moneymakers and contrasts their generally lavish style of living with that of the two brothers who starved on Mount Shouyang, Bo Yi and Shu Qi, who are the subjects of *Shiji* 61. Yang

也。[27] 佞幸。曰不料而已。[28]

11.18 或問近世社稷之臣。曰若張子房之智。陳平之無悟。[29] 絳侯勃之果。霍將軍之勇。終之以禮樂。則可謂社稷之臣矣。或問：公孫弘，董仲舒孰邇。曰仲舒欲為而不可得者也。弘容而已矣。[30]

11.19 或問近世名卿。曰若張廷尉之平。雋京兆之見。尹扶風之絜。王

27 However, both Li Gui and Wang Rongbao (1987, 17.460, 470) read *ling* 靈 as its homonym *ling* 令 (= *ming* 命), so that the sentence means "They stole [i.e., violated] the decrees of the kingdoms," in a manner similar to the Four Lords mentioned above.

28 L'Haridon (2006) prefers "incompetents." Han Jing (1992, 294n10) understands this to mean instead "These are people not worth talking about."

29 Editions vary, however, with some reading *wu* 忤 and some *wu* 牾 or *cheng* 悜 or *wu* 悟. The last would mean that Chen Ping was "never aware" of the Lü family designs on the Han throne, which seems unlikely.

30 *Hanshu* 58.2634 takes Dong Zhongshu and Ni Kuan to be the best of the Ru under Wudi. L'Haridon (forthcoming) takes this to mean that Gongsun Hong did not even aim to act properly.

"And the accommodating officials?"[71]

"Mere clerks."[72]

"The knights errant?"

"They stole the sacred spirit of the kingdoms."

"And the favorites?"

"Too numerous to count—that's all one can say!"

Someone asked me about the recent ministers serving the altars of grain and soil.[73] 11.18

"Were a man to take Zhang Liang's wisdom, Chen Ping's infallible tact,[74] Zhou Po's decisiveness,[75] and General Huo's courage,[76] and to the very end of his days bring them to fruition via performance of the rites and music,[77] then one could truly call him a fit 'minister of the altars of grain and soil.'"

Someone asked me about Gongsun Hong and Dong Zhongshu: "Who came closer to perfection?"[78]

"Dong wanted to become this sort of minister tending the altars of grain and soil, but he just couldn't do it. Gongsun Hong certainly had the appearance of being such a minister, but nothing more!"[79]

Someone asked me, "And what about the celebrated ministers of more recent times?" 11.19

"Were a person to have Judge Zhang's[80] sense of fairness, Capital

---

agrees with Sima Qian, however, in assuming that the good fortune of another tends to produce schadenfreude among the person's contemporaries.

71 The adjective does not mean "rule-abiding," because it refers to the good governors who accommodated local customs to some extent in their successful attempts to encourage the locals to accept the marriage and mourning rituals of the Central Plains. It is strange that Yang disparages these men; perhaps he believed that they were too accommodating.

72 Yang would have preferred the propagation of more classical forms of rites and music.

73 I.e., the symbols of the legitimacy of the ruling house.

74 Alternatively, "resourcefulness." For Chen Ping, see above.

75 Zhou Bo held several high offices under Liu Bang and his successors Dowager Empress Lü and Huidi. Upon the death of Dowager Empress Lü in 180 BCE, he and Chen Ping made sure that her clan members were executed. Both men also took steps to see that the King of Dai was installed as emperor (Wendi). Chen Ping and Zhou Bo were widely regarded as "meritorious ministers," even though neither made a move against the Lü clan until after Dowager Empress Lü's death. It is entirely possible that Yang is being sarcastic here.

76 Huo Guang was a famous minister for Wudi and regent for his successor. It is not clear which act(s) of courage in Huo's long career Yang is alluding to here.

77 Alternatively, "use ritual and music to see them [the attributes listed above] through from beginning to end."

78 I.e., which of them more closely approached the ideal of "the minister devoted to others"? Both men served Han Wudi. Both were specialists in the "Gongyang" traditions.

79 Yang Xiong mentions Zhang Tang elsewhere as a cruel official, and he couples Gongsun Hong's name with his. Therefore, he did not behave like a good official, in Yang's view.

80 I.e., Zhang Shizhi, who showed his mettle when he advised Wendi not to appoint a junior officer or to inflict a harsher punishment than the law required.

子貢之介。斯近世名卿矣。將。曰若條侯之守。長平,冠軍之征伐。博陸之持重。可謂近世名將矣。請問古。曰鼓之以道德。征之以仁義。輿尸血刃。皆所不為也。

11.20 張騫,蘇武之奉使也。執節沒身。不屈王命。雖古之膚使。[31] 其猶劣諸。

11.21 世稱東方生之盛也。[32] 言不純師。行不純表。其流風遺書。蔑如也。或曰隱者也。曰昔之隱者。吾聞其語矣。又聞其行矣。或曰隱道多端。[33] 曰固也。[34] 聖言聖行。不逢其時。聖人隱也。賢言賢行。不逢其時。賢者隱也。談言談行。而不逢其時。談者隱也。

31 Li Gui glosses *fu* 膚 as *mei* 美 (fine).

32 See *Hanshu* 65.2873–74, which also mentions Yang Xiong's disapprobation.

33 *Duan* 端 can refer to "pretext" or "reason" but also to "conduct" and "arrangements." Andrew Plaks (pers. comm.) prefers "multifarious."

34 However, Han Jing (1992, 301n5) defines *gu* 固 as *queshi* 確實(true, truly), following "song"; see Wang Rongbao (1987, 17.486).

Juan's[81] insight, Metropolitan Yin's incorruptibility,[82] and Wang Zigong's[83] uprightness, then one could truly call him a justly 'famous minister of recent times.'"

"And the generals?"

"Were a person to have Zhou Yafu's genius for defensive moves, the genius of Wei Qing and Huo Qubing in offensives,[84] plus Huo Guang's caution, then one could truly call him a 'famous general of recent times.'"

"May I ask about exemplary figures from antiquity?"[85]

"They were inspired by the Way and its Power; they launched punitive campaigns with humaneness and a sense of duty. What they *never* did was commit any deed that would end in cartfuls of corpses and bloodied blades."

Zhang Qian and Su Wu[86] were still holding their tallies as envoys when 11.20
they died;[87] never once did they disgrace their king's commands. Even the finest envoys of antiquity would, perhaps, be inferior to them!

"The whole world praises Dongfang Shuo's preeminence.[88] But his speech 11.21
was no pure model, and his conduct no pure standard. The fashions he set, like the writings he left behind, are nothing special."[89]

Someone remarked to me, "But he was a recluse!"

"The recluses of old—I have heard what they said and did, certainly, [and Dongfang cannot compare with them!]"

Someone said to me, "But with recluses, there are multiple reasons and modes."

"But there *is* one fixed rule: if one who is a sage in his speech and his conduct fails to meet with the proper time, then he becomes a sage in

---

81 Under Zhaodi, Juan Buyi served as Capital Overseer—hence the nickname. Juan was famous for having warned his peers about the dangers of excessive severity when administering the laws.

82 Yin Wenggui (d. 62 BCE) was in charge of one of the three metropolitan districts, Fufeng, under Han Xuandi. He was noted for his incorruptibility and for his rigorous use of punishments to maintain order. Yet because he eschewed factional politics, he avoided being classified as a "cruel official."

83 Wang Zun, Chancellor of Dongping and later Overseer of the Capital, was supposedly utterly fearless in his reports against offenders, even those in the highest places. Wrongly accused by a peer of defaming the empress, he was dismissed, to the sorrow of many, since he had shown himself highly capable of restoring order in the capital.

84 Zhou Yafu was one of the generals who helped to suppress the Seven Kingdoms Revolt in 154 BCE. For Huo Guang, cf. *Fayan* 10.21.

85 Adding "exemplary figures from," as implied.

86 Zhang Qian (d. 113 BCE) was envoy to the Western Regions; he visited Ferghana, Bactria, and possibly northern India and Persia; his reports included information on Wusun, Yuezhi, and Xiongnu customs. In 100 BCE Su Wu was sent out as envoy to the Xiongnu, where he was detained for some nineteen years. Throughout his time in captivity, Su Wu refused to defect to the enemies of Han.

87 Or "to the end of their lives."

88 Dongfang Shuo is known for the verbal pyrotechnics he unleashed against opponents and also for his blatant flattery of those in power. Dongfang fancied himself a "recluse at court," but he was craven in his desire for power. Liu Xiang, according to Ban Gu's account, collected the writings of Dongfang Shuo.

89 Literally, "did not amount to much."

昔者箕子之漆其身也。狂接輿之被其髮也。欲去而恐罹害者也。箕子之洪範。接輿之歌鳳也哉。[35]

或問東方生名過實者。何也。曰應諧不窮, 正諫穢德。應諧似優。[36] 不窮似哲。正諫似直。穢德似隱。請問名。曰詼達。惡比。曰非夷齊。而是柳下惠。戒其子以尚容。[37] 首陽為拙。柱下為工。[38] 飽食安坐。以仕易農。依隱玩世。[39] 詭時不逢。其滑稽之雄乎。或問柳下惠非朝隱者與。曰君子謂之不恭。古者高餓顯。[40] 下祿隱。

35 Following Han Jing (1992, 300n6), but alternatively "[How could Dongfang Shuo speak of] Jizi's 'Great Plan' and Jieyu's song about the phoenix [disparaging Kongzi] in one and the same breath?"

36 The commentators fight over whether Dongfang seems "like an entertainer" since they think that would be a slur cast on him. The objection to this reading lies in the logic of parallelism; the phrases "witty/wise, frank/straight, and hidden/self-deprecating" (哲、直、隱) represent positive qualities that Dongfang claims to possess, though he does not. By that logic, *you* 優 should mean something positive as well. This is why Han Jing (1992, 302n8) reads *you* 優 as *xianxia anyi* 閒暇安逸 (to be at ease).

37 Han Jing (1992, 304n11) reads this line as "He cautioned his sons to play it safe and go along with others." Similarly, Liu Shipei (1916) read *shang rong* 尚容 as *shang tong* 尚同 (valuing conformity). At this point, several passages in brackets were interpolated by Sima Guang, contra no fewer than three reliable editions with a much shorter version. The material within brackets appears in Ban Gu's *Hanshu* biography of Dongfang Shuo, which apparently cites Yang's language. Cf. *Taiping yulan* 459.7a.

38 Reading *zhu xia* 柱下 (lit., "below the pillar") as "staying at court." I have rejected "lying low" as a meaning since the binome *zhu xia* seems always to refer to some sort of court official. See Morohashi 14660.4–5. Some editions write Liuxia [i.e., Liuxia Hui] instead of *zhuxia*, but that is clearly a copyist's error.

39 Reading (tentatively) the single word *gui* 詭 in *gui shi* 詭世 as "cheat" and "pervert." The binome could also conceivably mean "defamed his contemporaries" or "exaggerated [to] his peers." I cannot find this compound explicated in Morohashi.

40 *Fengsu tongyi, juan* 2, sums up Yang Xiong's objections to the general commendation of Dongfang Shuo by saying that Yang considered Dongfang neither "pure in model [in his words] . . . nor pure in deed."

reclusion. And if a man of worthy speech and conduct fails to meet with the proper time, then he becomes a worthy man in reclusion.

A mere jester in his speech and his conduct who fails to meet with the proper time becomes nothing more than a jester in reclusion. Long ago, Jizi applied lacquer to his own body,[90] and Crazy Jieyu let his hair fall down his back to show his disdain for decorum.[91] Both wanted to leave their respective courts, lest they be ensnared and harmed. But what has Dongfang's talk to do with Jizi's "Great Plan" or Jieyu's Phoenix Song?"

Someone asked me, "So you mean that Dongfang Shuo's fame surpasses the reality?"

"There was his jesting repartee, his inexhaustible wit, his frank remonstrances, and his self-deprecation.'[92] His jests made him seem entertaining.[93] His inexhaustible wit made him seem wise. His frank remonstrances made him seem straightforward. And his self-deprecation made him seem a noble recluse."

"May I ask the source of his reputation?"

"He was a master of pleasantries."

"So who compares with him?"

"He denounced Bo Yi and Shu Qi and approved of Liuxia Hui.[94] He cautioned his sons to always go along with others.[95] He took the Mount Shouyang deaths to be the height of foolishness and staying at court to be the only skill of true value. [Eating his fill and sitting at his ease, he took official service in exchange for the farming life.] Using his pose as a recluse to toy with the world, he went against the times, though he met with no very great harm. He cheated and perverted his age, never finding a good time [to remonstrate]. Was he not the very finest example of a jester?"

Someone asked me, "But didn't Liuxia Hui also style himself a recluse at court?"[96]

"A noble man would deem him disrespectful.[97] In antiquity, people valued most those who achieved distinction by starving and despised those who claimed to be 'recluses at heart' while drawing fat salaries from the court."[98]

---

90 Jizi was a sage whom legend says lived at the very end of the Shang; he was supposedly the uncle of the bad, last king of Shang, against whose misconduct Jizi offered many remonstrances. To avoid discovery and almost certain death, he applied lacquer to his own person, thereby rendering himself unrecognizable. Some legends have him wearing his hair loose and down his back so that he looked like a madman or "barbarian."

91 Inserting "to show his disdain for decorum," as implied.

92 This description cites passages in Dongfang's biography in *Shiji* 126, as indicated by brackets.

93 Alternatively, "free-spirited."

94 Adding Shu Qi, Bo Yi's brother, who shared the same fate as Bo (see n. 70). Different editions of the *Fayan* give variant readings here. Liuxia Hui played a somewhat dubious role in late Zhanguo politics; he is now chiefly famous for showing no joy or regret when he gained or lost office.

95 Adding "always," as implied.

96 Like Dongfang Shuo.

97 Cf. *Mengzi* 2A.9.

98 The reference to starving presumably refers to the deaths of Bo Yi and Shu Qi on Mount Shouyang.

11.22 妄譽,仁之賊也。妄毀,義之賊也。賊仁近鄉原。賊義近鄉訕。[41]

11.23 或問子蜀人也。請人。曰有李仲元者。人也。其為人也。奈何。曰不屈其意。不累其身。曰是夷,惠之徒與。曰不夷不惠。可否之間也。如是。則奚名之不彰也。曰無仲尼。則西山之餓夫與東國之絀臣惡乎聞。曰王陽貢禹遇仲尼乎。曰明星皓皓。華藻之力也與。[42] 曰若是。則奚為不自高。曰皓皓者,己也。引而高之者,天

41 See Waley's translation of *Analects* 7.13 (p. 213), which translates *xiang yuan* as "honest villager" (with "narrow views" implied).

42 I take this to mean they did not need to rely upon Kongzi for their fame, but Li Gui takes the "flowery decoration" to belong to the shining stars, arguing that even they need to be right in the sky to be seen. See Wang Rongbao (1987, 17.491).

An undeserved reputation is the bane of humaneness.[99] And reckless slander does violence to a sense of duty. To harm humaneness approaches the smugly parochial,[100] and to harm a sense of duty makes the village gossip.[101] 11.22

Someone asked me, "You, sir, are a man of Shu. I beg to ask about its men." 11.23

"There was one Li Zhongyuan of Shu. He was quite a man."[102]

"In what way?"

"He did not bend his will, neither did he overtax his own person."[103]

"In that was he not the same sort of fellow as Bo Yi or Liuxia Hui?"

"He was like neither a Bo Yi nor a Liuxia Hui.[104] He occupied the narrow space between the permissible and the impermissible."[105]

"If this was so, then why is his name not especially illustrious?"

"Had there been no Zhongni, then no one would have heard of the men who starved on West Mountain or of the official dismissed in the east [in Lu]!"[106]

"But what if Wang Yang and Gong Yu[107] had been so fortunate as to meet up with Zhongni?"

"They were brilliant shining stars. Surely you do not mean to say that they had to rely on the force of flowery encomia?"

"Well, if that's the case, then why don't people like Li Zhongyuan make *themselves* famous?"[108]

"Li had that shining quality, because that was his own doing. But it is

99 Literally, "is a thief of" (meaning that it steals or prevents something); *zei* also implies violence in Han law, which is germane here. Cf. *Fayan* 11.3.

100 Or "conventional fellow," the person who never reexamines what passes for truth in his own narrow community. See *Analects* 17.13. *Mencius* 7B.37 contains a long discussion of this term.

101 Or "slanderer."

102 Li Zhongyuan (i.e., Li Hong) was famous in his native area for virtuous conduct and public service on behalf of others.

103 This is very close to the expression attributed to Kongzi in *Analects* 18.8.

104 See *Fayan* 11.21, where Bo Yi and Liuxia Hui are also taken as standards against which to judge a man's character. This coupling occurs also in *Analects* 18.8.

105 Perhaps the phrase "as defined by convention" is implied. Here we see Yang Xiong writing a variation on a famous line by Kongzi, recorded in *Analects* 18.8: "I have no things I deem improper or proper [meaning, no settled preconceptions or convictions before examining the precise context for acting or speaking]" (*wu ke wu bu ke* 無可無不可). In this Li is like Butcher Ding 丁, whom Zhuangzi praised for wielding his knife within the interstices of the oxen that he slaughtered. See also *Fayan* 6.19 for Bo Yi and Shu Qi.

106 Zhongni is the courtesy name of Kongzi. This is the same argument made by Sima Qian in *Shiji* 61. Note the contrast between east and west.

107 Wang Yang (aka Wang Ji) and Gong Yu were two contemporaries who served Xuandi (r. 74–48 BCE) as forthright remonstrants in their posts; both took great risks in urging unpopular reforms. As they were also close friends, they have a joint biography in *Hanshu*.

108 Li Hong was one of Yang Xiong's models according to *Huayang guozhi* (Ren Naiqiang ed.) 10A.533.

也。子欲自高邪。仲元[43]世之師也。見其貌者。肅如也。聞其言者。愀如也。觀其行者。穆如也。鄲聞以德詘人矣。未聞以德詘於人也。仲元畏人也。[44]

或曰育賁。曰育賁也。人畏其力而侮其德。請條。曰非正不視。非正不聽。非正不言。非正不行。夫能正其視聽言行者。昔吾先師[45]之所畏也。如視不視。聽不聽。言不言。行不行。雖有育,賁。其猶侮諸。

43 See also *Taiping yulan* 404.13b, which calls Li Hong "a teacher for all times." Wang Rongbao (1987, 17.495) says of Li Hong that he became famous thanks to the *Fayan*.

44 Cf. *Shangshu* 44.0200, 47.0458–70.

45 Han Jing (1992, 310n9) identifies the "old master" as Kongzi, but it could also be Li Hong or Yan Junping, given the preceding discussion.

heaven that elevates a person.[109] Would a true master ever want to elevate himself? [No!][110] Li Zhongyuan[111] was model for the age. When one saw his demeanor, it was reverent. When one heard his talk, it was eloquent. When one observed his actions, they were imposing and compelling. I have only heard that one uses virtue to make others submit. I have never heard that one uses virtue in order to submit to others. Li Zhongyuan was a person of truly awesome dignity."

Someone asked me, "But what about the legendary strong men Xia Yu and Meng Ben?"

"With those two, people found their physical strength awesome alright, but they despised their characters."

"May I ask for particulars?"

"One should not look upon anything that is not straight and true. One should not listen to anything that is not straight and true. One should not speak anything that is not straight and true. And one should not do anything that is not straight and true. Now, the persons who align their seeing, hearing, speech, and acts with what is straight and true—these my old master long ago regarded as truly compelling figures. But if a person sees and hears what should not be seen and heard, and speaks and acts what should not be said or done—well then, even if that person is another Xia Yu or Meng Ben, he will still be despised!"

---

109 Implying that Wang Yu and Gong Yu became famous not primarily because of their virtue but because of their high rank, which Li Zhongyuan lacked.

110 The true *junzi* (noble man) awaits his fate and cares little about reputation.

111 I.e., Li Hong.

卷第十二

君子

君子, 純終領聞。蠢迪撿押。
旁開聖則。譔君子。

12.1 或問君子言則成文。動則成德。何以也。曰以其弸中而彪外也。般之揮斤。羿之激矢。君子不言。言必有中也。不行。行必有稱也。[1]

---

1 *Cheng* 稱 can mean "appropriate," but the same character refers to balanced things or situations.

Chapter 12

The Noble Man

VERSE SUMMARY

The noble man who remains pure to the end earns a fine reputation. Malefactors wreaking havoc, they he constrains,[1] at every point developing the models of the sages. Thus, I have compiled chapter 12, "The Noble Man."

Someone asked me, "In his every speech, the noble man brings to perfection his visible refinements of character, and in his every action, he perfects his charismatic presence.[2] How does he do that?"[3] 12.1

"At his core, he is as taut and full as a stretched bow, and outwardly, he is as beautiful as a tiger skin.[4] He is another Lu Ban wielding an ax, another Hou Yi shooting arrows.[5] The noble man seldom speaks,[6] but

1 The phrase *chundi jianya* 蠢迪撿/檢押 is difficult to translate. In the *Fayan* itself (13/26), as well as in every other Han text, the phrase *chundi* is coupled with references to barbarian incursions. The phrase *jianya* elsewhere is used to mean "putting manacles and stocks on malefactors." David Knechtges, following most commentators cited in Wang Rongbao 1987, takes this four-character phrase to be a positive description: "All his acts follow standards and norms," presuming the noble man to be bound or constrained by the Way. However, the description is so negative in other texts that I have decided to reject the standard positive gloss.

2 This line may also refer not to words and acts but to the perfection of the noble man's inner training (he becomes an exemplary pattern). It is also often read to mean "When a noble man uses words, he creates literature," in the same way that when he moves, he creates virtue. For this reading, see Vervoorn 1996, 57.

3 Or "What does he use?"

4 See *Changes*, Hexagram 49 (Ge), Line text 5. Cf. Blake's poem: "Tyger, Tyger burning bright / In the forest of the night / What immortal hand or eye / Could frame thy fearful symmetry" (another reflection on ineffable perfection).

5 Meaning that he is reliably expert in all his activities. The analogy may hold only for his expertise; he realizes his virtue in right actions, as unerringly as Lu Ban with the ax or Hou Yi with the bow.

6 Cf. *Analects* 11.14. But the same *Analects* phrase is also taken to mean that "he did not

12.2 或問君子之柔剛。曰君子於仁也柔。於義也剛。

12.3 或問航不漿。衝不薺。[2] 有諸。曰有之。或曰大器固不周於小乎。曰斯械也。君子不械。

12.4 或問孟子知言之要。知德之奧。曰非苟知之。亦允蹈之。或曰子小諸子。孟子非諸子乎。曰諸子者, 以其知異於孔子者也。孟子異乎。不異。

12.5 或曰孫卿非數家之書。侻也。[3] 至于子思, 孟軻。詭哉。曰吾於孫卿。與見同門而異戶也。惟聖人為不異。

2 The commentators cannot agree on the significance of the second metaphor, *ji* 薺. Most think it refers to a pulling song used by charioteers—hence, the translation. However, Liu Shipei (1916), following Li Gui, believes it refers to the near impossibility that a big war chariot would be filled with greens or the stems of young garlic rather than weapons. L'Haridon (2006) concurs.

3 Reading *tui* 侻 as *hao* 好.

when he does, his words invariably hit the mark. He seldom acts, but when he does, his conduct has always been weighed."

Someone asked me about the relative "softness or hardness" of the noble man.[7] 12.2

"The noble man is soft insofar as he is benevolent and hard in that he does his duty."

Someone asked me, "Are there great battleships that do not rely on oars, 12.3
or ramming carts not pulled to the tune of "Shepherd's Purse"?[8]

"There are."

Someone remarked, "So you concede that a great vessel may be less well equipped than a small one for handling small tasks?"[9]

"We've been talking about tools and vessels. The noble man is no mere tool."[10]

Someone asked me, "Mencius knew the essentials of rhetoric,[11] but did he 12.4
understand the mysterious depths of charismatic virtue?"

"He not only understood it; he fully realized it."[12]

Someone asked me, "You disparage the various philosophical masters, but wasn't Mencius one of them?"

"The philosophical masters are defined by the points on which they diverged from Kongzi.[13] Did Mencius ever diverge? He did not."

Someone said to me, "In the many writings where Xun Qing[14] criticized 12.5
the various philosophical masters, he did well. But was he not perversely argumentative when it came to Zisi[15] and Mencius?"

---

speak [at all]," as in *Analects* 7.21.

7 "Hard" and "soft" refer not only to "yang" and "yin" respectively (as in the "Xici") but also to attitudes toward the use of the penal code to effect change.

8 A farmer would ordinarily pile garlic and greens onto an oxcart or a wheelbarrow, not a huge battleship meant to transport more important items. If that reading is right, parallelism suggests that the first three-character phrase should be read as "great multistoried battleships do not transport [unimportant] liquids" or, as Yu Yue (1874) suggests, "sauces." But see n. 2 on ji 薺.

9 With the implication that the noble man may not be as accomplished in some respects as lesser men.

10 Cf. *Analects* 5.4, which nonetheless says of Kongzi's disciple that he is a precious jade vessel.

11 Cf. *Mencius* 3B.9, where someone asks Mencius whether he is not "fond of disputation."

12 Meaning that he not only talked the talk but walked the walk.

13 Both "knowledge" and "understanding" are possible translations of *zhi* 知.

14 The traditional death dates for Xun Qing, the most influential philosopher to shape Western Han thought, are given as anywhere between 230 and 213 BCE. In his influential "Critique of the Twelve Thinkers," Xunzi lumped Mencius and Zisi with other thinkers, charging them with one-sided views. Mencius, for example, was said to be like Zhuangzi in paying too much attention to heaven (meaning here "the natural conditions") and thus too little to ritual.

15 Grandson of Kongzi and purported author of the "Zhongyong."

12.6 牛玄騂白。睟而角。其升諸廟乎。是以君子全其德。[4]

12.7 或問君子似玉。[5] 曰純淪溫潤。柔而堅。玩而廉。隊乎其不可形也。[6]

12.8 或曰仲尼之術。[7] 周而不泰。大而不小。用之猶牛鼠也。[8] 曰仲尼之道。猶四瀆也。經營中國。終入大海。他人之道者。西北之流也。綱紀夷貉。或入于沱。或淪于漢。

12.9 淮南說[9] 之用。不如太史公之用也。太史公,聖人將有取焉。淮南,鮮取焉爾。必也儒乎。乍出乍入。[10] 淮南也。文麗用寡。長卿也。多愛不忍。子長也。仲尼多愛。愛義也。[11] 子長多愛。愛奇也。[12]

---

4 Several commentators, including Tao Hongqing 陶鴻慶, cited in Wang Rongbao (1987, 18.502), append this passage to *Fayan* 12.3, while others (Song Xian 宋咸 and Wu Mi 吳祕) believe it belongs with *Fayan* 12.4. Wang Rongbao (1987) disagrees.

5 The analogies are also discussed in *Liji* 49.11 ("Bin yi" 賓義), which states that "the noble man's virtue compares to jade" (君子比德於玉).

6 Reading *dui* 隊 as *jui* 墜 (let fall), pertaining to the weight and heft of jade pendants, if we follow Sima Guang, cited in Wang Rongbao (1987, 18.503): 垂之如隊, 禮也. Yu Yue (1874) reads this as *zhong* 眾, on the basis of Song texts (none of which are specified); or as *sui* 燧, meaning "profound" or "deep" (hence "wise"). Wang Rongbao (1987, 18.503) glosses *dui* as *di* 棣, whose reduplicative form means "dignified and at ease."

7 Han Jing (1992, 317n1) takes "art" to mean "academic theories" (*xue shuo* 學說), but the phrase clearly refers more generally to conduct, including the performing of the polite arts.

8 According to Han Jing (1992, 318n1), *niu* 牛 should be read as a verb. Cf. *Fayan* 12.3. Alternatively, it could mean "using an ox in a rat's place" (meaning, not suiting the tool or method to the problem at hand).

9 *Shuo* 說 can refer to "explications" and "sayings"; hence, the translation.

10 Han Jing (1992, 319n2) takes this to mean that Liu An's text sometimes adopts the stance of a classicist and sometimes not. However, it could just as well mean that Liu An sometimes, because he is not a classicist, hones in on the core of a problem and sometimes not.

11 Reading *yi* 義 as "sense of duty" but with the added sense of *yi* 儀 (decorum). Han Jing (1992, 319n2) also expands *yi* to mean *ren yi* 仁義 (humaneness and duty).

12 See Liu Rulin 1935, 2.109.

"What do I think of Xun Qing? I see him as a different door in the same gate.[16] Only a sage does not diverge in the slightest from the sage."[17]

The sacrificial ox can be black, reddish, or white.[18] So long as its hide is a single color and it has horns, it is fit to be offered at the temple. This explains why the noble man keeps his character whole and pure. 12.6

Someone asked me about the noble man's resemblance to jade.[19] 12.7

"It is glossy and pure, warm and lustrous, soft yet solid. It is pleasing to roll it around in the hand,[20] yet it has straight edges.[21] Its heft and depth are beyond description."

Someone said to me, "The arts of Zhongni may have been comprehensive, yet unattainable.[22] Great they may be but unsuited to small schemes. Were one to employ them every day,[23] it would be like using a sacrificial ox to catch a rat." 12.8

"The Way of Zhongni is like the Four Great Rivers,[24] which work their way deliberately through the Central States before finally entering the sea. The ways ascribed to others are like the rivers of the far northwest, which crisscross the territories of the Yi and Mo before draining into the Tuo or flowing into the Han.[25]

The theories of Huainan[26] are not as useful as those of the Senior Archivist.[27] From the Archivist, even a sage can draw some inspiration and erudition, but from Huainan, very little can be gotten. What one needs to be is a classicist! Hit or miss—that's the style of Huainan. Ornate patterns of little real utility—that's Sima Xiangru for you.[28] Enthralled with everything and everyone,[29] and incapable of holding back—that's Sima 12.9

16 I.e., in the same philosophical line as Kongzi.

17 I.e., Kongzi.

18 Cf. *Analects* 6.6. According to, e.g., *Liji*, "Tangong, xia," 3.13/12/6, the Xia favored black, the Yin favored red, and the Zhou favored white, and these preferences were reflected in their choice of sacrificial animals. Cf. Dong Zhongshu's theories of the Three Powers of Black-Red-White in his *Chunqiu jieyu*.

19 Cf. *Analects* 5.4. Jade is supposedly soft to the touch with fine veins running throughout.

20 Or "polished to roundness."

21 Meaning that it can be cut so as to have straight angles, whose straightness symbolizes punctiliousness, scrupulousness, and incorruptibility.

22 See *Changes*, Hexagram 11 (Tai).

23 Adding "every day" (meaning "in every situation"), as implied.

24 The Yangzi in the east, the Ji in the north, the Huai in the south, and the Yellow River in the west.

25 Both the Tuo and the Han River are tributaries of the Yangzi River. The Tuo flows in Sichuan, and the Han, in Hubei, two parts of the Han empire regarded then as frontier zones.

26 I.e., Liu An, compiler of the *Huainan zi*.

27 I.e., Sima Qian (and possibly also his father, Tan), authors of the *Shiji*. This is the second time Yang compares Sima Qian and Huainan.

28 *Fayan* 2.2 seems more positive about Sima Xiangru.

29 This is a very loose translation for *duo ai* 多愛. Quite possibly, the two-character phrase means "overly empathetic," but as Kongzi was not known to be that, I have given the phrase a more neutral meaning. Cf. *Zuozhuan*, Lord Wen, Year 1.

12.10 或曰甚矣。傳書之不果也。[13] 曰不果則不果矣。人(=又?)以巫鼓。[14]

12.11 或問聖人之言。炳若丹青。有諸。曰吁。是何言與。丹青初則炳。久則渝。渝乎哉。

12.12 或曰聖人之道若天。天則有常矣。奚聖人之多變也。[15] 曰聖人固多變。子游,子夏得其書矣。未得其所以書也。宰我子貢得其言矣。未得其所以言也。顏淵閔子騫得其行矣。未得其所以行也。聖人之書言行。天也。天其少變乎。

---

13 Trying to capture both senses of *guo* 果 as (1) the substantial or real, and (2) factual, as the phrase *ze bu guo yi* 则不果矣 plays on both senses of the word *guo*. Andrew Plaks (pers. comm.) prefers "the unverifiability of the transmitted writings." If they don't pan out, they do not bear fruit.

14 Andrew Plaks (pers. comm.) prefers "Some of them are no better than wizards drumming." Wang Rongbao (1987, 18.508), cited in Han Jing (1992, 320n2), would read *ren* 人 as *you* 又 (also, moreover), believing *ren* to be a mistake in transcription, but I see no reason to emend the text. This is possibly an attack on the *fangshi* 方士 and the apocrypha, as drumming was used to excite people, and so to propagate ideas (*gu chui* 鼓吹), even when they were just false show. This line was used without attribution by *Wenxin diaolong* 9.1/89/1, which is devoted to "literary flaws."

15 The word "changes" (*bian* 變) can imply "violent changes" or even "destruction," in contrast to *hua* 化, which implies "evolution." For this, see "Xici" A.11.

Qian all over. Kongzi had many enthusiasms, but what he truly loved was a sense of duty. Sima Qian had many enthusiasms, but what he loved best were oddities and curiosities.[30]

Someone said to me, "Such a grave problem—the inaccuracies and lack of substance in the transmitted texts." 12.10

"If they are that way, they will not bear fruit. But some get all worked up by magicians drumming!"[31]

Someone asked me, "Has there ever been a case where a sage's words were as striking as a painting of red and green mineral pigments?"[32] 12.11–12

"Huh! What sort of talk is this? Cinnabar and malachite may be brilliantly colored at first, but after a while their color fades.[33] Do *those* words also fade?"

Someone asked me, "If the Way of the Sages is like heaven, and heaven has its regular, constant laws, then why do the sages undergo so many transformations?"[34]

"The sages do indeed undergo many changes. Ziyou and Zixia certainly got the Master's writings,[35] but they never truly apprehended his reasons for writing.[36] Zai Wo and Zigong certainly got his talent for speechifying, but they never truly apprehended his reasons for speaking. Yan Yuan and Min Ziqian certainly got his mode of conduct, but they never truly apprehended his reasons for acting as he did. The sages' writings, speeches, and conduct are truly like heaven![37] Surely you don't mean to say that heaven undergoes only a few transformations?"[38]

---

30 I.e., departures from regular patterns. This comment may represent Yang's swipe at Liu Xin, his contemporary, or at the academic establishment. When Liu Xin handed the throne a copy of the *Classic of Mountains and Seas* (Shanhai jing 山海經) produced under his direction, the *Shanhai jing* became all the fashion at court. It is said that the *wenxue* 文學 and the great classicists (Ru) all read and learned it because they "took it for a curiosity" in which one could learn about anomalous things.

31 Translation tentative. Alternatively, "Inaccuracies *are* inaccuracies. Worse yet is the magicians' drumming that magnifies these flaws!"

32 Cf. *Fayan* 2.6.

33 This stock theme is seen, for example, in *Huainan zi* 213/20/22–23. An aesthetic discourse in the classical era cast painting as unlike music in that painting does not convey temporal dimensions well; that it is stuck in one time helps to explain why painting fades over time.

34 This may refer not just to the *shen* (godlike) quality of the sages but also to the way the portrayals of them change over time.

35 Meaning "Kongzi's writings." *Analects* 11.2 names Ziyou and Zixia as the two disciples known for their "culture and learning" (*wenxue* 文學).

36 Or, more generally, "why [the sages] wrote," taking here and below Kongzi as a sage.

37 The phrase *tian ye* 天也 is ambiguous; it means "they come from heaven" or "they imitate heaven." Here I take it to mean that the sage's model is constant, perfect, and all-encompassing, like heaven.

38 Heaven is constant, perfect, and all-encompassing. Implicit here is the debate begun at least as early as Xunzi about whether one should speak about "constants" or about "changes" and unforeseen events; there is also a nod to Han debates over the relative reliability of portents versus ordinary events. The parallel between the sage's Way and the cosmic Way is a given. The unnamed interlocutor is focusing on only one aspect of heaven (that its movements exhibit certain regularities) while ignoring others.

12.13 或曰聖人自恣與。何言之多端也。[16] 曰子未覩禹之行水與。一東一北。行之無礙也。君子之行獨無礙乎。如何直往也。水避礙則通于海。君子避礙則通于理。[17]

12.14 君子好人之好。而忘己之好。小人好己之惡。而忘人之好。

12.15 或曰子於天下則誰與。曰與夫進者乎。[18] 或曰貪夫位也。慕夫祿也。何其與。曰此貪也。非進也。夫進也者。進於道。慕於德。殷之以仁義。進而進。退而退。[19] 日孳孳而不自知勸者也。或曰進進則聞命矣。[20] 請問退進。曰昔乎顏淵以退為進。天下鮮儷焉。或

16 *Duan* 端 is an extraordinarily difficult term to translate, as it has so many meanings, including "a beginning," "an extremity," "a direction," "a clue," "a reason," or "a rationale," "what is correct or proper or properly arranged," or even "an important point."

17 Cf. *Fayan* 7.5, where *li* 理 is associated with the *Annals* purportedly compiled by Kongzi; cf. "Zhongyong" 32.30/147/11, 17.

18 The antonyms *jin* and *tui* 進退 refer to "engagement and disengagement" with public life.

19 However, Sima Guang, cited in Wang Rongbao (1987, 18.512), would read this line not as *tui er tui* 退而退 (as in my translation) but as *tui er jin* 退而進, making a demotion or a withdrawal also an advance; Sima Guang advises one "not to consider advancement and demotion according to salary and rank, but simply to devote all one's energies to [apprehending and implementing] the Way and virtue." See Han Jing (1992, 324n2), which cites Sima Guang's and Wang Rongbao's (1987) approval of this explication, and relates it to the interlocutor's next speech, which mentions *tui jin* 退進. The line would then read, "If advancement realizes the Way, then one advances, and if withdrawal fulfills the Way, then one withdraws."

20 Han Jing (1992, 324n3) glosses *wen ming* 聞命 as "heard what you have said before."

Someone asked me, "Do sages follow their own inclinations? If not, how are we to explain the many directions their words take?"[39] 12.13

"Did you never see the way that Yu guided[40] the waters? Now to the east and now to the north, he channeled the waters so that their courses would meet with no obstructions. How can you possibly claim that the noble man in his conduct avoids all obstacles in his path? In what sense[41] do such men proceed straight toward their goal? Only when the water's path avoids obstructions does it get through to the sea. And only when the noble man avoids obstacles does he see clear through to the inherent patterns and principles in things and people."[42]

The noble man likes the good in other people, but he forgets the good in himself.[43] The petty man likes his own worst qualities, and he tends to forget the good in other people.[44] 12.14

Someone asked me, "Master, vis-à-vis the realm, whose side are *you* on?" 12.15

"I'm with those who advance!"[45]

Someone asked me, "The greedy get positions; the ambitious get official ranks and salaries. Why be on *their* side?"[46]

"That is greed, not advance. Now 'advance' to me means 'advancing in the Way,'[47] and 'admiring and emulating men of virtue' and 'attaining eminence through humaneness and a sense of duty.' If one would advance, one should advance in this way. Then a setback becomes a real setback. Hence the phrase, 'exerting oneself to the utmost every single day without ever feeling weary.'"[48]

Someone said to me, "Well, I have heard what you have to say about advancing in the one to advance in the other. So let me ask about the reverse: retiring from public life in order to advance in the Way."

"Long ago, Yan Yuan took retiring from public life to be an advance, and few in the world can compare with him!"[49]

---

39 Translation tentative.

40 Both meanings—"to travel along" and "to guide"—are conveyed by the single word *xing* 行.

41 Meaning "There *are* obstructions." They do confront obstacles.

42 Adding "in things and people" for clarification.

43 Meaning that he does not think particularly highly of himself, but he is inclined to be generous in his assessments of others.

44 On the rarity of finding an individual capable of assessing his own faults, see *Analects* 5.26. Cf. *Analects* 1.16.

45 An earlier version of mine used both "advance" and "engagement" to translate *jin* because the character also means "advancing in office."

46 Or "Why should they be approved?" Yang is playing with two senses of *jin*, as "progress in" and "advance [in office]."

47 Cf. *Analects* 4.5: "Riches and honors are what all men want, but if they cannot be had without doing violence to the Way, then they must be renounced.

48 Cf. the description of Kongzi and the noble man as men who "never felt weary" so long as they were promoting the Way (*Analects* 7.2, 7.34, 12.14, 13.1).

49 Meaning that Yan Yuan (i.e., Yan Hui) did not equate seeking power and rank with moral advance. Strictly speaking, Yan did not ever have an office, so I have taken this to refer more broadly to engagement in public life versus disengagement.

曰若此。則何少於必退也。曰必[21] 進易儷。必退易儷也。進以禮。退以義。難儷也。[22]

12.16 或曰人有齊死生。同貧富。等貴賤。何如。曰作此者其有懼乎。信死生齊貧富同, 貴賤等。則吾以聖人為囂囂。[23]

12.17 通天, 地, 人。曰儒。通天, 地而不通人。曰伎。

12.18 人必先作。然後人名之。先求。然後人與之。人必其自愛也。而後人愛諸。人必其自敬也。而後人敬諸。自愛, 仁之至也。自敬, 禮之至也。未有不自愛, 敬而人愛, 敬之者也。

12.19 或問龍, 龜, 鴻鵠不亦壽乎。曰壽。曰人可壽乎。曰物以其性。人以其仁。[24]

---

21 Han Jing (1992, 325n4) defines *bi* 必 as "finds it necessary to."

22 *Hanshu* 72.3097 says that the *shi* who retire to the mountains and forests cannot return to court, and those at court, once they enter, cannot go out again.

23 Han Jing (1992, 326n2) glosses this blandly as "He probably would have his cares and concerns, no?"

24 Unlike Han Jing (1992, 327n2), I do not think that Yang is saying here that an individual's longevity depends upon that person's morality.

Someone asked me, "Well, if it is as you say, why belittle those who must retire or retreat?"

"It's easy to equal those who are forced to advance or retreat. But it is very hard to find Yan's equal in advancing as propriety dictates and retreating as duty dictates!"[50]

Someone asked me, "How would it be if I thought life and death, poverty and wealth, high rank and low, all were equal?"[51] 12.16

"Isn't there something truly horrible[52] about acting this way?[53] If I truly deemed life and death to be equal, and poverty and riches to be just the same, and high and low rank comparable, then I would have to think the sages just so much hot air!"[54]

Someone who thoroughly understands heaven, earth, and human beings we call a true classicist.[55] Someone who comprehends heaven and earth, but not people, we term a mere technician.[56] 12.17

People must first do something before others grant them a good name. They must first seek something before others will give it to them. People must love themselves before others will love them.[57] They must have self-respect before others will respect them. To love oneself is the ultimate expression of humaneness, just as self-respect is the ultimate expression of ritual decorum. There has never been a person who failed to love and respect himself who was loved and respected by others.[58] 12.18

Someone asked me, 'Are not the dragon, turtle, and crane each long-lived?" 12.19

"They are."

"Can people live long?"

"Those creatures live long because of their inborn natures, whereas people live long because of their humaneness."[59]

---

50 Both ways of life have their shortcomings.

51 Of course, the second chapter of the *Zhuangzi* comes to mind.

52 Or "terrifying" or "a source of grave concern."

53 Alternatively, "Didn't he who wrote this [also] feel terror?" which is Sima Guang's preferred reading, cited in Wang Rongbao (1987, 18.513).

54 Or "clamor," "din."

55 *Ru* 儒, here a follower of Kongzi.

56 For the many possible translations of *ji* (伎 = 技?), see the notes to *Fayan* 10.16.

57 And so spare themselves (here and below), since *ai* means both "to love" and "to spare."

58 Cf. *Xunzi* 56/15/66–67, where Yan Yuan says, "The truly wise know themselves; the truly humane love themselves."

59 Good or bad conduct is not always requited. Yang recognizes the role of fate, so he is trying to move the conversation away from longevity, which is a poor measure of human worth because it is beyond human control. Yang here most likely recalls *Analects* 6.23 (*renzhe shou* 仁者壽); at most, all other things being equal, the good man has a chance to live longer, since he has not sought to destroy others in his group.

12.20 或問人言仙者。有諸乎。吁。吾聞宓羲神農歿。黃帝, 堯, 舜殂落而死。文王。畢。孔子。魯城之北。獨子愛其死乎。[25] 非人之所及也。仙亦無益子之彙矣。或曰聖人不師仙。厥術異也。聖人之於天下。恥一物之不知。仙人之於天下。恥一日之不生。曰生乎。生乎。名生而實死也。或曰世無仙。則焉得斯語。曰語乎者。非嚚嚚也與。惟嚚嚚能使無為有。或問仙之實。曰無以為也。有與無。非問也。問也者, 忠孝之問也。忠臣孝子偟乎不偟。

25 Andrew Plaks (pers. comm.) prefers "not willing to play your dying card" or "waste your death," as he thinks (rightly) that *ai qi si* means "wants his death to count for something."

Someone asked me, "People say there are immortals. Is there anything to such stories?" 12.20

"Hmm. I have heard that

Fuxi and Shennong perished;
Huangdi, Yao, and Shun all passed away.
King Wen expired in Bi,[60] and
Kongzi was buried north of the Lu capital walls.[61]

Are you the only person to begrudge his own death? Immortality is not something people can attain. Nor is immortality the sort of thing that would do the likes of you any good!"[62]

Someone said to me, "The sages do not model themselves upon immortals, their arts and methods being quite different. The sage's regard for the world is such that he is ashamed of not understanding every single creature,[63] while the immortal's relation to the world is such that he is ashamed to not be alive for a single day."

"Life! Life! [The search for immortality] may claim to be about life, but in truth it is a kind of death."

Someone asked me, "If there have really never been immortals in this world, why is there talk of them?"

"It's all just talk—meaningless babble, no? Only such babble could confuse the nonexistent with what's real!"

Someone asked me, "What *is* the true story, then, about immortals?"

"Don't proceed in this way![64] Whether immortals exist or not—that is not the question to ask. What one should inquire about is loyalty and filial duty.[65] Would loyal officials and the filial sons waste time asking about this[66] when they feel they have not a moment to waste?"

---

60 East of present-day Xianyang.

61 I.e., north of the walls of Qufu.

62 Cf. poem 15 of the Nineteen Old Poems, which is equally skeptical about the possibility of immortality.

63 Literally, "ashamed of a single thing's being unknown" or, alternatively, "ashamed at a single creature's being left unknowing," which reading would emphasize the sage's responsibility to enlighten everything.

64 Cf. *Analects* 19.24. Or "There is no way for them to exist." Knechtges (1968, 134n216) translates instead: "There is nothing to say about them. Their existence or non-existence is not something to ask [about]."

65 Having seldom talked about filial duty (*xiao* 孝), the *Fayan* takes this up, presumably to lay the ground for the next chapter.

66 Adding "about this," as implied.

12.21 或問壽可益乎。曰德。曰回, 牛之行德矣。曷壽之不益也。曰德。故爾。如回之殘, 牛之賊也。焉得爾。[26] 曰殘賊或壽。[27] 曰彼妄也。[28] 君子不妄。

12.22 有生者必有死。有始者必有終。[29] 自然之道也。

12.23 君子忠人。況己乎。小人欺己。況人乎。

26 *Er* 爾 (lit., "like this" 如此), according to Han Jing (1992, 331n2), refers in the first instance to the terrible fates they endured "like this" and, in the second instance, to the splendid reputations that Yan Hui and Ran Boniu achieved for virtue in later ages. The phrase *yan de er* means "How could they have attained / merited that?"

27 L'Haridon (2006, vol. 2, 104) reads, "If Yan Hui had been cruel and Ran Boniu false, how would they have ever been able to obtain *that*?"

28 Li Gui, cited in Wang Rongbao (1987, 18.510), cites *Analects* 6.19: "Man's very life is honesty, in that without it he will be lucky indeed if he escapes with his life." Some editions read *wang* 妄 as *wang* 罔 (without), but the emendation is unnecessary; *wang* here means "not straight," "baseless," "undeserved."

29 The same statement appears in *Shiji* 75.2362. The line may also play on the *Daode jing*, sec. 33: "To die but not be forgot is to be immortal" (死而不亡者壽).

Someone asked me, "Can the length of one's life span be increased?" 12.21
"By virtue, yes."
"But surely Yan Hui and Ran Boniu acted virtuously![67] Why was there no increase to *their* life spans?"
"Their name for virtue has lasted for a long time, surely![68] Had Yan Hui's humaneness been damaged, or Boniu's dutifulness impaired, how could they have ever gained their immortal reputations?"
"But some damaged and impaired people *do* live long."
"Those are freak accidents.[69] The noble man does not interest himself in such."

Whatever is born is bound to die. Beginnings all have their endings.[70] 12.22
That is the way things are.

"The noble man is loyal to others, and all the more so to himself! The 12.23
petty man deceives himself, and all the more so others!"

---

67 Two disciples of Kongzi.

68 The sentence could mean either that Yan Yuan and Ran Boniu did have their life spans extended by their virtue, since their lives would have been cut short at an even earlier time had they been less virtuous, or that they have lived on through the ages by means of their posthumous good names. Alternatively, the line means they deserved their reputation for virtue but not their illnesses and early deaths.

69 Or simply "irregular events." This argument recalls arguments made in the *Xunzi*, chap. 17 ("On Heaven" [Tian lun])

70 Yang Xiong here clearly refers to the Ru theory that argued, contra the Mohists, that a person's death has its predetermined time. See *Lunheng* 6/14/20–23, on the Ru theories.

卷第十三

孝至

孝莫大於寧親。寧親莫大於寧神。
寧神莫大於四表之歡心。譔孝至。

13.1 孝。[1] 至矣乎。一言而該。聖人不加焉。[2]

1 The *Xiaojing*, sec. 9, describes *xiao* in the following terms: "Of all things in heaven and earth, humans are the most valuable. No behavior is greater than filial devotion. No devotion is greater than reverently attending to one's father, and no reverent attention is better than making that parent the coadjutor of heaven itself" (天地之性人為貴。人之行莫大於孝。孝莫大於嚴父。嚴父莫大於配天). According to Wang Rongbao (1987, 19.523), this last chapter comes full circle with the first, showing the practical sociopolitical applications of the cultivation advocated in the first chapter of the *Fayan*.

2 Cf. the *Xiaojing*, sec. 9, which says, "Besides, what can be added to/greater than filial devotion?" (又何以加於孝乎). This line recalls the praise Kongzi supposedly accorded the Way of Zhougong in *Kongzi jiayu* 10/10 ("Haosheng" 好生), describing King Wen's Way (文王之道) as something to which nothing can possibly be added (其不可加焉).

Chapter 13

Honoring the Ancestors, the Ultimate Duty

VERSE SUMMARY

For filial duty, nothing is greater than comforting parents. For comforting parents, nothing is greater than comforting the spirits.[1] And for comforting spirits, nothing is better than cheering the hearts of the whole realm. Thus, I have compiled chapter 13, "Honoring the Ancestors, the Ultimate Duty."[2]

Filial duty is surely best of all![3] All is encompassed in that single word 13.1
xiao 孝, meaning "honoring the ancestors and family reverence." No person, not even the sage, could say or do anything more than that![4]

---

1 *Zuozhuan*, Zhao 20.6, talks of the denizens of the spirit realm refusing to consume the domain's sacrifices whenever they felt that the ruler was not worthy enough. As seen below, this becomes an important theme in the chapter.

2 *Fayan* 13 presents filial duty not as the foundation of morality, as in *Analects* 1.2, but as the "ultimate" achievement of the moral and political life, as in the Han dynasty text the *Xiaojing* 孝經. However, Yang also redefines filial duty, as noted in Nylan, forthcoming-b. Notably, the last chapter contains key historical assessments and a return to "honoring the ancients" (e.g., Yao, Shun, Tang, King Wen, Kongzi) as a final refuge and comfort; in this Yang may be imitating the last chapter of the *Xunzi*, which ends with "Questions for Yao."

3 Yang here may be thinking of the "Xici" formulation that says that the *Changes* is "the ultimate" or "best" (易其至矣乎) or the *Analects* line that gives the same praise to the "centered usages" (*zhong yong* 中庸). The phrase *qi zhi yi hu* occurs many times in the *Fayan*.

4 This translation is an expanded version of the more literal "Nothing can be added [i.e., thought superior] to it."

13.2 父母，子之天地與。無天何生。無地何形。天地裕於萬物乎。萬物裕於天地乎。裕父母之裕。不裕矣。事父母自知不足者。其舜乎。

13.3 不可得而久者。[3] 事親之謂也。孝子愛日。

13.4 孝子有祭乎。有齊乎。夫能存亡形，屬荒絕者。惟齊也。故孝子之於齊。見父母之存也。[4] 是以祭(=齊?)不賓。[5] 人而不祭。豺獺乎。[6]

13.5 或問子。曰死生盡禮。可謂能子乎。

13.6 曰石奮石建。父子之美也。無是父。無是子。無是子。無是父。

3 See *Hanshi waizhuan* 7.7/51/5, speaking of a filial paragon's view of one's parents: "Once gone, they cannot be brought back" (*wang er be ke huan zhe* 往而不可還者).

4 Li Gui's commentary, cited in Wang Rongbao (1987, 19.525), refers to the fast, where on the third day, the fasting person sees the object of cult. Therefore, Andrew Plaks (pers. comm.) prefers "he sees them as alive."

5 However, Sima Guang, cited in Wang Rongbao (1987, 19.525–26) reads this as "That is why, in offering sacrifice, he does not revert to the formality of host and guests," arguing that the filial son does not wish to treat his parents with the formality due guests, since his love for his parents exceeds his feelings for guests. In some sense, Sima Guang's reading follows more logically from the preceding phrase (見父母之存也). Still, Yu Yue (1874) objects to Sima Guang's reading, on the grounds that it imagines a regrettable departure from the old precepts embodied in the *Yi li*; Yu Yue therefore reads *bu bin* as I have, "not entertaining guests."

6 See, e.g., Huainan zi 5/39/5 (時則訓).

"Parents are heaven and earth to their children.[5] Without heaven, how could they be born? Without earth, how would they have assumed form? Are heaven and earth generous toward the myriad things, or are the myriad things generous towards heaven and earth? To be generous to the parents who have shown generosity to oneself is not generosity at all![6] Was it not Shun who 'in serving his parents came to recognize his own inadequacy'?[7] Serving parents is rightly called 'the duty that cannot be sustained for long enough.'[8] The filial child regards every single day that he has to express his love as precious." 13.2–4

"Does the filial child[9] offer sacrifices? Does he fast?"

"Only fasting and sacrifice can preserve those who no longer have form and are already relegated to a shadowy realm. Therefore, the filial child in fasting and sacrifice makes his parents appear before him as they were in life.[10] That is why he does not entertain guests during the times of sacrifice.[11] To be human yet to fail to make the offerings—is that not to be even less than the jackal or otter?[12]

Someone asked me about good sons. 13.5

"In death and in life, can we not call those who carry out the rites fully[13] 'capable sons'?"

"Shi Fen and Shi Jian represent the ideal father-son relation. Without such a father there would never have been such a son, and vice versa!"[14] 13.6

"So you think it always depends on the pairing of father and son?"

---

5 Han discussions on morality often claim that one party is "heaven" (*tian* 天) to another; parents are to be regarded as heaven by their children, and husbands, by their wives. Yang explains the particular sense in which he means this; many other passages do not. As parents have conferred all blessings on the child, including the gift of life, the child has no way to adequately repay the parents, let alone confer greater blessings on them. All possible benefits and more are owed to them.

6 As Sima Guang, cited in Wang Rongbao (1987, 19.524), says, "to confer benefits" mean to "give lavishly more than is due."

7 Shun is regarded as the perfect exemplar of filial duty in such texts as the *Mencius* because his father and mother were awful people, perhaps even would-be murderers, but Shun nonetheless served them with perfect deference. *Mencius* 5A and 7A treat Shun repeatedly as exemplary person.

8 Since the older generation inevitably dies. Adding "enough," as implied.

9 It is not only filial sons who sacrificed to ancestors in Han times—hence my use of the word "child."

10 The *Liji* chapter entitled "Meaning of Sacrifice" (Ji yi 祭義) has the filial child, no matter what his age, visualizing his parents, so that they appear to come alive before his very eyes during the sacrifice.

11 The idea here is that while fasting, he does not entertain guests.

12 Adding "even less than," for sense. The two animals were thought to offer sacrifice; in that single feature, they were like good men, even if they were in other aspects inauspicious. Jackals typically do not consume all of their victims immediately, so people thought they were setting aside a portion of the kill for blood sacrifices. The otter was widely believed to offer sacrifices of fish to its ancestors.

13 Cf. *Analects* 2.4.

14 Shi Fen, ally of the Han founder; Shi Jian was the eldest son of Shi Fen.

或曰必也兩乎。曰與堯無子。舜無父。不如堯父舜子也。

13.7 子有含菽縕絮而致滋美其親。將以求孝也。人曰偽。如之何。曰假儒衣, 書。服而讀之。三月不歸。孰曰非儒也。[7] 或曰何以處偽。[8] 曰有人則作。無人則輟之謂偽。觀人者。審其作。輟而已矣。

13.8 不為名之名。其至矣乎。為名之名。其次也。

13.9 或問忠言嘉謀。曰言合稷契謂之忠。[9] 謀合皋陶謂之嘉。或曰邵如之何。曰亦勗之而已。庳則秦儀鞅斯, 亦忠嘉矣。

13.10 堯舜之道皇兮。夏殷周之道將兮。[10] 而以延其光兮。或曰何謂也。

---

7 Cf. *Yantie lun* 5.7/36/3–5: "To wear Ru clothes and to wear Ru caps but not to be able to carry out the Ru Way—that is not what we mean by Ru."

8 Andrew Plaks (pers. comm.) prefers "subsume it under the false." Yu Yue (1874) defines *chu* 處 (place, stance) as "the place things reside in"; also "causing each thing to get its proper place." Yu says that *chu* therefore means *duan* 斷 ("to decide"; i.e., "to investigate").

9 Wang Rongbao (1987, 19.532–33) and Han Jing (1992, 340n2) remind us that the present-day "Gao Yao mo" chapter in the *Documents*—or at least its division into two sections—dates to the Jin dynasty (265–420), so it may be difficult to decide what Yang Xiong intends to draw to his readers' attention.

10 Reading *jiang* 將 as synonym for *huang* 皇 or *da* 大.

"Yao had no Shun for a son, and Shun had no Yao for a father. It's better to have fathers like Yao paired with sons like Shun."[15]

"Let us suppose a son were to seek to express his filial devotion by subsisting on beans and pulses and wearing frayed clothes in order to give his parents the finest foods and clothes. If others said that it was all an act, what would you think?" 13.7–8

"What would you say about a person who borrowed the robes and writings of the classicist, wearing the one while reciting the other, for three straight months without returning them?[16] Who would deny that such a person is a classicist?"[17]

Someone asked me, "But then how is one to spot a faker?"[18]

"If a person does certain things when others are present but stops doing them whenever nobody else is looking, he should be called a faker. In assessing others, attend to the contexts in which a person does something and stops doing it—that's all there is to it!"

"Surely it is best to have the reputation of not acting merely for the sake of a good name! To gain a reputation for acting merely for the sake of a good name—that is decidedly worse!"[19]

Someone asked me about loyal speech and commendable plans. 13.9

"Speech that is in accord with that of Hou Ji and Xie[20]—that we call loyal! Plans consonant with those of Gao Yao—those we call commendable!"[21]

Someone asked me, "Is there no alternative to aiming so high?"

"It's simply a question of making the effort. Lower your sights, and you will find Su Qin, Zhang Yi, Shang Yang, and Li Si sufficiently loyal and commendable."

The Way of Yao and Shun—how elevated it was! 13.10
The Ways of Xia, Yin, and Zhou—how splendid they were!
And so one may extend their shining glories to the present age![22]

Someone asked me, "What do you mean?"

---

15 This means that failing to have the ideal pairing of a Yao as a father and a Shun as a son, one should still strive to be a father like Yao and a son like Shun, instead of claiming that it always takes two to achieve real excellence.

16 Doing something for three months in the *Analects* indicates fixity of purpose.

17 *Mencius* 6B.2 says, "If you wear the clothes of Yao, speak the words of Yao, and behave the way Yao behaved, then you *are* a Yao." *Mencius* 7B.30 (speaking of Yao and Shun) says, "If a man borrows a thing [referring to "ways of acting virtuously"] and keeps it long enough, how can one be sure that it will not become truly his?"

18 Much of Han thought presumes that a human being will reveal himself, sooner or later, in his actions.

19 Cf. *Mencius* 7B.11 on the person willing to give up his entire kingdom for this end. Cf. *Zuozhang*, Lord Xiang 24.1(1), which puts "establishing words" (*li yan* 立言) behind "establishing one's character" (*li de* 立德) and "establishing one's merit" (*li gong* 立功).

20 Dynastic founders of the Zhou and Shang lines respectively.

21 If extant materials are any guide to past practices, the most commonly cited chapter of the *Documents* in Han times was "Counsels of Gao Yao." See *Fayan* 6.8, 11.3.

22 Adding "to the present age," as implied, as the Li Gui commentary suggests.

曰堯舜以其讓。夏[11] 以其功。殷周以其伐。

13.11 或曰食如螘。衣如華。朱輪駟馬。金朱煌煌。無已泰乎。曰由其德。舜禹受天下不為泰。不由其德。五兩之綸。[12] 半通之銅。亦泰矣。

13.12 天下通道五。[13] 所以行之一。曰勉。[14]

13.13 或曰力有扛洪鼎。揭華旗。智,德亦有之乎。[15] 曰百人矣。德諧頑嚚。[16] 讓萬國。[17] 知情天地,形不測。[18] 百人乎。[19]

13.14 或問君。曰明光。問臣。曰若禔。敢問何謂也。曰君子在上。則明而光其下。在下。則順而安其上。

---

11 Reading "Yu of Xia" instead of just "Xia," on the basis of the commentators cited in Wang Rongbao 1987 (19.534).

12 Cf. *Hou Hanshu* 49.1651n1. Li Gui says that the half-size bronze seal and the green silk belt were worn by local bailiffs, as mentioned in the commentary to the "Black Robes" (Ziyi 緇衣) chapter of the *Liji*. See Wang Rongbao (1987, 19.536).

13 Li Gui identifies the Five Modes of Virtuous Conduct as "practicing humaneness, doing one's duty, and observing ritual decorum, wisdom, and trustworthiness."

14 Cf. the "Zhongyong," *Liji zhushu* 52.10–11a: "It is all one whether one understands the Way from birth, realizes it with ease, or realizes it with great difficulty."

15 Han Jing (1992, 346n5) takes *yi you zhi hu* 亦有之乎 to mean "Are there also men who so surpass others [in these aspects of virtuous conduct]?"

16 See "Yao dian," *Shangshu* 01.0399. Cf. *Zuozhuan*, Lord Xi 24, which defines *wan* 頑 as referring to one's attitude, and *yin*, to one's speech; *Lunheng* 27/118/24 plays off this passage.

17 "Yao dian," *Shangshu* 01.0052, 54, where the phrase is *wan bang* 萬邦, not *wan guo* 萬國; presumably Yang observes a Han taboo. Or, as Han Jing (1992, 345n3) prefers, "to cede the throne [to Yu]," with its myriad states.

18 In "Xici" A.5, *bu ce* 不測 is the phrase often used to describe "unfathomably great" processes of yin-yang and the cosmic forces (*shen* 神), which the sage can nonetheless penetrate. See Peterson 1982.

19 Following Wang Rongbao (1987, 19.539).

"By ceding the throne, as Yao and Shun did. By dint of hard work, as did Yu of Xia. Or by punitive campaigns, as did Yin and Zhou."[23]

Someone asked me, "Would it not be excessive if a person were to feast on the finest foods and wear the most sumptuous robes, and if his carriages drawn by teams of four had red lacquer wheels, and if he had the shining gold seals of office suspended on red ribbons?" 13.11

"Depending on one's charisma and character, even receipt of the whole realm, as with Shun and Yu, would not be too much! But if a person does not abide in virtue, it is a great deal too much if he receives even a green braided silk belt of office and the small bronze seal of the petty functionary!"[24]

The great ways in the realm are five in number,[25] but the means to proceed along those paths is only one—that called "exertion." 13.12

Someone asked me, "With feats of strength, there's shouldering a great tripod or bearing aloft a gorgeous battle standard. Are there likewise acts that similarly outdo all others when it comes to wisdom and virtue?" 13.13

"Those equal to the force of a hundred men! Compelling virtue renders the nasty and quarrelsome compliant, as Shun once did.[26] It makes 'the myriad states accede to its rule.' And wisdom 'fathoms the true conditions in heaven-and-earth,' giving form to the unfathomable. This force surely equals that of a hundred other men!"

Someone asked me about good rule. 13.14

"Bright and enlightened."

"And ministers?"

"Compliant."

"I beg to ask what you mean by this."

"When a noble man is on high, he brings light to and enlightens those below. When he is in a subordinate position, he complies in order to make his superiors secure."

---

23 As each of the times differed, their paths to glory differed as well. Yin and Zhou unleashed punitive campaigns against rebellious subjects within their own domains.

24 I take the first question to come from a Mohist stance: that the emperor and the nobility should redistribute more wealth to their subjects rather than engaging in conspicuous consumption. It may be a swipe at Wang Mang or other high livers at court. As for the response, the lowest grade of officer wore a belt of woven green silk (*lun* 綸). The same hierarchy stipulated that the highest-ranking members of the realm would have gold seals; the next, silver seals; and the lowest, bronze; but there were two kinds of bronze seals, the square and the rectangular (the latter being one-half the size of the square, or *ban zhang* 半章).

25 Other commentaries take this as a reference to the Five Orders of ruler-subject, father-son, husband-wife, elder-younger brother, and friendly relations, on the basis of the "Zhongyong," which calls these the *dadao* 達道 (roads that go to the final destination), a synonym for *tong dao* 通道. It is clear that "way/Way" is to be used in both the literal and the metaphorical senses.

26 Legend calls Shun's father nasty and his mother quarrelsome (*wan yin* 頑嚚); hence, I have added the phrase "as Shun did," which seems implied. The phrase below describes Zhou.

13.15 或曰聖人事異乎。曰聖人德之為事。異亞之。[20] 故常修德者,[21] 本也。見異而修德者,末也。本末不修而存者。未之有也。

13.16 天地之得。[22] 斯民也。斯民之得。一人也。[23] 一人之得。心矣。

13.17 吾聞諸傳。[24] 老則戒之在得。[25] 年彌高而德彌卲者。是孔子之徒與。[26]

13.18 或問德有始而無終。與有終而無始也。孰寧。曰寧先病而後瘳乎。寧先瘳而後病乎。

13.19 或問大。曰小。問遠。曰邇。未達。曰天下為大。治之在道。不

---

20 See *Hanshu*, "Wuxing zhi," *zhongxia*; Liu Rulin 1935, vol. 1, 121. Thus, to constantly cultivate virtue is the fundament (lit., "the root"), and to cultivate virtue after seeing anomalies is but an offshoot (lit., "the tip of the branch").

21 *Xiu* 修 means "to prolong" or "continue" and "to cultivate" or "make grow."

22 But Han Jing (1992, 347n1), citing Gao Yu's commentary to the *Lüshi chunqiu*, suggests that *de* 得 be read as *zhong* 中, "center," so that the line means "In the midst of heaven-and-earth are these people." L'Haridon (2006, vol. 2, 144) agrees, following Liu Shipei (1916), but she reads *zhong* as "axis."

23 Following the sense of many commentators, including Li Gui, who equate the "one man" with the ruler. Cf. the *Zuozhuan*, where the Zhou king repeatedly refers to himself as "one man" (*yu yi ren* 余一人), as in, for example, Lord Cheng 13.3b.

24 *Chuan/zhuan* 傳 refers to both "traditions" in general and "commentaries" in particular.

25 Cf. *Analects* 16.7, a direct quote: 戒之在德. Wang Rongbao (1987, 19.540) and Han Jing (1992, 348n1) would have us read *de* 得 (acquisitiveness) as *de* 德 (virtue, character).

26 Han Jing (1992, 349n3) reads *tu* 徒 as "followers" or "disciples."

Someone asked me, "Does the sage preoccupy himself with curiosities and anomalies, thinking them portents?"[27] 13.15

"As the sages take doing good to be their chief task, anomalies are no more than secondary concerns.[28] Therefore, the root is the continual cultivation of charismatic virtue. And they think it treating the symptom[29] when a person cultivates virtue only after he has seen an anomaly. There has never been a single case when a person neglects these primary and secondary tasks but still is preserved from harm."[30]

From heaven-and-earth come these people,[31] and from them comes the one man, the ruler. And from the true ruler one gets the heart![32] 13.16

I have heard the traditions and commentaries say, "An old person must take great care not to be covetous." But couldn't the saying "The older he is, the nobler his character" be used of those who are truly in the camp of Kongzi?[33] 13.17

Someone asked me, "Which is preferable: to start out with charismatic virtue but be without it at the end[34] or the reverse?" 13.18

"Which would be preferable: to be sick first and later be cured, or to be healthy first and later fall ill?"

Someone asked me about greatness. 13.19

"It's small."

"What about distance?"

"It's near."

"I don't get it."

"However vast the realm, ruling it well depends upon the one Way, so it is manageable enough, is it not?[35] Whatever the distance between the

---

27 *Yi* 異 refers to "the strange," i.e., anomalies and curiosities that seem portentous.

28 Yang Xiong was consulted at least once about an omen: a drum that spontaneously sounded in the palace.

29 Literally, "getting [only] at the tip (i.e., what is secondary)." If the sages are not the subject, the line reads, "Thus, to constantly cultivate virtue is the root, and to cultivate virtue upon seeing anomalies is but the tip of the branch." (However, could the latter activity be so unimportant?)

30 Predictably, the commentators tie these lines to Wang Mang's propensity to focus on omens.

31 "These people" can refer to the "subjects" of the ruler or to the "king's men" of exemplary virtue.

32 An alternative reading would be "What heaven and earth obtain/depend upon is these people, and what these people obtain/depend upon is one man, the ruler. And what this one man obtains/depends upon is his heart." Unfortunately, the first clause of the three makes little sense, for it is unclear how anything in heaven or earth depends upon the people, or how these superior entities would obtain anything from the people.

33 As Yang Xiong elsewhere seems to disparage the people who were disciples of Kongzi (*Fayan* 1.2), the character *cong* 從 perhaps should be taken in the broader sense of "those who are like him." My translation seeks to capture both senses.

34 "End" can refer both to a "goal" and a finishing point such as death.

35 Cf. *Analects* 3.11 on the ancestral sacrifice: one who knew that could rule the state as

亦小乎。[27] 四海為遠。治之在心。不亦邇乎。

13.20 或問俊哲洪秀。曰知哲聖人之謂俊。秀穎德行[28] 之謂洪。

13.21 君子動則擬[29] 諸事。事則擬諸禮。

13.22 或問群言之長。群行之宗。曰群言之長。德言也。群行之宗。[30] 德行也。

13.23 或問泰和。[31] 曰其在唐虞成周乎。[32] 觀書及詩。溫溫乎其和可知也。[33]

13.24 周康之時。頌聲作乎下。關雎作乎上。習治也。齊桓之時縕。而春秋美邵陵。[34] 習亂也。故習治則傷始亂也。習亂則好始治也。

---

27 See Wang Rongbao (1987, 19.541).

28 Reading *ying* 穎 as "a full head of grain or grain in the ear, bent over by its own weight" (i.e., "what has fully flowered").

29 Reading *ni* 擬 as "to deliberate" or "mull over," "to take the measure of," and so "emulate." However, the Wu Mi edition, cited in Wang Rongbao (1987, 19.542), writes *ning* 凝 ("to accomplish" or "to perfect") instead, possibly on the basis of the phrase 苟不至德, 至道不凝焉.

30 However, Han Jing (1992, 351n1) glosses *zong* 宗 as *gen ben* 根本 (basis), rather than as "most compelling [model]," since *zong* can refer to the "most distinguished or honored."

31 Taihe 泰和. Yang asks about this, rather than Taiping 太平 (Great Peace), perhaps because the phrase "Taiping" had become too closely associated with Gan Zhongke 甘忠可 and other figures suspected of treason against the Han throne. See Arbuckle 1995.

32 Han Jing (1992, 352n2), among others, identifies "Cheng" as King Cheng of Zhou, but that would be to skip a dynasty—hence my decision to take Cheng as Cheng-Tang 成湯. The term "Zhou" does not necessarily refer only to the Duke of Zhou but to early Zhou rule in general. The text also refers to Yao as Tang and to Shun as Yu.

33 Wang Rongbao (1987, 19.543) punctuates differently than Han Jing (1992, 352) does. If Wang Rongbao is followed, the lines mean "Observing how gracious the *Documents* and the *Odes* are, one can know the harmony of those eras."

34 See CHAC, p. 556.

four seas at the ends of the earth , ruling them well depends upon the one heart, so it is very near, is it not?"

Someone asked me about surpassing wisdom and great accomplishments. 13.20

"'Surpassing' wisdom means being smart enough to see the wisdom[36] in the sages. 'Great' accomplishment means cultivating one's conduct until it bears fruit."[37]

The noble man, when he comes to act, takes the measure of the circumstances he confronts and, in his own actions, the measure of the rites. 13.21–22

Someone asked me, "Which is the most commanding of all possible speeches, and which the most compelling of all possible deeds?"

"The most commanding speeches speak of virtue, and the most compelling acts practice virtue."

Someone asked me about the term "Grand Harmony." 13.23–24

"Did it not exist in the time of Yao, Shun, Tang, the Shang founder, and Zhou? Peruse the *Documents* and the *Odes*, and one may know how gracious was the harmony that prevailed during those eras!"

During the reign of King Kang of Zhou, the music for the Hymns was composed below, and the "Guanju" ode was composed above, at court[38]—so accustomed were they to good rule then. The messy entanglements of the reign of Lord Huan of Qi were such that the *Annals* praises the treaty of Shaoling[39]—so accustomed by then were those of the time to misrule. Therefore, those used to good rule regard the first signs of chaos as an affliction,[40] while those used to misrule look favorably upon even the first and weakest signs of order.

---

easily as he could roll something in the hand. However, Li Gui takes "small" to refer to the "subtle" art of governance.

36 Or "credit [the sages] with practical wisdom" (*zhe* 哲).

37 One could translate this loosely as "those who fully realize themselves in virtuous conduct."

38 "Below" refers almost certainly to "those not at court," while "above" means "at court." Hence, I have added the phrase "at court" to the translation. Many other *Odes* traditions, including that of Zheng Xuan (127–200), follow Mao in ascribing the composition of the "Guanju" to the reign of King Wen instead. Also in dispute is the intended meaning of the ode. The Mao tradition treats "Guanju" as a praise poem, while the Lu tradition (followed by Sima Qian in the *Shiji*) interprets the ode as criticism. Yang Xiong seems to follow the Lu tradition (習治則傷始亂), taking "Guanju" as a poem that "mourns disorder." Still, the Lu version of the *Odes* attributes the (laudable) impulse to compose the ode to a desire to remonstrate with King Kang of Zhou and the ladies of his back apartments.

39 Shaoling is the treaty signed between Qi and various powers in 656 BCE; it represents the first compulsory meeting attended by heads of state at the behest of the de facto leader, or hegemon. The word "they" here refers to "the authors and their peers." Lord Huan originally led the armies of eight states to punish Cai for joining in an alliance with Chu; Chu bowed to the threat, however, and, admitting its errors, entered into a treaty with Qi. For this achievement, Lord Huan was recognized as hegemon by many states.

40 Or they "bemoan" them.

13.25 漢德其可謂允懷矣。黃支之南。[35] 大夏之西。東鞮, 北女。來貢其珍。漢德其可謂允懷矣。世鮮焉。

13.26 荒荒聖德。遠人咸慕。上也。武義璜璜。兵征四方。次也。宗夷猾夏。[36] 蠢迪王人。屈國喪師。無次也。

13.27 麟之儀儀。鳳之師師。[37] 其至矣乎。螭虎桓桓。鷹隼䎃䎃。未至也。

13.28 或曰訩訩北夷。被我純繢。帶我金犀。珍膳寧餬。[38] 不亦享乎。曰

---

35 *Hanshu* 28.1671 records a gift of a rhinoceros to the Han court under Pingdi, as does *Hanshu* 99A.4077: "Huangzhi presented a live rhinoceros as tribute from 30,000 li away." (This event occurred prior to 4 CE.) See Bielenstein 1986, 239; Cui 2007, 211–20; Li Dalong 2006, 162–93.

36 The phrase *manyi hua Xia* 蠻夷猾夏 is a set phrase, and Wang Rongbao (1987, 20.548–49) suggests *zongyi* 宗夷 is a variation of *manyi*, following the "Yaodian" chapter of the *Shangshu*, where *zong* probably means *zhong* 眾 (the many).

37 Usually the reduplicative *shi shi* 師師 means "many" or "flourishing" or "resplendent." However, subcommentary in Wang Rongbao (1987, 20.550) insists that *shishi* "refers to phoenixes flying and birds flocking together in the tens of thousands; it is like looking at an army in formation." My translation tries to get at the moral sense, as found in "teacher-teacher/model-model."

38 The commentators cannot agree on what type of fine food is indicated by the expression *ninghu* 寧糊, but most think it refers to fermented milk products.

Han charismatic rule—how "truly cherished" it may be said to be! People from the lands south of Huangzhi and west of Daxia,[41] in Dongti,[42] all come with the Northern Xiongnu[43] to the Han court bringing rare items as tribute.[44] Han charismatic rule—how "truly cherished" it may be said to be! Few ages have witnessed such charismatic rule![45] 13.25–27

The very best situation is one where the sage-ruler's charismatic virtue is so fabled[46] as to elicit the admiration of all the faraway peoples. The next best is awesome military might, with troops engaged in punitive campaigns in every direction. What hardly rates as glorious is the many Yi wreaking havoc on the Central States with their incursions,[47] their rapacious encroachment upon the king's men, and their bringing humiliation to our domains and death to our legions.

The unicorn, superbly decorous,[48] and the resplendent legions of phoenixes—these are the very finest of their species! Neither fierce tigers, in their mad rampages, nor eagles and falcons, in all their predations, can ever measure up to them![49]

Someone asked me, "The brutish Northern Yi wear the finest embroidered silk robes of ours; they wear at their belts our best golden buckles and swords decorated with wild animals.[50] They enjoy our finest delicacies along with their fermented mare's milk.[51] How can they *not* be enjoying themselves hugely?"[52] 13.28

---

41 Huangzhi is usually thought to be located in northern India (Tamil Nadu?). Daxia is usually thought to be Bactria. East Di is located beyond Kuaji, beyond the sea (Taiwan?).

42 Dongti is supposedly the name of a group of people divided into over twenty countries or tribes and living on islands corresponding to Taiwan and nearby islands. The location of Beinü (lit., Northern Girl) is unknown, but the *Shanghai jing* ("Haiwai xijing") speaks of a land of females far to the northwest, where the Xiongnu (often called the Northern Yi) are in control. The term *beinu* 北奴 (northern slaves) is the standard term for the Xiongnu on the northern frontier. In Chengdi's reign, in 25 BCE, the Xiongnu leader came to the Han court to pay his respects.

43 Here called by the perjorative term *beinu* 北奴 (northern slaves).

44 Adding, "to the Han court," as implied by the verb "to come."

45 One might compare the foregoing with *Lunheng* 57, "Touting the Han" (Xuan Han 宣漢).

46 Literally, "great." I use "fabled," since this reduplicative describes what is deep, far away, remote, wide ranging, or huge.

47 Adding "with their incursions," as implied.

48 The unicorn is the symbol of humane rule.

49 See *Fayan* 13.28–30, where the language of birds and beasts clearly refers to non–Central States nomads and others without sedentary agriculture or the Central States system of rites and music.

50 Literally, "bovine animal with a single horn" (rhinocerus?) but here rendered "wild animals" to suggest the "animal-combat style" favored in Han. Interestingly, Yang claims such items for the Han, but they are almost certainly of foreign (i.e., Scythian) origin. Possibly, this phrase could also refer to belts made of animal hides, with gold or silver decorations.

51 Some commentators assume that this criticizes the fine treatment some nomads were given as a result of the Han appeasement policies.

52 Translation tentative, implying that these inferior people are living it up, though they

昔在高文武。實為兵主。今稽首來臣。稱為北蕃。是為宗廟之神，社稷之靈也。可不享。[39]

13.29 龍堆以西。大漠以北。鳥夷獸夷。[40] 郡[41] 勞王師。漢家不為也。

13.30 朱崖之絕。[42] 捐之之力也。否則介鱗易我衣裳。[43]

---

39 L'Haridon (2006, vol. 2, 146) translates, "Are these not too many honors?" In any case, this sentence must be read in light of Hanshu 94B.3812, Yang Xiong's memorial on Xiongnu affairs. The character *xiang* 享 has confounded many commentators, with Yu Yue (1874), among others, suggesting that it be read instead as *heng* 亨 (to savor, to accept as sacrifice) or *hou* 厚 (generous). Yu Yue (1874) therefore reads, "Isn't our treatment of them excessively generous?" (*chanyu lai chen, li zhi tai hou* 單于來臣，禮之太厚?). *Taiping yulan* 811.8a–8b reads it as 厚, while Sima Guang, cited in Wang Rongbao (1987, 20.552), prefers to read it as *heng* 亨 (see below). Liu Shipei (1916), after seeming initially to favor the reading of *hou* 厚, eventually concludes that *xiang* 享 is correct after all. An alternative reading of the last line could be "Is this not very like making sacrifices [*xiang* 享] to the gods?" (Reply:) "In the time of Emperors Gao [i.e., Liu Bang 劉邦, r. 202–195 BCE], Wendi [r. 180–157 BCE], and Wudi [r. 141–87 BCE], they were indeed our enemies in war. But now they have come and prostrated themselves as subjects, declaring themselves our northern vassals." Still, Liu's interpretation seems flawed, if it implies that "the gods will be appeased if the nomads are appeased," even if that formula means simply that the improved Han-Xiongnu relations have the sanction of the gods.

Sima Guang, cited in Wang Rongbao (1987, 20.551), says that reading *xiang* as *hou* would make the line mean "How can we *not* treat them generously?" In Sima Guang's view, for access to the throne to be offered on such cheap terms, when the barbarians have already submitted, is to be "penny wise and pound foolish" (愛小費而就大患乎). See *Taiping yulan* 811.8a–8b.

40 See Wang Rongbao (1987, 20.554). These phrases come from the memorial of Jia Juanzhi recorded immediately below.

41 Liu Shipei (1916), cited in Wang Rongbao (1987, 20.554) would read *jun* 郡 as *qun* 群/羣 (many, masses), and similarly, Wang Niansun would read *jun* 郡 as *shu* 數 ("repeatedly" or "in great numbers"), on the grounds that the "kingly" and "commandery" systems did not coexist. Both scholars ignore the continuance of many preunification terms in the mixed Han imperial system. However, Li Gui's reading has the line meaning "To make the royal/imperial army toil in order to turn such lands into commanderies—the Han ruling house should not act in this way."

42 *Hanshu* 6.188 has Wudi setting up Zhuya and many other commanderies in the extreme south. See *Hanshu*, "Dili zhi," for Zhuya 朱[珠]崖 as the name of the old commandery on what is modern-day Hainan Island.

43 One might compare this comment with *Zuozhuan*, Lord Zhao, *fu* 3, and *Hanshu* 29.1698, which say that if it were not for the sage-ruler Yu's merit, all the people of the Central States would have become fish.

"Long ago, during the reigns of Han Gaozu, Wendi, and Wudi, the Xiongnu really were the strongest military force. Now they bow their heads and come as subjects of Han rule, proclaiming themselves our 'Northern Defenders.'[53] This is attributable to the divine power of our ancestral temple and also to the spirit efficacy of the altars of grain and soil. Is *that* not an experience to be savored *by us*?"[54]

As they say, "From White Dragon Dunes[55] to the west and the Great Des- 13.29–30
ert to the north, in the home of the Bird Yi and Beast Yi,[56] the commanderies bear the burden of the care and feeding of the king's troops.[57] The Han ruling house should not act in this way."

"The end to Zhuya came through Jia Juanzhi's forcefulness.[58] Had it been otherwise, we would all have been exchanging our caps and gowns for fish scales and diving suits!"[59]

---

do not deserve such favors.

53 In 3 CE, the Xiongnu sent a letter to Aidi's court asking to come to court. In a memorial Yang Xiong protested the initial decision not to invite the Xiongnu leader, a decision made on the feeble grounds that such a visit would be a waste of resources. The same faction was ready enough to go to war when it suited their purposes.

54 Adding "by us," as implied. This line recalls the "Pan Geng" chapter of the *Documents*: "When I offer the great sacrifices to the former kings, your forefathers join in to share the sacrificial feast" (*Shangshu* 16.0836). L'Haridon (2006, vol. 2, 147) translates as "Must one not do honor to those . . . ?" Judging from the extant records, Yang Xiong seldom intervened in Han policy making, but he sent a letter (unsolicited?) in 3 BCE remonstrating against the ministers' decision not to allow the Xiongnu *chanyu* to come to the Han court. To Yang's way of thinking, however expensive such a diplomatic visit might prove to be, it would most likely save money in the end, if it cemented better relations between the powers. Yang's advice was taken, and he was duly awarded ten *jin* of metal (gold?). In some sense, nearly all of chapter 13 of the *Fayan* can be read as an elaborate critique of Han Wudi, insofar as it asks for a reevaluation of the throne's duties to the imperial ancestors. Wudi once, in 112 BCE, used the solemn obligations owed the ancestral temple as a pretext to depose over 100 local lords (*zhuhou*), saying that the "gold vessels" that the lords contributed to the throne were not sufficiently grand to please the ancestors.

55 Adding the phrase "as they say," referring to Jia Juanzhi's memorial against a southern expedition. Jia Juanzhi, the great-grandson of the statesman Jia Yi (see the Glossary), sought to rebut the memorials of hawks urging the emperor to launch a punitive campaign against the south. The Great Desert is the Gobi, and the "barbarians" to its north were the Xiongnu. This passage speaks of the desert from White Dragon Dunes 白龍堆, in the old Western Regions (*xiyu* 西域), in modern-day southeastern Xinjiang, to the northeast of Lop Nor (a former salt lake now dried up), and on east to Gansu, with its Jade Gate (玉門) Pass. This swath of territory would include the various statelets of the Tarim Basin (i.e., the Western Regions), which lay west of these Dunes. Another way to think of this is that it describes the desert stretching from the western foothills of Daxing'an 大興安 to the eastern foothills of the Tianshan 天山 range.

56 The exact meanings of "Bird Yi and "Beast Yi" are uncertain; the terms may be derogatory but that is far from certain. One interpretation is that their peoples are "men clothed in bird feathers and animal skins."

57 The main idea is clear: the Han should not burden the people with expansionist policies.

58 Or "Jia Juanzhi's great contribution was [to cause] the abandonment of Zhuya [commandery]."

59 Meaning that "we would all have become less than fully civilized," on a par with the

13.31 君人者務在殷民阜財。明道[44]信[45]義。致帝者之用。成天地之化。使粒食之民粲也。[46]晏也。享于鬼神。不亦饗乎。

13.32 天道勞功。[47]或問勞功。日日一日(=曰?)勞。考載曰功。或曰君逸臣勞。何天之勞。曰於事則逸。於道則勞。

13.33 周公以來。未有漢公之懿也。[48]勤勞則過於阿衡。

13.34 漢興二百一十載而中天。其庶矣乎。[49]

---

44 *Ming dao* 明道 refers to both meanings.

45 Reading *xin* 信 as *shen* 伸, as is common in Yang's *Supreme Mystery*.

46 *Can* 粲 refers to "the materials for a feast," but it also means "bright," "splendid," and "laughing."

47 Cf. the "Image" for Hexagram 1 (Qian) in the *Changes*: 天行健. Heaven's own strength is said to give the ruler/noble man (*junzi*) the strength to work tirelessly "without stopping" on behalf of others (君子以自強不息).

48 See Knechtges 1968, chap. 1; also 1977.

49 Li Gui, cited in Wang Rongbao (1987, 20.562), says, e.g., "How numerous and prosperous its people!" while Sima Guang, also cited in Wang Rongbao (ibid.) says, "It is a nearly perfect realization of good government!"

The ruler of men works hard to make the people prosper and to increase their wealth, to clarify the Way and to clearly exemplify it, and to extend a sense of justice and duty to all, so as to achieve efficacy in the lordly functions and so accomplish the transformation of all things in heaven and earth. In this way, the ruler causes the sedentary grain eaters [of the Central Plains][60] to laugh[61] and feel at ease, so that when offerings are presented to the spirits, the spirits will certainly accept them![62] 13.31

"Heaven's Way is to work hard and so achieve." 13.32

Someone asked me, "What do you mean by 'hard work' and 'achievement'?"

"Each and every day heaven advances one degree [out of 360 in a year]. That is what I call 'hard work.' By year's end, we have what we call an 'achievement,' that is, the harvest."[63]

Someone asked me, "The ruler takes his ease while his officers and subjects work hard. In what sense, then, is heaven working hard?"

"With respect to the day-to-day management of affairs, the ruler takes his ease, but if we talk of the Way, then the true ruler labors hard and long."

Since the Duke of Zhou, none have had the charismatic virtue of Wang Mang, Lord of Han.[64] By the intensity of his efforts, he surpasses Yi Yin.[65] 13.33–34

The Han dynasty was founded 210 years ago. It soars to the heavens, and its years seem to approach the culmination.[66]

---

inhabitants of the far southeast, since caps and gowns are emblems of Central States civilization. Sometimes it is said of southerners diving for pearls that they had virtually become fish. The term "fish scales" describes any seaworthy creature or object, including boats and the special garb worn by pearl divers.

60 Literally, the "grain-eating people" (i.e., the people whose diet consists mainly of grains).

61 The common people are "laughing" because they have enough to eat. They do not curse their rulers, so the state sacrifices are acceptable to the gods and spirits.

62 Cf. *Analects* 6.22, 11.12.

63 Adding "that is, the harvest," as implied.

64 In 4 CE, Wang Mang gave himself the title "Lord Who Secures the Han" (*An Han gong* 安漢公). These lines in the *Fayan* have been used to support different readings: (*a*) this is a heartfelt statement in praise of Wang; (*b*) this is an unmarked citation of another's praise of Wang; (*c*) this phrase is sarcastic, since the praise is overdone (e.g., it implies Wang was more of a sage than Kongzi); and (*d*) the specific wording of this praise, while fairly formulaic, insists on Wang continuing to serve the Han, since A Heng himself, however good an official, never became emperor.

65 Yi Yin (i.e., A Heng) was minister to the founder of the Shang dynasty. To compare Wang to Yi Yin is possibly less than complimentary to Wang.

66 The phrase is perfectly ambiguous: it could mean that the Han dynasty is "nearly there" (at the zenith of its power and virtue) or is "nearly over" (at its end). The phrases that follow suggest a positive reading, however, as do the chief commentators.

辟廱以本之。
校學以教之。
禮樂以容之。
輿服以表之。
復其井刑。[50]
勉人役。[51]
唐矣夫。[52]

50 Reading *xing* 刑 as *xing* 型, contrary to Han Jing (1992, 368n6), who follows Wang Rongbao (1987, 20.563) in retaining *xing* in the meaning of "[mutilating] punishments," despite the evidence for Wang Mang's policies on penal law. If Han and Wang are correct, then the line should read, "It restores the proper well-field system and penal laws."

51 L'Haridon (2006, vol. 2, 149) reads, "Reducing the commerce in slaves," attributing this to Wang Mang.

52 As noted by Han Jing (1992, 368n8), most of the early commentators explained "Tang" 唐 here not as "splendid and great!" but as a reference first to the legendary sage-king Tang-Yao 堯, ultimate founder of the Han line, according to some traditions, and also to Shun (reading the last line as *tang yu fu* 唐虞夫). Li Gui, for example, glosses the last line as "[The Han dynasty] has no reason to envy the ages of Yao and Shun." Wang Rongbao (1987, 20.565), following *Shuowen jiezi*, reads *tang* as *da yan* 大言 (great words), meaning "high praise [belongs to Han]."

The Circular Moat[67] is taken as the basis for it.
The schools at the local and capital level are used to propagate moral teachings to them, the people.[68]
Rites and music are used to impart a grand appearance to it.
Carriages and robes,[69] to make clear standards for it.
It restores the framework of the well-field system,[70]
Encouraging the people to serve.
Splendid and great,[71] is it not?

67 The Biyong, or Circular Moat, was a ritual center erected south of the Han capital during the regency of Wang Mang.

68 "It" in the previous line refers to "Han rule," whereas "them" in this line probably refers to "the people" but could also be translated "for it [the Han dynasty]."

69 I.e., sumptuary regulations.

70 According to *Hanshu* 99A.4110–11, Wang Mang called for the reinstitution of the well-field system in 9 CE.

71 For the importance of this last line for the correct reading of this encomium, see Nylan, forthcoming-b.

Glossary of Names, Legendary and Historical

A Heng 阿衡. More commonly known as Yi Yin 伊尹; minister to Tang the Victorious (tradit. 1800 BCE), founder of the Shang dynasty (tradit. 1800–ca. 1050 BCE). A Heng's name is sometimes coupled with that of Guan Zhong 管仲 (see below), with both regarded as extraordinary ministers whose wise policies brought prosperity to the realm. According to the "Nan yan" 難言 chapter of the *Han Feizi*, A Heng tried no fewer than seventy times to have an audience with his ruler, but in the end, he persuaded his ruler to listen to him only because of his skills as a butcher and cook. A Heng hardly enjoyed a good reputation in all texts, however. *Fayan* 13.33.

[Bao]bo Lingzhi 鮑白令之. An officer, probably an Academician, at the Qin court who reprimanded the First Emperor (then the King of Qin) and miraculously lived to tell the tale. *Fayan* 10.16.

Bian Que 扁鵲 (5th cent. BCE). According to legend, one name for Qin Yueren 秦越人, an innkeeper in Zheng (?) who received from an old man (an immortal?) important texts on medicine and healing along with a drug that improved his powers of understanding. As a result, Bian Que could see into the viscera of his patients. By some accounts, Bian was the first master of pulse theory. He was assassinated by the chief physician at the court of predynastic Qin, who was jealous of his abilities. *Fayan* 10.2.

Bing Ji 丙/邴 吉. Played a number of important roles during several Western Han reigns, beginning with that of Wudi (r. 141–87 BCE). In 91 BCE, the Wei heir apparent and Empress Wei were forced to commit suicide in related crises. The Wei grandson was jailed, but Bing Ji offered him his care and protection. Later, when that grandson (posthumously titled Xuandi) was elevated to the Han throne, Bing Ji was hailed as the emperor's savior, though Bing Ji had been too modest to mention his role in saving the life of the Wei grandson.

Bing served as Superintendent of the Palace (*guanlu xun*) during the reign of Zhaodi (r. 87–74 BCE), and he attained the two highest-ranking posts in the bureaucracy under Xuandi (r. 74–48 BCE). While holding the post of Chancellor in 59 BCE, he initiated a policy forbidding senior officials from impeaching their own subordinates. He was a supporter of Han Yanshou 韓延壽, however, who was accused of misusing public funds. Seriously ill by 55, he recommended three people to Xuandi to succeed him in the post of Chancellor. By the time of his death, he had become such a venerable statesman that by imperial edict his portrait was displayed during the state visit of the Xiongnu *chanyu* to the capital in 51 BCE. See *Hanshu* 74.3142. *Shuoyuan* ("Fu en" 復恩) calls him Jing 景 Ji to avoid a taboo character. *Fayan* 10.27.

Bo Gui 白圭. Legendary moneymaker whose biography identifies him as a contemporary of Li Ke 李克 and Marquis Wen of Wei 魏文侯 (r. 449–396 BCE). He was known to be such a good judge of human excellence that the state of Qin did not dare attack the state of Wei while he was in its service. Bo reportedly formulated a number of infallible rules for buying and selling at a profit by observing the regularities in the universe. See *Shiji* 129.3258–59. *Fayan* 1.21.

Bo Qi 白起 (modern pronunciation Bai Qi; aka the Lord of Wuan 武安). Qin general during the late Zhanguo reign of King Zhao 昭, Bo was the commander-in-chief responsible for leading the attack against the major cities of the Han 韓 state after 293 BCE; he decimated the Han forces at the battle of Changping, where his army reportedly slaughtered some hundreds of thousands of the enemy who had already surrendered. Bo Qi then attacked Chu and took their capital city of Ying. Because of the machinations of his rival Fan Sui 范睢, Lord of Ying 應, Bo Qi was eventually exiled and forced to commit suicide. *Qianfu lun* 11/18/24 blamed the Qin for assessing the quality of its generals on the basis of how many people the generals killed. (多殺者為賢.白起蒙恬, 秦以為功,天以為賊.) During four separate campaigns over three decades, including one that destroyed the state of Yan, Bo reportedly was responsible for killing over a million combatants and civilians. Bo Qi and Meng Tian are therefore often singled out for their violence. See *Shiji* 73.2331. *Fayan* 11.12.

Bo Yi 伯夷 and Shu Qi 叔齊 (fl. ca. 1050 BCE). Two famous princes who "refused to eat the grain of Zhou" when King Wu of Zhou rebelled against his Shang overlord; they then starved to death on Mount Shouyang. According to legend, their father, the Lord of Guzhu 孤竹, wanted to override the order of legitimate succession by placing the younger brother, Shu Qi, on the throne. After their father's death, Shu Qi decided to flee the kingdom rather than assume a place that was rightfully that of his elder brother. Bo Yi, however, refused to disobey his father's wishes, so ultimately the two brothers both abandoned the state of Guzhu altogether. These brothers are controversial figures, insofar as they epitomize the sort of moral purity that puts principle above practical considerations. Bo Yi and Shu Qi are the subject of *Shiji* 61, the first of the biographical chapters. They also receive mention in *Analects* 5.23, 7.15, 16.12, 18.8. See *Fayan* 6.19, 11.21, 11.23.

Bu Shang 卜商. See Zixia.

Bu Shi 卜式. Made a vast fortune from raising sheep; often contributed his own funds to help pay expenses incurred in the campaigns against the Xiongnu. Both standard histories agree that Bu Shi's early claim to fame rested on his ability to attract money into the district where he was first appointed prefect. Wudi eventually rewarded Bu Shi with a post as his Imperial Counselor (*yushi daifu*), the second-highest post in all the land. In 110 BCE, however, Bu Shi objected to Wudi's economic policies, especially the monopolies on salt and iron; Wudi quickly retaliated by demoting Bu. As Bu held Sang Hongyang 桑弘羊 responsible for "turning government officials into merchants," Bu took advantage of a severe drought to criticize Sang, saying, "If the imperial representatives at the local level (*xianguan* 縣官) were forced to live on a low rate of taxes [rather than relying on the monopolies], and Sang Hongyang were to be tried and boiled alive, . . . the heavens would send down rain." See *Shiji* 129.1431 and *Hanshu* 24B.1167. Bu Shi also won fame for his skill in argumentation, according to *Kongzi jiayu* 38/66/20. *Fayan* 7.21.

Bu Yi. See Juan, Capital.

Cai 蔡, Master. After Xiang Yu's 項羽 destruction of the Qin palace at Xianyang in 206 BCE, Master Cai suggested that Xiang would be well advised to establish his seat in the old Qin capital of Xianyang because of its strategic advantages. Xiang Yu ignored his advice, however, in part because he had already butchered Xianyang's inhabitants and in part because he wished to return to his homeland in the south. Xiang Yu later executed Cai for an impertinent remark comparing Xiang Yu to "a monkey with a hat on" (*Shiji* 7.315). The *Hanshu* calls Master Cai Master Han 韓, for reasons not clearly understood. *Fayan* 10.17.

Cai Ze 蔡澤. Chancellor serving several kings of Qin, most famously King Zhao of Qin (r. 306–251 BCE), shortly before unification in 221 BCE. See the entry on Fan Li. See *Shiji* 79.2418. *Fayan* 5.15.

Cao Shen 曹參. Along with Xiao He, minister and trusted adviser to the Han founder. Enfeoffed as Marquis of Pingyang, Cao succeeded to Xiao's post as Chancellor after Xiao's death in 193 BCE. Cao Shen is mainly known for his noninterventionist policies with regard to the economy. Legend has him "borrowing his techniques for good rule from the Yellow Lord" (*Shiji* 54.2021). *Fayan* 11.17.

Changgong. See Luoxia Hong.

Chao Cuo 鼂錯 [= 晁/朝錯] (d. 154 BCE). As senior official under Jingdi (r. 157–141 BCE), Chao submitted a number of valuable policy proposals to the Han throne on subjects as various as the security of the dynasty, the qualities required of a good ruler, the duties of senior officials, the necessity to reduce the power of the kings and nobles, economic security, and military strategy in the northwest frontier zone. Trained in the teachings of Shen Buhai 申不害 and Shang Yang 商鞅 (see below), Chao was a strong proponent of centralizing policies. Despite opposition to Chao from Yuan Ang 爰盎, Shentu Jia 申屠嘉, and Dou Ying 竇嬰, Chao rose steadily through the ranks until, in 155 BCE, he was appointed Imperial Counselor (*yushi daifu*), the second highest bureaucratic office in the land. In 154, Yuan Ang and Dou Ying were able to persuade Jingdi that the Seven Kingdoms Revolt could be traced to Chao's policies to suppress the power of the kings. Chao was then executed, despite his exemplary record of service to two Han emperors. *Fayan* 11.17 calls Chao Cuo "obtuse," either because he was a cruel official or because he failed to see the enmity his policies were engendering.

Chaofu 巢父. See Nest, Father.

Chen Ping 陳平 (d. 178 BCE). Reportedly devised the remarkable Six Schemes that allowed the commoner Liu Bang 劉邦 to wrest control of the empire; later Chen served as senior adviser in the administrations of Liu Bang, his wife Dowager Empress Lü, and son Huidi (r. 195–188 BCE). The *Fayan* cites an incident when Zhang Biqiang, son of Zhang Liang, reported to Chen Ping and Zhou Bo 周勃 the lack of real sorrow displayed by Liu Bang's widow upon her husband's death in 195 BCE (an indication that she and her family might soon revolt). Chen Ping was also instrumental in putting the King of Dai on the throne as Emperor Wen of Han. See *Shiji* 56.2051–58. *Fayan* 10.18, 11.18.

Chen She 陳涉. See Chen Sheng.

Chen Sheng 陳勝 (aka Chen She 涉). A peasant plowman, who happened to be named head of a corvée team that later was caught in a rainstorm soon after the death of the First Emperor, in 209 BCE. Realizing that his late arrival at his assigned destination would most probably mean his prompt execution for dereliction of duty, Chen led the group of men in his charge in a revolt against Qin. Though Chen was soon killed by his own carriage driver, Chen's revolt set in motion the train of events that eventually brought down the Qin Empire and ushered in the Western Han dynasty. Accordingly, the *Shiji* assigns Chen She a "Hereditary House" for his role in these dramatic events, on the pretext that Chen She had named himself King of Chu. Significantly, however, the *Hanshu*, probably under Yang Xiong's influence, accorded Chen no such honors. See *Shiji* 48.1949. *Fayan* 10.6.

Chen Tang 陳湯 (courtesy style name Zigong 子公). First appointed to the junior staff of the Privy Treasurer (*shaofu* 少府), in which post he failed to distinguish himself, Chen requested that he be posted to the Western Regions during the reign of Xuandi (r. 74–48 BCE). Later, under Chengdi (r. 33–7 BCE), Chen Tang was appointed Lieutenant Colonel of the Western Regions, where he fought in several campaigns against the Xiongnu. He was renowned for his ability to draft memorials, and some legends have Chen Tang bringing back Roman legionnaires from Central Asia. Once, Chen forged an imperial decree ordering him to call out all the Han and non-Han forces in the area, in order to overcome the hesitation of a fellow frontier officer, Gan Yanshou 甘延壽, to undertake a massive call-up of local forces against the Xiongnu. After the levy, Chen confessed to the illegal act. At court, Shi Xian 石顯 and Kuang Heng 匡衡 promptly accused Chen of two crimes: forging an imperial edict and misappropriating property. Liu Xiang, however, defended both Chen Tang and Gan Yanshou on the grounds that the two generals had restored Han prestige in the frontier zone and so rendered incomparable service. As a result of this defense, all charges against the two were dropped, and Chen was even awarded the rank of Noble of the Interior (*guannei hou* 關內侯), as recounted in *Hanshu* 70.3007. However, Chen Tang was ultimately punished for arranging a real-estate development deal in connection with a second mausoleum complex built during the reign of Chengdi. *Fayan* 9.21.

Chen Yu 陳餘. Erstwhile friend of Zhang Er, who later became his enemy, and powerful military commander who rebelled against the Qin while in the service of Chen Sheng 陳勝. See Zhang's entry. *Fayan* 10.23.

Cheng Tang 成湯 (Tang the Victorious). Founder of the Shang dynasty (tradit. 1800 BCE). *Fayan* 1.13, 4.24, 6.10, 8.1, 9.4, 10.11.

Cheng Ying 程嬰. Friend of and fellow Counselor with Gongsun Chujiu 公孫杵臼 in Jin during the Chunqiu period. At the time of Duke Jing 景 of Jin (r. 599–581 BCE), the counselor Tu Anjia 屠岸賈 tried to exterminate all the heirs to the ruling Zhao clan. The sole survivor of the massacre was Zhao Shuo's 趙朔 former consort, who was then pregnant by her lord. She managed to hide herself in the palace, and eventually she bore a son known as Zhao Wu 武. Cheng Ying had decided that if she bore a son, he would somehow protect the Zhao lineage, but if it was a girl, he would kill the child.

Gongsun Chujiu came up with the plan that ultimately saved the child. He had another person's son take the place of the child Zhao Wu. He then had Cheng Ying report the existence of Zhao Wu's double to Tu Anjia, figuring that if Tu killed the putative son, along with his guardian Gongsun Chujiu, Tu would surely think he had succeeded in exterminating the Zhao heir. Cheng Ying meanwhile spirited Zhao Wu away to a remote mountain location, where he could raise Zhao Wu in safety. Many years later, when a Jin counselor killed Tu Anjia, Duke Jing of Jin recalled Zhao Wu and restored him to his rightful position as heir. Cheng Ying promptly announced that his mission had been accomplished, and that he would commit suicide to tender his apologies to Zhao Shuo, whose life he had been unable to save. See *Zuozhuan*, Lord Cheng 8.226/Cheng 8/6 Zuo, where the story differs slightly from that told in *Shiji* 43.1783–85. (This story is the subject of the 2010 film *Sacrifice*.) *Fayan* 10.24.

Chi You 蚩尤. Legendary rebel who tried but failed to overthrow Huangdi, the

Yellow Emperor; often identified as an early god of war. See *Shiji* 1.1–2. *Fayan* 11.12.

Chong 重. Legendary Regulator of the South (Nanzheng 南正), supposedly the astronomical official charged with the task of calculating the path of the sun. Some legends cast Chong and Li as the Directors of Wood and Fire [Phases] respectively. Sima Qian in *Shiji* 130 took the Nanzheng office to be a precursor to his own office of *taishi ling* 太史令 (Senior Archivist). *Hanshu* 21A.973 claims that the legendary sage-ruler Zhuanxu was the first to set Chong and Li up in office, but then their offices were temporarily suspended. Later, the sage-king Yao supposedly restored their descendants to office, however. Another legend collapses Chong and Li into one person, Chongli (*Shiji* 40.1689), making him the grandson of Zhuanxu, who is buried at the base of Mount Heng; see Shen Hongzhi's *Jingzhou ji*, cited in *Hanshu* 59.1922, n. 3. *Fayan* 10.1.

Chunshen 春申, Lord of (d. 237 BCE). Named Huang Xie 黃歇; an important official in the state of Chu 楚 who served as regent and Chancellor under King Kaolie 考烈. He dismissed Xunzi 荀子 from his post at Lanling on account of slander. *Fayan* 11.7.

Chunyu Yue 淳于越. A native of Yue who served the First Emperor in an advisory post as part of a corps of Academicians (*boshi* 博士). In 214 or 213 BCE he urged the First Emperor to restore the system of vassalage inherited from the previous Zhou dynasty. His proposal left him open to the accusation by his rival Zhou Qingchen 周青臣 that he was a traitor to the new regime. Li Si 李斯, then Chancellor in Qin, rejected Chunyu Yue's proposal outright. See *Shiji* 6.254, 87.2546. *Fayan* 10.16.

Dan 旦, King, of Yan 燕 (not to be confused with Prince Dan of Yan). Son of Emperor Wu (r. 141–87 BCE) who was accused by Huo Guang 霍光, his enemy, in 80 BCE of joining several members of the Shangguan 上官 family and Sang Hongyang 桑弘羊 in a plot to depose Zhaodi, kill Huo Guang, and install himself on the imperial throne. King Dan of Yan was doubtless angry that he had been passed over, and another of Wudi's sons appointed heir. All those engaged in the plot were executed or forced to commit suicide, along with their clan members (*zongzu* 宗族) and supporters, and no fewer than twenty of King Dan's consorts and close advisers committed suicide with him. *Fayan* 10.21.

Daowu 悼武, King, of Qin. See King Wu of Qin.

Di Ya. See Yi Ya.

Dong Zhongshu 董仲舒 (179–104 BCE). A native of Guangchuan (present-day Hebei), Dong was an expert in the "Gongyang" tradition for the *Annals*, especially with respect to legal matters. Dong authored several treatises on omens, in which the variations of yin and yang (but not the Five Phases) figure prominently. He was also the putative author of the *Chunqiu fanlu* 春秋繁露, most of whose chapters almost certainly postdate the Han period. See *Shiji* 121.3127; *Hanshu* 56, 88.3615. While serving as prime minister in Jiangdu, he taught his students from behind a curtain, presumably to indicate his lofty disinterest in mundane matters. Now widely regarded as the most famous philosopher of Han times, Dong began to be elevated to the higher authority of a classical master only during late Western Han and Eastern Han, judging from his *Hanshu* biography and other early works reviewed in Michael Loewe's recent monograph on Dong. As Dong's elevation began with Yang Xiong, it is ironic that Dong's reputation grew in inverse proportion to that of Yang. *Fayan* 3.11, 11.16, 11.18.

Dongfang Shuo 東方朔 (ca. 160–ca. 93 BCE). Of Pingyuan; known for the verbal pyrotechnics he unleashed against opponents and his blatant flattery toward those in power. Both approaches assured him ready favor at the court of Wudi (r. 141–87 BCE), for Wudi admired Dongfang Shuo's talents in composition and was hardly averse to enjoying the cruel tricks that Dongfang Shuo sometimes played on dwarves and court entertainers. Dongfang fancied himself a "recluse at court," but by most accounts, he was craven in his desire for power. However, Dongfang did venture to register a protest against Wudi's plan to expand Shanglin Park and its palace facilities, arguing that such an expansion would withdraw farmland from the local residents. He also complained about Wudi's favoritism toward Dong Yan 董偃, the lover of Wudi's aunt (ca. 129 BCE), as well as the general extravagance of Wudi's court. The *Hanshu* includes two essays attributed to Dong, both in dialogue form, which attempt to explain why he did not reach higher rank in office despite his evident brilliance. See *Shiji* 126.3205; *Hanshu* 65.2841; *Hanshu buzhu* 30.47b, note. *Fayan* 11.21.

Dou Ying 竇嬰. Famous for his friendship with Guan Fu, in which the two friends supported each other through the vicissitudes of fortune (*Shiji* 107.2856). During Wendi's reign (r. 180–157 BCE), Dou Ying, as a cousin of Wendi's empress, served as Chancellor of the Wu kingdom. After Jingdi ascended the throne in 157 BCE, the dowager empress tried to get Dou Ying appointed Chancellor (a post that many did not survive), but Jingdi appointed Wei Wan instead. Dou Ying then proceeded to argue against the naming of a much beloved son of Dowager Empress Dou as heir, a protest that so angered the dowager empress that Dou Ying was banished from court. Somewhat later, ca. 154 BCE, Dou Ying was the only person bold enough to protest Chao Cuo's 鼂錯 plan to reduce the power of the local kings in the Liu clan. When the Seven Kingdoms Revolt broke out in 154 in response to the implementation of Chao's plan, Dou was in a comparatively secure position at court, and from that position, he recommended a number of good officials, including Yuan Ang 爰盎 and Luan Bu 欒布. After the revolt was suppressed, Dou was given the title of Lord of Weiqi (Weiqi hou 魏其侯) and appointed tutor for Liu Rong 劉榮, who was then heir apparent.

After Wudi's accession to the throne in 141 BCE, Dou Ying and Tian Fen 田

蚡 seem to have joined forces temporarily, both being supporters of the court classicists against the faction surrounding the woman who now assumed the title of Grand Dowager Empress Dou. But as other members of the Dou family under her protection grew ever more corrupt, Dou Ying found himself increasingly isolated from the power-holders at court, including the members of his own clan and Tian Fen. In 139, Dou Ying retired, and he was thereafter shunned by nearly all his former supporters, except for Guan Fu. *Fayan* 10.23.

Duanmu Ci. See Zigong.

Fan Ju 范睢 (also pronounced "Fan Sui"). Along with Cai Ze 蔡澤, served King Zhao 昭 of Qin (r. 306–251 BCE). As the first adviser to Qin to promote the goal of unremitting expansionism for that state, predicated on Qin's need for "alliance with the distant powers and war with its neighbors," Fan was often held responsible for persuading Qin to undertake this policy change. See *Shiji* 129.3257. Yang Xiong mentions both Fan and Cai in his "Dispelling Ridicule" (Jie chao) *fu*: see Knechtges 1982a, 48, 302 (nn. 402–4). *Fayan* 5.15.

Fan Kuai 樊噲 (d. 189 BCE). A dog butcher who became an early supporter of Liu Bang 劉邦. Fan fought with considerable success against some of the most famous Qin generals. Perhaps more importantly, Fan Kuai's quick-wittedness saved Liu Bang, who might otherwise have fallen into a trap when Xiang Yu 項羽 entertained him at a banquet in 206 BCE. Later Fan Kuai fought several campaigns against Xiang Yu and his generals. After Han unification, Fan fought against many rebel leaders, from Zang Tu 臧荼 in 202 to Lu Wan 盧綰 in 195. See *Shiji* 95.2651; *Hanshu* 41.2067. *Fayan* 11.17.

Fan Li 范蠡 (aka Tao Zhu, or "Adaptable Old Wineskin"). Legendary moneymaker of the fifth century BCE who began life as a native of Chu named Xin Yan 辛研. When Fan Li came to the court of Yue, the forces of King Guojian 句踐 of Yue were being besieged by the Yue forces at the top of Mount Kuaiji. Fan Li advised the new king how to make his country rich enough to withstand all external attacks and eventually launch a successful attack against Wu, the major rival power in the southeast. Later, when King Goujian forced Fan Li's friend Wen Zhong 文種 to commit suicide, Fan Li decided to abandon his post and try his luck elsewhere. Some stories ascribe his decision to leave Wu to his keen insight about his ruler's failings; King Goujian was someone to share adversity but not prosperity with, Fan Li said.

Fan soon amassed a very large fortune in Tao, and in this later persona he was known as "Sire Zhu of Tao" (Tao Zhu Gong 陶朱公). Fan Li is often identified as a Chinese Croesus, since legend credits him with making three separate fortunes totaling a thousand units (catties?) of gold each over nineteen years. Twice he gave these fortunes away to his poor friends and distant relatives. Accordingly, *Shiji* 129.3257 praised Fan as "a rich man who likes implementing his virtue and favor" (*fu hao xing qi de zhe* 富好行其德者). Despite the general consensus that Fan deserved high praise, Yang Xiong denounces him in *Fayan* 5.15.

Fan Sui 范雎. See Fan Ju.

Fan Yuqi 樊於期 (sometimes read as Fan Wuqi; d. 227 BCE). Qin general who had served a predecessor of Ying Zheng (the future Qin Shihuang, or First Emperor, r. 221–210 BCE) before taking refuge in Yan in the household of the Yan heir, Prince Dan 丹. As a young and ambitious king, Ying Zheng repeatedly pressed Yan for the gift of Fan Yuqi's head, but the ruler of Yan ignored such requests until Prince Dan hatched a plot to assassinate Ying Zheng. Fan Yuqi then saw how useful it would be if the assassin were to carry Fan's head to Ying Zheng in a box, so as to gain entrance to the Qin court and obviate suspicion. Without hesitation, like a true warrior, Fan committed suicide to further the plot, but the assassin, Jing Ke 荊軻, failed to accomplish his mission. *Fayan* 11.13.

Feng Tang 馮唐. Native of Dai; grandson of the Chancellor of Dai kingdom. Appointed adviser to the Han court, Feng Tang insulted Wendi (r. 180–157 BCE) by saying that he would not know how to use such first-rate generals as Lian Po 廉頗 or Li Mu 李牧 properly, were they to be enlisted in his service. When Wendi asked Feng Tang to explain his remarks, Feng replied that military law was being so scrupulously enforced that his generals' severity was ruining any chance for Han successes in the field. Wendi accordingly ordered Feng Tang to convey his pardon to a competent governor who had been charged with a slight infraction. Feng's name was put forward for consideration for a top post after Jingdi's accession in 156 BCE, but because he was already around ninety years of age by then, he did not take up the office. See *Shiji* 102.2757; *Hanshu* 50.2312. *Fayan* 10.22.

First Emperor (259–210 BCE). Ascended to the throne of Qin in 246 BCE. Unification came in 221 BCE. For events in his reign, see *Shiji* 6 for his "Basic Annals." *Fayan* 10.7, 10.9, 10.16–17.

Four Graybeards (Dongyuan Gong 東園公, Qili Ji 騎里季, Xiahuang Gong 夏黃公, and Master Jiaoli/Luli 角里). Exemplary recluses who were persuaded to leave their retreat on Mount Nan 南 (South) in order to advance the cause of the future Huidi (r. 195–188 BCE), whom they championed as a worthy heir apparent to the Han founder (r. 206–195 BC). See *Shiji* 55.2045–56. *Fayan* 11.16.

Fu Xi 伏羲. Legendary sage-ruler in primordial times (tradit. ca. 3000 BCE). According to legend, Fu Xi taught men how to hunt, fish, herd, and make musical instruments. He is also credited with "inventing" the Eight Trigrams that became the basis for the sixty-four hexagrams of *Changes*. *Fayan* 4.10, 12.20.

Gan De 甘德. According to rival traditions, a Zhanguo astronomer who was a native of Qi, Chu, or Lu. Perhaps he traveled to all these states. A *Divining the Stars* (Xing zhan 星占) manual, in eight *juan* 卷 (scrolls), is ascribed to him. The extant work entitled *Gan Shi xing jing* 甘石星經 is believed to be a later forgery. *Fayan* 8.14.

Gan Luo 甘. At the age of twelve *sui*, finally managed to persuade Lü Buwei, Chancellor of Qin during Ying Zheng's reign prior to unification, that he, Gan, could persuade Zhang Tang 張唐 to serve as Chancellor in Yan 燕. Gan then alerted Lü Buwei to Zhang Tang's actions as Chancellor in Yan, in particular Zhang's seizure of Zhao 趙 territory. Lü Buwei thought Gan too young to be an effective speaker, but Gan tartly reminded him that Kongzi himself had listened to a child prodigy who was only seven *sui*. These stories are not precisely dated; they occurred ca. 247 BCE, some decades prior to unification. See *Shiji* 71.2319–21. *Fayan* 10.18.

Gan Mao 甘茂. Grandfather of Gan Luo; influential official in the states of Qi and Chu. *Fayan* 10.18.

Gao Yao 皋陶 (tradit. d. 2204 BCE). Native of Qufu (present-day Shandong and the home of Kongzi); served as minister during the reign of the legendary sage-king Yu. Legend credits him with being the first to introduce laws designed to deter criminal behavior. He is purportedly the author or protagonist of "Gao Yao mo" 皋陶謨, the most frequently cited *Documents* chapter during Han times. *Fayan* 6.8, 11.3, 13.9.

Gaoxin 高辛. Great grandson of Huangdi, the Yellow Emperor; otherwise known as Lord Ku 嚳. *Fayan* 10.11.

Gaoyang 高陽. Grandson of Huangdi, the Yellow Emperor; otherwise known as Zhuanxu 顓顼. *Fayan* 10.11.

Geng Zhongcheng 耿中丞 (aka Geng Shouchang 壽昌 or Geng Shou 耿壽, if we follow *Hanshu buzhu* 30.68a–b in taking Chang 昌 to be the style name of one whose personal name was Shou). Mathematician under Xuandi (r. 74–48 BCE) and assistant to the Superintendent of Agriculture (*da sinong* 大司農). (However, the *Jinshu* "Treatise on Astronomy" makes Geng a contemporary of Luoxia Hong and Xianyu Wangren decades earlier, ca. 104 BCE.) In the years 57–54, Geng proposed practical measures to prop up the price of grain, benefit the economy, and reduce the amount of labor needed for the transport of grain to the metropolitan area from the east. He imposed a threefold increase on the taxes paid by fisheries while funding the construction of "ever normal" granaries at the frontier. As a result of the popularity and efficiency of these schemes, Geng was granted the noble rank of Noble of the Interior (*guannei hou* 關內侯) in 54 BCE. Geng Shouchang also submitted one memorial in 52 BCE about the movements of the moon. Two treatises of calendrical science are ascribed to him in *Hanshu* 30.1766. *Fayan* 10.3.

Ghost Valley Master 鬼谷子 (Guigu zi). Purportedly the Zhanguo author of a text on strategies, including military and rhetorical strategies. *Fayan* 11.14.

Gong Sheng 龔勝 and Gong She 舍 (Brothers Gong). Famous as remonstrants when serving as Palace Counselors under Aidi (7–1 BCE), the Brothers Gong supposedly were loathe to serve Wang Mang, who as regent had arrogated supreme power to himself under Pingdi (1–6). At that point, they quit their posts and retired to their native lands. Gong Sheng died ca. 6 CE, and Gong She then committed suicide in ca. 11 CE. The brothers were also famous for their frugality. *Fayan* 6.19.

Gong Yixiu. See Gong Yizi.

Gong Yizi 公儀子 (aka Gong Yixiu 公儀休). Native of Lu; served as prime minister under Duke Mu of Lu (r. 415–383 BCE), in which capacity he supposedly refused to have members of his own family engage in farming or weaving, on the grounds that a member of the duke's court should never compete for profit with the common people, as he would enjoy an unfair advantage over them. Gong Yizi won fame for rejecting a bribe of fish, despite his love of fish. When a disciple asked him why he did not take the bribe, he replied, "It is because I am fond of fish that I refused the fish. Now, as Chancellor, I can supply my own fish. If I were to accept the fish, and then be dismissed from office for that offense, I would never find anybody to supply me with fish afterward!" See *Shiji* 119.3101–3. *Fayan* 3.11.

Gong Yu 貢禹. Native of Langya; identified as one of the most prominent Ru who held ministerial rank under Xuandi (r. 74–48 BCE) and Yuandi (r. 48–33 BCE). He and other like-minded officials advocated a reduction in government expenditures, the freeing of over 100,000 government slaves, and the institution of a series of ritual reforms designed to "restore" a system of ancestral and sacrificial cults that was associated with antiquity. See *Hanshu* 25B.1253. During Gong Yu's lifetime the Han court often ignored Gong's ritual prescriptions, but some of Gong's proposals were instituted after his death, if only briefly. *Fayan* 11.23.

Gongshu Ban 公輸般 (aka Lu Ban 魯班). Carpenter and rough contemporary of Mozi. The epitome of the master craftsman, Ban was supposedly able to build a "cloud ladder" that could scale the highest defensive walls. The Lu Ban Gate in the Weiyang Palace was named after him. *Fayan* 1.7.

Gongsun Chujiu 公孫杵臼. Friend of Cheng Ying; see Cheng's entry. *Fayan* 10.24.

Gongsun Hong 公孫弘. Specialist in the "Gongyang" tradition who served Han Wudi (r. 141–87 BCE) in a variety of posts; a "law-and-order" judge responsible for the executions of many officers at court, and an early proponent of classical learning. As Gongsun Hong began as a pig farmer, his rise to fame and fortune was considered especially remarkable. *Fayan* 11.18.

Gongsun Long 公孫龍 (fl. 320–250 BCE). Master rhetorician famous for his paradoxes; perhaps the most famous sophist of the Zhanguo period. *Fayan* 2.7.

Gongzi Lu. See Meng Xizi.

Gongzi Xi. See Meng Xizi.

Guan Fu 灌夫. One of a pair of famous friends at the time of Han Wudi; able

Han commander who won renown for his bravery and success in quelling the Seven Kingdoms Revolt of 154 BCE. See Dou Ying for further details. *Fayan* 10.23.

Guan Ying 灌嬰. Originally a silk merchant; early supporter of Liu Bang 劉邦. By 208 BCE, Guan, in his capacity as cavalry general, had helped Liu Bang incite a successful rebellion against Qin, for Guan handily defeated several Qin generals. After 206 BCE, Guan acted as imperial envoy in charge of settling the old metropolitan area. Later, as Imperial Counselor (*yushi daifu* 御史大夫), Guan helped Han Xin 韓信 defeat Tian Heng 田橫 and Tian Guang 田光, who had been the de facto rulers of Qi. Guan then turned his forces against Chu, where he promptly took the cities of Pengcheng and Shouchun. Under Han Gaozu, Guan also defeated the forces loyal to two rebels, Zang Tu 臧荼 and Han Xin, for which he was made a noble at Yingyin 穎陰. Following the death of Dowager Empress Lü in 180 BCE, Guan Ying acted in concert with Zhou Bo 周勃 and Chen Ping 陳平 to install the King of Dai 代 as emperor. Appointed Supreme Commander (*taiwei* 太尉) under Wendi in 179 BCE, Guan Ying colluded with Zhou Bo to oppose the recommendations offered by the junior officer Jia Yi 賈誼 and also (more helpfully) to deny important posts to the younger members of the Dou 竇 family. Guan Ying's final campaign in 177 BCE forced the Xiongnu to withdraw, but he was ordered to disband his forces during the revolt of the King of Jibei in that same year. When he died in 176, he was buried with the honors customarily given a Chancellor and posthumously awarded the title of Noble of the Interior (*guannei hou*). See *Shiji* 95.2667, 84.2492; *Hanshu* 41.2080. *Fayan* 11.17.

Guan Zhong 管仲 (Yiwu 夷吾; d. 645 BCE). Perhaps the most famous statesman in early China, who served Duke Huan of Qi 齊桓公 (r. 684–643 BCE), the first of the Chunqiu hegemons, as Chancellor. Kongzi, in *Analects* 14.18, credited Guan Zhong with saving the traditions of rites and music, even as he criticized Guan's extravagances and sycophancy (e.g., 3.22, 14.17). The *Guanzi*, a set of writings ascribed to Guan, was compiled centuries after his death. See *Shiji* 62.2131–34. *Fayan* 9.11.

Gui, Cinnabar. See Bo Gui.

Guigu zi 鬼谷子. See Ghost Valley Master.

Han Anguo 韓安國 (fl. 160–150 BCE). Envoy to King Xiao of Liang, uncle of Jingdi, who felt free to flaunt the Han laws and sumptuary regulations, since he presumed upon the love and support of his sister, Jingdi's mother. As Jingdi's suspicions and anger were quickly aroused by King Xiao's inappropriate behavior, Han Anguo arranged an interview with Jingdi's sister, during which he pleaded the king's innocence, after which Jingdi somewhat relaxed his guard. A skilled negotiator and diplomat, Han Anguo then turned his skills to persuading King Xiao to exercise better judgment in future. Han was also responsible for recommending many good men for office during the reign of Jingdi's successor, Wudi. However, eventually Han was defeated by the Xiongnu in battle, and he reportedly died of mortification. See *Xinxu* 10.13/60/4–61/18 ("Shan mou" 善謀); *Shiji* 108.2857, 110.2905; *Hanshu* 52.2394, 94A.3765. *Fayan* 10.26.

Han Feizi 韓非子 (d. 233 BCE). Legalist thinker from the predynastic state of Han, who studied with Li Si 李斯 under Xunzi 荀子. Like Li Si, Master Han Fei found favor at the court of Ying Zheng, the future First Emperor (Qin Shihuang), and, like Li, Han Fei eventually was executed. Han's writings were predicated on two views: (1) humans in general will compete against each other and destroy society if strict laws do not prevent criminal behavior; and (2) the emperor must hide his activities, so as to make it hard for his subjects either to criticize or to placate him, even while he ensures that his administration justly distributes rewards and punishments to encourage more constructive behavior. A set of fifty-five essays is ascribed to him under the title *Han Feizi*. *Fayan* 6.22.

Han Kui 韓傀. See Han Lei.

Han Lei 韓纍 (aka Han Kui or Lei 韓傀 or Xia Kui or Lei 俠傀) (fl. ca. 350 BCE). Originally a counselor in the service of Jin, Han ultimately became Chancellor of the state of Han. While serving in that capacity, he was assassinated by Nie Zheng 聶政, who was working on behalf of a rival Han minister, Yan Sui 嚴遂. *Fayan* 11.13.

Han Wudi (r. 141–87 BCE). Most famous of the Western Han rulers aside from Liu Bang 劉邦, the Han founder, Wudi managed to extend the territories under the direct control of the imperial house, especially in the northwest and in Central Asia, though the six major offensives he personally organized were far less successful than the northern campaigns led by skilled generals. *Fayan* 13.29.

Han Xin 韓信 (d. 197 BCE). A superb strategist who played a major role in Liu Bang's 劉邦 eventual victory over his rivals. Initially in the service of Xiang Liang 項梁 and Xiang Yu 項羽, he transferred his loyalties to Liu Bang when he found that his advice to the Xiangs was repeatedly ignored. By contrast, Liu Bang's adviser, Xiao He, recognized Han Xin's merits and treated him extremely well. As Liu Bang's ally, Han Xin was appointed to several high offices, first as King of Chu, and later as King of Qi. After his ascension to the Han throne, in 201 BCE, Liu Bang came to suspect Han Xin of plotting rebellion. Initially, Han suffered only a minor reduction in territories and in rank, followed by a demotion to the rank and title of Noble of Huaiyin. But when Chen Xi 陳豨 decided to rebel in 197, Han Xin joined forces with him. Ultimately, Han Xin was executed as a traitor, along with all the members of his family. See *Shiji* 92.2609; *Hanshu* 30.1762–64. *Fayan* 10.15.

Han Yanshou 韓延壽 (d. 56 BCE). A native of Duling, Han was an example of a good governor of erudition who raised cultural standards in the areas he administered and who led by personal example. First appointed to the post of Governor of Huaiyang, Yingchuan, and Dong commanderies, Han continued the same style of administration when he was promoted to the post of Overseer of one of three capital districts under Han Xuandi in 59 BCE. Supposedly, "his sense of obligation and trust extended to some twenty-four counties" under his jurisdiction, so much so that the people in the countryside quit their land disputes and urban-dwellers, their lawsuits. When Han Yanshou was in his capital post, he heard that Xiao Wangzhi 蕭望之 was about to undertake an investigation into Han's conduct as Governor of Dong commandery, and so Han preemptively charged Xiao with the misuse of funds while in office. The investigation ended with Han, rather than Xiao, being charged with misuse of funds—perhaps wrongly. As a result, Han was executed in 56 BCE for the capital crime of "great treason" (*dani wudao* 大逆無道). Not surprisingly, many grieved over his death, and Han's three sons obeyed his dying wish that they never serve in office. *Fayan* 10.27.

Helü 闔閭, King, of Wu (r. 514–496 BCE). *Fayan* 11.13.

He's 和 jade. Priceless jade taken by Bian He 卞和 (sometimes rendered as Mr. He 和) from the mountains in the Chu kingdom. Bian tried to present the fabulous jade to two successive kings of Chu, King Li and his brother King Wu (r. 740–690 BCE), each of whom regarded the proferred jade as nothing more than an ordinary stone of little or no value, for which they punished Bian by amputating first his left and then his right foot. Only when Bian submitted the jade a third time to the court of Chu did anyone trouble to have the jade carefully examined. Naturally, it was found to be of priceless value. "He's jade," in consequence, became a much-used metaphor for something or someone whose value has been seriously underestimated. *Fayan* 6.19.

Hong Gong 弘恭. Hong Gong of Pei 沛 commandery, along with Shi Xian 石顯 of Ji'nan, was one of the first eunuchs to exercise real power at the Han court. During Xuandi's reign (74–48 BCE), Hong, who was an expert in legal matters and drafting documents, became Director of the Palace Writers (*zhong shu ling*). Shi Xian is usually treated as the much more problematic figure of the two, but the coupling of Hong Gong and Chen Tang is surely meant to be derogatory. See *Hanshu* 98.4015. *Fayan* 9.21.

Hou Ji 后稷 (Lord Millet). Legendary predynastic founder of the Zhou dynasty (ca. 1050–256 BCE). *Fayan* 13.9.

Hou Yi 后羿. Also known as Archer Yi; legendary archer who in primeval times shot down the ten suns, thereby rendering the world habitable. *Fayan* 1.7, 12.1.

Hu, Tiger. See Yang Hu.

Huan 桓, Duke, of Qi (r. 685–643 BCE). First and most famous of the hegemons or overlords nominally committed to propping up the authority of the Zhou royal house. Duke Huan, with the aid of Guan Zhong 管仲, secured the throne of Qi and for many years ruled his state wisely and well. He managed to suppress potential invaders on his western and northern frontiers.

He originally led the armies of eight states to punish Cai for joining an alliance with Chu. Cai fell and it looked as if Chu would be punished for its failure to supply the house of the Zhou king with its annual tribute of white reeds. Chu bowed to the threat, however, and, admitting its errors, entered into a treaty with Qi. For this achievement, see Loewe and Shaughnessy 1999, 556; also the entry on Guan Zhong. *Fayan* 7.5, 9.4, 11; 13.24.

Huan, Lord of Lu (r. 711–694 BCE). First of the Lu rulers recorded in the *Annals* ascribed to Kongzi.

Huangdi. See Yellow Emperor.

Huhai 胡亥 (d. 207 BCE). Disrespectful term for the Second Emperor of Qin, who has an entry below. *Fayan* 10.21.

Hui 惠 or Huiwen 惠文, King, of Qin. See Lord Huiwen of Qin.

Huiwen 惠文, Lord, of Qin (r. 337–311 BCE). The duke ruled as "lord" (*jun* 君) from 337 until 324 BCE, when he proclaimed himself king. Thereafter, he ruled as King Huiwen for thirteen more years, until 311 BCE. King Huiwen is famous for refusing Su Qin's 蘇秦 advice to adopt an offensive policy toward his neighbors and also for the incident recorded in *Fayan* 11.9.

Huo Guang 霍光 (d. 68 BCE). Younger half brother of Huo Qubing 霍去病, Huo Guang was one of the most famous ministers of Han times. He witnessed the Han throne reach the apogee of its power (ca. 104 BCE) and also subsequent calls for retrenchment. During the dynastic crisis of 91 BCE (the so-called witchcraft incident; see Loewe 1974), Huo Guang, then about forty years of age, oversaw the peaceful nomination of a new heir, Liu Fuling 劉弗陵, son of Consort Zhao, at which point Wudi asked Huo to assume the role of regent when that son succeeded to the throne. During the young Zhaodi's reign (r. 87–74 BCE), Huo's relations with his fellow regents Jin Midi 金日磾 and Sang Hongyang 桑弘羊 were strained, with only Sang capable of initially providing a counterbalance to Huo, in that he was senior to Huo and responsible for so many of Wudi's successful economic policies. Nor did Huo get along much better with the powerful Shangguan Jie 上官桀 and the Shangguan 上官 Princess.

Upon the death of Jin Midi in 86 BCE, Huo Guang took almost all power into his own hands, over the strenuous objections of the Princess, Shangguan Jie, and Sang Hongyang. Huo's relations with the Shangguans and with Sang thereafter steadily deteriorated, especially after the debacle of the brief installation of the Prince of Changyi as emperor for a few months in 74 BCE. Portents in 78 BCE were read as critiques of Huo Guang's regency, since Huo and his allies had been behind the deposition of the prince and the subsequent enthronement of Wudi's great-grandson, Liu Bingyi 劉病 (the future Xuandi), in the same year. But Huo remained the power behind the throne until his death in 68 BCE, despite accusations that Huo had engaged in various types of illegal and immoral conduct, including turning a blind eye to the machinations of his wife, Huo Xian 顯, who was finally, in 66 BCE, after Huo's death, charged with plotting rebellion and using poison to kill Xuandi's empress, Lady Xu 許. (Huo Xian was then executed, along with other members of the Huo clan accused of plotting to overthrow the Han.)

Huo Guang enjoyed a very mixed reputation in Han times (see *Hanshu* 68.2931, 8.247, 27A.1335, 66.2899; Loewe 1974, chap. 4). Some hailed him as the epitome of loyalty faithful to the self-abnegating model of that other celebrated regent, the Duke of Zhou. Others, however, condemned him as a high-ranking official of little merit, loyalty, and wisdom who did nothing to stop either Wudi's excesses or his own wife's attempts to install their daughter as empress, although he must have known that the installation would ultimately threaten the supremacy of the Han ruling house. Huo Guang also receives blame for not promptly handing over his authority to Xuandi when he came of age in 73 BCE. Ban Gu's appraisal of Huo's contributions is therefore markedly ambivalent (*Hanshu* 68.2967). *Fayan* 1.18–19, 10.21, 11.19.

Huo Qubing 霍去病 (d. 117 BCE). Along with his nephew, Wei Qing 衛青, one of the most successful generals serving under Han Wudi (r. 141–87 BCE), whose campaigns substantially reduced the Xiongnu threat to the Han Empire's northern frontiers. After Huo's aunt was named empress in 128, he advanced quickly through the ranks, with the result that he was given noble titles, surrendered tribesmen, and the best cavalry and infantry units. With such crack troops under his command, Huo began in 121 BCE to push far into Central Asia, using Zhang Qian's 張騫 (see below) descriptions of those distant lands, which had been submitted to the throne two years earlier. In 119 BCE, Wudi unfairly blamed Wei Qing for not capturing the Xiongnu supreme leader, a poor showing nearly guaranteed by the failure of two of Wei's generals to rendezvous with him at the appointed time, after which Huo Qubing saw his influence surpass that of Wei Qing. Two years later, Huo died. See *Shiji* 111.2928, 60.2105, 109.2875; *Hanshu* 55.2478. *Fayan* 11.19.

Huo Xian. Wife of Huo Guang. See his entry and *Fayan* 10.21.

Huozheng, or Fire Regulator. See Li, Regulator of the North.

Ji An 汲黯 (d. 108 BCE). Usually identified as a Huang-Lao proponent (as if that would automatically mark him as an enemy of all classicists), Ji An served during the reign of Jingdi (r. 157–141 BCE) and Wudi (r. 141–87 BCE). Initially, Ji's employment in the heir apparent's establishment, and possibly that adherence to Huang-Lao, may have encouraged Gongsun Hong 公孫弘 and Zhang Tang 張湯 to regard him as an enemy, one of many in Dowager Empress Dou's faction. In any case, when Gongsun Hong became Chancellor in 124 BCE, he persuaded Wudi to transfer Ji to the potentially dangerous post of Metropolitan Superintendent of the Right (*you neishi* 右內史), charged with overseeing one of the three capital areas. Probably in 118 BCE, after the death of Gongsun

Hong, he was appointed Governor of Huaiyang and, sometime later, of Donghai. Ji An was famous for his forthright remonstrations protesting Wudi's enormous appetites and lack of humaneness, as well as for his ardent support for Wudi's *heqin* 和親 treaty with the Xiongnu.

Shiji 24.1179 recounts the story of Ji An's famous rebuke of Wudi, who had lyrics composed and sung to celebrate the acquisition of two "divine horses," one from the Wowa River valley and one from Pushao. According to the *Shiji*, Ji An said, "In general, kings compose music in order to present it to their ancestors above or reform the common people below. Now Your Majesty obtains some horses, and he then writes a set of lyrics. . . . How are the deceased emperors and his subjects among the Hundred Surnames to understand these sounds?" Loewe (2000) suspects that this passage is a later interpolation, but van Ess (2005) disagrees. *Fayan* 11.16.

Ji Bu 季布 (fl. 210–ca. 160 CE). General under Xiang Yu 項羽 who several times besieged Liu Bang's 劉邦 forces, before joining the Han administration. After Xiang Yu's defeat, Liu Bang put a price on Ji's head, so Ji sold himself into slavery, hoping thereby to escape the attention of the authorities. Only later, after a pardon was issued by the Han founder, did Ji come to serve the Han in various offices, the highest of which was Governor of Hedong. Thanks to Cao Qiusheng 曹丘生 and Sima Qian 司馬遷, Ji Bu came to be seen as a person capable of enduring early humiliations and achieving high rank, but incapable of determining the manner of his own end, due to his drunkenness. See *Shiji* 100.2729, 100.2745; *Hanshu* 62.2733 ("Letter to Ren An"). *Fayan* 10.25.

Ji Dan 姬丹 (aka Prince Dan of Yan). See entry for Jing Ke. *Fayan* 11.13.

Ji Shi 姬奭. See Shaogong.

Jia Juanzhi 賈捐之. Great-grandson of the far more famous Jia Yi 賈誼 (200–167 BCE). Jia Juanzhi's own contribution came while he was young. Determined to rebut the memorials of hawks urging his emperor to launch a punitive campaign against a group of southern rebels, Jia offered the throne a strongly worded memorial that instead urged withdrawal from Zhuya commandery altogether. To Jia's way of thinking, those lands to the far south supplied little of real utility to the throne, unlike the Han territories to the north and northwest. (*Hanshu* 69, the biography of Zhao Chongguo 趙充國, recounts the rebellion and subsequent campaign and provides an invaluable record of the total expenditures in grain, salt, and fodder used by the Han expeditionary forces.) Despite his early promise, Jia Juanzhi failed to make a fine career at court, due to his frequent criticisms of Shi Xian 石顯, the imperial favorite. *Fayan* 13.30.

Jia Yi 賈誼 (200–168 BCE). One of the most famous rhetoricians and reformers of early Western Han, during the reign of Wendi (r. 180–157 BCE); a wunderkind whose policy proposals irritated all the senior advisers at court. *Fayan* 2.3.

Jiang Taigong 姜太公. See Taigong.

Jiaoli 角里. See Four Graybeards.

Jie Yu 接輿 (Crazy Jie Yu) (5th cent. BCE). Legendary recluse and eccentric. *Analects* 18.5 contains a famous exchange between Kongzi and Jie Yu in which Jie tells Kongzi that he is like a phoenix in decline, and he should stop trying to save the world, for "great is the peril of those who fill office." Cf. *Analects* 17.16, which portrays Jie Yu as a fanatic who nonetheless has a useful point to make. *Fayan* 11.21.

Jin Midi 金日磾 (d. 86 BCE). A Xiongnu prince, who was enslaved and assigned the job of Keeper of the Stables. As Jin had saved Wudi from an assassination attempt in 91 BCE, he was named coregent with Huo Guang 霍光 for Han Wudi's successor, but Jin died within a year of Wudi. *Fayan* 10.27.

Jing Chai 景差. Famous *fu* writer whose works are no longer extant. Wang Yi's 王逸 (fl. 114–19) preface to the *Chuci* states that some traditions ascribe the "Great Summons" poem to Jing Chai. *Fayan* 2.2.

Jing Fang 京房. Disciple of the *Changes* teacher Zhao Yanshou 趙延壽, who held the post of governor during the reign of Yuandi (r. 48–33 BCE). Jing Fang was famous, according to Christopher Cullen (2010), for criticizing Five Phases cosmological theories, though he upheld yin-yang explanations in his readings of portents. *Fayan* 11.16.

Jing Ke 荊軻. Undoubtedly the most famous assassin-retainer of the late Zhanguo period. A native of Wei 衛, Jing entered the service of Prince Dan of Yan 燕太子丹, who asked him to kill Ying Zheng, the future First Emperor of Qin, whose expansionist policies threatened Yan. Having gained admittance to the Qin court in 227 BCE, Jing Ke was foiled in his assassination attempt, after which he was slain. *Fayan* 11.4.

Jizi 箕子 (aka Xu Yu 胥餘). The legendary Viscount of Ji, imprisoned for speaking out against the last king of Shang. After the downfall of Shang ca. 1050 BCE, Jizi supposedly fled to the territory that is now Korea, rather than serve King Wu of Zhou, whom he deemed a usurper. Eventually, however, King Wu won his allegiance, with the result that Jizi presented him with the text of the "Great Plan" chapter of the *Documents*. *Fayan* 6.8, 11.21.

Juan, Capital (Buyi) 雋不疑, whose personal name means "No Doubt." During the reign of Han Wudi (r. 141–87 BCE), the future Capital Juan was a student of the *Annals*. He later served as Inspector (*cishi* 刺史) for Qingzhou 青州, after which he served Wudi's successor, Zhaodi (r. 87–74 BCE), as Capital Overseer. Juan was famous, first, for his warnings to fellow bureaucrats about the dangers of overly severe application of the laws and, second, for having the audacity to refuse the hand of Huo Guang's 霍光 daughter (see above). The incident mentioned in *Fayan* 11.19 apparently refers to the good judgment he showed in imprisoning a man who falsely claimed to be Prince Li, former heir to Han Wudi. Juan died in 81 BCE, and his biography appears in *Hanshu* 71.3035.

Kang 康, King, of Zhou (tradit. r. 1078–52 BCE). *Fayan* 13.24.

Kuai Tong 蒯通/徹 (fl. early 2nd cent. BCE). A native of Fanyang who was originally named Kuai Che 徹, but since this given name was the same as that of Han Wudi (Liu Che), Kuai's name was posthumously changed to avoid the prohibition against using an imperial name. Kuai was a strategist whose persuasive powers stemmed from his ability to clearly lay out the benefits and disadvantages of a given course of action. In what was perhaps his most famous briefing, he persuaded Han Xin 韓信 (d. 197 BCE) to proceed with his planned attack on Qi on behalf of Liu Bang 劉邦, despite negotiations then under way with Li Yiji 李食其. Kuai is equally famous for *failing* to dissuade Han Xin from rebelling against Liu Bang. (See *Shiji* 89.2574, 92.2620; *Hanshu* 45.2159.) In *Shiji* 77, Kuai Tong's persuasion is first marked by insinuations (君背貴不可言) and then by the grand vision of the tripartite division of the empire. *Wenxin diaolong* 4.3/46/14 says of Kuai that he barely escaped the cauldron (i.e., being boiled alive for treason). He purportedly wrote a book on diplomacy that was listed in Liu Xin's 劉歆 "Seven Summaries" under the rubric of military writings but was reclassified in Ban Gu's *Hanshu* catalog, which eliminated military writings as a separate classification. *Fayan* 10.20.

Kuang, Music Master. See Shi Kuang.

Kui 夔, Music Master. Legendary musician at the court of the sage-king Shun. *Fayan* 7.22.

Li 黎, Regulator of the North (Beizheng 北正; aka Huozheng 火正). Official in charge of the second star in the Xin 心, or Heart, constellation. See also Chong. *Fayan* 10.1.

Li Guangli 李廣利 (d. after 90 BCE). A general who served the Han court with great distinction in Central Asia during the years 104–90 BCE. Li was ultimately condemned, however, for defecting to the Xiongnu enemy after his wife and children were taken into official custody (and almost certainly enslaved) when Wudi began having second thoughts, in the wake of bloody witchcraft trials in the Han capital, about installing as his heir Li's nephew, the King of Changyi 昌邑. Li was later executed by the Xiongnu, after being slandered by a jealous rival. *Fayan* 10.27.

Li Hong 李弘. See Li Zhongyuan.

Li Lou 離婁 (aka Li Zhu 離朱). Legendary figure who was famed for his extraordinarily acute eyesight and who lived during the reign of the equally legendary Yellow Emperor. According to *Hanshu* 86B.3565, "Li Lou could spy into a cranny a thousand miles away." *Fayan* 2.3.

Li Mu 李牧 (d. 229 BCE). General in the service of Zhao during the late Zhanguo period; especially famous for organizing and training a Zhao cavalry division that was used with great success against Xiongnu raiding parties. The *Shiji*'s "Hereditary House of Zhao" (34.1559–60) chapter tells the story of Li Mu's execution on the orders of the Zhao king, who unjustly suspected Li of treason on the basis of slanderous reports circulated by agents from the rival state of Qin. *Fayan* 10.22.

Li Shang 酈商 (d. 179 BCE). Younger brother of Li Yiji 李食其 who was inspired by Chen Sheng's 陳勝 rebellion to lead a rebellion of his own against the Qin. Having brought some four thousand men over to join the forces under Liu Bang 劉邦, Li was duly appointed Commandant (*duwei* 都衛) of Longxi, with authority over the northwest corridor. After unification in 206 BCE, he fought against the rebel Zang Tu 臧荼, then campaigned alongside Zhou Bo 周勃 in the north. In 196 BCE, he participated in the campaigns to suppress the rebels Chen Xi 陳豨 and Ying Bu英布, for which he received a second noble title. *Fayan* 11.17.

Li Si 李斯 (280?–208 BCE). A native of Shangcai, in Chu 楚 (present-day Henan). About to be expelled from Qin in 237 BCE as an "alien," Li submitted a strongly worded remonstrance urging the Qin ruler to rescind his order. Li eventually rose to the highest post in the land, that of Chancellor, during the last years of the First Emperor's reign; but after the First Emperor's untimely death in 210 BCE, Li colluded with the evil eunuch Zhao Gao 趙高 in demanding the execution of the real heir and in tricking General Meng Tian into committing suicide. Li Si is credited or vilified with many of the signature measures of the Qin, such as the unification of the bureaucratic script, standardization of weights and measures, and the Burning of the Books, whose principal aim seems to have been to rid the newly unified state of "private learning" from its former rivals that could be cited against the state's interests. Li Si was eventually executed for treason, after he proposed halting the construction of the Epang Palace south of the Wei River.

Li is generally portrayed in the *Shiji* as an able administrator prey to some weaknesses. He is further celebrated as compiler of at least part of the *Cangjie pian* 倉頡篇, an early lexicon. See *Shiji* 6.254–55, 112.2954, 87.2546–47, for somewhat varying accounts; also Derk Bodde's essay on Qin in Loewe 1986. *Fayan* 6.7, 10.21, 13.9.

Li Yiji 麗食其 (fl. end of the 3rd cent. BCE). A native of Gaoyang (Chenliu 陳留), Li was dismissed as a poor bookworm until the rebellions of Chen She 陳涉, Xiang Yu 項羽, and others led him to enter service in Liu Bang's 劉邦 camp. Soon afterward he had persuaded the locals of Chenliu to ally themselves with Liu Bang, the future Han founder, and then with Tian Guang 田廣 and Tian Gou 田構, King and Chancellor of Qi. But when Han Xin 韓信 (see above) sent troops to attack Qi, the King of Qi concluded that he had been tricked by Li Yiji and ordered Li boiled alive. A nobility was conferred upon Li's son by Liu Bang in recompense for his father's unjust death (*Shiji* 97.2705). *Fayan* 10.19.

Li Zhongyuan 李仲元 (aka Li Hong 李弘, teacher of Yang Xiong). A native of Shu 蜀 (present-day Sichuan), Li was appointed to the local Bureau of Merit in recognition of his great virtue but, according to legend, left office before the month was out. Whenever consulted on public matters, he remonstrated on behalf of the common people. As with another master, Yan Junping (discussed in *Fayan* 6.19), Li's model of upright conduct was often compared with that of Bo Yi and Shu Qi, the two princes who famously refused to "eat the grain of Zhou." Chapter 10 of the *Huayang guozhi* gives an account of Li's activities. The historical figure of Li Hong was later conflated by some religious Daoists with an avatar of the deified Laozi. *Fayan* 11.23.

Li Zhu 離朱. See Li Lou.

Lian Po 廉頗. Successful general working for the state of Zhao 趙 during the late Zhanguo period. As long as Zhao kept Lian Po as its general, the state remained strong, but eventually, King Xiaocheng 孝成 of Zhao (r. 265–245 BCE) was persuaded that Lian Po was seeking to avoid battle, at which point the king named Zhao Kuo as his chief military commander to replace Lian Po. A rumor circulated by enemy spies alleged that Lian Po planned to surrender the 400,000 soldiers under his command to the enemy state of Qin. Almost immediately after Lian's dismissal, the fortunes of the Zhao state declined precipitously. Perhaps the most famous story involving Lian Po tells of how he came to befriend Lin Xiangru 藺相如 (*Shiji* 81.2442). *Fayan* 10.22, 10.26.

Lin Xiangru 藺相如. Minister in Zhao, primarily under King Huiwen (r. 298–266 BCE). Lin Xiangru ferreted out the truth about Qin's duplicity to Zhao and used a ruse to see that the Zhao state treasure, "He's 和 *bi* jade disk," was returned by Qin to Zhao. On a later occasion, when the rulers of Qin and Zhao met at Min Lake, Lin saved his ruler from suffering a studied insult by Qin. At first General Lian Po 廉頗, then serving Zhao and inclined to be self-aggrandizing, often picked fights with Lin Xiangru, who always managed to avoid an open break. Judging Lian to be a good general, with many victories under his belt, Lin Xiangru refused to treat General Lian Po as a rival, lest such a rivalry damage the political fortunes of his home state of Zhao. Eventually, Lian Po, realizing the error of his ways, apologized to Lin Xiangru, and the two became fast friends until their deaths. *Fayan* 10.26, 11.5.

Ling 靈, Duke, of Wei (r. 534–493 BCE). *Fayan* 8.3.

Ling 靈, King/Duke, of Qin (r. 424–415 BCE). *Fayan* 10.8.

Liu An 劉安 (d. 122 BCE). King of Huainan, uncle to Han Wudi, and putative patron-compiler of the philosophical classic *Master Huainan* (Huainan zi), dated to 138 BCE. A patron of scholars and advisers, Liu An was supposedly interested in alchemical works. He was eventually charged with treason and executed. *Fayan* 5.16, 12.9.

Liu Bang 劉邦 (249–195 BCE, r. 202–195 BCE). High Founder or Ultimate Ancestor (Gaozu 高祖) of the Western Han dynasty, Liu rose steadily up from the rank of commoner when leading a major rebellion against Qin. He served the rebel cause, first as Governor of Pei 沛 and then as King of Han (206 BCE). After defeating his chief rival, Xiang Yu 項羽, in battle in 202 BCE, he was crowned emperor of the Han. In 195 BCE, he was killed by a stray arrow in a border skirmish, which left his wife, Empress Lü, to dominate the court for the next sixteen years, although Liu Bang's son nominally ruled as Huidi (r. 195–188 BCE). See *Fayan* 10.9, 10.10, 10.14, 10.19, 13.28.

Liuxia Hui 柳下惠 (personal name Zhan Huo 展獲). Local ruler in the Liuxia district in Lu during the Chunqiu period (770–481 BCE). A figure of dubious reputation, Liuxia Hui was perhaps most famous for gaining and leaving high office without joy or regret (*Fengsu tongyi*, chap. 5). In the *Analects*, he is listed simply as a sometime recluse from society who was willing to enter the service of anyone, no matter how good or bad. Other legends, however, claim that he was so virtuous that a young lady once sat in his lap without any salacious rumors spreading. When he died, his wife gave his funeral oration, since she claimed that none knew his merits as well as she. See *Analects* 15.14, 18.2, 18.8; *Mencius* 2A.9, 5B.1, 6B.6, 7A.2, 7B.28. *Fayan* 11.21, 11.23.

Lou Jing 婁敬 (fl. early 3rd cent. BCE). Dissuaded Liu Bang from making Luoyang his capital, even as he persuaded Liu Bang to contract *heqin* 和親 marriage alliances with the Xiongnu. For his unfailingly good advice, the imperial family granted Lou Jing the signal honor of using the imperial family name of Liu as his own. See *Shiji* 99.2715; *Hanshu* 43.2119; and *Hanshu* 30.1726, for a three-*pian* work (now lost) ascribed to Lou. *Fayan* 11.16.

Lu Ban 魯班. See Gongshu Ban.

Lü Buwei 呂不韋 (d. 235 BCE). A rich merchant operating in Han who traveled to Zhao, where he met Zichu 子楚, one of the sons of the King of Qin who was in virtual exile there. Lü put his entire fortune at Zichu's disposal so that Zichu might bribe his way into the favor of Lady Huayang, the favorite of the reigning Qin king, who saw that Zichu was eventually named heir to the throne. Meanwhile, Lü supposedly introduced his own newly pregnant concubine into Zichu's household, where she quickly became Zichu's favorite. After the birth of the child, Zichu naturally mistook the child sired by Lü to be his own son, and when he assumed the throne as King Zhuangxiang (r. 249–247 BCE) a mere three years later, Zichu named Lü's putative son as his heir. When Zhuangxiang died not long afterward, this heir of Zichu, known as Ying Zheng, ascended the throne. Ying Zheng later went on to unify the Central States and name himself the First Emperor of Qin (Qin Shihuang). Lü, initially elevated to noble rank, was in the end exiled to Shu, where he was forced to commit suicide after being accused of treason. All the members of his clan were then executed. See *Shiji* 85.2505. *Fayan* 10.18, 11.9.

Lu Jia 陸賈 (ca. 228–140 BCE). Among many accomplishments, Lu Jia persuaded Zhao Tuo 趙佗 (r. 210–137? BCE), the self-proclaimed King of Nanyue, to ally himself with the Han. With no less art, Lu also convinced Liu Bang that the latter could not rule an empire solely "on horseback" (i.e., through war) and persuaded Chen Ping 陳平 to destroy the entire Lü family after Dowager Empress Lü's death in 180 BCE. He was often consulted by Wendi (r. 180–157 BCE). Later Han legends portray Lu urging Liu Bang to study the *Odes* and *Documents* in order to become a better ruler, and Wang Chong 王充 (27–97) called Lu "a straight-talking man of service" (*zhi yan zhi shi* 直言之士). Lu is moreover the putative author of *New Talk* (Xinyu 新語), on general policy making, and three other texts (all now lost): *The Annals of Chu and Han* (Chu Han chunqiu 楚漢春秋) in nine bamboo bundles; a set of *fu* in three bundles; and a book devoted to military strategy. See *Shiji* 97.2697; *Hanshu* 43.2111. *Fayan* 11.16.

Lü Wang 呂望. See Taigong.

Lu Zhonglian 魯仲連 (fl. mid-3rd cent. BCE). A man of Qi famous for his high principles and refusal to hold office. The Lord of Pingyuan (d. 251 BCE) in Zhao wanted to confer a settlement on him, along with a thousand pieces of gold. Lu purportedly scoffed at the generous offer, saying, "I would rather be poor and of low status and be able to look down on the world and do as I please than be rich and distinguished but have to yield to others" (*Shiji* 83.2459–69). Because Lu is associated with Fan Li, they are mentioned together in Su Shi's essay "On Fan Li." Tao Yuanming's poems sometimes mention him as a model as well. *Fayan* 11.5.

Luan Bu 欒布. During the early Western Han period, a paragon of loyalty toward his friend and patron, Peng Yue 彭越, King of Liang, who sent him to serve Qi. Before Luan was able to return home from that mission, the Han court charged Peng Yue with treason and executed him. The Han court then issued an edict forbidding anyone to render posthumous offerings to Peng's exposed and severed head. In defiance of that edict, upon his return to the capital, Luan publicly wept in front of the mutilated head, after which he made offerings to its spirit. He was promptly arrested for this act of disobedience, but when he obtained an interview with the Han founder, Luan reminded Gaozu that it had been Peng Yue who had arrested Liu Bang's rival, Xiang Yu 項羽. Because of his spirited defense of Peng Yue, Luan was ultimately released, and afterwards he served the Han house in various posts, including that of Chancellor of Yan under Wendi (ca. 166 BCE). He also played a role in suppressing the Seven Kingdoms Revolt in 154 BCE. Shrines were therefore erected in his memory in both Yan and Qi. See *Shiji* 100.2733; *Hanshu* 4.126, 37.1980, 52.2006. *Fayan* 10.26.

Luoxia Hong 落下閎 (aka Changgong 長公). A native of Ba commandery in southern Sichuan, Luoxia made calendrical calculations during the reign of Han Wudi, working with the Senior Archivist (*taishi ling* 太史令, presumably Sima Qian 司馬遷, but possibly his father) to devise the Taichu 太初 calendar promulgated in 104 BCE. Like Yang Xiong, a native of neighboring

Shu, Luoxia Hong is credited with the invention of the armillary sphere (*Shiji* 26.1260). See chapter 10 of *Huayang guozhi*. *Fayan* 10.3.

Mao Jiao 茅焦 (fl. end of 3rd cent. BCE). A native of Hebei, Mao, as an officer under the First Emperor of Qin (Qin Shihuang), protested the emperor's decision to publicly execute Lao Ai 嫪毐 and two of his own younger brothers and transfer the dowager empress to another palace on account of her affair with Lao Ai. *Shuoyuan* 9.8/69/15 offers details, including the statement that no fewer than twenty-seven people who remonstrated with the emperor about his handling of the affair were summarily executed—hence Yang Xiong's reference to corpses flung everywhere on the path into the palace audience hall. *Fayan* 10.17.

Marquis Sui's 隨 pearl. A legendary treasure of comparable value with He's 和 fabulous *bi* 璧 jade disk. *Fayan* 6.19.

Mei Cheng 枚乘 (usually rendered Sheng) (d. ca. 140 BCE). Famous *fu* writer and a native of Huaiyin best known for his failure to dissuade Liu Pi 劉濞, King of Wu (r. 195–153), from leading the Seven Kingdoms Revolt of 154 BCE. After the rebellion broke out, Mei transferred his allegiance to the King of Liang (r. 168–44), who remained loyal to the Liu clan forces. Of several works attributed to him, Mei's "Seven Stimuli" (Qifa 七發) is the most intriguing. *Fayan* 2.2.

Mencius (Meng Ke 孟軻) (tradit. 390–305 BCE). Self-proclaimed Confucian and defender of Kongzi's teachings against the allegedly more popular theories of Mozi 墨子 and Yang Zhu 楊朱. Mencius was a native of Zou in Shandong, which is within an hour's walk of Qufu, the Lu capital and home of Kongzi. See *Fayan* 2.19, 6.4, 11.4.

Meng Ben 孟賁 (aka Meng Yue 孟說/悅). Legendary strong man; a native of Qi during the late Zhanguo period, noted for his physical strength and courage. In one legend, he competed with King Wu of Qin (r. 310–307 BCE) in lifting heavy bronze ritual tripods. *Fayan* 11.23.

Meng Ke. See Mencius.

Meng Tian 蒙恬 (d. 210 BCE). Son and grandson of two famous generals under King Zhao of Qin (r. 306–251 BCE) and King Zhuangxiang (r. 249–247 BCE), and a deservedly renowned general under the First Emperor. He was Metropolitan Superintendent (*neishi* 內史) for the Qin capital as well. In 215 BCE the First Emperor ordered Meng to take north a force of 300,000 to be used against the Xiongnu. Along the border, Meng built long defensive lines (reportedly part of the Qin dynasty Great Wall), which stretched from Lintao to Liaodong, after which he distinguished himself in attacks on the Xiongnu forces. In 212 BCE, Fusu 扶蘇, then heir to the First Emperor, vigorously protested Qin's suppression of learning, after which he was consigned to Meng's care and supervision. In 210 BCE, following the untimely death of the First Emperor (Qin Shihuang), Zhao Gao 趙高 and Li Si 李斯 thought that Fusu and Meng stood in the way of usurpation; Zhao and Li naturally preferred to place Huhai 胡亥, a less independent-minded candidate, on the throne. Eventually, Fusu was executed, at which point Meng Tian swallowed poison. Both Sima Qian and Ban Biao 班彪 blamed Meng Tian for creating many hardships for conscript laborers. Legend, however, tends to celebrate Meng for overseeing the construction of a Great Wall, which project supposedly employed some 300,000 laborers. See *Shiji* 6.252, 88.2565; *Wenxuan* 9.233; Knechtges 1982b–, vol. 2, 167. *Fayan* 11.10.

Meng Xizi 奚斯 (aka Gongzi Xi 公孫奚 or Gongzi Lu 公子魯). Supposedly composed the Lu Hymns on the model of the Shang Hymns during the reign of Lord Zhao (r. 541–510 BCE) of Lu (*Zuozhuan*, Zhao 7, 6). *Fayan* 1.18.

Meng Yue 孟悅. See Meng Ben.

Mengchang 孟嘗, Lord of (fl. 301–284 BCE). Named Tian Wen 田文, the Lord of Mengchang served as Chancellor under King Min 泯 of Qi 齊 (r. 300–284 BCE). Sima Qian (*Shiji* 75.2363) says that he "attracted the families of perhaps 60,000 highwaymen and criminals to Xue [his fief]"—not much of a recommendation! *Fayan* 11.6.

Min Sun 閔損. See Min Ziqian.

Min Ziqian 閔子騫 or Min Sun 損 (early 5th cent. BCE). Disciple of Kongzi usually identified as a paragon of filial devotion; also known for his refusal to serve corrupt lords, for which he is praised in the *Analects* (11.4, 11.14, and implicitly in 6.9). A fragment from Liu Xiang's *Shuoyuan* tells the story of Min Ziqian's mistreatment at the hands of his wicked stepmother, the subsequent anger of Min Ziqian's father at his son's ill-treatment, and Min Ziqian's intervention to prevent a divorce, lest his younger siblings suffer unduly from being motherless. In *Shiji* 67, which is devoted to the disciples of Kongzi, the biography of Min Ziqian follows that of Yan Hui, Kongzi's most beloved disciple, which may explain why the two names are coupled in the title of chapter 11 in the *Fayan*. *Fayan* 11.1, 12.12, 14.11.

Mo 墨子, Master. See Mo Di.

Mo Di 墨翟 (aka Mozi 墨子, or Master Mo) (tradit. 480–420 BCE). One of the most influential thinkers of the early Zhanguo period; a native of Song 宋. Originally trained as a classicist (Ru 儒), Mo Di came to object to the expense of court ceremonies, which extracted money and time from the hard-pressed common people. *Fayan* 2.20.

Mu 穆, Duke, of Lu (r. 407–377 BCE). An oblique reference to this ruler appears in *Fayan* 7.16.

Mu 穆, Duke, of Qin (r. 659–621 BCE). Famous for extending the Qin territory on its western frontiers via annexation of twelve other small states (*Zuozhuan*,

Lord Wen 6) and for demanding that several of his court favorites follow him to the grave at his death. *Fayan* 10.24.

Nan 赧, King, of Zhou (r. 314–256 BCE). The last Zhou king. *Fayan* 10.8, 11.9.

Nanzi 南子 (Child of the South). Consort of Duke Ling of Wei (r. 534–493 BCE), known for her licentiousness. Both the *Analects* 6.26 and *Shiji* 47.1920–21 refer to an interview that took place between Nanzi and Kongzi, for which Kongzi's disciple Zilu 子路 berated him, saying such a meeting would ruin his master's impeccable reputation, if the word got out. Kongzi did not actually see Nanzi herself, since ritual dictated that she conduct the interview from behind a screen. Because he could hear the sounds of her girdle ornaments, however, Kongzi knew that Nanzi had bowed twice in response to his greetings. Later, Nanzi tried to use the fact of their meeting to imply Kongzi's support for her own designs. *Fayan* 8.3.

Nest, Father (Chaofu 巢父). A legendary recluse at the time of the sage-king Yao; gained his nickname by living in a tree. (The term "Father" is simply used of someone who is older.) As Chaofu blamed Xu You for inviting Yao's attention, he purportedly washed out his ears to purify himself of the taint linked to Xu You. *Fayan* 6.20.

Nie Zheng 聶政 (d. 379 BCE). Zhanguo period assassin who killed the Han minister Han Lei 韓累 (aka Xia Kui 俠傀) on behalf of Yan Sui 嚴遂, a Han counselor. (When Jin was partitioned in the mid-fifth century BCE, the state of Han was formed, which lasted from 402 to 230 BCE.) To protect his elder sister from implication in his crime, Nie disfigured himself, but his sister proudly proclaimed her relation to Nie, knowing that it would mean certain death. *Fayan* 11.13.

Pang Meng 蓬蒙. Legendary archer whose name is often linked with that of Hou Yi. *Fayan* 1.7.

Peng Yue 彭越. See Luan Bu.

Ping 平, King, of Chu (r. 528–516 BCE). Executed Wu Zixu's father and elder brother in 522 BCE. *Fayan* 10.5.

Pingyuan 平原, Lord of (d. 251 BCE). Named Zhao Sheng 趙勝, the Lord of Pingyuan served three successive kings of Zhao 趙 as Chancellor. He accepted a proposal to turn the territory of Shangdang 上黨 (then in Han territory) over to Zhao in order to forge an alliance against Qin, which ultimately led to a Qin attack on Shangdang and the disastrous defeat of the Zhao troops at nearby Changping 長平. It was in this sense that the Lord of Pingyuan's failure "to see things in the broadest possible light" paved the way for Qin's final victory over all the rival six states in 221 BCE. *Fayan* 11.6.

Prince Dan 丹 of Yan 燕. Late Warring States prince who hired the assassin Jing Ke to kill the First Emperor of Qin. See Jing Ke. *Fayan* 11.3.

Qian Lou 黔婁 (late 5th cent. BCE). Native of Qi at the end of the Chunqiu period. As the story goes, the rulers of both Qi and Lu wanted him to become a minister in their states, but Qian Lou steadfastly refused to serve either. He was never afraid of poverty, and his wife supposedly encouraged him in this attitude. Qian Lou is often described as a dear friend or disciple of Zengzi 曾子, who was himself a disciple of Kongzi. For further details, see *Fengsu tongyi*, chap. 3, p. 25; *Lie nü zhuan* 2.11/19/8; Huangfu Mi's 皇甫謐 "Gaoshi zhuan" 高士傳. *Fayan* 10.26.

Qin, Second Emperor of. See Second Emperor of Qin.

Qin Shihuang. See First Emperor.

Qin Yueren 秦越人. See Bian Que.

Qing Bu 黥布 (Tattooed Bu or Ying 英 Bu) (d. 196 BCE). Acquired his name after suffering the punishment of tattooing in his youth. Condemned to work on the First Emperor's mausoleum at Lishan, Qing/Ying participated in an uprising soon after the emperor's death, joining forces with Wu Rui 吳芮, whose daughter he married. He managed to assemble a huge army, which he led north after Chen Sheng's 陳勝 fall to attack the Qin forces. Eventually, he joined up with Xiang Liang 項梁 and, later, Xiang Yu 項羽, who made him a general. But by 206–205 BCE, Qing Bu was hedging his bets about the rival contenders for the imperial throne, and he was finally persuaded to join Liu Bang's camp in 204 BCE. In 203 BCE, he was made King of Huainan, from which kingdom he recovered much of his former territory, until then in Xiang Yu's hands. In 196 BCE, Qing Bu was accused of fomenting rebellion against the house of Han because he failed to seek permission before executing his counselor Fei He 肥赫, who had been dallying with one of his consorts. *Fayan* 10.15.

Qingji 慶忌. Son of King Liao 僚 of Wu; forced to flee Wu after King Helü 闔閭 (r. 514–496 BCE) killed his father and made himself king. *Fayan* 11.13.

Qu Yuan 屈原 (d. 278 BCE). Supposed author of the poem "Encountering Sorrow" (Li sao). Qu took his own life after being slandered by a jealous rival at the court of King Huai of Chu. Yang Xiong criticizes Qu for being excessively emotional. *Fayan* 2.6.

Ran Niu/Ran Boniu 冉伯牛 (late 5th cent. BCE?). Faithful disciple of Kongzi; died young, possibly from leprosy. *Fayan* 6.11, 12.21.

Ren Bi 任鄙 (late 4th cent. BCE). Along with Wu Huo 烏獲, Ren Bi was one of the many strong men who attained high office under King Daowu of Qin (r. 310–307 BCE) and whose strength became proverbial in late Zhanguo and Han times. *Fayan* 11.4.

Righteous Emperor 義帝. Grandson of King Huai of Chu (r. 328–299 BCE); appointed by Xiang Yu 項羽 as his puppet ruler. *Fayan* 10.14.

Sang Hongyang 桑弘羊 (152–80 BCE). Member of a merchant family of Luoyang who showed particular aptitude for keeping accounts. At the age of fourteen, Sang was appointed Palace Attendant. By 110 BCE, he was responsible for much of the work of the Superintendent of Agriculture (*da sinong* 大司農). Together with Kong Jin 孔僅, he instituted a number of measures to resolve the fiscal problems caused by Wudi's expansionist policies, including price stabilization for some basic commodities, new methods of transport, and the imposition of state monopolies for salt, iron, and wine. He also urged that government offices be sold in return for "gifts" of grain and proposed the establishment of sponsored agricultural colonies (*tun tian* 屯田) in the northwest (*Shiji* 30.1428; *Hanshu* 24B.1164, 63.2754). Sang Hongyang probably was also behind Wudi's decision to demote over one hundred nobles and princes (*zhuhou* 諸侯) on the pretext that the annual tribute they offered to the imperial ancestral temples—small vessels of bronze or other metals—was of insufficient weight; at one stroke, Wudi's administration saved itself millions of cash. Given Yang Xiong's views on the proper relation between the ruler and his imperial ancestors (the subject of chapter 13 in the *Fayan*), this last initiative would have served as sufficient reason to deplore the close cooperation between Sang and Han Wudi. Sang was accused by Huo Guang 霍光 of treason in 80 BCE and promptly executed. *Fayan* 7.21.

Second Emperor of Qin (r. 210–207 BCE). Named Huhai 胡亥, the second son of Qin Shihuang was elevated to the throne through a palace coup shortly after his father's death. During his three-year reign, Huhai proved to be such an incompetent and murderous ruler that the eunuch Zhao Gao 趙高, one of the powers behind the throne who had originally elevated him, decided that he was a severe liability. A second coup therefore ended with Huhai being replaced by a young child who reigned during the year before the final collapse of the Qin dynasty. *Fayan* 10.21.

Shang Yang 商鞅 (aka Wei Yang 衛鞅 or Gongsun 公孫 Yang) (d. 338 BCE). Legendary chief minister of the predynastic Qin state, who in ca. 350 BCE effected a number of reforms, including the organization of collective-responsibility groups and the imposition of direct taxation on lands organized in commandery-county units. His teachings are supposedly gathered together in the *Book of Lord Shang* (Shang jun shu 商君書), which has been translated into English. *Fayan* 13.9.

Shangguan Jie 上官桀. In 80 BCE, Huo Guang 霍光 claimed to discover a plot involving several members of the Shangguan family, Sang Hongyang, and King Dan of Yan. All were summarily executed, along with their clan members (*zongzu* 宗族) and supporters. *Fayan* 10.21.

Shao, Lord of. See Shaogong.

Shaogong 召公 (or Ji Shi 姬奭) (fl. mid-11th cent. BCE). Brother of the Duke of

Zhou, and founder of the Yan 燕 state (around present-day Beijing). Shaogong was known for his fair judgments in trials and cases of arbitration. *Fayan* 9.4.

Shen, Master (Shen Pei 申培). A man from Lu who served both the Qin and early Western Han courts in the capacity of Academician. Master Shen was famous for his teaching of the *Odes* and possibly the *Annals* as well. He also served as a wise tutor to several princes of the Liu clan, one of whom had Shen mutilated (castrated?). Shen was understandably loathe to continue in office after that punishment, but Shen's pupils included key officials such as Wang Zang 王臧 and Zhao Wan 趙綰. Like Wang and Zhao, Shen incurred the wrath of Dowager Empress Dou, particularly for his advice regarding the erection of a Spirit Hall (Mingtang 明堂). Shortly after angering the dowager empress, he died of natural causes. *Fayan* 11.16.

Shen Buhai 申不害 (d. 337 BCE). Legalist philosopher known for his theories on the importance of *shi* 勢 (circumstance, position), who served as Chancellor for Marquis Zhao 昭 of the Han state. The *Shenzi* 申子 bears his name and presumably describes his major teachings. Unlike many of the Zhanguo masters, Shen Buhai died a natural death. *Fayan* 4.22, 4.24–25, 8.28.

Shen Pei 申培. See Master Shen.

Shenjing 慎靚, King, of Zhou (r. 320–315 BCE). Also known as Shunjing 順靚 of Zhou. *Fayan* 11.9.

Shennong 神農. Legendary sage-ruler credited with the invention of sedentary agriculture, the so-called "basis" for the distinctive Central States civilization. *Fayan* 12.20.

Shentu Jia 申屠嘉. Served Han Wendi (r. 180–157 BCE) as Chancellor and Imperial Councilor, for which he was made a noble. Shentu won a reputation for bravery as he criticized the influence of the emperor's male favorite, Deng Tong 鄧通. Many regard him as one of the most upright and honest of the early Han Western officials. *Fayan* 11.16.

Shi Fen 石奮 (d. 124 BCE). Joined the Han founder's camp at the age of fifteen and rose steadily through the ranks until he was appointed Senior Tutor for Wendi's (r. 180–157 BCE) heir, the future Jingdi (r. 157–141 BCE). His eldest son was Shi Jian 建 (see below). Shi Fen's four sons, like their father, rose to ranks that commanded a salary of 2,000 bushels or *shi*, hence Shi Fen's nickname "10,000 Bushel Lord." *Fayan* 13.6.

Shi Jian 石建. See Shi Fen.

Shi Kuang 師曠. Music master known for his extraordinary connoisseurship. *Fayan* 2.3.

Shi Qing 石慶 (d. 103 BCE). Youngest of Shi Fen's four sons (all of whom rose to be ministers ranked at 2,000 bushels). Shi Qing was appointed in 139 BCE as one of the Metropolitan Superintendents under Han Wudi (r. 141–87 BCE).

Noted for his honest and cautious nature, Shi Qing was elevated to the rank of Senior Tutor to Wudi's heir apparent in 122 BCE. One time, when several teams of horses pulling the imperial carriage were careening wildly, Shi Qing himself took over the reins from the frightened charioteer. In Wudi's later years, Shi's advice was often passed over in favor of that of Ni Kuan 兒寬 and others, however. He died in office. *Fayan* 10.27.

Shi Shen 石申. Native of Wei during the Zhanguo period. Putative author of *Heaven's Patterns* (Tian wen 天文), an astronomical manual in eight scrolls, or *juan*. This work is no longer extant, but the Tang star manual *Divination Classic of the Kaiyuan Reign* (Kaiyuan zhan jing 開元占經) supposedly incorporates its views. See Sun and Kistemaker 1997. *Fayan* 8.14.

Shizhi 釋之. See Zhang, Judge.

Shu Qi. See Bo Yi.

Shun 舜 (tradit. 2317–2008 BCE). Legendary sage-king and successor to Yao; renowned for the devotion he displayed to the members of his family, who were uniformly awful. *Fayan* 4.1, 4.9, 4.17, 4.21, 6.20, 8.1, 9.8, 10.11, 10.13, 11.3, 12.20. 13.2, 13.6, 13.10, 13.11, 13.13, 13.23.

Shusun Tong 叔孫通. Usually dubbed "the ancestor" of the Ru (i.e., a founder of their fortunes); first served the Qin dynasty as court Academician (*boshi* 博士) under the Second Emperor. When he saw that the dynasty was collapsing, Shusun decided to flee to his native Xue but found the area had already surrendered to Chu (i.e., Xiang Liang 項梁 and his brother Xiang Yu 項羽), whose administrations he served until 205 BCE, when he transferred his allegiance to Liu Bang 劉邦, who eventually founded the Han dynasty. By 202 BCE, the Han founder had commissioned Shusun Tong to devise the Han court ceremonial for audiences. His success in that endeavor was so great that Shusun Tong was appointed Superintendent of Ceremonial (*feng chang* 奉常). In that capacity Shusun Tong was also asked to establish the proper ceremonies for Liu Bang's funeral. Yang's *Fayan* harshly criticizes Shusun Tong, but the criticism is more muted in Yang's *Hanshu* biography, where the line reads, "If someone had composed the rituals of Shusun Tong during the Xia or Yin dynasties, he would have been deemed misguided." These lines come from Yang's "Dispelling Ridicule" (Jie chao) *fu*. *Fayan* 11.17.

Sima Qian 司馬遷 (aka Zizhang 子長). China's most famous historian, who reportedly completed the *Shiji* sometime after 104 BCE (some say by 92 BCE). *Fayan* 5.16, 7.8, 12.9.

Sima Xiangru 司馬相如 (179–117 BCE). One of the most famous of the *fu* writers, who, like Yang Xiong, hailed from Shu (present-day Sichuan). In a memorial, Sima Xiangru quoted others as saying, "We have heard that the Son of Heaven's relationship with the foreign Yi and Di should follow the proverb 'a loose rein is not broken'" [*jimi wujue* 羈縻勿絕], an encouragment to the throne to give more slack to the nomadic frontier groups, lest they revolt" (*Shiji* 117.3049). *Fayan* 2.2, 12.9.

Song Yu 宋玉. Warring States *fu* writer said to write in the same style as Qu Yuan 屈原. Tradition ascribes several extant works to Song Yu, including a *fu* entitled "Deng Tuzi Loves Sex" (Deng Tuzi hao se 登徒子好色); the "Summoning the Soul" (Zhao hun 招魂) poem; "The Gaotang" 高唐 *fu*; and the "Divine Woman" (Shennü 神女) poem. *Fayan* 2.2.

Su Qin 蘇秦 (d. 317 BCE). "Itinerant persuader" (i.e., professional orator and strategist for hire) whose name is typically coupled with that of Zhang Yi 张儀 (d. 309 BCE), a fellow student under Master Ghost Valley (Guigu). Like Zhang Yi, Su Qin allegedly believed that loyalty to any one ruler or principle was of questionable utility or value. As legend has it, Su Qin became the major architect of the anti-Qin "vertical" alliance, after he failed to persuade King Hui 惠 of Qin (r. 337–311) to adopt a more aggressive military posture against his neighbors. Su Qin made a brilliant career, especially in Zhao. Zhang Yi, who became Chancellor of Qin, was sent as envoy to Zhao, Chu, and Han on Qin's behalf. The result of the various alliances formed by both men was that Wei, the first leading opponent of Qin, was broken by Qi (301–284 BCE), which itself was ultimately toppled, after a period of Zhao ascendancy (284–260 BCE), by an alliance under the leadership of Yan. Meanwhile, over the course of the century spanning 350 to 249 BCE, Qin was nearly continuously acquiring territory at the expense of its neighbors, even if most early works blamed Qin's aggression primarily on Su Qin and Zhang Yi. Some recent works have argued, however, that Qin already was virtually the sole superpower after the decline of Wei in 364 BCE. *Fayan* 11.9, 11.14–15.

Su Wu 蘇武. General under Han Wudi and loyal patriot. In 100 BCE, Su was sent as envoy to the Xiongnu, where he was detained for nineteen years. Nonetheless, Su refused to defect to the enemies of Han. When relations between the Han and Xiongnu improved under Zhaodi (r. 87–74 BCE), Su was finally allowed to return home to the Han capital at Chang'an (*Shiji* 110.2917; *Hanshu* 54.2459, 7.240). *Wenxuan* 29 contains the texts of three poems addressed by Li Ling to Su Wu and four by Su Wu, which Chavannes (1895–1905, vol. 1, cv, note) implies were composed in Eastern Han times. *Fayan* 11.20.

Sunwu Zheng 孫無政. See Wang Liang.

Taigong 太公 (aka Jiang Taigong 姜太公, Lü Wang 呂望, or Lü Shang 呂尚). Legendary figure, supposedly a Shang official who joined the Zhou side during the reign of the predynastic King Wen. Taigong then served King Wu (King Wen's son) as chief strategist for the Zhou victory in ca. 1050 BCE. Several years later, after the untimely death of the founder King Wu, Taigong also helped to stabilize the Zhou polity. According to legend, Taigong was himself named founder of the Qi 齊 vassal state. Famed for his military stratagems,

Taigong is the putative author of the *Six Stratagems* (Liu tao 六韜), in six scrolls (*juan*). *Fayan* 7.16.

Tang Le 唐勒. A *fu* writer; contemporary of Jing Chai; court counselor in his native state of Chu, who is said to have written his works after the death of Qu Yuan (d. 278 BCE). None of Tang's works are extant. *Fayan* 2.2.

Tang the Victorious. See Cheng Tang.

Tao Zhu 陶朱. See Fan Li.

Tian Guangming 田廣明 (d. 71 BCE). A Han official who maintained good order only by using the most draconian methods. Within a year of his appointment Tian had arrested one rebel, an action that got him appointed to the post of Superintendant of State Visits in 89 BCE. He then was sent to suppress rebels in Yizhou, and for his success there he was duly rewarded with the rank of Noble of the Interior (*guannei hou* 關內侯), despite the accusation that he had misused his troops. In 72 BCE, the Han court sent Tian off to lead some 40,000 cavalry to help the Wusun cause in a fight against their mutual enemies, the Xiongnu. Enroute to his destination, Tian summoned the recently bereaved widow of the Commandant of Shoujiang and dallied with her, with the result that Tian failed to make a previously arranged military rendezvous. Charged with the failure to engage the enemy, he chose to commit suicide. See *Huayang guozhi* 4.2a. *Fayan* 10.27.

Tiger Hu. See Yang Hu.

Wang Ji 王吉. See Wang Yang.

Wang Jian 王翦 (d. before 210 BCE). Native of Qin, from the northwestern part of present-day Shaanxi; a famous general who conquered the kingdoms of Zhao, Wei, Chu, and Yan during the years 236–223 BCE. Most spectacular was Wang's defeat of the Chu state in 223 BCE, when he led some 600,000 men (possibly most or all of the Qin army) to defeat Qin's chief longtime rival. Wang enjoyed favor at the First Emperor's court until his death. See *Shiji* 73.2338. *Fayan* 11.12.

Wang Liang 王良 (aka You Wuxu 郵無恤 and Sunwu Zheng 孫無政). Legendary charioteer for Prince Jian 蕑 of Zhao; after his death supposedly served as charioteer for the Lord of Heaven, living his afterlife either as the five-star constellation corresponding to Cassiopeia or as the single star beside the Celestial Quadriga (Milky Way). *Fayan* 1.7.

Wang Ling 王陵 (d. 180 BCE). One of Liu Bang's most trusted allies; enfeoffed as Noble Pacifying the Realm 安國 in 201 BCE; assisted Chancellor Cao Shen 曹參 as Chancellor of the Right under (r. 195–188 BCE), from which post he courageously resisted the efforts of Dowager Empress Lü and her family to seize the throne from the ruling Liu clan. See *Shiji* 8.360, 381, 391; *Hanshu buzhu* 40.17a, note. *Fayan* 11.16.

Wang Mang 王莽 (d. 23 CE). Regent for the last Han emperor; in 4 CE conferred upon himself the title of "Lord Who Secures the Han" (An Han gong 安漢公). A line from Yang's *fu* entitled "Excoriating Qin while Praising Xin" (Ju Qin Mei Xin 劇秦美新 (compiled 14 CE?) intoned, "Since the creation, I have never heard of anyone greater [than you, Wang Mang]." But Yang's hyperbolic praise of Wang Mang most likely registered sarcasm. See *Fayan* 13.33. A number of passages in the *Fayan* are said by various commentators to refer to Wang, including *Fayan* 2.12, 5.26, 9.16–17, 10.1–2, 10.4, 10.11, 10.15, 13.7, 13.11, 13.17–18, 13.25, 13.28–29, 13.34.

Wang Yang 王陽 (aka Wang Ji 吉 or Ziyang 子陽). Like Gong Yu 貢禹, an upright official in serving Xuandi (r. 74–48 BCE) who took great risks in urging unpopular reforms. They were also close friends (hence their joint biography in *Hanshu* 72.3058–80). Wang Yang showed his independence by retiring to his natal home when Xuandi refused to listen to his advice. He agreed to return to office under Yuandi (r. 48–33 BCE) but died en route to the capital to take up his new position. Wang Yang taught the Qi version of the *Analects*. *Fayan* 11.23.

Wang Zigong 王子貢 (Wang Zun 王尊). Born to a family of shepherds; during the reign of Yuandi (r. 48–33 BCE) became Chancellor of Dongping 東平, in present-day Shandong. Wang Feng 王鳳, probably the most powerful man at the court of Chengdi (r. 33–7 BCE), trusted Wang Zigong and appointed him to suppress bandits in the Chang'an metropolitan area. Wang took up various high offices, including that of Overseer of the Capital (*jingzhao yin*), in which posts Wang was ready to charge his superiors with misconduct as necessary. In general, Wang Zigong was known for his harsh administration. Accused by a peer of defaming the empress, his dismissal brought sorrow to many, since he had shown himself capable of restoring order in the capital. He was ultimately saved from disgrace by a man who submitted a claim reporting that a former subordinate of Wang, who held a grudge against him, was responsible for many of the slanders circulating about him. He was then appointed Inspector of Xuzhou and Governor of Dong commandery. Wang also won renown for his refusal to move from a dangerous site when the Yellow River threatened to burst its banks in 29 BCE. *Fayan* 11.19.

Wang Zun 王尊. See Wang Zigong.

Wei Qing 衛青 (fl. 129–106 BCE). With Huo Qubing 霍去病, one of the two best generals serving Han Wudi (r. 141–87 BCE). After 119 BCE, probably because of Wei Qing's failure to capture the Xiongnu leader, or *chanyu*, Huo came to surpass Wei Qing in influence. See the entry on Huo Qubing. *Fayan* 11.19.

Wei Xiang 魏相 (d. 59 BCE). Governor of Henan during the reign of Zhaodi (87–74 BCE); Chancellor (along with other posts) under Xuandi (r. 74–48 BCE). As Chancellor Wei Xiang launched an inquiry into an accusation that Zhao Guanghan 趙廣漢 had allowed one of his subordinates to slay an innocent man. Zhao, seeking a way to prevent Wei Xiang from continuing the investigation into his misconduct, falsely reported that Wei Xiang's wife had killed a slave. When matters were investigated, Zhao was tried for perjury and executed (sometime between 66 and 64 BCE), one of his chief accusers being Xiao Wangzhi 蕭望之. *Fayan* 10.27.

Wei Xuancheng 韋玄成. Younger son of Wei Xian 韋賢; nearly named by Wang Mang as heir to Xian after Wei Xian's death. Wei Xuancheng feigned madness, however, so that his brother might inherit the noble rank instead. Eventually, Wei Xuancheng succeeded to his father's title (ca. 61 BCE), then served in a variety of different posts, including that of Chancellor in 42 BCE. *Fayan* 10.26.

Wen 文, King/Duke, of Qin (r. 765–716 BCE). *Fayan* 10.8.

Wen, Lord, of Jin. Second of the Chunqiu period hegemons who propped up the authority of the Zhou royal house. *Fayan* 7.15.

Wen of Zhou 周文王, King (fl. ca. 1050 BCE). Also known as Lord Protector of the West; predynastic king; ruler of Qi 岐 under the last Shang emperor, Zhou 紂. He was imprisoned at Youli 羑里, during which time he supposedly worked on parts of the *Changes*. See *Shiji* 4. *Fayan* 1.13, 6.10, 8.1, 10.8, 12.20, 13.28.

Wen Zhong 文種. Also known by his style name of Ziqin 子禽, an officer of Chu, who served King Goujian 句踐 of Yue for over twenty years alongside Fan Li (also of Chu), superintending the rise of the Yue state among the southern powers after Yue suffered the fall of its capital of Kuaiji to Wu. Eventually, thanks to the efforts of Wen Zhong and Fan Li, Yue proved strong enough to destroy its rival Wu and restore its honor. In 494 BCE, after suffering a major defeat, Wen Zhong was sent by King Goujian to Wu to seek a peace treaty with King Fuchai. Goujian later forced Wen Zhong to commit suicide, as Fan Li had predicted he would. See the entry on Fan Li. *Fayan* 10.5.

Wu 武, King, of Qin (aka King Daowu) (r. 310–307 BCE). Renowned for his physical strength, the king appointed a number of strong men to high office, three of whom are named in the *Fayan*: Ren Bi 任鄙, Wu Huo 烏獲, and Meng Ben 孟賁. Little else is known of King Wu, as the *Shiji* allots a mere page (*Shiji* 5.209) to his reign. *Fayan* 11.3.

Wu 武, King, of Zhou (aka Ji Fa 姬發) (fl. ca. 1050 BCE). Founder of the Zhou dynasty and brother of Zhougong. See *Shiji* 4.120–32. *Fayan* 1.13, 6.8, 8.1, 9.4, 10.8, 13.28.

Wu Guang 吳廣 (fl. late 3rd cent. BCE). Leader of a peasant revolt under Qin, though far less famous than Chen She 陳涉. At one point, Wu held a position as "king" under Chen She that allowed him to supervise the other commanders in a concerted attack on Xingyang. Unable to take the city, Wu Guang fell victim to a plot led by Tian Zang 田臧, after which he was killed. Tian Zang then sent Wu's head to Chen She, who rewarded him with the post of

Senior Minister (*lingyin* 令尹) of Chu. At one point, the combined troops under Chen and Wu numbered only some nine hundred men hiding out in the Great Marsh (Daze 大澤, present-day Anhwei). See *Fayan* 10.6.

Wu Huo 烏獲 (late 4th cent. BCE). One of several strong men favored by King Daowu of Qin (r. 310–307 BCE) whose strength became proverbial by late Zhanguo and Han times. *Fayan* 11.4.

Wu Ji Zha 吳季札. See Yanling Jizi.

Wu of Wei 魏武侯, Marquis (r. 396–371 BCE). Ruler for Wu Qi and Tian Wen (see below). *Fayan* 7.13.

Wu Qi 吳起. A native of Wei 衛, a general, who defeated the Qin army and occupied the Xihe region on behalf of Wei 魏. Wu Qi also served Lu 魯 and Chu 楚 at various points in time. In Chu, ca. 401 BCE, he instituted a set of famous reforms. Ultimately, however, the Chu ruler, concerned with Wu's cunning and willingness to exploit expedience and strategic advantage, ordered Wu Qi torn limb from limb. Wu Qi is the putative author of the work *Master Wu's Military Strategies* (Wuzi bingfa 吳子兵法). *Fayan* 1.7, 7.13.

Wu Zixu 伍子胥. Legendary official who helped Wu defeat Chu. Wu Zixu's father, Wu She, was minister and tutor to the heir of King Ping of Chu (r. 528–516 BCE), Prince Jian. Nonetheless in 522 BCE King Ping had both the father and brother of Wu Zixu killed. Seeking revenge, Wu set out to destroy the Chu kingdom, which he nearly accomplished while adviser to King Helü 闔閭 of Wu (r. 514–496 BCE). After Helü's death, his son Fuchai (r. 495–473 BCE) succeeded to the throne of Wu. As a result of Wu Zixu's many sharp rebukes of King Fuchai's chosen strategy, which ignored Wu Zixu's advice to confront Yue and stop attacking Qi, relations between Fuchai and Wu Zixu became so strained that Fuchai finally, in 485 BCE, asked Wu Zixu to commit suicide by falling on his sword. By then Wu Zixu had become so anxious for revenge and angry at Fuchai for doubting his loyalty that he reportedly asked his men to affix his eyeballs after his death to the east gate of Wu's capital, so that he might personally watch the coming invasion of Wu by the state of Yue. That invasion eventually occurred, as Wu Zixu had predicted.

The "Wu Speeches" section of the *Guoyu* contains several long stories that depict Wu Zixu's attempts to persuade King Fuchai not to extend his ambitions to the far north, since Wu's real enemy was nearby Yue. As noted above, King Fuchai ignored that advice, to his peril. Wu Zixu is typically regarded as a hero in the early sources, including the *Xunzi*. Yang Xiong says of Wu in his own autobiography, "After Zixu died, Wu perished" (*Hanshu* 87B.3568), but *Fayan* 10.5 disputes the laudatory assessments.

Xia Kui 俠傀. See Han Lei.

Xia Yu 夏育. Legendary strong man who defied all dangers. *Fayan* 11.23.

Xiahou Sheng 夏侯勝 (fl. 74–51 BCE). Native of Dongping, known as Xiahou the

Elder, in contrast to Xiahou the Younger (Xiahou Jian 夏侯建), both of whom were appointed Academicians in 51 BCE; nephew to Xiahou Shichang 始昌, who had served Han Wudi as an expert in the *Documents* classic and in yin/yang theory. Xiahou Sheng clearly continued the family tradition of *Documents* study, especially its omen interpretations, but he was also reportedly an expert in some of the rites, and he was, perhaps, the first expert of record for the Lu version of the *Analects*. All his teachings had a great influence upon Xiao Wangzhi 蕭望之 and Huang Ba 黄霸 (d. 51), exemplary officials at the court of Xuandi (r.74–48 BCE). As one of the most famous classical masters, Xiahou Sheng was invited to participate at the Shiqu Pavilion conference convened by Xuandi in 51 BCE, along with his cousin Xiahou Jian 建. But Xuandi eventually threw Xiahou Sheng in prison for criticizing Xuandi's forebear, Han Wudi (r. 141–87 BCE) in the strongest possible terms; he languished in prison for a full three years before being released. Yang Xiong shared Xiahou Sheng's view of Wudi, which explains his praise of the man. *Fayan* 11.16.

Xiahou Ying 夏侯嬰 (d. 172 BCE). Called Teng 滕 in the *Fayan* after the name of the place where he served as Prefect; considered one of the meritorious officials in early Western Han. Once engaged in the transport business, Xiahou Ying fought alongside Xiao He 蕭何 to defeat several Qin generals or force their surrender. During the wars leading up to unification under Han, Xiahou Ying recommended Han Xin 韓信 for office and helped to secure a pardon for Ji Bu 季布. He also, in a crisis, managed to save two of Liu Bang's children, including the future Huidi (r. 195–188 BCE), whom Bang had been ready to abandon. (For this, he earned the undying gratitude of both Huidi and Huidi's mother, Dowager Empress Lü, whom he later served as Superintendent of Transport.)

After unification under Han in 206 BCE, Xiahou Ying fought with distinction against both the Xiongnu and the rebels Chen Xi 陳豨 and Ying Bu 英布. Shortly after 206 BCE he was given the title of Noble of Zhaoping (*Zhaoping hou* 昭平侯) and later, ca. 202, the kingdom of Ruyin 汝陰, with five thousand households attached to it. After the death of Dowager Empress Lü in 180 BCE, he oversaw the purification of the imperial palace, the deposal of the infant heir, and the enthronement of the King of Dai (i.e., Wendi). He died eight years after Wendi's ascension. Xiahou Ying was one of those rare individuals who managed "to maintain his position of favor . . . from before the foundation of the Han dynasty throughout the turbulent upsets that ensued from the death of Gaodi [Gaozu, Liu Bang] until the accession of Wendi" (Loewe 2000). *Fayan* 11.17.

Xian 顯, King, of Zhou (tradit. r. 368–321 BCE). In 360 BCE, the king sent Duke Xiao of Qin (r. 361–338 BCE) a portion of the set of sacrificial meats that had been originally offered to Kings Wen and Wu; in 334 BCE, the Zhou king also sent some meats to King Hui 惠 of Qin. *Fayan* 10.8.

Xiang 襄, King/Duke, of Qin (r. 777–766 BCE). *Fayan* 10.8.

Xiang Yu 項羽 of Chu (d. 202 BCE). Chief rival of the Han founder after the collapse of the Qin Empire in 210 BCE. In the first month of the first year of the reign of Qin Yidi 義帝, the so-called Righteous Emperor, Xiang Yu set up eighteen kingdoms, with Liu Bang as overlord of the kingdom of Han. Xiang Yu was later defeated by Liu Bang at Gaixia, when his forces were surrounded and far outnumbered. *Fayan* 10.9–10, 10.14, 10.17, 10.25.

Xianyu Wangren 鮮于妄人. Court astronomer who flourished 78–75 BCE, during Wudi's reign. *Fayan* 10.3.

Xiao 孝, Duke, of Qin (r. 361–338 BCE). Principally famous for employing Shang Yang 商鞅 ca. 350 BCE to change the laws, bureaucratize government service, institute private property directly taxed by the court (thereby "opening the fields"), and give rich rewards to those with demonstrated achievements in battle and in farming, thereby paving the way for Qin's supremacy over its rivals. His achievements are recorded in *Shiji* 5, the "Basic Annals of Qin." *Fayan* 10.7.

Xiao He 蕭何 (d. 193 BCE). Native of Pei 沛, the birthplace of the Han founder, generally remembered as one of the finest ministers the Central States have ever produced. Instrumental in the Han founder's rise to power, he persuaded Liu Bang that he must secure the area within the passes if he was to supplant his rival Xiang Yu. In 205 BCE, Xiao He, left alone to defend the metropolitan area while Liu Bang was fighting elsewhere, used his position to establish the ancestral shrine as well as the altars to the gods of soil and grain, to erect the main Han palaces and the capital walls, and to regularize many aspects of the administration. In addition, he was soon able to send to Liu Bang at Xingyang a relief force he had recruited from peasants who had been exempted from corvée service. Xiao also counseled Liu Bang on the rewards to be given his allies, thereby obviating many problems in maintaining those alliances. There was occasional friction between Xiao He and Liu Bang, however, for example, on the occasion when Liu Bang refused Xiao's advice to turn Shanglin Park over to the inhabitants of Chang'an (at which point Xiao was temporarily put under arrest). Later, at a banquet, Liu Bang himself acknowledged that Xiao He was superior to him in many ways. Xiao He died two years after Liu Bang. See *Lunheng* 36/176/5–7; 38/181/11–14. *Fayan* preface to 11, also *Fayan* 11.17.

Xiao Wangzhi 蕭望之. See the entry for Han Yanshou.

Xie 契. Legendary founder of the Shang line (tradit. 1800-ca. 1050 BCE). *Fayan* 13.9.

Xinling 信陵, Lord of (d. 242 BCE). Named [Gongzi] Wuji [公子] 無忌); younger son of King Zhao of Wei 魏昭王 (r. 311–279 BCE). In 257 BCE at Handan, one of the largest cities within the Central States, he led the allied forces in resisting a siege by the Qin army. A later literary piece has Wuji "riding a four-horse chariot to save Handan from the siege." Unfortunately, this initial success soon prompted a sweeping counteroffensive by Qin launched against the allied forces of Wei, Han, Zhao, and Chu. The Lord of Xinling is therefore criticized as short-sighted in *Xunzi* 50/13/19, 46. *Fayan* 11.6.

Xu You 許友/由. Recluse who, according to some legends, lived at the time of sage-ruler Yao. *Fayan* 6.19–20.

Xu Yu 胥餘. See Jizi.

Xuan 宣, King/Duke, of Qin (r. 675–664 BCE). *Fayan* 10.8.

Xun Qing 荀卿. See Xunzi.

Xun Xi 荀息/叔 (fl. mid-7th cent. BCE). Presented as an adviser in the Chunqiu state of Jin in the *Zuozhuan* and *Gongyang* commentaries for Lord Xi. When Duke Xian of Jin (d. 651 BCE) killed his heir apparent, Shen Sheng, and raised Xiqi 奚齊, son of his favorite concubine (Lady Li), to be heir, he asked for and got Xun Xi's complete support. When, after Duke Xian's death, Li Ke 李克 then murdered Xiqi, Xun Xi put on the throne a second son of Lady Li, named Dao 卓/悼子. Li Ke then proceeded to kill Daozi and possibly Xun Xi as well. Legend has Xun Xi taking his own life, however, on the grounds that he had been unable to execute his promise to the dying duke. The larger (or deeper) question raised by the commentaries is whether keeping a promise matters when the promise itself is misguided. In some stories, Xun Xi admonishes Duke Ling of Jin (r. 620–607 BCE) for building a nine-tiered terrace. *Fayan* 10.24.

Xunzi 荀子 (aka Xun Qing 荀卿 or Minister Xun) (d. 238 BCE). Follower and promoter of the Confucian Way; also the teacher of Han Feizi and Li Si. *Fayan* 12.5.

Yan Hui 顏回 (aka Yan Yuan 顏淵). Most beloved and best disciple of Kongzi. *Fayan* 1.7, 1.8, 4.24, 5.1, 6.11, 11, 12.12.

Yan Junping 嚴君平 (aka Zhuang Zun 莊尊) (fl. mid-1st cent. BCE). Yang Xiong's teacher; famous for working in the marketplace telling fortunes in such a way as to encourage the Chengdu locals to practice morality. At one time, Li Qiang of Duling, who was on friendly terms with Yang Xiong, thought to secure Yan's services as Regional Commissioner for Yizhou (Sichuan), but Yan refused. Yan was famous for combining mastery of the *Changes*, the *Laozi*, and the *Zhuangzi*. *Fayan* 6.19.

Yan Pingzhong 晏平仲. See Yanzi.

Yan Yuan 顏淵. See Yan Hui.

Yang Gui 楊貴. See Yang Wangsun.

Yang Hu 陽虎 (aka Tiger Hu; Yang Huo 陽貨). Nominally Steward for the Ji 季 (Jisun 季孫) clan, one of the three leading clans that held power in the state of Lu during Kongzi's (551–479 BCE) lifetime, but actually dictating its policies. Once, in order to avoid paying his respects to Tiger Hu, Kongzi pretended that he was not at home when Yang brought him a gift of a suckling pig. Eventually, however, Kongzi felt he had to see Yang, if his Way was to have any chance of succeeding in Lu. For details, see *Analects* 17.1. *Fayan* 8.3.

Yang Wangsun 楊王孫 (Yang Gui 貴; Wangsun was his style name) (2nd cent. BCE). Born into a rich family, Yang Wangsun was nevertheless so fond of certain Huang-Lao 黃老 ideas that he left orders that he should be buried in the simplest possible way, without a coffin, so that his body could make direct contact with the earth. His son and heir asked a noble of Qi to dissuade Yang Wangsun from such an extreme act, but Yang insisted and his request was honored after his death. Ban Gu so deplored this action that he lumped Yang Wangsun together with the First Emperor of Qin. See *Hanshu* 67.2907, 67.2928; *Hanshu buzhu* 67/14a, note. *Fayan* 10.29.

Yang Zhu 楊朱 (4th cent. BCE). Influential thinker who argued that the common good would be best served if each person would always act with supreme selfishness. According to his classic formulation (supposedly designed to counter the influence of Mozi 墨子, who advocated extremes of altruism), if every person refused to offer even a single hair from his or her head in return for saving the world, it would mean that no man would have to die needlessly for his country or for honor. Book 7 of the *Liezi* is devoted to his sayings. *Fayan* 8.28.

Yanling Jizi 延陵季子 or Wu Ji Zha 吳季札 (fl. mid-6th cent. BCE). Younger son of King Shoumeng 壽夢 of Wu (r. 585–561 BCE); enfeoffed at Yanling, hence his name. When Yanling Jizi traveled to Lu as envoy for Wu in 544 BCE, he asked to see various odes performed, then assessed the performance, as recorded in *Zuozhuan*, Lord Xiang 29/8. For this reason, he was regarded as an archetypal connoisseur of music. Aside from his expertise in music, Yanling Jizi was most famous for refusing the throne of Wu, since his elder brother by rights should succeed to it, "with the result that the people who pursued lawsuits about land boundaries dropped them." Sima Qian considered him an exemplary statesman (*Shiji* 31.1475), as does *Liji* chapter "Tangong." Legend also had him giving up his sword to a man in order to fulfill a promise, though the man was already in the grave; thus, for many, he epitomizes the highest virtue. *Fayan* 5.21.

Yanzi 晏子 (aka Yan Ying 晏嬰; Yan Pingzhong 晏平仲 (posthumous name) (fl. 556 to ca. 500 BCE). By most accounts, exemplary minister of Qi in the sixth century BCE, praised by the Kongzi of the *Analects* for his ability in making and keeping friends and allies: "However long the relation lasted, he treated [the person(s)] with the same reverence" (*Analects* 5.17; *Shiji* 62.2134–37). At the same time, other traditions blame Kongzi's failure to attain high position in Qi on this prime minister. Aside from his ability to eliminate potential rivals at court, Yanzi is now principally known as author or inspiration for the *Yanzi* (now known as the *Yanzi chunqiu*), which contains a number of loyal remonstrances supposedly addressed by Yan to his ruler. In the pre-Han and Han periods, Yan was equally famous for his extreme frugality; allegedly, he would not allow two kinds of meat to be served at his table, nor would he allow the women in his family to wear silk. He himself wore the same fox-fur garment for thirty years. *Fayan* 8.28.

Yao 堯. Legendary sage-king, now chiefly remembered for his disinterestedness in choosing Shun, an able minister, to be his heir rather than his own son. He is the fourth of the Five Lords (*wu di* 五帝). *Fayan* 1.13, 4.1, 4.17, 4.21, 4.24, 6.16, 6.20, 8.1, 9.4, 10.11–12, 12.20, 13.6, 13.10–11, 13.23.

Yao Li 要離. Native of Wu 吳 kingdom, late fifth-century BCE assassin-retainer. According to legend, Yao told his ruler, King Helü 闔閭 of Wu (r. 514–496 BCE), to first kill Yao Li's wife and children and then burn their corpses, since these acts would allow Yao Li to pretend to be a man bearing a grudge against the king, by which ruse Yao Li might win the trust of the ambitious prince Qingji 慶忌. Then, having won the prince's confidence, Yao Li assassinated Qingji at the very first opportunity, when the prince was en route to Wu to seize power. See the *Wushi chunqiu,* "Loyal and Incorrupt" chapter. *Fayan* 11.13.

Yellow Emperor (Huangdi). By some accounts, the ultimate progenitor of all the Central States peoples. *Fayan* 4.9, 10.2, 10.11, 12.20.

Yi Ya 易牙 (aka Di Ya or Yongwu 雍巫). A celebrated cook who, according to most sources, was in the service of Duke Huan of Qi (r. 684–642 BCE), whom Yi Ya reportedly served with excessive slavishness, since he was willing to cook his own son to provide his lord with a new taste sensation. *Fayan* 5.11.

Yi Yin 伊尹. See A Heng.

Yidun 猗頓. A legendary moneymaker from the state of Lu who traded in salt, probably during the fourth century BCE. See *Shiji* 129.3259. *Fayan* 1.22.

Yin 尹, Metropolitan (Yin Wenggui 尹翁歸; nicknamed Yin Fufeng 扶風 (d. 62 BCE). In charge of Fufeng, one of the three metropolitan capital districts, under Han Xuandi (r. 74–48 BCE). Yin was noted for his incorruptibility and for his strict punishments to maintain order; he was also one of the few ministers who eschewed all forms of political intrigue. By maintaining good relations with his colleagues, he avoided being classified as a "cruel official." All three of his sons rose to high office. *Fayan* 11.19.

Yin Jifu 尹吉甫. Minister to King Xuan of Zhou (r. 827–781 BCE); supposedly composed at least two of the Zhou Hymns included in the *Odes*: "Song gao" 崧高 and "Zheng min" 蒸民. *Fayan* 1.18.

Yin Wenggui 尹翁歸. See Yin, Metropolitan.

Ying Bu 英布. See Qing Bu.

Ying Shuli 嬴樗里. Younger brother of King Huiwen of Qin 秦惠文 (r. 337–311 BCE) by a different mother; served both Kings Wu and Zhao of Qin as Chancellor. Ying was considered so wise that many called him a "wisdom bag"; legend even has him predicting the precise location of his tomb, also that imperial palaces would be built on either side of his grave. *Fayan* 11.8.

Ying Zheng 應政. Disrespectful way to signify the First Emperor of Qin (d. 210 BCE), since the family and personal names of an emperor are usually tabooed. *Fayan* 10.7, 10.9, 10.16–17.

Yiwu 夷吾. See Guan Zhong.

Yongwu 雍巫. See Yi Ya.

You Wuxu 郵無恤. See Wang Liang.

Youxiong 有熊. Legendary ruler in primeval times; see Huangdi. *Fayan* 10.11.

Yu 禹. Legendary sage-ruler, flood-queller, and putative author of the "Tribute of Yu" (Yugong 禹貢) chapter in the *Documents*. Another *Documents* chapter, entitled "Counsels of Great Yu" (Da Yu mo 大禹謨) is also ascribed to him, but this is a post-Han forgery or pastiche. *Fayan* 10.2 identifies Yu by his clan name, Si 姒. *Fayan* 1.13, 4.16, 5.9, 6.8, 8.1, 9.8, 10.2, 10.12, 11.3, 12.13, 13.10, 13.11.

Yuan Ang 爰[袁]盎. Appointed Gentleman of the Palace (*zhonglang* 中郎) at a fairly young age, thanks to his elder brother's influence, Yuan warned Wendi (r. 180–157 BCE) that Zhou Bo 周勃 (see below) was not altogether loyal, for which remonstrance he earned Zhou's implacable hatred. Nonetheless, when later Zhou was accused of plotting rebellion, Yuan Ang intervened on his behalf, and thereafter the two men joined forces. In 177 BCE, Wendi's half brother, Liu Chang, King of Huainan, murdered Shen Yiji 審食其, who had been Chancellor three years before. Three years later, in 174 BCE, when Liu Chang plotted revolt, Yuan Ang urged Wendi to treat the king with great leniency, lest his subjects assume that Wendi wanted to kill Liu Chang by sentencing him to a harsh exile. Wendi followed this advice. But Yuan Ang's repeated protests about a host of policy matters, including the imperial visits to Shanglin Park, eventually cost him favor at court. Yuan was then appointed Chancellor to Chu and Wu (at that time ruled by Liu Pi 劉濞, who was already plotting revolt). In 155 BCE, at the young Jingdi's court, Chao Cuo 鼂錯 charged Yuan Ang with receiving bribes from Liu Pi, but Yuan Ang's sound advice at the outbreak of the Seven Kingdoms Revolt in 154 BCE proved so invaluable to Jingdi that the emperor granted Yuan Ang a private audience. Then, with the help of Dou Ying 竇嬰, Yuan Ang blamed the whole revolt on Chao Cuo's mishandling of the local kings' grievances. After the defeat of the rebels, Yuan Ang was appointed Chancellor to the newly appointed King of Chu, in which post he was frequently consulted by Jingdi. Around 150 BCE, Liu Wu 劉武, King of Liang, had Yuan Ang executed on the grounds that Yuan had blocked his appointment as Jingdi's heir.

Yuan Ang had the reputation of a forthright man of high moral principles, but his reputation may not have been earned, given his willingness to blame the entire Seven Kingdoms Revolt on his enemy. The *Hanshu* is much more positive than either the *Shiji* or Yang Xiong on the subject of Yuan Ang (contrast *Shiji* 101.2745 with *Hanshu* 49.2303); the *Hanshu* compliments Yuan Ang for the "generosity of his heart," even as it criticizes Chao Cuo for devising far-ranging plans for the future while failing to see the danger near at hand. *Fayan* 11.17.

Yuan Gu 轅固. See Yuangu, Master.

Yuan Taotu 轅涛塗. High-ranking officer in Chen, a state near Chu. In 656 BCE, Lord Huan 桓 of Qi (d. 672 BCE) attacked Chu. Upon his return home, he wanted to take a route through Chen, but Councilor Yuan Taotu persuaded the ruler of Chen that it would be unwise to let Lord Huan and his armies enter the state, whereupon the furious Lord Huan seized Yuan. See the *Zuozhuan* and *Gongyang* commentaries for Lord Xi 4, whose stories show minor variations. *Fayan* 9.4.

Yuangu 轅固, Master (sometimes rendered as Yuan Gu). A master in Shen Pei's 申培 interpretation of the *Odes*; served the court of Jingdi (157–141 BCE) as Academician, where he won fame for his defiant critique of the *Daode jing* before Dowager Empress Dou. For this offense the dowager had him locked into a pen with one or more wild boars. Had Jingdi (r. 157–141 BCE) himself not given Yuangu a dagger to kill the animal(s), he would certainly have been gored to death. Later he was appointed senior tutor to the King of Qinghe 清河. See *Shiji* 121.3122; *Hanshu* 88.3612. *Fayan* 11.16.

Zai Wo 宰我 (aka Zaiyu 宰予 and Ziwo 子我). A famously lazy disciple of Kongzi. Zai Wo eventually became leader in Linzi 臨淄, the capital of Qi, and took part in the rebellion of Tian Chang 田常 in 481 BCE, which action shamed his teacher, Kongzi. *Fayan* 12.12.

Zaiyu 宰予. See Zai Wo.

Zhan Huo 展獲. See Liuxia Hui.

Zhang 張, Judge (Shizhi 釋之). A native of Nanyang who bought his first office and was ignored for nearly a decade by his emperor, Wendi (r. 180–157 BCE). Zhang was just about to retire from public life when Yuan Ang 爰盎, recognizing his abilities, appointed him Imperial Messenger (*ye zhe* 謁者), in which office he became famous for his determination to uphold the laws, even at the risk of endangering himself. For example, he once charged the future Jingdi and the King of Liang with the capital crime of "disrespectful conduct," since they had failed to dismount from their carriages at the gates of the imperial palace. Zhang Shizhi also showed his mettle when he advised Wendi not to appoint a junior officer or to inflict a harsher punishment than the law required. Such actions won Zhang Shizhi the admiration of Zhou Yafu 周亞夫, his contemporary. Under Han Jingdi (r. 157–141 BCE), Zhang was demoted to Chancellor of Huainan. The explorer Zhang Qian 張騫 may have been his descendant. See *Shiji* 1–2.2751; *Hanshu* 50.2307. *Fayan* 11.19.

Zhang, Colonel. See Zhang Anshi.

Zhang Anshi 張安世 (d. 62 BCE). Son of Zhang Tang 唐; held a number of ministerial posts under three successive emperors, Wudi (r. 141–87 BCE), Zhaodi (r. 87–74 BCE), and finally Xuandi (r. 74–48 BCE). After Huo Guang's 霍光 death in 68 BCE, Zhang Anshi became the most powerful official at court, who was put in charge of all construction and the defense of the capital and its palaces. Zhang won renown for his frugality and modesty; he was inclined to hide others' faults and advertise their good points. This is probably how he escaped trouble even though his granddaughter was married to a relative of the Huo clan, and nearly everyone linked to the Huo clan was ultimately executed. Zhang Anshi was eventually named Marquis of Fuping, and by imperial edict his portrait was displayed on the occasion of the visit of the Xiongnu leader or *Chanyu* in 51 BCE. Zhang Anshi's tomb and that of his wife were recently found in Xi'an. See *Kaogu* 2009:8, for reports. *Fayan* 10.27.

Zhang Biqiang 張辟強 (2nd cent. BCE). Precocious son of Zhang Liang 張良 (d. 187 BCE), who was a senior minister in the early Western Han court. *Fayan* 10.18.

Zhang Er 張耳. Both Chen Yu 陳餘 and Zhang Er hailed from Zhao 趙 (present-day Kaifeng, in Henan), and both initially supported the claims of Zhao Xie 趙歇 to become the "restored" king of Zhao after the collapse of Qin power in 210 BCE. But when Handan, the former capital of the old Zhao state, was retaken by a Qin general, both men fled to Julu 鉅鹿, where they and their forces were besieged again by a second Qin general, Wang Li 王離. Unable to decide what to do next, the two friends had a falling out, after which Zhang Er joined the camp of Xiang Yu 項羽. Appointed King of Changshan (in the old territory of Zhao), Zhang Er was unable to keep those lands. Eventually he was defeated by a combined forced led by Chen Yu and Tian Rong 田榮 of Qi. Zhang Er then joined Liu Bang's army and was named king of Zhao under Liu Bang's protection in 203 BCE. He died a year later. (Meanwhile Chen Yu's troops were defeated and he was killed.) See *Kaogu* 1980.1, 52–55, for excavations at his tomb. *Fayan* 10.23.

Zhang Liang 張良 (d. 185 BCE). Born to a well-to-do family in Han 韓; a staunch ally of Liu Bang in his rise to power. After Liu Bang's death in 195 BCE, Zhang Liang held the post of Chancellor under Liu Bang's successors, Huidi 惠帝 (r. 195–188 BCE) and Dowager Empress Lü (in power, 188–180 BCE). Li Yiji 李食其 had urged Liu Bang to grant fiefs to some surviving members of the pre-imperial kingdoms, but Zhang Liang, equally well versed in historical precedents, argued that semi-independent princes tended to try to usurp power. Zhang Liang also urged Liu Bang to make his capital at Chang'an rather than Luoyang. Zhang declined several grants of households, either by directing the grants to his peers or refusing them outright. Considered so wise that some said that he had become an immortal after his death, Zhang is credited, along with Xiao He and Cao Shen 曹參 and others, with putting the Han dynasty on a secure footing. He is also said to have "won victory from afar, while sitting in his tent" (*Wenxin diaolong, juan* 26, final appraisal). *Fayan* 10.18, 11.18.

Zhang Qian 張騫 (d. 113 BCE). Served Han Wudi as envoy to the Western Regions; lived as a virtual prisoner of the Xiongnu for about ten years and married a Xiongnu woman. Eventually, however, Zhang managed to escape, after which he went on to complete his missions to Ferghana, Bactria, and possibly northern India and Persia, though he and a single guide were the sole survivors of a mission that originally numbered more than a hundred people. After his return to the Han court, Zhang's detailed reports included information on the customs of the Wusun, Yuezhi, and Xiongnu peoples. Epitaphs celebrating him are listed in *Lishi* 12.1b. *Fayan* 11.20.

Zhang Shizhi 張釋之 (style name Ji 季). Han official who, thanks to patronage by Yuan Ang 爰盎, served Wendi (180–157 BCE) as Superintendent of Trials (*tingwei* 廷尉), in which position he was an upright defender of justice, who resisted any and all attempts to interfere with sentencing, even those by the emperor himself. *Fayan* 11.19. See Zhang 張, Judge.

Zhang Yi 張儀. See Su Qin.

Zhao Gao 趙高 (d. 207 BCE). Evil eunuch who seized power during the reign of the Second Emperor of Qin; blamed for many tyrannical acts, perhaps because he was a eunuch. Reportedly, he conspired with Li Si 李斯 to have Huhai 胡亥 placed on the throne as the Second Emperor of Qin, only to later kill Huhai. In any case, Zhao himself fell victim to a plot in 207 BCE. Zhao Gao is also named as the compiler of a short work on script forms entitled *Yuan li* 爰歷. *Fayan* 10.21.

Zhao Guanghan 趙廣漢 (fl. 57–49 BCE). Overseer of the capital during the reigns of Zhaodi and Xuandi (87–74, 74–48 BCE, respectively), hence his nickname "Capital Zhao." Zhao, then regarded as a promising junior official, became one of the signatories of the indictment against the King of Changyi in 74 BCE. Promoted to be Governor of Yingchuan and then Noble of the Interior (*guannei hou*), Zhao put down bandits and led a force against the Xiongnu before returning to become acting governor of the capital in 71 BCE. Once back in the capital, Zhao failed to rein in his own subordinates, which led to a direct conflict with Chancellor Wei Xiang 魏相, who launched an inquiry into an accusation that Zhao Guanghan had murdered an innocent man. Anxious to prevent Wei Xiang from pursuing this investigation further, Zhao falsely reported that Wei Xiang's wife had killed a slave. Further investigations (between 66 and 64 BCE) ended in Zhao's trial for perjury and his execution. Notably, when Zhao was about to be executed, a crowd of men offered to die in his place, but the court refused to grant him a substitute. *Fayan* 10.27.

Zhaoxiang 昭襄, King, of Qin (r. 306–251 BCE). Also known simply as King Zhao, he disputed with the Confucian master Xunzi 荀子 concerning the ultimate utility of appointing classicists to his court. *Fayan* 11.9.

Zheng Kaofu 正考父 (tradit. fl. 799–728 BCE). According to legend, counselor to Lord Xiang 襄 of Song and the seventh-generation ancestor of Kongzi; arranger of the Shang Hymns section of the *Odes*. Zheng Kaofu's son was the famous general Kong Fujia 孔父嘉, commander-in-chief of the Song forces. *Fayan* 1.18.

Zheng Pu. See Zheng Zizhen.

Zheng Zizhen 鄭子真 of Guokou (style name of Zheng Pu 鄭樸). During the reign of Chengdi (r. 33–7 BCE), Zheng supposedly refused the blandishments of Wang Feng 王鳳, the power behind the throne, who tried to lure him to court with promises of honors and high rank. *Hanshu* 72.3056 associates him with Yan Junping, Yang's teacher in Chengdu, Sichuan, as does Xun Yue's *Hanji*, *juan* 24. *Fayan* 5.25.

Zhi Buyi 直不疑. Sometime during the reign of Wendi (r. 180–157 BCE), Zhi was wrongly accused of stealing his neighbors' money, and yet he undertook to repay the money that had gone missing. Zhi "Not Suspect" became famous for his honesty and also for his refusal to defend himself against the charges leveled against him during his lifetime. He was appointed to several high offices, including that of Imperial Counselor (*yushi daifu* 御史大夫) in 154 BCE. In 140, he was dismissed, along with Wei Wan 衛綰, for unspecified faults. *Fayan* 10.26.

Zhongni 仲尼. Courtesy title for Kongzi (Confucius).

Zhou, Duke of. See Zhougong.

Zhou Bo 周勃. A native of Pei 沛 (like Liu Bang), Zhou earned his living in a variety of low professions until he decided to join the forces of Liu Bang against Qin and Xiang Yu 項羽. During the years 209–202 BCE, until Xiang Yu's death, Zhou fought in the field., but after unification under the Han in 202 BCE, he fought against a variety of purported traitors, all former allies of Liu Bang, as well as against the Xiongnu. Zhou Bo was one of the few early supporters of Liu Bang who managed to survive the various coups and countercoups during the early Western Han period. At the defeat of Zang Tu 臧荼 in 201 BCE, Zhou was given a noble title and over eight thousand households. Five years later, in 196, he was appointed Supreme Commander (*taiwei* 太尉), a position he continued to hold under Huidi (r. 195–188 BCE). Upon the death of Dowager Empress Lü in 180 BCE, he and Chen Ping 陳平 made sure that the Lü clan members were executed. He also took steps to see that the King of Dai was installed as the new emperor (posthumously named Wendi). Under Wendi, Zhou Bo served as Chancellor of the Right, while Chen Ping became Chancellor of the Left; both Zhou and Chen vetoed any policy proposals offered by the young Jia Yi 賈誼. But in 177 BCE, Zhou retired, hoping to set a good example for those nobles who refused to leave the court. Once he took up residence in Hedong, he was charged with inciting rebellion, and he was pardoned only after complex negotiations entailing a large transfer of cash. Zhou Bo was widely regarded as a "meritorious minister," even though he did not move against the Lü clan until after the death of the dowager empress. *Fayan* 10.18.

Zhou Chang 周昌 (d. 191 BCE). Rebuked Liu Bang for his partiality toward Lady Qi's son and his consequent failure to favor his son by his legal wife. Liu Bang named Zhou Chang Chancellor for King Ruyi 如意 of Zhao, and later, when Dowager Empress Lü wanted to kill Ruyi, Zhou Chang prevented the king from entering the Han capital. Eventually, after Ruyi's death by poisoning, Zhou Chang, fearful of the dowager empress, pleaded illness and left the court. *Fayan* 11.16.

Zhou Xin 纣辛 (d. ca. 1050 BCE). The last king of Shang, remembered for his lust and cruelty. *Fayan* 4.17.

Zhou Yafu 周亞夫. Son of Zhou Bo; one of the generals sent to fight the Xiongnu under Han Wendi (r. 180–157 BCE). Under Jingdi, Zhou Yafu helped to suppress the Seven Kingdoms Revolt in 154 BCE. See Yuan Ang. *Fayan* 10.22.

Zhougong 周公 (aka Duke of Zhou). By legend, the primary model and inspiration for Kongzi. Whether the duke himself arrogated the powers of the Zhou king or not (a point of contention in Han and pre-Han texts), Zhougong as regent moved quickly to suppress the rebellions led by two of his brothers, Guan Shu 管叔 and Cai Shu 蔡叔, and by the son of the last king of Shang, Huo Shu 霍叔. For debates on the Duke of Zhou, and whether he became king or not, see Nylan 2009. *Fayan* 7.16.

Zhu Jia 朱家 (early 2nd cent. BCE). Knight errant in early Western Han and contemporary of Liu Bang; won renown for his refusal to take credit for any of his meritorious acts, including advancing the career of Ji Bu 季布. *Fayan* 10.26.

Zhuang Zhou 莊周 (aka Zhuangzi 莊子) (tradit. 4th cent. BCE). Thinker from Chu; usually regarded as one of the greatest logicians and rhetoricians of all time. The first seven chapters (Inner Chapters) of the book ascribed to him are remarkable tours de force. Yang, like his teachers, seems to have admired some of Zhuangzi's teachings (especially the injunction to reduce one's desires) while deploring others (e.g., seeing things as equal). *Fayan* 3.20, 4.24–26, 5.27, 8.29.

Zhuang Zun 莊尊. See Yan Junping.

Zhuangzi 莊子. See Zhuang Zhou.

Zigong 子貢 (Duanmu Ci 端木賜). Kongzi's richest and most successful disciple, whom early sources credit with making Kongzi's reputation. The sources record Zigong's travels as itinerant persuader to Qi, Wu, Yue, and Jin, during which time he incited several wars between Wu and the other states—wars whose final result was to preserve Lu, weaken Qi, destroy Wu, and make the Yue ruler a hegemon. *Analects* 13.20 records Zigong's speech about shame. *Fayan* 11.14, 12.12.

Ziqian 子騫. See Min Ziqian.

Zisi 子思. Grandson of Kongzi by the name of Kong Ji 孔伋; putative author of the "Doctrine of the Mean" (Zhongyong 中庸); served Duke Mu of Lu (r. 407–377 BCE). *Fayan* 12.5.

Ziwo 子我. See Zai Wo.

Zixia 子夏 (aka Bu Shang 卜商, Yan Yan 言偃, or Ziyou 子游). According to *Analects* 11.2, Ziyou and Zixia were two disciples of Kongzi known for their "culture and learning" (*wenxue* 文學). Zixia was known to be sarcastic, scornful, and critical of others. Some sources make him author of a preface to the *Odes*. *Fayan* 12.12.

Ziyou. See Zixia.

Zizhang 子長. See Sima Qian.

Zou Yan 鄒衍 (ca. 305–240 BCE). A native of Zou 鄒, near Qufu, home of Kongzi, and the same state where Mencius was born; won renown as an astronomer, cosmologist, and adviser to kings and princes, for whom Zou functioned as an expert in "things beyond the sea that people cannot see" (*ren zhi suo bu neng du* 人之所不能睹). Mere fragments of the writings once ascribed to him survive. Zou thought the Central States occupied only one part in eighty-one of the earth. Like Kongzi, he was famous as one whose theories frightened rulers. *Fayan* 4.26, 5.27, 8.28.

Zou Yang 鄒陽 (fl. early 2nd cent. BCE). Native of Qi; an itinerant adviser who, along with Mei Cheng, served Liu Pi 劉濞, king of Wu (r. 195–154 BCE), sometime near the end of that king's reign. Zou Yang composed a memorial designed to dissuade Liu Pi from revolting against the Han throne; the memorial's rather circuitous logic failed to convince the king of the futility of revolt. While serving in a later post in Liang, Zou made the mistake of advising the ruler about policy matters before he had gained his ruler's confidence and, as a result, was thrown into prison. But thanks to his moving letter to the ruler, Zou Yang not only avoided execution but went on to become marquis in the Liang state. *Wenxin diaolong*, *juan* 18, praises Zou's "clever metaphors and irrefutable logic." *Fayan* 11.6.

Zuo Qiuming 左邱明. Putative author of the *Zuozhuan*; according to some legends, a contemporary of Kongzi, and according to others, a disciple. *Fayan* 10.30.

Abbreviations

CHANT: Chinese Ancient Texts database, Research Centre for Chinese Ancient Texts, Institute of Chinese Studies, Chinese University of Hong Kong.

DRK: All references to Knechtges' translation of the *Hanshu* biography of Yang Xiong; see Knechtges 1982a.

ECT: *Early Chinese Texts: A Bibliographic Guide.* Berkeley: Society for the Study of Early China, 1993.

e-*SKQS*: Electronic database based on the printed Wenyuange edition of *Siku quanshu* 四庫全書. Hong Kong: Chinese University of Hong Kong and Digital Heritage Publishing, 1999–.

Fayan: Han Jing 韓敬. *Fayan zhu* 法言注. Beijing: Zhonghua shuju, 1992.

HJAS: *Harvard Journal of Asiatic Studies.*

HYSIS: Harvard-Yenching Sinological Index Series.

JAOS: *Journal of the American Oriental Society.*

KGYWW: *Kaogu yu wenwu* 考古與文物.

Bibliography

MAJOR COMMENTARIES TO THE *FAYAN*

Han Jing 韓敬. *Fayan zhu* 法言注 (Commentary on *Fayan*). Beijing: Zhonghua shuju, 1992.

Li Gui 李軌. *Yangzi Fayan zhu* 揚子法言注 (Commentary on Master Yang's *Fayan*). 13 *juan* (scrolls?). In Sibu beiyao 三四部備要 ed.

Liu Shipei 劉師培. *Fayan bushi* 法言補釋 (Supplementary Explications for the *Fayan*). Dated 1916. In *Liu Shenshu yi shu* 劉申叔遺書 (1936). Cited in Wang Rongbao 1987.

Ma Zong 馬總. *Fayan yaoyu* 法言要語 (The *Fayan,* Important Phrases). Originally 15 *juan*. Dated 786. Fragments cited in Wang Rongbao 1987.

Sima Guang 司馬光. *Yangzi Fayan ji zhu* 揚子法言集注 (Collected Commentaries on Master Yang's *Fayan*). 10 *juan*. Dated 1081. Now in the Wenyuange ed. of *Siku quanshu* 四庫全書.

Song Zhong 宋衷. *Yangzi Fayan zhu* 揚子法言注 (Commentary on Master Yang's *Fayan*). Originally 13 *juan*. Dated 219. Fragments in Ma Guohan 1967, 1.112–16; also cited in Wang Rongbao 1987.

Sun Yirang 孫詒讓. *Fayan zha yi* 法言札迻 (Notes on the *Fayan*). Dated 1904. Cited in Wang Rongbao 1987.

Wang Rongbao 汪榮寶. *Fayan yishu* 法言義疏 (Commentaries on the *Fayan*). Comp. 1899, notes added 1911, orig. pub. 1933. 2 vols. Beijing: Zhonghua Shuju, 1987.

Wu Mi 吳祕. *Yangzi Fayan zhu* 揚子法言注 (Commentary on Master Yang's *Fayan*). Dated 1081. Fragments now known from Sima Guang and from Wang Rongbao 1987.

Yinyi 音義: *Yangzi Fayan yinyi* 揚子法言音義 (Sound Glosses for Yang's *Fayan*). By a Song dynasty author, whose name has been lost. Cited in Wang Rongbao 1987.

Yu Xingwu 于省吾. *Fayan xinzheng* 法言新證 (New Evidence for the *Fayan*). 1 *juan*. Dated 1938. In Yu's *Zhuzi xinzheng* 諸子新證 (New Evidence for the Masterworks), also 1938.

Yu Yue 俞樾. *Zhuzi pingyi* 諸子平義 (Critical Reflections on the Meanings in the Masterworks). Dated 1874. Cited in Wang Rongbao 1987.

OTHER PRIMARY SOURCES

Analects 論語. See *Lunyü*. All references are cited according to standard chapters and paragraphs.

Ban Si 班嗣. "Sheng xian gao shi zhuan" 聖賢高士傳. All references are to e-*SKQS*.

Baoshan Chu mu 包山楚墓. Ed. Hubei sheng Jingsha tielu kaogu dui. 2 vols. Beijing: Wenwu 1991.

Beitang shuchao 北堂書鈔. Comp. Yu Shinan 虞世南. Beijing: Qinghua daxue, 2003.

Bielu 別錄. Comp. Liu Xiang. Fragments preserved in *Bielu, Qilue jiben* 別錄七略輯本. Taipei: Guangwen, 1969.

Bohu tong 白虎通. Comp. Ban Gu 班固. All references are to CHANT.

Bowu zhi 博物志. Zhang Hua 張華. Ed. Fan Ning 范寧. Beijing: Zhonghua shuju, 1980.

Cao Pi 曹丕. "Lun wen" 論文. All references are to e-*SKQS*.

Cao Zijian ji 曹子建集. By Cao Zhi 曹植. All references are to e-*SKQS*.

Changes 易經. See *Yijing*.

Chunqiu fanlu 春秋繁露. Attributed to Dong Zhongshu 董仲舒. All references are to CHANT.

Da Dai Liji 大戴禮記. All references are to CHANT.

Daode jing 道德經. Traditionally assumed to have been authored by Laozi 老子. All references are to standard sections as given in CHANT; refer also to Wu Cheng 吳澄, *Daode zhen jing zhu* 道德真經注. Taipei: Yiwen yinshuguan, 1965.

Documents Classic. See *Shangshu*.

Dong Zhongshu 董仲舒. *Chunqiu jieyu* 春秋決獄. Quoted in Ma Guohan 1967, 2.1180–81; also *Guoxue jiben congshu* 國學基本叢書, vol. 38. Taipei: Commercial Press, 1968.

Dongguan Hanji 東觀漢記. Compilation ascribed to Liu Zhen 劉珍. All references are to CHANT.

Ershi wushi bubian 二十五史補編. All references are to the 1956 six-volume edition. Beijing: Zhonghua shuju, 1956.

Fengsu tongyi 風俗通義. By Ying Shao 應劭. All references are to CHANT.

Fu Sheng 伏勝. See *Shangshu dazhuan*.

Ge Hong 葛洪. *Baopuzi* 抱朴子. All references are to e-*SKQS*.

Gongkui ji 攻媿集. Comp. Lou Yue 樓鑰. Sibu Congkan ed.

Gongyang zhuan 公羊傳. All references are to *Chunqiu jingzhuan yin de* 春秋經傳引得, HYSIS.

Guangya 廣雅. All references are to e-Siku.

Guliang zhuan 穀梁傳. All references are to CHANT.

Guodian 郭店. All references are to *Guodian Chu mu zhu jian* 郭店楚墓竹简, ed. Jingmen shi bowuguan. Beijing: Wenwu chubanshe, 1998.

Guoyu 國語. All references are to CHANT.

Han Changli quanji 韓昌黎全集. By Han Yu 韓愈. Beijing: World Books, 1935.

Han Feizi 韓非子. All references are to CHANT.

Han guan yi 漢官儀. In *Hanguan jiuyi* 漢官舊儀.

Han Yu 韓愈. "Song Meng Dongye xu" 送孟東野序; "Yuan dao" 原道: See *Han Changli quanji* 韓昌黎全集 19.11a-16a.

———. "Yuan dao" 原道: See *Han Changli quanji* 韓昌黎全集, vol. 1, 11.1–7a.

Hanguan jiuyi 漢官舊儀. Ed. Ji Yun 紀昀. All references are to CHANT.

Hanshu 漢書. By Ban Gu and others. Beijing, Zhonghua shuju, 1962 (except for references to Yang Xiong's *Hanshu* biography, for which see Knechtges 1982a).

Hanshu buzhu 漢書補注. Comp. Wang Xianqian 王先謙. Changsha: Wangshi, 1900.

Hou Hanshu 後漢書. Fan Ye 范曄 et al. See the 1965 Beijing: Zhonghua shuju ed., 12 vols.

Huainan zi 淮南子. If commentary is needed, references are to the standard citation text: Liu Wendian 劉文典, *Huainan honglie jijie* 淮南鴻烈集解, citing by *juan* and page. Otherwise, all references are to CHANT.

Huangfu Mi 皇甫謐, *Gaoshi zhuan* 高士傳. All references are to e-*SKQS*.

Huayang guozhi 華陽國志. By Chang Qu 常璩. All references are to Liu Lin 劉琳, annot., *Huayang guozhi jiaozhu* 華陽國志校注. Taipei: Xinwenfeng chuban gongsi, 1988; unless ascribed to Ren Naiqiang 任乃強, annot. Shanghai: Shanghai guji chubanshe, 1987.

Jiaoshi yilin 焦氏易林. By Jiao Yanshou 焦延壽. All references are to CHANT.

Jinshu 晋書. By Fang Xuanling 房玄齡. Beijing: Zhonghua shuju, 1974.

Kongzi jiayu 孔子家語. All references are to CHANT.

Laozi Daode jing. See *Daode jing*.

Lie nü zhuan 列女傳. Comp. Liu Xiang 刘向. All references are to CHANT.

Liji 禮記. All references are to CHANT. If commentary is needed, references are to Ruan Yuan 阮元, ed., *Liji zhushu*, in *Shisan jing zhushu* 十三經注疏, vols. 10–12: see *Shisan jing zhushu*. For an English translation, see Legge 1967.

Lishi 隸釋. Comp. Hong Gua 洪适. All references are to e-*SKQS*.

Lu Jia 陸賈. *Xinyu* 新語, *juan* 10. All references are to CHANT. For an English translation, see Ku 1990.

Lunheng 論衡. By Wang Chong 王充. All references are to CHANT.

Luo Yue 樓鑰. *Gongkui ji* 攻媿集. Sibu Congkan ed.

Lüshi chunqiu 吕氏春秋. Annot. Chen Qiyou 陳奇猷. All references are to the standard paragraphing used in Knoblock and Riegel 2000, and CHANT. Chen Qiyou 陳奇猷, *Lüshi chunqiu jiaoshi* 吕氏春秋校釋. Shanghai: Xinhua shudian, 1984 is cited only where reference to commentaries is helpful (as noted).

Lüshi chunqiu jiaoshi. See *Lüshi chunqiu*.

Ma Guohan 馬國翰, comp. *Yuhan shan fang ji yi shu* 玉函山房輯佚書. 6 vols. Taipei: Wenhai chubanshe, 1967.
Maoshi zheng yi 毛詩正義. See *Odes.*
Mencius 孟子. All references are cited according to the standard chapters and paragraphs.
Ming shi 明史. All references to Yangmingshan: Guofang yanjiuyuan ed. of 1962–63.
Mozi 墨子. All references are cited according to HYSIS.
Odes 詩經. All references are cited according to the Mao numbers and stanzas, as cited in *Mao shi yin de* 毛詩引得 (HYSIS). See also Ruan Yuan 阮元, ed. *Maoshi zheng yi* In *Shisan jing zhushu* 十三經注疏, vols. 3–5. See *Shisan jing zhushu.*
Ouyang Xiu 歐陽修. *Ouyang Wenzhong quanji* 歐陽文忠全集. Taipei: Taiwan Zhonghua shu ju, 1965.
Pei Ziye 裴子野. "Diao chong lun" 雕蟲論. All references are to CHANT.
Qianfu lun 潛夫論. By Wang Fu 王符. All references are to CHANT.
"Qiong da yishi" 窮達以時: See *Guodian.*
Quan Han wen 全漢文. See Yan Kejun.
Quan Hou Han wen 全後漢文. See Yan Kejun.
Quan Jin wen 全晉文. See Yan Kejun.
Quan Wei wen 全魏文. See Yan Kejun.
Sanguo zhi 三國志. By Chen Shou 陳壽. 5 vols. Beijing: Zhonghua shuju, 1959.
Shanghai bowuguan cang Zhanguo Chu zhushu 上海博物館藏戰國楚竹書. Edited by Ma Chengyuan 馬承源. 8 vols. Shanghai: Shanghai guji chubanshe, 2001–8.
Shangshu 尚書. References are to Gu Jiegang 顧頡剛, *Shangshu tongjian* 尚書通檢. Taipei: Chinese Materials and Research Aids Service Center, 1966. If commentary is needed, references are to Sun Xingyan 孫星衍, *Shangshu jinguwen zhushu* 尚書今古文注疏, 2 vols. Taipei: Guan wen shuju, n.d.
Shangshu dazhuan 尚書大傳. By Fu Sheng 伏勝. All references are to CHANT.
Shangshu quanjie 尚書全解. Comp. Lin Zhiqi 林之奇. All references are to e-*SKQS.*
Shen jian 申鑒. By Xun Yue 荀悅. All references are to CHANT.
Shen Yue 沈約. *Shen Yue ji jiao* 沈约集校. All references are to e-*SKQS.*
Shi ming 釋名. All references are to CHANT.
Shiji 史記. By Sima Qian 司馬遷. Beijing: Zhonghua shuju, 1956.
Shiji suoyin 史記索隱. By Sima Zhen 司馬貞. Cited in the *Shiji* ed. and in Wang Rongbao 1987.
Shiqu baoji 石渠寶笈. All references are to e-*SKQS.*
Shisan jing zhushu fu jiaokanji 十三經注疏附校勘記, 20 vols. Annot. Ruan Yuan 阮元. Preface 1815. Reprint, Beijing: Zhonghua shuju, 1980.
Shishuo xinyu 世說新語. Comp. by Liu Yiqing 劉義慶, annot. Liu Xiaobiao 劉孝標. Taipei: Qiming shuju, 1960.
Shitong 史通. References are to Liu Zhiji 劉知幾, *Shitong tongshi* 史通通釋, annot. Pu Qilong 浦起龍. Taipei: Yiwen yinshuguan, 1974. Cf. *Shitong xin*

jiaozhu 史通新校注, annot. Zhao Lüfu 趙呂甫 (Chongqing: Chongqing chubanshe, 1985); and Hong Haopei, *Shitong suoyin* (Taipei : Xinxing shuju, 1959).
Shuo[*Shui*]*yuan* 說苑. Comp. Liu Xiang 劉向. All references are to CHANT.
Shuowen jiezi 說文解字. Comp. Xu Shen 許慎. All references are to e-*SKQS*.
Sima Guang (not the *Fayan* commentary). See *Zizhi tongjian*.
Songshi 宋史. By Tuotuo 脫脫. 20 vols. Beijing: Zhonghua shuju, 1977.
Su Shi 蘇軾. "Da Xie Minshi shu" 答謝民師書. Cited in Han and Zhao 2010.
Su Shi wenji 蘇軾文集. Ed. Kong Fanli 孔凡禮. Beijing: Zhonghua shuju, 1986.
Sui shu 隋書. Comp. Wei Zheng 魏徵. Beijing: Zhonghua shuju, 1973.
Taiping yulan 太平御覽. Comp. Li Fang 李昉. Beijing: Zhonghua, 1995. Reprint of Sibu Congkan ed.
Taixuan jing 太玄經: See Nylan 1994.
Tanaka Masami 田中麻紗巳. *Hōgen: Mōhitotsu no Rongo* 法言: もうひとつの論語. Tokyo: Kōdansha, 1988.
Tiandi kunchong tuce 天地昆蟲圖冊. Beijing: Kexue, 1978.
Wang Qi 王圻. *Xu Wenxian tongkao* 續文獻通考 (between 1621 and 1644), available in e-*SKQS*. Wang Yinzhi 王引之. *Jingyi shu wen* 經義述聞. 2 vols. Taipei: Taiwan Commercial Press, 1968.
Wei shu 魏書. By Wei Shou 魏收. 5 vols. Beijing: Zhonghua shuju, 1975.
Wenxin diaolong 文心雕龍. By Liu Xie 劉勰. All references are to CHANT.
Wenxuan 文選. By Xiao Tong 蕭統. All references are to e-*SKQS*.
Wenzhang bianti huixuan 文章辨體彙選. Comp. Hu Fuzheng 賀復徵. All references are to e-*SKQS*.
Wenzi 文子. All references are to CHANT.
Wu Chaoqing 吳朝請. *Ji* 集. All references are to e-*SKQS*.
Wu Mi 吳祕. *Yangzi Fayan zhu* 揚子法言注 (now known only from fragments).
Xiaojing 孝經: All references are cited according to HYSIS.
"Xici" 繫辭. See *Yijing*.
Xijing zaji 西京雜記. In *Han Wei congshu* 漢魏叢書, vol. 1, 664–687. Ed. Cheng, Rong 程榮. Taipei: Xinxing shuju, 1966.
Xin lun 新論. By Huan Tan 桓譚. All references are to Pokora 1975.
Xin Tangshu 新唐書. By Ouyang Xiu 歐陽修; annot. Song Qi 宋祁. Beijing: Zhonghua shuju, 1975.
Xinyan 新言. See *Taiping yulan, juan* 795.
Xinxu 新序. Comp. Liu Xiang 劉向. All references are to CHANT.
Xun Yue 荀悅. See *Shen jian*.
Xunzi 荀子. All references are cited according to HYSIS.
Yan Kejun 嚴可均, comp. *Quan shanggu Sandai Qin Han Sanguo Liuchao wen* 全上古三代秦漢三国國六朝文. 9 vols. Taipei: Shijie shuju, 1961.
Yan Lingfeng 嚴靈峯. *Zhou Qin Han Wei zhuzi zhijian shumu* 周秦漢魏諸子知見書目. Beijing: Zhonghua shu ju, 1993.
Yanshi jia xun 顏氏家訓. By Yan Zhitui 顏之推. All references are to CHANT.
Yantie lun 鹽鐵論. All references are to CHANT.
Yijing 易經. All references are cited according to HYSIS.

Yili 儀禮 All references are to CHANT.
Yilin 意林. Ascribed to Jiao Yanshou 焦延壽. All references are to CHANT.
Yiwen leiju 藝文類聚. By Ouyang Xun 歐陽詢. Beijing: Zhonghua shuju, 1965.
Yu Xingwu 于省吾. *Shuangjian jijin wenxuan* 雙劍吉金文選. 2 vols. Beiping: n.p., ca. 1929, 1933.
"Yucong" 語叢. See *Guodian*.
Zach, Erwin von, trans. *Yang Hsiung's "Fa-yen" (Worte strenger Ermahnung): Ein philosophischer Traktat aus dem Beginn der christlichen Zeitrechnung*. Sinologische Beiträge 6.1. Batavia: Drukkeriji Lux, 1939.
Zhang Boxing 张伯行. *Jinsilu jijie* 近思錄集解. All references are to e-*SKQS*.
Zhang Yi 張揖. *Shang Guangya biao* 上廣雅表. In *Huang Qing jing jie* 皇清經解 667A.
Zhanguo ce 戰國策. All references are to CHANT, unless the Shanghai: Guji, 1985 ed. is noted.
Zheng Qiao 鄭樵. *Tongzhi* 通志. All references are to e-*SKQS*.
Zhengtong Daozang 正統道藏, vol. 20. Taipei: Xingwen, 1988.
"Zhongyong" 中庸. See *Liji*.
Zhouli/Zhouli zhushu 周禮注疏. All references are to e-*SKQS* or Ruan Yuan 阮元, ed., *Zhouli/Zhouli zhushu*, in *Shisan jing zhushu* 十三經注疏, vols. 6–7. See *Shisan jing zhushu* (as noted).
Zhu Xi. See *Zhuzi yulei*.
Zhuangzi 莊子. All references are cited according to HYSIS. If commentary is needed, references are to Guo Qingfan 郭慶藩, comp., *Zhuangzi jishi* 莊子集釋. Beijing: Zhonghua shuju, 1993.
Zhuzi yulei 朱子語類. By Zhu Xi 朱熹. All references are to e-*SKQS*.
Zizhi tongjian 資治通鑑. Comp. Sima Guang 司馬光. 4 vols. Changsha: Yuelu shushe/Hunan sheng xin hua shu dian jing xiao, 1990.
Zuozhuan 左傳. All references are to *Chunqiu jingzhuan yin de* 春秋經傳引得 (HYSIS).

SECONDARY SOURCES

Adorno, Theodor W. *Aesthetic Theory*. Trans. Robert Hullot-Kentor. Minneapolis: University of Minnesota Press, 1997.
Ames, Roger T. *Confucian Role Ethics: A Vocabulary.* Hong Kong: Chinese University of Hong Kong, 2011.
Arbuckle, Gary. "Inevitable Treason: Dong Zhongshu's Theory of Historical Cycles and Early Attempts to Invalidate the Han Mandate." *JAOS* 115, no. 4 (1995), 585–97.
Ashmore, Robert. *The Transport of Reading: Text and Understanding in the World of Tao Qian (365–427)*. Harvard East Asian Monographs, 327. Cambridge, MA: Harvard University Asia Center, 2010.
Bagley, Robert W. "Anyang Writing and the Origin of the Chinese Writing System." In *The First Writing: Script Invention as History and Process*, ed. Ste-

phen D. Houston, 190–237. Cambridge: Cambridge University Press, 2004.
———. "Percussion." In *Music in the Age of Confucius*, ed. Jenny F. So. Washington, DC: Freer Gallery of Art, 2000.
Barnes, Jonathan, ed. *The Complete Works of Aristotle: Revised Oxford Translation*. 2 vols. Princeton, NJ: Princeton University Press, 1984.
Bartsch, Shadi. *The Mirror of the Self: Sexuality, Self-Knowledge, and the Gaze in Early Modern Europe*. Chicago: University of Chicago Press, 2006.
Bauer, Wolfgang. *China and the Search for Happiness: Recurring Themes in Four Thousand Years of Chinese Cultural History*. New York: Seabury Press, 1976.
Berkowitz, Alan. *Patterns of Disengagement: The Practice and Portrayal of Reclusion in Early Medieval China*. Stanford, CA: Stanford University Press, 2000.
Berry, Mary Elizabeth. *Japan in Print: Information and Nation in the Early Modern Period*. Berkeley and Los Angeles: University of California Press, 2006.
Bielenstein, Hans. *The Bureaucracy of Han Times*. Cambridge: Cambridge University Press, 1980.
———. *Restoration of the Han Dynasty, with Prolegomena on the Historiography of the Hou Han shu. Bulletin of the Museum of Far Eastern Antiquities* 26 (1953): 1–209; 31 (1959): 1–286; 39 (1967): 1–198.
———. "Wang Mang, the Restoration of the Han Dynasty, and Later Han." In *The Cambridge History of China*, vol. 1, *The Ch'in and Han Empires, 221 BC–AD* 220, ed. Denis Twitchett and Michael Loewe, 223–90. Cambridge: Cambridge University Press, 1986.
Blitstein, Pablo. "Pei Ziye (469–530), and his 'Diao chong lun ' 雕蟲論." Unpublished paper, 2009.
Bodde, Derk. *Festivals in Classical China: New Year and Other Annual Observances during the Han Dynasty, 206 B.C.–A.D. 220*. Princeton, NJ: Princeton University Press, 1975.
Boodberg, Peter. "The Semasiology of Some Primary Confucian Concepts." *Philosophy East and West* 2, no. 4 (1953), 317–32.
Bottéro, Françoise. "Les 'Manuels de caractères' à l'époque des Han occidentaux." In *Éducation et instruction en Chine*, vol. 1, *L'éducation élémentaire*, ed. Christine Nguyen Tri and Catherine Despeux. Paris: Éditions Peeters, 2003.
Bulling, Anneliese. "Notes on Two Unicorns." *Oriental Art* 3 (1966), 109–13.
Cao Daoheng 曹道衡. "Guanyu Pei Ziye shiwen de jige wenti" 關於裴子野詩文的幾個問題.In *Zhonggu wenxue shi lunwen ji* 中古文學史論文集, 296–305. Beijing: Zhonghua shuju, 2002.
Carruthers, Mary Jean. *The Book of Memory: A Study of Memory in Medieval Culture*. Cambridge: Cambridge University Press, 2008.
Chan, Wing-tsit, trans. *Reflections on Things at Hand: The Neo-Confucian Anthology*. New York: Columbia University Press, 1967.
Chavannes, Édouard. *Les mémoires historiques de Se-ma-Ts'ien*. 5 vols. Paris: E. Leroux, 1895–1905.
Chen, Jack W. "Diao Chong lun, Notes and Translation." In *Early Medieval China: A Reader*, ed. Wendy Swartz. Forthcoming.
Chen Shixiang. "The *Shih-ching*: Its Generic Significance in Chinese Literary

History and Poetics." In *Studies in Chinese Literary Genres*, ed. Cyril Birch, 8–41. Berkeley and Los Angeles: University of California Press, 1974.

Cheng, Anne. "Review of *From Chronicle to Canon: The Hermeneutics of the Spring and Autumn, according to Tung Chung-shu*, by Sarah A. Queen. *Early China* 23–24 (1998–99), 353–66.

Cherniack, Susan. "Book Culture and Textual Transmission in Sung China." *HJAS* 54, no. 1 (1994), 5–126.

Chongqing Zhongguo Sanxia bowuguan 重庆中國三峡博物館. Ed. Chongqing bowuguan. Beijing: Kexue chubanshe, 2003.

Colvin, Andrew. "Patterns of Coherence in the *Fayan* of Yang Xiong." PhD diss., University of Hawaii, 2001.

Connery, Christopher. *The Empire of the Text: Writing and Authority in Early Imperial China*. Lanham: Rowman and Littlefield, 1998.

Creel, Herrlee G. *What Is Daoism? and Other Studies in Chinese Cultural History*. Chicago: Midway Reprint, 1970.

Cui Mingde 崔明德. *Liang Han minzu guanxi sixiang shi* 两汉民族关系思想史. Beijing: Renmin chubanshe, 2007.

Cullen, Christopher. "Numbers, Numeracy, and the Cosmos." In *China's Early Empires*, ed. Michael Nylan and Michael Loewe, 323–39. Cambridge: Cambridge University Press, 2010.

Davidson, James N. *Courtesans and Fishcakes*. London: St. Martin's Press, 1997.

Declerq, Dominic. *Writing against the State: Political Rhetoric in Third and Fourth Century China*. Leiden: Brill, 1998.

Despeux, Catherine, ed. *Éducation et instruction en Chine*. Vol. 1, *L'éducation élémentaire*. Paris: Éditions Peeters, 2003.

DeWoskin, Kenneth. *A Song for One or Two: Music and the Concept of Art in Early China*. Ann Arbor, MI: Center for Chinese Studies, 1982.

Drège, Jean-Pierre. *Les bibliothèques en Chine au temps des manuscrits (jusqu'au Xe siècle)*. Paris: École française d'Extrême-Orient, 1991.

Dubs, Homer H., trans. *The History of the Former Han Dynasty, by Pan Ku*. 3 vols. Baltimore, MD: Waverly Press, 1938–55.

Dudbridge, Glen. *Lost Books of Medieval China*. London: British Library, 2000.

Durrant, Stephen. *Cloudy Mirror: Tension and Conflict in the Writings of Sima Qian*. Albany, NY: SUNY Press, 1995.

Erkes, Eduard. "Si er bu wang." *Asia Major*, n.s., 3 (1953), 156–61.

Farmer, J. Michael. "Art, Education, and Power: Illustrations in the Stone Chamber of Wen Weng." *T'oung Pao* 86, no. 1/3 (2000): 100–35.

———. *The Talent of Shu: Qiao Zhou and the Intellectual World of Early Medieval Sichuan*. Albany, NY: SUNY Press, 2007.

Farquhar, Judith. "Eating Chinese Medicine." *Cultural Anthropology* 9, no. 4 (1994), 471–97.

Feeney, D. C. *Caesar's Calendar: Ancient Time and the Beginnings of History*. Berkeley and Los Angeles: University of California Press, 2007.

Fingarette, Herbert. *Confucius: The Secular as Sacred*. New York: Harper Torchbooks, 1972.

Finley, Moses I. *The Use and Abuse of History*. London: Chatto and Windus, 1975.
Fischer, Steven Roger. *A History of Reading*. London: Reaktion Books, 2003.
Fu Yuzhang 傅玉璋. *Zhongguo gudai shixue shi* 中國古代史學史. Hefei: Anhwei daxue, 2008.
Fukui Shigemasa 福井重雅. *Kandai Jukyō no shiteki kenkyū: Jukyō no kangakuka o meguru teisetsu no saikentō* 漢代儒教の史的研究: 儒教の官學化をめぐる定說の再檢討. Tokyo: Kyūko Shoin, 2005.
———. "Rikukei, rikugei to gokei: Kandai ni okeru gokei no seiritsu" 六經六藝と五經漢代における五經の成立. *Chûgoku shigaku* 中國史學 4 (1994), 139–64.
Gadamer, Hans-Georg. *Truth and Method*. London: Sheed and Ward, 1975.
Galambos, Imre. *Orthography of Early Chinese Writing: Evidence from Newly Excavated Manuscripts*. Budapest: Department of East Asian Studies, 2006.
Gao Guangfu 高光復. *Lidai fu lun xuan* 歷代賦論選. Harbin: Heilongjiang renmin chubanshe, 1990.
Gao Heng 高亨. *Guzi tongjia huidian* 古字通假會典. Jinan: Qi Lu shushe, 1989.
Geaney, Jane. "Grounding 'Language' in the Senses: What the Eyes and Ears Reveal about Ming 名 in Early Chinese Texts." *Philosophy East and West* 60, no. 2 (2010).
———. *On the Epistemology of the Senses in Early Chinese Thought*. Albany, NY: SUNY Press, 2002.
Genette, Gérard. *Paratexts: Thresholds of Interpretation*. Trans. Jane E. Lewin. Cambridge: Cambridge University Press, 1997.
Geng Zhanjun 耿占軍 and Yang Wenxiu 楊文秀. *Han Tang Chang'an de yuewu yu baixi* 漢唐長安的樂舞與百戲. Xi'an: Xi'an chubanshe, 2007.
Gentz, Joachim. "The Ritual Meaning of Textual Form: Evidence from Early Commentaries of the Historiographic and Ritual Traditions." In *Text and Ritual in Early China*, ed. Martin Kern, 124–48. Seattle: University of Washington Press, 2005.
Giele Enno. "Signatures in Early Imperial China." *Asiatische Studien/Études asiatiques* 59, no. 1 (2005), 353–87.
Goldin, Paul. "The Motif of the Woman in the Doorway and Related Imagery in Traditional Chinese Funerary Art." *JAOS* 121, no. 4 (2001), 539–48.
Gong Kechang. *Studies on the "Han fu."* Trans. David R. Knechtges et al. New Haven, CT: American Oriental Society, 1997.
Graham, A. C. "The Classical Chinese Topic-Marker *fu*." *Bulletin of the School of Oriental and African Studies* 35, no. 1 (1972), 85–110.
———. *Disputers of the Tao: Philosophical Argument in Ancient China*. La Salle, IL: Open Court, 1989.
———. *Later Mohist Logic, Ethics and Science*. Hong Kong: Chinese University Press, 1978.
———. "Taoist Spontaneity, 'Is,' and 'Ought.'" In *Experimental Essays on Zhuang Zi*, ed. Victor Mair, 3–23. Honolulu: University of Hawaii Press, 1983.
Greatrex, Roger. "An Early Western Han Synonymicon: The Fuyang Copy of the *Cang Jie pian*." In *Outstretched Leaves on His Bamboo Staff: Studies in Honour

of Göran Malmqvist on His 70th Birthday, ed. Joakim Enwall, 97–113. Stockholm: Association of Oriental Studies, 1994.

Gu Ming Dong. *Chinese Theories of Reading and Writing*. Albany, NY: SUNY Press, 2005.

Gu Yisheng 顧易生 and Jiang Fan 蔣凡. *Xian Qin Liang Han wenxue piping shi* 先秦兩漢文學批評史. Shanghai: Shanghai guji chubanshe, 1990.

Guan Xihua 管錫華. *Zhongguo gudai biaodian fuhao fazhanshi* 中國古代標點符號發展史. Chengdu: Ba Shu shushe, 2002.

Guo Shaoyu 郭紹虞. *Zhongguo lidai wenlun xuan* 中國歷代文論選. Vol. 1. Shanghai: Shanghai guji chubanshe, 1979.

Hadot, Pierre. *The Present Alone Is Our Happiness*. Stanford, CA: Stanford University Press, 2009.

Han Zhaoqi 韓兆琦 and Zhao Guohua 趙國華. *Qin Han shi shiwu jiang* 秦漢史十五講. Nanjing: Fenghuang chubanshe, 2010.

Henry, Eric. "'Junzi yue' versus 'Zhongni yue' in *Zuozhuan*." *HJAS* 59, no. 1 (1999), 125–61.

Hervouet, Yves. *Un poète de cour sous les Han: Sseu-ma Siang-jou*. Paris: Presses universitaires de France, 1964.

Hsing I-t'ien. "Handai Cang Jie, Jijiu, bati he shishu wenti: Zai lun Qin Han guanli ruhe xuexi wenzi" 漢代倉頡, 急就, 八體和史書問題: 再論秦漢官吏如何學習文字. In *Paleography and Early Chinese History* 古文字與古代史, no. 2, ed. Li Zong-kun 李宗焜, 429–70. Taipei: Symposium Series of the Institute of History and Philology, Academia Sinica, 2009.

Hsu Fu-kuan. See Xu Fuquan.

Huizinga, Johan. *Homo ludens: A Study of the Play-Element in Culture*. London: Routledge and Kegan Paul, 1949.

Inglis, Alister D. *Hong Mai's Record of the Listener and Its Song Dynasty Context*. Albany, NY: SUNY Press, 2006.

Jacob, Christian, and François de Polignac. *Alexandria, Third Century BC: The Knowledge of the World in a Single City*. Alexandria: Hapocrates Publishing, 2000.

Jiang Fan 蔣凡. *Xian Qin Liang Han wenxue piping shi* 先秦兩漢文學批評史. Shanghai: Shanghai guji chubanshe, 1990.

Johnson, David. "Epic and History in Early China: The Matter of Wu Tzu-hsu." *Journal of Asian Studies* 40, no. 2 (1981), 255–71.

Kalinowski, Marc. "La production des manuscrits dans la Chine ancienne: Une approche codicologique de la bibliothèque de Mawangdui." *Asiatische Studien/Études asiatiques* 57, no. 4 (2003), 849–80.

Kaogu 1980.1, 52–55.

Kaogu yu wenwu 考古與文物 2009:5, 111–12, "Xi'an Fenglouyuan Xi Han mudi tian ye kaogu fajue shouhuo" 西安鳳棲原西漢墓地田野考古發掘收穫, comp. Shaanxi Archaeological Bureau 陝西省考古研究院.

Kern, Martin. "Western Han Aesthetics and the Genesis of the Fu." *HJAS* 63, no. 2 (2003), 383–437.

Kieschnick, John. "*Analects* 12.1 and the Commentarial Tradition." *JAOS* 112, no. 4 (1992), 567–76.

Knechtges, David R. "Exemplary Sayings." In *The Columbia Anthology of Traditional Literature*, ed. Victor Mair, chap. 2. New York: Columbia University Press, 1994.

———. *The Han Rhapsody: A Study of the* Fu *of Yang Hsiung, 53 B.C.–A.D. 18.* Cambridge: Cambridge University Press, 1976.

———, trans. *The "Han shu" Biography of Yang Xiong (53 B.C.–A.D. 18).* Tempe: Arizona State University, Center for Asian Studies, 1982a.

———. "The Liu Hsin/Yang Hsiung Correspondence on the *Fang yen.*" *Monumenta Serica* 33 (1977–78), 309–25.

———. "Uncovering the Sauce Jar: A Literary Interpretation of Yang Hsiung's 'Chü Ch'in mei Hsin.'" In *Ancient China: Studies in Early Civilization*, 229–52. Hong Kong: Chinese University Press, 1977.

———. *Wen xuan, or Selections of Refined Literature.* 3 vols. to date. Princeton, NJ: Princeton University Press, 1982b–.

———. "Yang Shyong, the *Fuh*, and Hann Rhetoric." PhD diss., University of Washington, 1968.

Knoblock, John, and Jeffrey Riegel, trans. *The Annals of Lü Buwei: A Complete Translation and Study.* Stanford, CA: Stanford University Press, 2000.

Konstan, David. *The Emotions of the Ancient Greeks: Studies in Aristotle and Classical Literature.* Toronto: University of Toronto Press, 2006.

Kroll, Jurij. "The Life, the Views, and the Poem of Yang Yün, Ssu-ma Ch'ien's Grandson." In *China and Around: Mythology, Folkore, Literature; on the Occasion of the 75th Anniversary of Academician B. L. Riftin*, 297–337. Moscow: Institute of Oriental and Classical Studies, 2010.

Kroll, Paul. "Literary Criticism and Personal Character in Poetry, ca. 100–300 CE." In *China's Early Empires*, eds. Michael Nylan and Michael Loewe, 517–33. Cambridge: Cambridge University Press, 2010.

Ku, Mei-kao. *An Introduction to the Study of the "Hsin yü" of Lu Chia.* Singapore: Hsin she, 1990.

Kuriyama, Shigehisa. *The Expressiveness of the Body and the Divergence of Greek and Chinese Medicine.* New York: Zone Books, 1999.

Lai, C. M. "Messenger of Spring and Morality: Cuckoo Lore in Chinese Sources." *JAOS* 118, no. 4 (1998), 530–42.

Legge, James. *The Chinese Classics.* Vol. 3, *The Shoo King.* Vol. 5, *The "Ch'un Ts'ew" with the "Tso Chuen."* 2nd ed. Oxford: Clarendon Press, 1893. Reprint, Hong Kong: Hong Kong University Press, 1960.

———. *Li Chi: Book of Rites, an Encyclopedia of Ancient Ceremonial Usages, Religious Creeds, and Social Institutions.* Ed. Ch'u Chai and Winberg Chai. 1885. 2 vols. Reprint, New York: University Books, 1967.

Lei Hanqing 雷漢卿. *Shuowen 'Shi' buzi yu shenling jisi kao* 說文示部字與神靈祭祀考. Chengdu: Ba-Shu shushe, 2000.

L'Haridon, Béatrice 羅逸東. "Le *Fayan* de Yang Xiong and le questionnement confucéen de l'histoire." *Études chinoises* 24 (2005), 233–47.

———. "La recherche du modèle dans les dialogues du *Fayan* de Yang Xiong (53 av. J.-C.–18 apr. J.C.): Écriture, éthique, and réflexion historique à la fin des Han occidentaux." 2 vols. PhD diss., Institute National des Langues and Civilisations Orientales, 2006.

Li Dalong 李大龙. *Han-Tang fanshu tizhi yanjiu* 汉唐藩属体制研究. Beijing: Zhongguo shehui kexue chubanshe, 2006.

Li Jixiang 李紀祥. *Shiji xue yu shijie Hanxue lunji* 史記學與世界漢學論集. Taipei: Tonsan Publications, 2011.

Li Zehou 李澤厚. *Lunyu jin du* 論語今讀. Hong Kong: Tiandi tushu, 1998. Reprint, Taipei: Yunzhen wenhua, 2000.

Lien, J. Edmund. "Wei Yao's Disquisition on 'Boyi.'" *JAOS* 126, no. 4 (2006), 7–78.

Liu Rulin 劉汝霖. *Han Jin xueshu bian nian* 漢晉學術編年. 2 vols. Shanghai: Shangwu yinshuguan, 1935.

Liu Shi Shun, trans. *Chinese Classical Prose: Eight Masters of the T'ang-Sung Period*. Hong Kong: Renditions, 1979.

Liu Xingjun 劉興均. *Zhouli mingwuci de yanjiu* 周禮名物詞研究. Chengdu: Ba-Shu shushe, 2001.

Loewe, Michael. *Biographical Dictionary of the Qin, Former Han, and Xin Periods*. Leiden: Brill, 2000.

———. *The Cambridge History of China*, vol. 1, *The Ch'in and Han Empires, 221 BC–AD 220*, ed. Denis Twitchett and Michael Loewe. Cambridge: Cambridge University Press, 1986.

———. *Crisis and Conflict in Han China*. London: Allen and Unwin, 1974.

———. *Dong Zhongshu, a "Confucian" Heritage and the "Chunqiu fanlu."* Leiden, Brill, 2011.

———. *Early Chinese Texts: A Bibliographical Guide*. Berkeley: Society for the Study of Early China, 1993.

———. *The Government of the Qin and Han Empires: 221 BCE–220 CE*. Indianapolis: Hackett, 2006.

———. "On the Terms *Bao Zi*, *Yin Gong*, *Yin Guan*, *Huan*, and *Shou*: Was Zhao Gao a Eunuch?" *T'oung Pao* 91 (2005), 301–19.

Loewe, Michael, and Edward L. Shaughnessy. *The Cambridge History of Ancient China: From the Origins of Civilization to 221 B.C.* Cambridge: Cambridge University Press, 1999.

Louie, Kam. *Critiques of Confucius in Contemporary China*. New York: St. Martin's Press, 1980.

Lowenthal, David. *The Past Is a Foreign Country*. Cambridge: Cambridge University Press, 1985.

Lu Qinli 逯欽立. *Xian Qin Han Wei Jin Nanbeichao shi* 先秦漢魏晋南北朝詩. Beijing: Zhonghua shuju, ca. 1983. Reprint, 2006.

Lu Xun 魯迅. *Hanwen xueshi gangyao* 漢文學史綱要. Hong Kong: Shenghuo, dushu, xinzhi Sanlian shu dian, 1958.

Lyotard, Jean-François. *The Inhuman: Reflections on Time*. Cambridge: Polity Press, 1991.

Ma Jigao 马积高. *Fu shi* 赋史. Shanghai: Shanghai guiji chubanshe, 1987.

Mair, Victor, ed. *The Columbia Anthology of Traditional Literature*. New York: Columbia University Press, 1994.

Marsili, Fillipo. "On Tripods." In *Recarving China's Past: Art, Archaeology, and the Architecture of the "Wu Family Shrines,"* ed. Cary Liu et al., 315–21. Princeton, NJ: Princeton University Press, 2005.

Mather, Richard. *The Age of Eternal Brilliance: Three Lyric Poets of the Yung-ming Era (483–493)*. Leiden: Brill, 2003.

Matsukawa Kenji 松川健二. *Rongo no shisōshi* 論語の思想史. Tokyo: Kyūko Shoin, 1994. (Translated into Chinese by Lin Qingzhang 林慶彰. Taipei: Wanjuan lou tushu, 2006.)

McDermott, Joseph. *A Social History of the Chinese Book*. Hong Kong: Hong Kong University Press, 2006.

McKenzie, D. F. *Bibliography and Sociology of Texts*. London: British Library, 1986.

Mittag, Achim. "Change in *Shijing* Exegesis: Some Notes on the Rediscovery of the *Odes* in the Song Period." *T'oung pao* 79 (1993), 4–5, 197–224.

———. "The Qin *Bamboo Annals* from Shuihudi: A Random Note from the Perspective of Chinese Historiography." *Monumenta Serica* 51 (2003), 543–70.

Naquin, Susan. Review of *Commerce in Culture: The Sibao Book Trade in the Qing and Republican Periods*, by Cynthia Brokaw. *HJAS* 68, no. 1 (2008), 203–12.

Needham, Joseph. *Science and Civilisation in China*. Vol. 3, *Mathematics and the Sciences of the Heavens and the Earth*. Cambridge: Cambridge University Press, 1954.

Nylan, Michael. *"The Canon of Supreme Mystery," T'ai hsüan ching, by Yang Hsiung; a Translation with Commentary*. Albany, NY: SUNY Press, 1993.

———."The Classical Master in Yang Xiong's 揚雄 *Exemplary Figures* (*Fayan* 法言): An Inquiry and a Speculation." In *Literary Forms of Argument*, ed. Dirk Meyer and Joachim Gentz. Leiden: Brill, forthcoming-a.

———. "Classics without Canonization: Reflections on Classical Learning and Authority in Qin (221–210 BC) and Han (206 BC–AD 220)." In *Early Chinese Religion*, pt. 1, *Shang through Han (1250 BC –AD 220)*, ed. John Lagerwey and Marc Kalinowski, 721–77. Leiden: Brill, 2008.

———. *The Five "Confucian" Classics*. New Haven, CT: Yale University Press, 2001a.

———. "Han Ideas of Qin: A Revisionist History." *Bulletin of the Museum of Far Eastern Antiquities* 79 (2013).

———. "Legacies of the Chengdu Plain." In *Ancient Sichuan: Treasures from a Lost Civilization*, ed. Robert W. Bagley. 307–28. Seattle: Seattle Art Museum; Princeton, NJ: Princeton University Press, 2001b.

———. "The Many Faces of the Duke of Zhou." In *Statecraft and Classical Learning: The "Rituals of Zhou" in East Asian History*, ed. Benjamin Elman and Martin Kern, 94–128. Leiden: Brill, 2009.

———. "The Politics of Pleasure." *Asia Major* 14, no. 1 (2001c), 73–124.

———. "A Problematic Model: The Han 'Orthodox Synthesis,' Then and Now." In *Imagining Boundaries: Changing Confucian Doctrines, Texts, and Hermeneutics*, ed. Kai-wing Chow, On-cho Ng, and John B. Henderson, 17–56. Albany, NY: SUNY Press, 1999.

———. *The Shifting Center: The Original "Great Plan" and Later Readings*. Sankt Augustin: Institut Monumenta Serica, 1992.

———. "Textual Authority in Pre-Han and Han." *Early China* 25 (2001d), 1–54.

———. *Yang Xiong on the Pleasures of Reading and Classical Learning*. New Haven, CT: American Oriental Society, 2011.

———. "Yang Xiong's 揚雄 Final *Fayan* 法言 Chapter: Rhetoric to What End and for Whom?" Forthcoming-b (for a volume edited by Garrett Olberding for the Harvard East Asian monograph series).

———. "Ying Shao's *Fengsu tongyi*: An Exploration of Problems in Han Dynasty Political, Philosophical and Social Unity." PhD diss., Princeton University, 1983.

Nylan, Michael, and Harrison Huang. "Mencius on Pleasure." In *Polishing the Chinese Mirror: Essays in Honor of Henry Rosemont*, ed. Marthe Chandler and Ronnie Littlejohn, 1–26. La Salle, IL: Association of Chinese Philosophers of America and Open Court, 2007.

Nylan, Michael, and Michael Loewe, eds. *China's Early Empires*. Cambridge: Cambridge University Press, 2010.

Nylan, Michael, with Thomas A. Wilson. *Lives of Confucius*. New York: Doubleday/Random House, 2010.

Owen, Stephen. *Readings in Chinese Literary Thought*. Cambridge, MA: Council on East Asian Studies, Harvard University, 1992.

———. *Remembrances: The Experience of the Past in Classical Chinese Literature*. Cambridge, MA: Harvard University Press, 1986.

Pan Meiyue 潘美月. *Songdai zangshujia kaolue* 宋代藏書家考. Taipei: Xuehai chubanshe, 1980.

Peterson, Willard J. "Making Connections: 'Commentary on the Attached Verbalizations' of the *Book of Change*." *HJAS* 42, no. 1 (1982), 67–116.

———. Review of *Chinese Ideas about Nature and Society, Studies in Honour of Derk Bodde* , ed. Charles le Blanc and Susan Blader. *Journal of Asian Studies* 48, no. 2 (May 1989), 365–67.

Pfister, Rudolf. "The Production of Special Mental States." In *Love, Hatred, and Other Passions: Questions and Themes on Emotions in Chinese Civilization*, ed. Paolo Santangelo with Donatella Guida, 180–94. Leiden: Brill, 2006.

Pitner, Mark Gerald. "Embodied Geographies of Han Dynasty China: Yang Xiong and His Reception." PhD diss., University of Washington, 2010.

Plaks, Andrew H. "*Xin* as the Seat of the Emotions in Confucian Self-Cultivation." Paper presented at "Chinese Culture, Past and Present: An International Conference in Commemoration of Frederick W. Mote," National Central University, Taiwan, November 2006.

Pokora, Timotheus. *Hsin-lun* (*New Treatise), and Other Writings by Huan T'an (43 B.C.–28 A.D.): An Annotated Translation with Index*. Ann Arbor, MI: Center for Chinese Studies, University of Michigan, 1975.

———. "Huan T'an and Yang Hsiung on Ssu-ma Hsiang-ju." *JAOS* 91, no. 3 (1971), 431–38.

Pulleyblank, Edwin. *Outline of Classical Chinese Grammar.* Vancouver: University of British Columbia, 1995.
Queen, Sarah A. "Inventories of the Past: Rethinking the 'School' Affiliation of the *Huainanzi.*" *Asia Major* 14, no. 1 (2001), 51–72.
Rao Zongyi 饒宗頤. "Zhen de zhexue" 貞的哲學. *Huaxue* 華學 5 (2001), 1–13.
Ricoeur, Paul. "The Task of Hermeneutics." In *Hermeneutics and the Human Sciences: Essays on Language, Action, and Interpretation*, trans. John B. Thompson. Cambridge: Cambridge University Press, 1981.
Riegel, Jeffrey. "Eros, Introversion, and the Beginnings of *Shijing* Commentary." *HJAS* 31 (1997), 143–77.
Rosemont, Henry. "On Knowing (*Zhi*): Praxis-Guiding Discourse in the Confucian *Analects.*" Unpublished paper.
Schafer, Edward. *Pacing the Void: T'ang Approaches to the Stars.* Berkeley and Los Angeles: University of California Press, 1977.
Schneider, Laurence. *The Madman of Chu.* Berkeley and Los Angeles: University of California Press, 1980.
Serruys, Paul L.-M. *The Chinese Dialects of Han Time according to Fang yen.* Berkeley and Los Angeles: University of California Press, 1959.
Sivin, Nathan. "Preliminary Reflections on the Words *Pien* 變, *Hua* 化, and *T'ung* 通 in the "Great Commentary" to the *Book of Changes.* Unpublished paper, 31 December 1977.
Smith, Kidder, Jr., et al. *Sung Dynasty Uses of the "I Ching."* Princeton, NJ: Princeton University Press, 1990.
Steck, Odile Hannes. *Old Testament Exegesis: A Guide to the Methodology.* Atlanta, GA: Scholar's Press, 1998.
Stercyx, Roel. "Searching for Spirit: *Shen* and Sacrifice in Warring States and Han Philosophy and Ritual." *Extrême-Orient, Extrême-Occident* 29 (2007), 23–54.
Sukhu, Gopal. "Yao, Shun, and Prefiguration: The Origins and Ideology of the Han Imperial Genealogy." *Early China* 30 (2005–6), 91–153.
Sun Xiaochun and Jacob Kistemaker. *The Chinese Sky during the Han.* Leiden: Brill, 1997.
Taniguchi Hiroshi 谷口洋. "Fu ni jijo o tsukeru koto: RyōKan no majiwari ni okeru sakusha no mezame" 賦に自序をつけること: 兩漢の交における作者のめざめ. *Tōhōgaku* 東方學 119 (January 2010), 22–39.
Teng Ssu-yu. *Family Instructions for the Yen Clan.* T'oung Pao Monographs 4. Leiden: Brill, 1968.
Thern, K. L. *Postface of the "Shuo wen chieh tzu": The First Comprehensive Chinese Dictionary.* Wisconsin China Series 1. Madison: Department of East Asian Languages and Literature, University of Wisconsin, 1966.
Tian Xiaofei. *Tao Yuanming and Manuscript Culture: The Record of a Dusty Table.* Seattle: University of Washington Press, 2005.
Tiandi kunchong tuce 天地昆蟲圖冊. Beijing: Kexue, 1978.
Tsien, Tsuen-hsuin. *Written on Bamboo and Silk.* Chicago: University of Chicago Press, 2004.

van Ess, Hans. “Some Preliminary Notes on the Authenticity of the Treatise on Music in *Shiji* 24.” *Oriens Extremus* 45 (2005/6), 48–67.

Vankeerberghen, Griet. “Choosing Balance: Weighing (*Quan* 權) as a Metaphor for Action in Early Chinese Texts.” *Early China* 30 (2006), 47–89.

———. “Texts and Authors in the *Shiji*.” In *China's Early Empires: A Reappraisal*, ed. Michael Nylan and Michael Loewe, 461–79. Cambridge: Cambridge University Press, 2010.

Vendler, Helen. *The Art of Shakespeare's Sonnets*. Cambridge, MA: Harvard University Press, 1997.

Venture, Olivier. “Reflections about Western Zhou Elites' Relationship to the Past as Seen in Bronze Inscriptions.” Unpublished paper, draft 2005.

Vervoorn, Aat. *Men of the Cliffs and Caves: The Development of the Chinese Eremitic Tradition to the End of the Han Dynasty*. Shatin, N.T.: Chinese University Press, 1990.

———. “Music and the Rise of Literary Theory in Ancient China.” *Journal of Oriental Studies* (*Dongfang wenhua*) 43, no. 1 (1996), 50–70.

———. “Zhuang Zun: A Daoist Philosopher of the Late First Century B.C.” *Monumenta Serica* 38 (1998–99), 6–94.

Veyne, Paul. *Did the Greeks Believe in Their Myths? An Essay on the Constitutive Imagination*. Chicago: University of Chicago Press, 1988.

Vogelsang, Kai. “Prolegomena to Critical *Zuozhuan* Studies: The Manuscript Tradition,” *Asiatische Studien/Études asiatiques* 61 (2007), 941–88.

Wagner, Rudolf. *Craft of a Chinese Commentator: Wang Bi on the “Laozi.”* Albany, NY: SUNY Press, 2000.

Waley, Arthur. *The Analects of Confucius*. Trans. and annot. Arthur Waley. London: G. Allen and Unwin, 1938.

Wang Baoxuan 王葆玄. *Jin gu wen jingxue xin lun* 今古經學新論. Beijing: Zhong guo shehui kexue chubanshe, 1997. Reprint, 2004.

Wang Guowei 王國維. “Shi Zhou pian zhengxu” 史籀篇證序. In *Wang Guowei yishu* 王國維遺書, vol. 1, 5/17a–20a. Shanghai: Shanghai guji, 1983.

Wang Qicai 王啟才. *Handai zouyi de wenxue yiyun yu wenhua jingshen* 漢代奏議的文學意蘊與文化精神. Beijing: Renmin chubanshe, 2009.

Wang Wentai 汪文臺. *Qi jia Hou Han shu* 七家後漢書. Taipei: Wenhai chubanshe, 1972.

Wang Yunxi 王 運熙 and Gu Yisheng 顧 易生, eds. *Xian Qin Liang Han wenxue piping shi* 先秦 兩漢 文學 批評史. Shanghai: Shanghai guji chubanshe, 1990.

Watson, Burton, trans. *The Complete Works of Chuang Tzu*. New York: Columbia University Press, 1968.

Wilson, Thomas A. *Genealogy of the Way: The Construction and Uses of the Confucian Tradition in Late Imperial China*. Stanford, CA: Stanford University Press, 1995.

Wu Fusheng. “Han Epideictic Rhapsody: A Product and Critique of Imperial Patronage.” *Monumenta Serica* 55 (2007): 23–59.

Xia Nai 夏鼐. “Handai de yuqi: Handai yuqizhong chuantong de yanxu he bianhua" 漢代 的玉器: 漢代玉器中傳統的延續和變化. *Kaogu xuebao* 2 (1983), 125–46.

Xu Fuguan 徐復觀. *Liang Han sixiang shi* 兩漢思想史. Vols. 1–2. Hong Kong: Chinese University of Hong Kong, 1975. Reprint, Taipei: Student Bookstore, 1979.

———. "Yang Xiong lunjiu" 揚雄論究. *Dalu zazhi* 大陸雜誌 50, no. 3 (1975), 1–43.

Xu Rongsheng 許蓉生. "Qian tan liubo de chansheng yanbian ji yingxiang" 淺談六博的產生演變及影響. *Sichuan wenwu* 2005:6, 63–66.

Yan Lingfeng 嚴靈峯. *Zhou Qin Han Wei zhuzi zhijian shumu* 周秦漢魏諸子知見書目. Taipei: Zhengzhong shuju, 1979. Reprint, Beijing: Zhonghua shuju, 1993 (vol. 5 is on Yang Xiong).

Yang Haizheng 楊海峥. *Han Tang Shiji yanjiu lungao* 漢唐史記研究論稿. Jinan: Qi Lu shushe, 2003.

Yu, Jiyuan. *The Ethics of Aristotle and Confucius: Mirrors of Virtue*. London: Routledge, 2007.

Yuan Jixi 袁济喜. *Liuchao meixue* 六朝美學. Beijing: Beijing daxue/Xinhua shudian, 2000.

Zhang Zhenze 張震澤, comp. *Yang Xiong ji jiaozhu* 揚雄集校注. Shanghai: Shanghai guji chubanshe, 1993.

Zheng Yuyu 鄭毓瑜. "Chong fu duanyu yu fengtu biyu: Cong Shijing 'shan you . . . shi you . . . nan you' chongfu duanyu tanqi" 重複短語與風土比喻: 從詩經山有溼有南有重複短語談起. *Tsinghua Journal*, n.s., 39, no. 1 (March 2009), 1–29.

Zhongguo da baike quanshu 中國大百科全書. Beijing: Xinhua shudian, 1990.

Zhou Zumo 周祖謨. *Erya jiao jian* 爾雅校箋. Nanjing: Jiangsu jiaoyu chubanshe, 1984.

Index

The introduction is indexed by page number; the main body of *Exemplary Figures* is indexed by chapter and verse. The glossary is not indexed, nor are lesser figures about whom little is known. Also not indexed are the sage-kings listed separately, aside from Kings Wen and Wu of Zhou, Yu the Great, and Shun.

The verse summary for a given chapter is listed as VS–x (where *x* stands for the chapter number).